SO YOU WANT TO SING MUSICAL THEATRE

So You Want to Sing

Guides for Performers and Professionals

A Project of the National Association of Teachers of Singing

So You Want to Sing: Guides for Performers and Professionals is a series of works devoted to providing a complete survey of what it means to sing within a particular genre. Each contribution functions as a touchstone work not only for professional singers but also for students and teachers of singing. Titles in the series offer a common set of topics so readers can navigate easily the various genres addressed in each volume. This series is produced under the direction of the National Association of Teachers of Singing, the leading professional organization devoted to the science and art of singing.

So You Want to Sing Music Theater: A Guide for Professionals, by Karen S. Hall, 2013

So You Want to Sing Rock 'n' Roll: A Guide for Professionals, by Matthew Edwards, 2014

So You Want to Sing Jazz: A Guide for Professionals, by Jan Shapiro, 2015

So You Want to Sing Country: A Guide for Performers, by Kelly K. Garner, 2016

So You Want to Sing Gospel: A Guide for Performers, by Trineice Robinson-Martin, 2016

So You Want to Sing Sacred Music: A Guide for Performers, edited by Matthew Hoch, 2017

So You Want to Sing Folk Music: A Guide for Performers, by Valerie Mindel, 2017

So You Want to Sing Barbershop: A Guide for Performers, by Diane M. Clarke & Billy J. Biffle, 2017

So You Want to Sing A Cappella: A Guide for Performers, by Deke Sharon, 2017

So You Want to Sing Light Opera: A Guide for Performers, by Linda Lister, 2018

So You Want to Sing CCM (Contemporary Commercial Music): A Guide for Performers, edited by Matthew Hoch, 2018

So You Want to Sing for a Lifetime: A Guide for Performers, by Brenda Smith, 2018

So You Want to Sing the Blues: A Guide for Performers, by Eli Yamin, 2018

So You Want to Sing Chamber Music: A Guide for Performers, by Susan Hochmiller, 2019

So You Want to Sing Early Music: A Guide for Performers, by Martha Elliot, 2019

So You Want to Sing Music by Women: A Guide for Performers, by Matthew Hoch and Linda Lister, 2019

So You Want to Sing World Music: A Guide for Performers, edited by Matthew Hoch and Linda Lister, 2019

So You Want to Sing Spirituals: A Guide for Performers, by Randye Jones, 2019

So You Want to Sing with Awareness: A Guide for Performers, edited by Matthew Hoch, 2020

So You Want to Sing Cabaret: A Guide for Performers, by David Sabella and Sue Matsuki, 2020

So You Want to Sing Musical Theatre: A Guide for Performers, by Amanda Flynn, 2022

SO YOU WANT TO SING MUSICAL THEATRE

A Guide for Performers
Updated and Expanded Edition

Amanda Flynn

Allen Henderson
Executive Editor

Matthew Hoch
Series Editor

ROWMAN & LITTLEFIELD
Lanham • Boulder • New York • London

Published by Rowman & Littlefield
An imprint of The Rowman & Littlefield Publishing Group, Inc.
4501 Forbes Boulevard, Suite 200, Lanham, Maryland 20706
www.rowman.com

86-90 Paul Street, London EC2A 4NE

Copyright © 2022 by The Rowman & Littlefield Publishing Group, Inc.

All rights reserved. No part of this book may be reproduced in any form or by any electronic or mechanical means, including information storage and retrieval systems, without written permission from the publisher, except by a reviewer who may quote passages in a review.

British Library Cataloguing in Publication Information Available

Library of Congress Cataloging-in-Publication Data

Names: Flynn, Amanda, author.
Title: So you want to sing musical theatre : a guide for performers / Amanda Flynn [and four others].
Description: Updated and expanded edition. | Lanham : Rowman & Littlefield,
  2022. | Series: So you want to sing | Includes bibliographical references and index. | Summary: "Broadway vocal coach, voice teacher, and researcher Amanda Flynn provides the skills singers need to successfully sing musical theatre repertoire. The book is updated and expanded for musical theatre performance in the current era, covering a broader array of topics and including more in-depth discussion than the original edition" —Provided by publisher.
Identifiers: LCCN 2022005594 (print) | LCCN 2022005595 (ebook) | ISBN 9781538156315 (cloth) | ISBN 9781538156322 (paperback) | ISBN 9781538156339 (epub)
Subjects: LCSH: Singing—Instruction and study. | Musicals—Instruction and study.
Classification: LCC MT956 .F59 2022 (print) | LCC MT956 (ebook) | DDC 782.1/143—dc23
LC record available at https://lccn.loc.gov/2022005594
LC ebook record available at https://lccn.loc.gov/2022005595

∞™ The paper used in this publication meets the minimum requirements of American National Standard for Information Sciences—Permanence of Paper for Printed Library Materials, ANSI/NISO Z39.48-1992.

For Jones, who taught me how to be professional.
And for RR, who is my everything.

CONTENTS

List of Figures and Tables	xi
Series Editor's Foreword *Matthew Hoch*	xvii
Foreword *George Salazar*	xix
Acknowledgments	xxv
Online Supplement Note	xxvii
1 Musical Theatre History: A Brief Overview	1
2 Musical Genres	45
3 Singing and Voice Science *Scott McCoy*	71
4 Vocal Health for Singers *Wendy LeBorgne*	89
5 Using Audio Enhancement Technology *Matthew Edwards*	109

6	How Learning Works: An Introduction to Motor Learning Theory *Lynn Helding*	133
7	Musical Theatre Vocal Pedagogy	165
8	Musical Theatre Developmental Repertoire	211
9	The Musical Theatre Actor	255
10	The Musical Theatre Athlete	265
11	Young Musical Theatre Performers	287
12	Musical Theatre Auditions	305
13	Musical Theatre Profiles	339

Glossary	373
Index	389
About the Author and Contributors	415

LIST OF FIGURES AND TABLES

FIGURES

Figure 3.1	Location of diaphragm	73
Figure 3.2	Intercostal and abdominal muscles	75
Figure 3.3	External oblique and rectus abdominis muscles	76
Figure 3.4	Layered structure of the vocal fold	78
Figure 3.5	Cartilages of the larynx, viewed at an angle from the back	80
Figure 3.6	Primary modes of vocal fold vibration	81
Figure 3.7	Natural harmonic series, beginning at G2	82
Figure 3.8	Typical range of first and second formants for primary vowels	85
Figure 5.1	Compression and rarefaction	110
Figure 5.2	The figure shows two instruments playing the same pitch. The peak at the far left is the fundamental frequency, and the peaks to the right are harmonics that have been amplified and attenuated by the instrument's resonator resulting in a specific timbre.	112
Figure 5.3	Basic design of a dynamic microphone	114
Figure 5.4	Basic design of a condenser microphone	115

LIST OF FIGURES AND TABLES

Figure 5.5	Example frequency response graphs for the Oktava 319 and the Shure SM58	116
Figure 5.6	Example of a microphone polar pattern diagram	117
Figure 5.7	If the amplitude response curve intersected with point A, there would be a 10-dB reduction in the amplitude of frequencies received by the microphone's diagram at that angle.	118
Figure 5.8	Diagram 1 represents a bidirectional pattern; diagram 2 represents a cardioid pattern.	119
Figure 5.9	Diagram 3 represents a supercardioid pattern; diagram 4 represents a hypercardioid pattern.	119
Figure 5.10	Diagram 5 represents a shotgun pattern; diagram 6 represents an omnidirectional pattern.	120
Figure 5.11	The frequency amplitude curves show the effect of applying a shelf equalizer to an audio signal.	121
Figure 5.12	The frequency amplitude curves above display two parametric equalizer settings. The top curve represents a boost of +8 dB set at 1 kHz with a relatively large bell curve—a low Q. The lower curve represents a high Q set at 100 Hz with a cut of 6 dB.	122
Figure 5.13	An example of a parametric equalizer interface. The "LO CUT" button applies a shelf equalizer at 80 Hz when depressed.	122
Figure 5.14	Example of a graphic equalizer interface	124
Figure 5.15	This graph represents the effects of various compression ratios applied to a signal. The 1:1 angle represents no compression. The other ratios represent the effect of compression on an input signal with the threshold set at line A.	124
Figure 5.16	This diagram illustrates the multiple lines of reflection that create reverb.	126
Figure 5.17	This diagram illustrates how a direct line of sound followed by a reflected line of sound creates delay.	127
Figure 7.1	Singers can use a five- or eight-note scale depending on their comfortability.	176

LIST OF FIGURES AND TABLES

Figure 7.2	Descending five- or eight-note scales on easy vowels are a great way to begin vocalizing.	177
Figure 7.3	This exercise is a great way to begin to introduce vowels other than /u/ and /i/.	177
Figure 7.4	This exercise ascends into the higher range.	178
Figure 7.5	This pattern allows singers to begin working on ascending through their middle range.	178
Figure 7.6	This exercise is a great way to introduce a more rapid moving pattern that still feels descending in nature.	178
Figure 7.7	Simple five-note scale runs are a great way to introduce agility.	179
Figure 7.8	Using the hum to impact the lower singing range is a great way to find a connection between speaking and singing.	180
Figure 7.9	A simple exercise like this one can help a singer find their lower, chest voice.	180
Figure 7.10	Taking a spoken phrase and putting it on pitches is a great way for a singer to experience their speaking voice on pitch.	181
Figure 7.11	In this exercise, you want the lower notes to use the same clear, resonant speaking voice that has already been practiced, while the octave jump can flip into a lighter, more rounded, head voice.	181
Figure 7.12	The bottom note of this exercise should always be in chest voice, while the top note should always be in head voice.	183
Figure 7.13	The bottom note should always be chest voice and the top should always be head voice.	184
Figure 7.14	The bottom note should always be in chest voice with the higher notes lightening up accordingly.	184
Figure 7.15	Practice calling out, then try putting the call on pitches.	186
Figure 7.16	Adding in an ascending pattern can help folks who need a bit more chest connection.	186
Figure 7.17	This figure shows the various ways singers might explore the variations of belting.	187

Figure 7.18	Slide higher with no specific tempo while perceptually maintaining the same volume. Many singers will notice their tendency to get louder as they ascend.	188
Figure 7.19	Try doing this exercise twice in a row with the first time at forte (*f*) and the second at piano (*p*).	188
Figure 7.20	Leading with an /i/ or /u/ vowel in a speechlike pattern helps singers work on a closed vowel in their belt.	189
Figure 7.21	This exercise allows you to practice moving from a speechlike quality to a more call-like quality.	190
Figure 7.22	When attempting the sustained portion of this exercise, be sure and aim for the same resonance and energy of the shorter call.	196
Figure 7.23	Try to maintain energy and intention through the repeated notes at the beginning.	196
Figure 7.24	The vowels in this exercise are very flexible and should be tailored to each singer, but be sure you are executing these runs in a chest-, or speech-dominant laryngeal registration.	196
Figure 7.25	Adding in turns on a run is a great way to increase the skill level of the exercise.	196
Figure 7.26	This exercise is an excellent way to work through connecting the higher belt range to the lower belt range.	197
Figure 7.27	Using a blues scale is a great way for singers to practice moving through a scale that is non-diatonic.	199
Figure 7.28	This exercise allows you to practice sustaining a note and then moving quickly down the scale as if it were a quick run.	200
Figure 7.29	This exercise can be used to work on clean, breathy, or glottal onsets.	201
Figure 7.30	When the tongue is out, this exercise can help with onset as well as a general feeling of pharyngeal release.	201
Figure 7.31	The singer is singing into a small straw.	203
Figure 7.32	The regular-size straw can be used throughout the entire range.	204

LIST OF FIGURES AND TABLES

Figure 7.33	The singer is creating a seal around the mouth with the cup that has a small hole in the bottom.	205
Figure 7.34	The singer is closing off their mouth with the back of their hand to help increase the back pressure.	206
Figure 10.1	The band is tied gently over their ribcage to feel a full expansion on inhale.	270
Figure 10.2	The singer is leaning forward with a hunched back and arms rounded in front to feel a full expansion of the ribcage.	270
Figure 10.3	The singer is pulling the exercise band to feel more stabilization in the ribs and back.	273
Figure 10.4	The singer is actively twisting as they sing in order to feel the work move to their lower abdominals.	274
Figure 10.5	The singer has their body weight in their hands so that their abdominals can release and their ribcage can expand.	275
Figure 10.6	Singing with the tongue out can raise awareness of unintentional movement.	277
Figure 10.7	The tongue is in a rolled position, creating a deeper stretch in the middle.	278
Figure 10.8	The singer is applying gentle pressure in a forward motion in order feel gentle pressure in the temporomandibular joint.	279
Figure 10.9	The singer is applying pressure in a circular motion.	279
Figure 10.10	The singer is applying pressure upward to find the pterygoid muscle.	280

TABLE

Table 6.1	The Two Basic Modes of Human Information Processing and Their Attributes	136

SERIES EDITOR'S FOREWORD

So You Want to Sing Musical Theatre is a unique book in the So You Want to Sing series in that it is simultaneously the newest book in the series (the twenty-first) while also representing an expansion and revision of the first book, *So You Want to Sing Music Theater*, which was published in 2014 by founding series editor Karen Hall. After the publication of the twentieth book, *So You Want to Sing Cabaret*, in 2020, a decision was made to cap the series at twenty books for an indefinite amount of time to focus our efforts on the revision of previously published titles. As the first three books preceded my editorship (as well as the tenure of the current production team at Rowman & Littlefield), starting at the very beginning—with musical theatre—seemed like a very good place to start.

A lot has changed since 2014. As the So You Want to Sing series has evolved over the past decade, books have become longer and glossaries more expansive. Guest chapters have become commonplace, offering the opportunity for input from a diverse array of professionals who offer a variety of invaluable perspectives. The number of common chapters has expanded from two to four; the original essays on voice science and vocal health by Scott McCoy and Wendy LeBorgne, respectively, now coexist alongside two additional contributions: "Using Audio Enhancement Technology" by Matthew Edwards and "How Learning Works: An

Introduction to Motor Learning Theory" by Lynn Helding. The NATS website has also undergone a major revision, opening up new possibilities for the online resources that supplement each title in the series.

While most "second editions" of books share the same title as the first, you will note two changes with *So You Want to Sing Musical Theatre*. The first is the name of the genre itself. While NATS has long favored the more concise "music theater," a decision was made in late 2020 to change over to the industry-preferred "musical theatre." Moving forward, all So You Want to Sing books—as well as *Journal of Singing* articles and categories at NATS auditions) will consistently adopt this spelling. Second, this revision reflects the revised subtitle, "A Guide for Performers" (not "Professionals"), which has been in regular use since the fourth book in the series, *So You Want to Sing Gospel*.

The third change—and inarguably the most significant—is the engagement of a new author for this revised and expanded edition. In our discernment of possible writers, Amanda Flynn emerged as the perfect choice. With a wealth of experience that ranges from Broadway to academic conferences to pedagogical publications to offices in our nation's most important professional organizations, Amanda has built an impressive career that beautifully bridges the chasms that sometimes exist between pedagogy, practice, and industry. She brings a ground-level perspective to this project that will provide any reader—student, teacher, performer, or scholar—with a more thorough understanding of what it takes to sing musical theatre successfully.

The collected volumes of the So You Want to Sing series offer a valuable opportunity for performers and teachers of singing to explore new styles and important pedagogies. I am confident that voice specialists, both amateur and professional, will benefit from Amanda Flynn's important book. It has been a privilege to work with her on *So You Want to Sing Musical Theatre, Updated and Expanded Edition*.

Matthew Hoch
Series Editor

FOREWORD

George Salazar

"It takes one to know one."

I have been a musical theatre performer for twenty years, working professionally for fifteen of those years. Throughout my career, I've suffered ankle injuries, calf injuries, wrist injuries, and back injuries. These injuries were all taken very seriously by every employer I worked under. It's par for the course. It's understood that when you work six days a week performing a grueling eight-show schedule, muscles will get tweaked and sprained; the recommendation every time is: rest. That's why we have understudies!

But there's another type of injury that often gets swept under the rug, both by performers feeling ashamed or by producers who don't quite understand the instrument. I'm speaking of vocal injury. There has been a stigma stamped on such injuries and it is the most terrifying for any vocal performer to endure because, for whatever reason, it's shrouded in mystery and uncertainty.

We can and often do continue to perform on a bummed ankle, a weak back, but how does someone navigate a vocal injury?

"It takes one to know one."

In 2019, I was getting ready to open a labor of love on Broadway. Let's start at the beginning, though, to better understand the stress and pressure I felt in February of 2019. In early 2015, I was in the original cast of a musical called *Be More Chill*, which ran for a month at Two River Theater in Red Bank, New Jersey. The show received a less-than-favorable review from the *New York Times*, the fastest way to kill the future of a new musical. We were fortunate to have the opportunity to record a cast album after the show closed, something that hardly happens for a show that did not premiere in New York City. The recording was released on Halloween 2015 and much like the original production, the album hardly made a mark.

But then something miraculous happened.

In 2017, two years after we released the cast recording, the internet (unidentified musical theatre fans) discovered the album, particularly the big act 2 number that I sang, "Michael in the Bathroom," and—quite rapidly—the show was gaining a strange, unprecedented momentum. Social media was buzzing with fan art and blog posts written by people searching for bootleg recordings—slime tutorials as they are now lovingly referred to by theatre fans to avoid being found by legal teams representing writers. I was caught in the eye of the storm, and I loved every second of it.

You see, I'm a half-Filipino, half-Ecuadorian musical theatre performer. Growing up, there was no one doing what I do, no one to look up to, no one to say to me: "Look what I get to do and you can too!" So when I started my career, my goal and my dream was to somehow be that person for young people who looked like me. I witnessed, firsthand, the power that this musical and my character, a sweet loner named Michael Mell, had. I was receiving fan letters from young people who said the show saved their lives. I was meeting them on sidewalks, at Target, at the stage door for shows that were not *Be More Chill*. And of course, all this high-tech attention flew over the heads of many of the older theatre producers in New York who pour their money into tried-and-true advertising: buses, newspapers, magazines, those annoying TVs in the back of NYC cabs.

We were standing on the precipice of something new and unique to the times we live in. And no one knew what to do with it. I worked closely with Joe Iconis to try to build momentum in hopes of attracting a producer to bring the show to New York, and eventually, in 2018, that dream came true. Our show was brought to NYC by Jerry Goehring, a producer and educator who mounted an amateur production of the show at the college where he teaches and saw fans flying in from all over the world to see his students do *Be More Chill*.

We ran off-Broadway at the end of 2018 and secured a Broadway transfer that would start rehearsals in January of 2019. This little show that could was making it to Broadway! It would mark composer Joe Iconis's Broadway debut as well as the Broadway debuts for book writer Joe Tracz, director Stephen Brackett, and countless others. It was my second Broadway show, my first being *Godspell* which opened and closed seven years prior.

I was doing loads and loads of press, singing "Michael in the Bathroom" on morning shows (which tape before 9:00 a.m.), and living the Broadway life I had always dreamed of. But the song itself, one I had sung hundreds of times over the span of five years by this point, was a difficult song to sing. It lived in the upper quarter of my range and was extremely emotionally charged and required a lot of me vocally. On top of this, I was rehearsing the show six days a week—from 10:00 a.m. to 6:00 p.m. My voice only saw a break at night.

Imagine a dancer, doing the same complicated and difficult routine for eight hours a day, six days a week. There's only so much our bodies can take. But thank God for Amanda Flynn.

"It takes one to know one."

Amanda Flynn herself has a solid career as a musical theatre performer. Amanda spent some time covering the role of Glinda in *Wicked*. She understood the grueling schedule and the vocal and physical demands of being a performer. When our paths crossed, Amanda was running her voice studio, transitioning to helping performers sharpen their skills and do so safely. Amanda's top concern for her students: longevity. How can we make the task at hand manageable for an extended period of time?

Amanda had been coaching me on a weekly basis. But she goes above and beyond for her students. It wasn't just an hour session a week. It was, "Call me whenever if something feels off" or "Want me to meet you at the theatre to help relieve neck tension?" As I write this, I'm in the final week of the run of a musical, two years after my injury and it's only because of Amanda, her expertise, her care, and her friendship. Every performer needs an Amanda Flynn. And that's why I'm glad you're reading this book. The woman knows the ins and outs of musical theatre.

The day of our second preview was Valentine's Day 2019. I woke up at 7:00 a.m., after a full day of rehearsal and then our first public Broadway performance the night before. A camera crew and news anchor were coming to my apartment to follow me around for a feature on "a day in the life of a Broadway actor." They followed me until noon, when I had to head back to the Lyceum Theatre for preview rehearsal at 1pm. We ran through changes to the show and continued the tech process when I started to feel something weird with my voice. I called Amanda on a break to let her know something felt off and she walked me through exercises. Everything sounded OK. Fast forward to the evening.

We got to my big number in act 2, "Michael in the Bathroom," when for the first time in five years, I struggled to hit the high notes. It was more than a struggle really. It was virtually impossible. I had never experienced this before. The song is basically a panic attack set to music and I was *not* acting that night. I panicked as I got closer and closer to the end of the song, incapable of singing the high notes; I eventually surrendered to what was happening and just shouted the lyrics as very real tears streamed down my face. What was happening to me? I worked so hard to get here. Will I be able to do the show tomorrow night? People are counting on me. People flew to New York to see us. Maybe if I drank tea and went on vocal rest for a day, I'll be back to normal tomorrow? But what if things don't go back to normal? Will I ever be able to sing this again? What do I do if I can't do what I love? I was spiraling.

I communicated with Amanda after the show and she did her best to calm me down, but I knew something was very wrong. She told me to go home, shut down my voice, and keep in touch through the night. She made a late-night call to the receptionist at my ENT's office to try to get me a last-minute appointment and we had one scheduled for the very next morning.

Going to the ENT for a vocal injury is terrifying. You sit alone in that waiting room thinking the worst, you fill out the paperwork, and eventually you go in and the doctor (in my case, the amazing Dr. Lucian Sulica of the Sean Parker Institute for the Voice at Weill Cornell Medical College) inserts a scope with a tiny camera attached to it to observe your vocal folds. He looks at the monitor with almost no expression so as to not alarm his patients. And then he confirms your worst fear: a hemorrhaged vocal fold. A very small blood vessel in the vocal fold essentially exploded during the show the night before. But I *wasn't* alone for this appointment. Amanda met me in the lobby and was there with me the whole time. I cried. . . . No, I wept. But Amanda held me and assured me everything was going to be OK. That's Amanda: above and beyond.

The thought was that I'd need surgery to zap the blood vessel to keep it from bleeding. I'd need two weeks of complete vocal rest prior to the procedure and then two weeks of continued vocal rest for recovery and healing. Truly scary stuff, but I had the most incredible vocal coach in my corner. She went with me to pick out a dry erase board that I used to communicate so I wouldn't have to speak, she checked in with me daily, but most importantly, she communicated with my producers to keep them educated and up to date. I never once experienced pressure to return until I was physically ready to return. Those conversations would've been stressful if I had to be the one to have them, but Amanda took it all on because she cares for her friends and clients and because she *knows* what she's talking about. She came over to keep me company throughout my recovery while the show went on without me. She kept me distracted and taken care of and continued to accompany me at my ENT visits. At the two-week mark, we were all surprised and thrilled to learn that the hemorrhage had healed on its own. It was truly a miracle, but it only healed because of Amanda's help and guidance.

I returned to the show without any additional vocal injuries and spoke very publicly about what had happened to me because Amanda helped lift the stigma of vocal injuries in the building. She never once, even as the official voice consultant for *Be More Chill*, thought to just put me on steroids and send me back out. Longevity. That's what matters to her.

As a voice teacher running her own studio, I've watched Amanda's students go on to book some incredible jobs. On a recent trip to NYC (I live in Los Angeles now), I visited her new studio and clocked a book on her shelf that covers the intricacies of working with young trans singers undergoing hormone therapy. It brought a tear to my eye that even with the vast wealth of knowledge she already possessed, she continues striving to learn as much as she can to make sure she can help guide *all* artists to realize their dreams of a life in the musical theatre.

In our continued work together, we discovered that I have a slight vocal fold deformity called a sulcus. It's a groove or a furrow that keeps my vocal folds from closing tightly and completely. This creates a breathy quality when I'm singing softly or in falsetto, and once we made that discovery, Amanda formulated a whole new approach to working to strengthen my voice. She did the research because she cares.

There is a definite possibility that without Amanda, my career would look very different right now. But rather than waste my energy on the what if's, I choose to celebrate what *is*. Amanda Flynn is an incredible asset to the American musical theatre and I'm thrilled you've picked up this book to hear what she has to say.

"It takes one to know one," and Amanda Flynn is most certainly one of *us*.

ACKNOWLEDGMENTS

There's an old adage in musical theatre that says that writers never really finish writing a musical, but at some point, they have to stop working on it. After writing this book, I can attest to this. I'm a lifelong learner who's constantly reading books, trying new things in the studio, and opening my mind to new pedagogical concepts and approaches. This means that I could tweak and edit this book for the rest of my life and never feel finished. However, deadlines meant that at some point I had to stop working on it. You hold in your hands a labor of love that will hopefully provide you some valuable information about musical theatre singing. I wrote this book for voice teachers who are new to teaching musical theatre, or who are looking for a refresher. I also wrote this book for aspiring musical theatre singers. If you dream of being on Broadway, this book will hopefully give you some tips and tools to start laying the foundation for that dream.

I am thankful to Karen Hall for laying the groundwork with the first edition and to Matthew Hoch and Michael Tan for the opportunity to dig deeper for this revised and expanded edition. I have been fortunate to collaborate with and learn from the greatest voice professionals in the business over the years. These folks have been my community and my backbone throughout my career. Thank you Ellen Lettrich, Lucian

Sulica, Christine Estes, Babak Sadoughi, Christine Schneider, Paul Kwak, Shirley Gherson, Aaron Johnson, Milan Amin, Chris York, Erwan Noblet, Jeanne Goffi-Fynn, Dianna Heldman, Christine Reimer, Pam Phillips, Heather Petruzelli, and Chris Roselli. A special thanks to Jared Trudeau, my fellow voice nerd, research partner, and friend for being my sounding board for all things voice. Thank you to Maggie McNeil for keeping me and my voice studio organized and running. Thank you to Hannah Lundy Connell for being the best associate teacher there is and for teaching in my stead while I wrote this book. Thank you to Ken Bozeman and Melissa Foster for your expertise in crafting parts of this book. Thank you to Rachel Lee for being a wonderful collaborator in the field of diversity, equity, and inclusion. Thank you to Leana Rae Concepcion and Miles Josephson for being my models in this book.

Thank you to every single singer that has stood in front of me and shared part of yourself. I have learned something from each and every one of you. Thank you to every voice teacher that I have had the honor of guiding. You give me hope for the future of voice teaching.

My family has always been the most supportive. When I told them I was dropping out of college to move to New York and be on Broadway, they said OK and helped me pack. Without them, I wouldn't have had the opportunities I have had in my life and career. I also have the greatest partner in the world with my husband, Rob. He is my confidant, my biggest supporter, and my forever editor. Thank you for reading every word in this book and then suggesting different words to make my writing stronger. Thank you for your unconditional support when I say, "I've decided" followed by some grand plan, like "I've decided . . . to write a book!" Without your love and support, I would not be the person (or writer) I am today.

ONLINE SUPPLEMENT

So *You Want to Sing Musical Theatre* features an online supplement courtesy of the National Association of Teachers of Singing. Visit the link below to discover additional exercises and examples, as well as links to recordings of the songs referenced in this book.

http://www.nats.org/So_You_Want_To_Sing_Book_Series.html

A musical note symbol ♪ in this book will mark every instance of corresponding online supplement material.

MUSICAL THEATRE: A BRIEF HISTORY

Musical theatre has never been more popular. Hollywood has recently produced film versions of stage musicals like *Into the Woods*, *In the Heights*, and *Tick, Tick . . . Boom!*, in addition to creating new movie musicals such as *Enchanted* and *La La Land*. The song "Let It Go," from the animated Disney film *Frozen*, became the most streamed Disney song of all time before making its way to the Broadway stage in 2018.[1] Musical theatre is even on television with live productions like NBC's *Annie* and *Jesus Christ Superstar*, as well as Fox's *Grease*. Not to mention shows like *Smash*, *Glee*, *Crazy Ex-Girlfriend*, and *Zoey's Extraordinary Playlist* becoming weekly mainstays. This is all in addition to the boom of musicals on Broadway. The 2018–2019 season hosted 14,768,254 patrons on Broadway and grossed $1.8 billion.[2] Musical theatre is mainstream, and some might even say we are living in a "New Golden Age" of Broadway.[3]

Before we can understand how we got to this "New Golden Age," we need to start at the beginning of this uniquely American artform. Much like America itself, musical theatre is a mosaic of genre, style, storytelling, and origin. The development of musical theatre, like many artforms, was also heavily impacted by the sociopolitical climate of the time. The American musical took many years to find its own identity, much of which was influenced by earlier European artforms.

THEATRICAL BEGINNINGS

Storytelling has existed since time began. The earliest humans would gather around a campfire and share stories,[4] and music has been known to predate agriculture in the human species.[5] This need for community and storytelling is part of who we are as human beings.

Although musical theatre as we know it did not come to fruition until centuries later, music and drama have been interconnected across the globe for centuries. Drawings and wall paintings in African caves show people participating in theatrical rituals, complete with props, costumes, and scripts.[6] The Greeks included singing, dancing, instrumental music, and intoned oration in their theatrical events.[7] They considered oration to be of the utmost importance and would spend a great deal of time training their voices just as the Greek athletes would train for competition.[8]

Despite setbacks from the bubonic plague and the Dark Ages, theatre continued to flourish. The Renaissance saw "reworkings" of ancient Greek and Roman plays, and the need for new plays to be written for the many theatre companies that were being established at the time.[9] In the late 1500s, the Florentine Camerata began to gather. They were a group of humanists, musicians, poets, and intellectuals who came together to infuse the music of the day with elements of Greek storytelling.[10] While many composers had been experimenting with this new musical format, Monteverdi wrote the first fully realized opera, *L'Orfeo*, in 1607.[11] Opera quickly became a popular source of entertainment for the wealthy across Europe.

The Beggar's Opera

Although opera had become a famous pastime of the rich in England, the artform was not readily accessible to the lower classes. Most were performed in languages other than English and revolved around characters and themes that the common people would not find relatable. Journalist John Gay became inspired to create an opera for the working class. In 1728, *The Beggar's Opera* opened in London, becoming the first ballad opera. Ballad operas were racy with satirical plots. They used more familiar music styles than opera (including preexisting songs), were written in English, and even used dialogue between the songs.[12] *The Beggar's Opera* was a massive hit, proving that there was an audience for this type of English-language material, especially with its more approachable themes and content. *The Beggar's Opera* was one of the most produced shows in the British colonies during the eighteenth century.[13]

Although *The Beggar's Opera* is well known for its success, the first musical production on American soil occurred much earlier in 1735. *The Opera of Flora, or Hob in the Well* was staged in a Charleston, South Carolina, courtroom.

The year 1753 saw the first professional theatre company open in New York, the Theatre on Nassau Street, led by Lewis Hallam. Not long after, the theatre company moved to Philadelphia, where Dutch laws prohibited plays and operas from being acted out on stage. Not only were shows prohibited, but patrons were also fined if they attended. Hallam battled these laws for years. In 1767, the first musical written by an American, *The Disappointment or The Force of Credulity: A New American Comic Opera of Two Acts by Andrew Barton, Esq.*, was scheduled to open, but it was considered too crude to be seen by audiences, and thus closed before opening night. This type of censorship was the first time—but certainly not the last—that American puritanical values and societal issues directly impacted the American musical theatre.[14]

The American Revolution

During the American Revolution, there were laws enacted to restrict theatrical productions, although they began to disappear by 1793. America began to see a resurgence of theatrical performance, supported in part by President George Washington's regular theatre attendance. During this time, the American stage continued to rely mostly on imported forms such as British plays and European comic operas.[15] The comic opera was similar to the ballad opera, but as the name suggests, was more comedic in nature, typically without the provocative, often political plots. They used original music and always had a happy ending.

It was not uncommon to see music integrated into most theatrical productions of the 1800s. Plays would often include musical numbers between acts, and even some performances of Shakespearean tragedies were known to have included popular songs or musical numbers before or after the performance.[16] The spectacle of American musical theatre dates back to this era as well. Many theatres sat up to three times as many people as a modern-day Broadway theatre, so production elements had to be substantial to fill the space.[17] An exaggerated performance style was a necessity to hold the focus of the audience and to be seen and heard.

By 1822, New York City had become the economic and cultural center of the United States, due in part to the industrial revolution.[18] With population rising, the need for entertainment grew. New York City saw a boom of theatres being built across the city.

The African Theater

One such theatre was the African Theater. It was owned and operated by William Henry Brown and was the first Black theatre company in America.[19] Brown owned a tea garden around 1816 that would cater to Black patrons and featured food, drinks, and entertainment. The entertainment quickly became the star attraction. Brown formed an amateur theatre company that mounted more ambitious productions. By 1820, Brown had purchased a new space where he built a three-hundred-seat theatre to stage more professional productions.[20] The theatre company featured numerous Black actors, including Ira Aldridge, who would go on to become of the most famous, and well-respected, Shakespearean actors of all time. Aldridge would ultimately receive a plaque of distinction at the Shakespeare Memorial Theatre in Stratford-upon-Avon, the only actor of African American descent to receive this honor.[21]

As Brown's company began performing Shakespeare's plays, there was immediate backlash from the White community. Robert Hornback writes in his book *Racism and Early Blackface Comic Traditions*:

> At a time when "Shakespeare" was associated with the most eloquent oratory . . . the fact that some free black men and women were owning their freedom by voicing Shakespearean eloquence posed an extraordinary challenge to white supremacy. The black community in New York gravitated to Shakespeare not solely for entertainment purposes (one motive),

but also in support of a bolder agenda, in order to demonstrate that black Americans were in no way inferior to white Americans.[22]

Brown's productions quickly came under attack by the press, theatre owners, and citizens who would often mob the theatre, with no consequences by local law enforcement.[23] When Brown changed the name of the theatre to "The American Theater" in attempt to assert the equality of Black and White Americans, the attacks worsened, forcing the American Theater to close in 1823.[24]

Minstrel Shows

One of the ways the American Theater was attacked was by misrepresentation of the Black actors' talents, specifically their elocution. White journalists purposefully created a comedic, characterized dialect to demean the actors and bring an end to Brown's theatre. This racist dialect became standardized in print and a major part of minstrel shows, which were gaining popularity at the time.[25]

The minstrel show was an entertainment form based on the denigration of Black culture.[26] These minstrel shows attracted mostly White, male audiences and created harmful "malignant stereotypes"[27] of Black Americans. White performers would utilize the aforementioned dialect, in addition to "ill-fitting clothes . . . contorted movements,"[28] and blackface. New York City audiences supported the minstrel show for about twenty-five years, but the genre was kept alive by numerous troupes that toured and entertained the smaller cities and towns throughout the United States well into the twentieth century.[29] In the years following the Civil War, additional forms of entertainment began to rise in popularity. This led to many minstrel troupes looking to keep up with the changing times. This time period also saw a rise in minstrel shows that featured larger casts, all-female casts, and all-Black troupes, many of which still donned blackface.

The minstrel show was the first form of musical theatre born on American soil. The racist underpinnings of the minstrel show are another example of how intertwined the development of musical theatre is with the American sociopolitical climate. At the time, Black Americans were segregated, discriminated against, disenfranchised, and subjected to racially fueled violence that typically went unpunished.[30] In order to find success as a Black minstrel performer, these actors were forced to conform to these demeaning, harmful stereotypes to ensure the "White comfort"[31] of their audience. In fact, reinforcing negative stereotypes to play to the comfort of White, cisgender, nondisabled, and male audiences is an all-too prevalent theme in the American musical theatre. It would be many years before Black performers would be afforded the opportunity to perform as their authentic self on the musical stage.

Burlesque

Burlesque was another popular form of entertainment that first appeared in the United States in the 1840s. It was a type of variety show that typically involved elements of mockery of the upper class, provocatively dressed women, and striptease. Burlesque could take the form of short musical shows or could be stretched into longer productions. Most shows loved to mock the more serious subjects of the day. Many writers, performers, and designers gained early experience through burlesque before moving into vaudeville, theatre, film, and television.[32]

Laura Keene and the Extravaganza

One of the most successful producers of burlesque was Laura Keene. She is believed to be the first woman in America to run a professional theatre.[33] She was not only an accomplished actress but was considered one of the most important producers of the era, creating some of the more popular shows of the 1860s.[34] Her productions combined burlesque, ballet, music, and spectacular sets and costumes, giving way to a new type of entertainment: extravaganza, or sometimes called burlesque extravaganza. Complete with lavish staging, special effects, and opulent costumes, the comedic focus was often multifaceted, lampooning everyone and everything from famous persons to popular books, popular culture, and more.

Keene eventually opened her own theatre on Broadway, Laura Keene's Theater, in 1856. Her production of *The Elves* set the record as the first "long-running" musical on Broadway with a run of fifty performances. This was followed by an even more astonishing achievement when her show, *The Seven Sisters,* ran for an unprecedented 253 performances.[35]

The Civil War

During the time of the Civil War (1861–1865), most theatre productions were produced in the North because of bigger populations and wealth. During this time, audiences sought out entertainment that distracted them from the realities and ravages of the war. On April 14, 1865, Laura Keene's theatre company presented a benefit performance of the highly popular satirical comedy *Our American Cousin* at the Ford Theater in Washington, D.C. It was during this performance that John Wilkes Booth assassinated President Lincoln. It has been rumored that Laura Keene herself cradled the president as he died. In 1867, Keene became the first person to offer a cash prize of one thousand dollars to the writer of the best new American play.[36] This tradition of offering cash prizes, grants, and financial fellowships to support American writers continues to this day.

Vaudeville

In the 1850s, saloons began offering entertainment to attract customers. This entertainment typically consisted of skits, singing, dancing, juggling, or any other type of simple, short entertainment. It wasn't long before this casual format was formalized into vaudeville. The father of vaudeville was Tony Pastor, a performer who had spent years traveling as a ringmaster, minstrel, and clown. He created vaudeville shows with performing acts that would come and go throughout the run of the show. He chose to make vaudeville family friendly, even opening the doors to women, which was uncommon at the time. He could now sell tickets to the entire family, not just the men, which would prove more profitable. This family friendly entertainment set vaudeville apart from burlesque and minstrel shows, the other popular entertainment of the time.

Although the theatre was off-limits to smoking and drinking, Pastor found a pub in the same building to reserve for the male patrons. He created a separate entrance from inside the theatre to the bar so that they could drink and smoke freely. Pastor was able to make money on both the family ticket sales and the alcohol, a financial model that is still seen on Broadway today.[37]

Vaudeville became a popular form of entertainment, with many famous performers gaining valuable experience on the vaudeville circuit.[38] The performers would travel between theatres, sometimes up to forty weeks a year. Performances were divided into levels: "small time," "medium time," and "big time." The theatres and salaries improved with each level, ranging from small town theatres, which served as training grounds for newer performers, to the finer theatres in the biggest cities. The smaller the theatre and act, the shorter the run. These smaller acts would be subjected to "one-nighters" and split-week engagements, while larger, more famous acts might play a venue for weeks at a time.[39] To this day, it is not uncommon to see smaller musical theatre tours still adhere to the "one-nighter" and split-week model, while the larger, more profitable Broadway tours tend to play each venue anywhere from one week to six months.

Pantomime

Pantomime acts tell a story with body or facial movements and were often paired with other types of entertainment beginning in the 1700s. It became popular during the latter half of the nineteenth century and frequently centered around Mother Goose–themed characters. Pantomime had a mass appeal because you did not need to speak English to enjoy the show. Although pantomime went out of fashion in the United States by 1880, it is still an English holiday tradition. British families pile into theatres and village halls throughout England to see these holiday shows, which are still typically based on children's stories.[40] While the modern-day "panto" does include dialogue, it is a direct descendent of this popular entertainment style of the nineteenth century.

The Black Crook

The Black Crook is often considered the first American musical, despite not technically being a musical. In 1866, producer William Wheatley was in rehearsals for a new German drama, *The Black Crook* at his theatre, Niblo's Garden. At the same time, two other producers were importing a new ballet from a French ballet troupe to perform at the Academy of Music. Unfortunately, the academy suffered a devastating fire while the dancers were en route. Upon arrival to New York, the producers approached Wheatley about using his theatre for the premiere of their ballet. Wheatley agreed to take the ballet and insert it into the play. What resulted was a play with dancing, in addition to interpolated songs by popular composers, that lasted over five hours on opening night.

Despite the length, the show was a success. It ran for an unprecedented 474 performances and earned over one million dollars in the first year. One of the show's key features was the ballet dancers' flesh-colored tights. This was particularly shocking at the time and added sex appeal to the production. This type of scandal helped sell tickets and made *The Black Crook* the first show to combine drama, music, and dance on American soil.[41]

Operetta

Another form of entertainment that was wildly popular at the end of the nineteenth century was operetta. These light operas typically had a romantic plotline and an accessible, soaring score, always with a happy ending.[42] They often took place in lavish settings, like ballrooms and castles. Numerous writers found success writing operettas, such as Victor Herbert, Jacques Offenbach, and most famously, Gilbert and Sullivan.[43]

Gilbert and Sullivan

In the 1870s, British playwright William Schwenk Gilbert and British composer Arthur Sullivan began their famous collaboration. Their "comic opera," *H.M.S. Pinafore*, arrived in the United States in 1878 and was instantly a success. After its debut in Boston, productions of the show began popping up all over the states, sometimes including competing productions in one city. At one time, there were up to eight competing productions of *H.M.S. Pinafore* in New York City alone.[44] Unfortunately, Gilbert and Sullivan did not receive any royalty payments for these unofficial productions due to international copyright laws. The official production of *Pinafore*, mounted by Gilbert, Sullivan, and longtime producer Richard D'Oyly Carte, arrived in New York in 1879, after the States had seen upwards of 150 pirated productions.[45] This was the first production to pay royalties to Gilbert and Sullivan for their work. These laws were something Gilbert, an attorney, would fight in later years to protect the work of dramatic authors.[46]

One of the most important impacts Gilbert and Sullivan had on the creation of musical theatre was in the structure of their shows. Almost all their shows revolved around a plotline of boy meets girl, boy loses girl, boy gets girl. While this was not new at the time, their commitment to story was. Up until this point, most forms of entertainment focused on a variety of acts in one evening, but Gilbert and Sullivan focused on one plot. There were no acts hired to come in and entertain between scenes. The entire pace of the evening was dictated by the story. The dialogue and music all centered around the plot, no matter how convoluted.[47] Audiences fell in love with this new plot-driven format.

A NEW CENTURY

At the turn of the twentieth century, the economy was booming, and a young America was coming into its own. New York City had become the cultural hub of the nation and more than thirty Broadway theatres were in existence. The expansion of the subway system made Broadway more accessible to the public and more tourists were visiting on railways and steamships. The new century seemed to hold endless possibilities.

Floradora

The first big hit came in the 1900–1901 season. The imported, British show was called *Floradora*, which like *The Black Crook*, had a popular female ensemble. The "Floradora Girls" represented the ideal women of the time and were the focus of a substantial amount of press and publicity. *Floradora* was also one of the first shows to sell sheet music to Americans across the country, in addition to taking advantage of the fledgling recording industry by recording two hit songs for the public to hear.[48]

George M. Cohan

There is no one who captured the patriotic spirit and vigor of the new century better than George M. Cohan. Cohan was born into a family of Irish American vaudeville performers and spent his entire life performing. In 1903, he wrote, composed, directed, produced, and starred in his first Broadway success, *Little Johnny Jones*. The show featured two of his biggest hits "Yankee Doodle Boy" and "Give My Regards to Broadway." Cohan was known for the American themes that ran through his plots. Cohan's America was seen as the land of opportunity where anyone with enough determination and grit could find success.

Prejudice on the Stage

One aspect of this newfound patriotism in musical comedy was unfortunately the xenophobia that is still prevalent in American society today. As America gained power over foreign territories, the fear of the "other" contaminating American society became normalized. This unfortunately made its way onto the musical stage. Between 1902 and 1907, several musicals played Broadway that all had essentially the same plot: an American gets mixed up in foreign affairs, and all is lost until the US Navy arrives to rescue the lost American, all the while overtaking the foreign armed forces. Shows like *The Sultan of Sulu*, *The Runaways*, *The Isle of Spice*, and *The Royal Chef* were a few of these "gunboat musicals" of the era.[49]

The fear of the "other" that these musicals perpetuated was often reinforced by the harmful portrayal of non-White American characters, specifically those from Asian, Oceanic, and Latin American countries. A shared feature of these shows was that anyone who was not American, or a love interest of an American, was portrayed as "barbaric, bloodthirsty, or buffoonish."[50] Although America was becoming the home to thousands of immigrants, it was clear that the America painted by George M. Cohan was not available to all—only to those who passed as White. And while the communities and cultures misrepresented in these shows have seen more authentic representation on the Broadway stage recently, there is still so much room for growth in the way non-White stories are told in American musical theatre.

The Shuberts

Vaudeville was still popular in the early 1900s, but it had faced a major structural shift. Three businessmen purchased theatres across the country creating what they called "circuits." By doing this, they were able to control the bookings across their entire circuit. Their business model grew, and eventually they were booking all vaudeville acts for the entire country out of one central booking office. They had a monopoly on producing theatre.

The Shubert brothers—Sam, Lee, and Jacob—were determined to take on this monopoly. They began by operating theatres in upstate New York before moving into the city with a lease on the Herald Square Theatre in 1900. By 1904, they owned ten theatres in New York City, and by 1929 they controlled 60 percent of the legitimate theatres in the country.[51] Currently, the Shubert Organization is the largest theatre owner on Broadway, with seventeen Broadway and six off-Broadway theatres under their control.[52]

Williams and Walker

Bert Williams and George Walker were writers, producers, and directors, and were the first successful Black musical theatre team. In 1901, the duo became the first Black recording artists. Although the recording industry was new at the beginning of the century, they recorded twenty-eight records for the Victor Company.[53] As their career progressed, they were finally able to break away from the racial stereotypes that were expected in their early career. In 1906, Williams originated a song called "Nobody" in the show *Abyssinia*, which would become his stage persona for the rest of his career. This persona was the inspiration for the character Amos Hart in Kander and Ebb's musical *Chicago*. The song "Mr. Cellophane" is based on Williams's famous tune.[54] After the death of George Walker in 1911, Bert Williams went on to become one of the most beloved and popular entertainers of the twentieth century. Williams and Walker were instrumental in opening the doors for many Black Americans in the entertainment industry.

In Dahomey

New York had seen a few all-Black shows by the time the new century rolled around. Touring shows that had made stops in New York were *The Creole Show*, *The Octoroons*, *Oriental America*, and *Black Patti's Troubadors* starring Sissieretta Jones, one of the greatest opera singers of the twentieth century and one of the highest-paid Black performers of her time.[55]

In 1903, *In Dahomey* broke ground by being the first all-Black musical to play a major Broadway house. The show starred Williams and Walker, was a huge hit with its White audiences, and created a new international dance sensation out of a traditional African American dance, the cakewalk. Despite portraying the typical stereotyped characters, Williams and Walker were notably proud of being involved in a show that was written and performed by Black Americans and was the source of employment for so many Black artists.[56]

Victor Herbert

Despite the rumblings of new American voices on Broadway, the European artforms were still prevalent. The music of Rudolph Friml, Sigmund Romberg, Jacques Offenbach, Franz Lehár, and Johann Strauss remained popular in the United States.

Victor Herbert, another Irish American immigrant, quickly became one of the most popular operetta composers of the early twentieth century. Herbert was trained in the European styles of music but was inspired by the new sounds of America. He penned the scores to operettas such as *Prince Ananias*, *The Fortune Teller*, *Babes in Toyland*, *Naughty Marietta*, and *The Enchantress*.

Herbert was also notoriously protective of his scores. It was not uncommon at the time for producers to make constant changes to scores, including bringing in other composers to write songs to be interspersed into the show. Herbert insisted on his shows having one, unified musical voice. This quickly became the norm and allowed for the rise of "star" composers that would become a major aspect of the musical theatre industry.[57]

Tin Pan Alley

In the early twentieth century, most middle-class families had pianos. The recording industry had not yet taken off, so Americans relied on sheet music to learn the songs of the day.[58] Music publishers began to realize that they could encourage people to buy sheet music by introducing new songs to the public. New York City became the heart of the music publishing industry with most publishers located on 28th Street between Broadway and Sixth Avenue. One could walk down this block, commonly referred to as Tin Pan Alley, and hear music wafting from the windows as pianists tried out these new, American songs.

New American Music

The onset of World War I (1914–1918) brought about a halt to the imported, European forms of entertainment. After the *Lusitania* sank in 1915, all nonessential travel was banned for the entirety of the war. This meant that not only could tourists not visit New York or London, but that it was also virtually impossible to import European entertainment. The war also invigorated a patriot spirit in the American public, and they wanted "American voices speaking in American idioms, using the imagery of newly emerging American myths and archetypes."[59]

One such type of music was ragtime. The rhythms of ragtime were based on the music of Black Americans. These rhythms had been used in minstrel shows, unfortunately with the intention of parody, for many years.[60] In 1893, Scott Joplin, a Black composer and pianist, legitimized ragtime to White audiences with a successful performance at the Chicago World's Fair. In 1900 his piano piece "Maple Leaf Rag" was a huge hit with the sheet music for the song selling over half a million copies by 1909.[61]

Although Joplin made ragtime mainstream in America, it was another composer who turned the entire world on to ragtime. Irving Berlin published "Alexander's Ragtime Band" in 1911, which became a worldwide hit, thus making Berlin a household name. Berlin also became popular for writing patriotic songs during World War I, just as George M. Cohan did, and even enlisted to fight in the war. His first Broadway musical, *Watch Your Step*, was revolutionary for featuring the syncopated rhythms of ragtime on the Broadway stage.

Another American composer popular in the early twentieth century was Jerome Kern. Kern revolutionized dance music on Broadway by writing dance songs in 4/4 time instead of the popular 3/4 waltz. This led to the inclusion of jazz dance vocabulary on Broadway.[62] Kern was also a believer of storytelling through song. He felt the music should help further the plot or add to character development. Although we take this for granted in modern musical theatre, it was a radical concept at the time.

Kern teamed with Guy Bolton and P. G. Wodehouse to write a series of popular musicals commonly referred to as the Princess musicals, as they were written for the Princess Theatre. Because of the small size of the theatre, these shows had to focus on character and story instead of the lavish sets and spectacle that were common at the time. American audiences fell in love with this form of "American" entertainment, especially because they felt the characters were relatable to the American way of life. Kern was also a staunch advocate for composers' rights. He, along with Irving Berlin, Victor Herbert, and John Philip Sousa, was a founding member of The American Society of Composers, Authors, and Publishers (ASCAP), a society that began to collect royalty payments on behalf of the writers.[63]

Revues

Revues became the perfect place to showcase these new American composers. While revues had been around for a while, their popularity increased in this new century. They bore a resemblance to vaudeville by featuring a variety of skits, songs, and dance numbers, but had some clear differences. While vaudeville was family friendly entertainment, revues were more political and satirical, and they featured scantily clad women. Vaudeville also featured revolving acts that might come and go from week to week, but revues had a set running order with the same performers for the length of the run.

The most popular composers of the day had songs featured in revues. Audiences would go to the theatre to hear new tunes penned by Irving Berlin, Jerome Kern, and George and Ira Gershwin. Revues became the first playground for this new, American musical theatre sound. Numerous producers became famous for their lavish versions of revues. The Shuberts created *The Passing Show*, George White had *George White's*

Scandals, Earl Carroll produced *Earl Carroll's Vanities*, and Florenz Ziegfeld famously conceived *The Ziegfeld Follies*.

The Follies were the most successful of the revues and Ziegfeld was considered one of the greatest producers of the early twentieth century. The Follies notoriously put women at the center of the spectacle. They were dressed in opulent costumes and would parade around the stage with their exposed bodies on display. The Follies also boasted numerous stars of the day such as Fanny Brice, Will Rogers, Eddie Cantor, and Bert Williams, who became the first Black performer to share the stage with a White ensemble.[64] The Follies first appeared in 1907, with the final edition arriving in 1931.

THE JAZZ AGE

America was coming of age in the new century. Producers were creating new forms of entertainment and writers were taking ownership of the new, American voice they were creating. Actors were also taking charge by standing up against the ever-powerful producer. In 1913, Actors' Equity Association (AEA) was formed to create better working conditions for actors, including guaranteed pay. In 1919, AEA executed the first actor's strike with the demand of recognizing the union as the bargaining agency for professional actors. The strike lasted for thirty days and included both Actor's Equity and Chorus Equity, which were eventually merged into one union in 1955.[65] To this day, AEA is still the union of professional stage actors and stage managers.

The country was also ravaged by a flu pandemic from 1918 to 1919. Despite losing around 675,000 American lives, and at least 50 million people worldwide, Broadway refused to shutter.[66] Theatres across the country closed for fear of mass contamination, but the New York City Health Commissioner refused to close the main theatres in the city. Instead, theatres were subject to strict cleaning procedures, including ventilation by opening all windows and doors during off-hours.[67]

As America headed into a new decade, producers were trying to financially recover from World War I, the flu pandemic, and the formation of the union. While theatre had been focused on notable producers for the past twenty years, this new decade would provide a change.

Composers and writers became the main attraction in this new era of musical theatre.

The Roaring Twenties

The 1920s were a decade of "unprecedented prosperity and self-confidence."[68] America was thriving under its newfound isolationism after World War I. Many American women were granted the right to vote in 1920 and the country experienced a sexual revolution. The decade was also known for Prohibition, which did not stop people from consuming alcohol, it simply moved them into speakeasies across the country. Americans were venturing outside of their homes for entertainment in record numbers. There was a huge desire for sophisticated, fun entertainment. The 1920s saw the number of productions increase, as well as the profits, length of the runs, and the quality of the entertainment.[69]

Jazz Music and Broadway

Jazz was born in the Black community in New Orleans. It made its way to other cities, such as Chicago, Memphis, and Kansas City, where it was cultivated into a thriving musical artform. Like its predecessor ragtime, jazz was also co-opted by White artists.[70] Jazz music combined the familiar syncopated rhythms of ragtime, with an element of improvisation. The vocals were known to have the emotional cry often found in the blues. The lyrics felt contemporary and real, and the rhythms felt as alive and free as the American spirit. This new sound became the sound of Broadway.

Richard Rodgers and Lorenz Hart wrote twenty-eight musicals and over five hundred songs between 1919 and 1943. Rodgers's music was jazzy and captured the spirit of the decade. Hart's lyrics were witty, playful, and had the ability to capture the depth of the human spirit. They were two of the hottest writers during the 1920s with fifteen shows playing Broadway during the decade, and one show on the West End. Some of their shows during this time were *Fly with Me*, *The Girl Friend*, *Betsy*, *Peggy Ann*, *A Connecticut Yankee*, and *Present Arms*.

George and Ira Gershwin were a sibling songwriting team who rose to popularity in the 1920s. When he was nineteen years old, George had his first big hit when "Swanee" was published. He teamed with his brother, Ira, in 1924 for the Broadway musical *Lady Be Good*. George decided to move away from writing stand-alone songs for revues and instead focused on writing book musicals with Ira. Book musicals are musicals with fully integrated dialogue, music, and lyrics, all serving the plot or storyline. The book of the musical refers to the spoken dialogue in the show. The Gershwins wrote nine book musicals from 1924 to 1929.[71] George's music was heavily influenced by jazz, with some infusion of traditional Jewish music. Ira's lyrics were witty and known for their wordplay.[72] Some of their other shows during this era were *Funny Face*, *Oh, Kay!*, and the flops *Treasure Girl*, and *Show Girl*. The Gershwin's music would be the basis for the future jukebox musicals *Crazy for You*, *Nice Work If You Can Get It*, and *My One and Only*.

Noble Sissle and Eubie Blake were known on the vaudeville circuit as the "Dixie Duo" where they got their start as a songwriting team. Together with Flourney Miller and Aubrey Miles, they wrote *Shuffle Along*, the first Black production on Broadway in over a decade.[73] The show was a huge success on many fronts. It was financially successful, but it also broke new ground. Black patrons at the show were not seated in segregated areas near the back of the theatre, but instead were seated as close as the fifth-row orchestra. *Shuffle Along* was also the first time Broadway saw two Black actors engage in an earnest love song. Despite the show depicting the egregious stereotypes that were still expected in the era, White audiences at *Shuffle Along* were presented with moments of depth and sincerity expressed on stage by Black actors.[74] This was revolutionary at the time. The show also revived the excitement for all-Black productions. *Runnin' Wild* followed *Shuffle Along* on Broadway and gave the world the song "The Charleston," which led to the dance craze that was all the rage during the decade. An all-Black revue, *Blackbirds*, also ran in the 1920s with much success.[75] *Shuffle Along* was the focus of the 2016 Broadway production *Shuffle Along, or the Making of the Musical Sensation and All That Followed*, which had a revamped book by director George C. Wolf. The musical focused on the making of *Shuffle Along* and gave contemporary audiences a chance to experience the fantastic original score by Sissle and Blake.

Show Boat

In 1927, Jerome Kern partnered with lyricist Oscar Hammerstein II to write *Show Boat*. Hammerstein was born into a theatrical family and was known for writing both book and lyrics, which was not common at the time. Kern and Hammerstein took almost a year to write *Show Boat*, which was unheard of, as most musicals at the time were churned out in a few weeks.

Show Boat broke new ground for musical theatre in a few ways. First, it was plot centered, with all the music existing to further said plot. This had been done before, but *Show Boat* had clearer storytelling. The show also discussed themes that were unheard of in the theatre at the time such as race relations, spousal abuse, alcoholism, gambling, and miscegenation. The show's opening number did not open with the common up-tempo dance number, but instead, opened on the Black characters of the show mid-work on the boat. This was jarring to the audiences at the time, who were so stunned on opening night, they did not clap at the end of the show. Despite this reaction, the show was a hit.[76]

It should be noted that while *Show Boat* was groundbreaking and did change the artform, the Black characters in the show were still written in a stereotypical fashion.[77] Additionally, despite hiring both Black and White actors, the role of Queenie, a pivotal Black character, was played by a White actress in blackface under the stage name "Aunt Jemima."[78]

THE GREAT DEPRESSION

Theatregoers in the late 1920s were reveling in the excitement and success of *Show Boat*. Unfortunately, the Great Depression hit in 1929, leaving few people who could afford the theatre. Those that could afford it, were not interested in the weighty, topical issues of *Show Boat*. They wanted frivolous entertainment.

Talking Pictures

In 1927, Al Jolson's *The Jazz Singer* was released, making it the first full-length movie with sound. This changed the face of the entertainment industry. Hollywood began making films at a rapid pace and produced more than thirty new movie musicals every year throughout the 1930s. To produce so many musicals, Hollywood needed experienced writers. Irving Berlin, Jerome Kern, Rodgers and Hart, Oscar Hammerstein II, and the Gershwins all had songs in numerous films during the decade.

Movie musicals became a direct competition to live theatre, especially during the Great Depression. Film could capture all the spectacle that was possible at the time and only charge around fifty cents a ticket, which was nothing compared to a three-dollar theatre ticket.[79] Even though ticket sales suffered throughout the 1930s, theatre was still alive. There were fewer shows being produced in New York, but those that did get produced were well-crafted and smart, proving that musical theatre was still growing.

Music of the 1930s

Cole Porter's first Broadway show was *Paris* in 1928, which was followed the next year by *Fifty Million Frenchmen*. Porter hit his stride in the 1930s with numerous Broadway hits including *The New Yorker, Gay Divorce, Anything Goes, DuBarry Was a Lady*, and *Red, Hot, and Blue*. Porter was known for his jazzy melodies and clever, scandalous lyrics, and was one of the most successful composers of the 1930s.

The Gershwins continued to write Broadway hits in the 1930s including *Strike Up the Band* and *Girl Crazy*, which starred Ginger Rogers and Ethel Merman. They followed this success with their biggest hit to date, *Of Thee I Sing*. The musical was a political satire and was the first musical to win the Pulitzer Prize for Drama. They followed this with a sequel called *Let 'Em Eat Cake*, which was one of the first Broadway musical sequels. In 1934, they dove into working on a project that would become *Porgy and Bess*. Based on the novel *Porgy* by DuBose and Dorothy Heyward, the show featured an all-Black cast. People still debate whether *Porgy and Bess* is an opera or a musical, with many considering it to be the first "great American opera."[80] The Gershwins moved completely away from satire for this show and focused on dramatic storytelling. The show ran for four hours and was mildly successful on Broadway, but the subsequent tour streamlined the show, proving more successful. *Porgy and Bess* was George Gershwin's last musical. He died suddenly of a brain aneurysm in 1937 while working on a film in Hollywood.

The Cradle Will Rock

In 1935, President Franklin Roosevelt created the Works Progress Administration (WPA), an initiative to create work opportunities for Americans. One branch of the WPA was the Federal Theatre Project (FTP), which helped fund theatrical productions across the country. The FTP funded a new musical by Marc Blitzstein titled *The Cradle Will Rock*. The musical had political themes and revolved around a fictional US town called "Steeltown, USA." In the show, the factory owner battled with the head of the workers union. However, real union talks were heating up in the steel industry at the time, so the WPA considered the show too controversial.[81] They closed the production and the theatre the day before opening night.

On opening night, director Orson Welles met the cast and audience in front of the theatre and walked them all uptown to an empty theatre. Because AEA had not approved the venue change for the production, the actors were not allowed to step foot on stage. Welles had them all take seats with the audience and proceeded to have them perform the show from the house, with Blitzstein accompanying the show from the lone piano on stage. The show was a massive success and provided one of the most exciting, interesting evenings at the theatre. It ran for 109 performances and has been revived several times off Broadway, often with the original, unintentional staging of placing the actors in seats on the stage or across the theatre.[82]

World War II

In 1939, World War II (1939–1945) began. America was still battling the Great Depression but found itself in the familiar throes of patriotism. Tin Pan Alley songwriters began writing patriotic tunes by the dozen. Irving Berlin, once again, became one of the most prolific songwriters of patriotic and war-related tunes.[83] While there were a few patriotic shows on Broadway during this time, they were not as common as during World War I. During the first war, theatre was the main source of entertainment for the American people. Shows featured patriotism and war-related themes to relay a patriotic spirit to the nation. During World War II, politicians in Washington created committees that oversaw Hollywood, radio broadcasts, songwriters, and the recording industry to make sure they kept the war at the forefront of their entertainment. By the 1940s, the government felt Broadway no longer had the same reach of the more popular forms of entertainment. This allowed producers to continue to produce the shows they wanted with no required patriotism. This led to the war consuming so many forms of entertainment, that the theatre became one of the few places where you could go and not be blasted with war propaganda.

Broadway had seen a steady decline in shows being produced during the Great Depression. However, despite fewer shows running during World War II, there was an increase in attendance. This was due partly to the escapism that Broadway offered, but also due to a boost in the wartime economy. There were also fewer number of shows to choose from, which meant that shows ran longer and ticket prices increased.[84]

THE GOLDEN AGE

In the 1940s, American musical theatre continued to mature. Broadway saw a few major shifts in storytelling. *Cabin in the Sky* was a musical that featured an all-Black cast including Ethel Waters, Todd Duncan, Dooley Wilson, and Rex Ingram. The show was written by Lynn Root, John LaTouche, and Vernon Duke. The creative team had George Balanchine, founder of New York City Ballet, at its center. He choreographed the entire show with seamless, dance-based transitions and set changes. He used dance to move the plot forward in new, inventive ways. He also collaborated with Katherine Dunham and her dance company to bring a Black voice to the choreography. He co-choreographed many numbers with Dunham, allowing her and her dancers to create movement that he then put in context of the balletic storytelling of the show. Although Dunham never received credit for her choreographic collaboration, she was a featured member of the cast.[85]

Pal Joey was a Rodgers and Hart collaboration that was also groundbreaking for a few reasons. First, Joey was an unlikable lead character. He was the first "antihero" on the Broadway stage.[86] He manipulated people and never found success. This was not the typical leading man of 1940s Broadway. The show also used dance in new ways. Many of the numbers took place in a nightclub, which impacted the choreographic language used in the show, in addition to featuring a dream sequence at the end of act 1.

Oklahoma!

Richard Rodgers was given the script to the play *Green Grow the Lilacs* by the Theatre Guild's director, Theresa Helpburn. He was immediately taken with the story and approached Lorenz Hart about working on an adaptation. Hart's mental and physical health had been declining, and it was clear that he would not be able to adapt the story. Rodgers approached Oscar Hammerstein II about adapting the work, and a new collaboration was born.

Oklahoma! opened on Broadway in 1943 and was a huge hit. It broke all box office records at the time. *Oklahoma!* was groundbreaking in many ways. It featured an opening number with only two people on stage instead of the entire chorus dancing. It was fully integrated, with all scenes and songs propelling the plot forward. Because Hammerstein wrote book and lyrics, he was able to seamlessly transition between dialogue and song. The show also featured a plot and a subplot that both resolved by the end of the show. And most notably, the choreography was fully integrated, including an act 1 finale "dream ballet" where Laurey contemplates her future. While each of these features had been seen on stage before (*Louisiana Purchase* had an opening number with only two people, *Pal Joey* and *Cabin in the Sky*'s choreography moved the plot forward, *Show Boat* had a main plot and subplot, and *Lady in the Dark* featured musical and dance numbers that explored the leading lady's psyche), *Oklahoma!* was the first show to incorporate all these elements into a commercially successful production. The show's success was not only in the writing, but in the choreography of the legendary Agnes DeMille. The Broadway audience of the 1940s was ready for this type of sophisticated entertainment. Future musicals would be expected to offer this type of integrated, plot-driven storytelling, with the composers acting as dramatists, not just songwriters.[87] *Oklahoma!* ushered in Broadway's "golden age," which continued until the mid-1960s.

After *Oklahoma!*

While the golden age of Broadway brought about new writing teams, some successful composers of the 1920s and 1930s tried their hat at writing in this new integrated fashion. Irving Berlin wrote *Annie Get Your Gun* in 1946, his first and only attempt at a book musical. The show received tepid reviews but was adored by audiences. The show was also a star vehicle for Ethel Merman. Like Berlin, Cole Porter was reticent to try his hand at this new form. His attempt in 1948, *Kiss Me, Kate*, would be one of his greatest successes. Rodgers and Hammerstein also continued to write musicals together. *Carousel*, *Allegro*, *South Pacific*, *The King and I*, *Me and Juliet*, *Flower Drum Song*, and *The Sound of Music* all appeared on Broadway in the 1940s and 1950s.

The Tony Awards

The Tony Awards also came to be during the golden age. The Tony Awards recognize excellence in Broadway theatre and are named after Antionette Perry, cofounder of the American Theatre Wing. The first ceremony was held in 1947 in a ballroom at the Waldorf Astoria Hotel, with seven awards being presented.[88] The Tony Awards continue to this day. Although they are no longer the only award show that recognizes the efforts of the theatrical community, they are the most widely recognized due to their national television broadcast.

A New Era for Choreography

Agnes DeMille was responsible for ushering in a new era of dance in musical theatre. After her success with *Oklahoma!*, she went on to choreograph shows such as *Bloomer Girl*, *Carousel*, *Brigadoon*, *Allegro*, *Gentlemen Prefer Blondes*, *Paint Your Wagon*, and *110 in the Shade*. Musical theatre was now expected to have dance numbers that furthered the plot, thanks to DeMille's revolutionary work.

Jerome Robbins was another monumental choreographer and director of the golden age era. His first hit was *On the Town*, which had a score by Leonard Bernstein, with book and lyrics by Betty Comden and Adolph Green. He went on to direct and/or choreograph musicals such as *West Side Story, Gypsy, Fiddler on the Roof, The King and I, Call Me Madame*, and *The Pajama Game*. Jerome Robbins is considered a genius, although he was known for being particularly cruel to his co-workers, especially the dancers he employed.[89]

New Writers of the Golden Age

The golden age not only brought about a new form for the American musical, but it also brought new writing teams to the scene. Leonard Bernstein was successful in the world of classical music and musical theatre. He wrote the score to *On the Town, Wonderful Town, Candide, West Side Story, Trouble in Tahiti*, and *1600 Pennsylvania Avenue*.

The lyricist and book writing team of Betty Comden and Adolph Green wrote the lyrics and books to some of the most popular musicals of the era. Their career was born in the golden age but continued through the 1990s. They wrote the lyrics and/or book to *Wonderful Town, Peter Pan, Bells Are Ringing, Do Re Mi, Applause, On the Twentieth Century*, and *The Will Rogers Follies*. They also wrote the screenplays to *Singin' in the Rain* and *The Band Wagon*.

The golden age also saw Alan Jay Lerner and Frederick Loewe begin their successful collaboration. They wrote the music, book, and lyrics to some of the biggest hits of the golden age including *Brigadoon, My Fair Lady, Paint Your Wagon, Finian's Rainbow*, and *Camelot*. *My Fair Lady* was the biggest hit of all, running for over seven years and making more money than any theatrical show to date.[90] Their success continued through 1960 with *Camelot*. The show had clear metaphors for Kennedy's America, and was even a favorite of the president. As Thomas L. Riis and Ann Sears state in *The Cambridge Companion to the Musical*, "The public's willingness to associate a new Broadway show with a contemporary presidency reveals the extent to which America was attuned to New York's theatrical life in its heyday."[91]

Jule Styne was a British-born, American-raised composer. After a successful career as a songwriter, he began writing musicals. His musicals included *High Button Shoes*, *Gentlemen Prefer Blondes*, *Hazel Flagg*, *Peter Pan*, *Bells Are Ringing*, *Gypsy*, *Do Re Mi*, *Subways Are for Sleeping*, *Funny Girl*, and *Hallelujah Baby!*.

Composer Frank Loesser also popped onto the scene with *Where's Charley?* in 1948. This was followed by *Guys and Dolls*, *The Most Happy Fella*, *Greenwillow*, and *How to Succeed in Business without Really Trying*.

Richard Adler and Jerry Ross were a composer and lyricist team that rose to fame with *The Pajama Game* in 1954, which was the first show produced by legendary director/producer Harold (Hal) Prince. *The Pajama Game* was directed by Jerome Robbins and choreographed by first-time choreographer, Bob Fosse. The following year, Adler and Ross had another hit with *Damn Yankees*, again with Bob Fosse as choreographer.

Composer, lyricist, and book writer Meredith Willson found success with his musical *The Music Man* in 1957. He was one of the few writers of the era who wrote all aspects of his musicals. He also wrote *The Unsinkable Molly Brown* and *Here's Love*, an adaptation of the film *It's a Wonderful Life*.[92] *The Music Man* had the first female full-time conductor on Broadway with Liza Redfield, who would continue to work as a conductor through the 1980s.

Bock and Harnick began writing in 1957. Their first hit was *Fiorello!* in 1959, which won the Pulitzer Prize for Drama. They followed this with *Tenderloin* and then *She Loves Me*. Their biggest hit was in 1964 with *Fiddler on the Roof*, which was known for bringing the experience of Jewish immigrants in Ukraine to the Broadway stage.

Composer Charles Strouse, lyricist Lee Adams, and book writer Michael Stewart wrote *Bye Bye Birdie*, which premiered on Broadway in 1960. The songs of Broadway had been the popular music of the day since the beginning of the century, but that began to change in the 1950s. The popularity of rock and roll began to rise, which appealed to the young people of the day.[93] *Bye Bye Birdie* featured a score of mostly musical theatre inspired songs, with the exception of those sung by Conrad Birdie, the fictional rock star in the story. His songs were parodies of the rock music of the day. Although it was intended to be a satire, this was one of the first times rock and roll was heard on Broadway.[94] This was a precursor of things to come as Broadway moved away from the golden age.

Jerry Herman's career began at the end of the golden age with *Milk and Honey* in 1961. He followed with *Hello, Dolly!*, which was his first hit. *Hello, Dolly!* won ten Tony Awards, which was the record for the most Tony awards until *The Producers* took home twelve in 2001.

The Golden Age Producers

The golden age brought two major producers onto the scene. The first was David Merrick. He produced eighty-eight shows on Broadway over the span of only fifty-four years.[95] Merrick was known for his outbursts, lack of collegiality, and willingness to go to any length for publicity. When *Subways Are for Sleeping* was on track to receive negative reviews, Merrick found seven locals who had the same names as the seven main theatre critics. He wined and dined them, gave them the best seats in the house, and then asked them their thoughts on the show. They unanimously raved about the production. Merrick had their quotes printed in an ad in a local paper. The stunt nearly cost him membership in the League of Broadway Producers and Theatres, but Merrick defended his antics. He said, "My own group of drama critics are real people, and I think far more representative of the tastes of the community."[96] This was not the only stunt that Merrick would pull off in his notorious career.

Hal Prince began his career as an assistant stage manager for George Abbott, one of the most prolific directors of the golden age. He began producing musicals in 1954 with *The Pajama Game* and moved into directing in 1963 with *She Loves Me*. Prince played a major role in musical theatre throughout the golden age and beyond.

A CHANGING ART FORM

As America headed into the 1960s, the country was changing. The Civil Rights Act of 1964 was passed and second-wave feminism gave many women the motivation to push for equal rights. The era of "free love" was officially in full swing. There were also stirrings of an antiestablishment movement called the counterculture that gained momentum as the United States went to war in Vietnam. Young people in America had more disposable income than any other era, so their preferred music, rock and roll, became the popular music of the day.[97] Musical theatre songs had been the mainstream music for decades, but that was beginning to slip away.

There were many writers in the 1960s that continued to write musicals in the style of the golden age. *Fiddler on the Roof*, *Golden Boy*, *She Loves Me*, *Man of La Mancha*, *Sweet Charity*, and *Mame* all opened in the 1960s. While these shows were written in the form and style of the earlier golden age musicals, many shows were already beginning to push the boundaries of what musical theatre could be.

The Concept Musical

In 1966, Kander and Ebb's *Cabaret* opened on Broadway, and a new type of musical was born: the concept musical. Producer Hal Prince was instrumental in creating the concept musical. Plot had been the defining feature of the golden age of Broadway, but in this new form, the concept would take center stage. In *Cabaret*, there are plot driven songs as you would expect in a musical, but there are also interspersed songs throughout the musical that comment on what is happening. Much of the show takes place in a nightclub, which allowed for a seamless transition into these commentary songs. Kander and Ebb became masters of writing songs that sounded like good, old fashioned showtunes, but underneath, they were motivated by painful, heartbreaking moments of character development. The title song in *Cabaret* was no exception. It's an up-tempo tune about finding joy in your life, but it's sung after the title character has faced numerous heartbreaks. This type of sophistication would carry into the next decade of musical theatre writing.

Off and Off-Off-

Off Broadway was born in the 1950s as a response to the commercialism and expense of Broadway. Broadway shows were becoming more and more expensive to produce, which meant that shows had to sell tickets to the general theatre-going audiences. This led to the material becoming more and more commercial to appeal to the masses. Off-Broadway spaces became a place where shows cost less to produce, and theatre makers could experiment more with content. The first successful off-Broadway musical was a revival of *The Threepenny Opera* in 1954, which showed that musicals could be financially successful off Broadway.[98]

By the 1960's many experimental theatre artists were becoming frustrated with off Broadway as it started to commercialize. Off Broadway had long been a training ground for younger artists, but as off Broadway grew, this was no longer the case. Many younger artists, especially those interested in more experimental theatre, were no longer being offered roles in off Broadway productions. Many of these young artists began to create their own theatre spaces in basements, cafes, and lofts, mostly in the downtown, bohemian neighborhoods of Greenwich Village and the East Village. This movement coincided with the counterculture movement of the 1960s. This led to a whole new generation of theatre makers who were not focused on commercial success.[99] The off-off-Broadway movement saw the birth of theatres such as the Judson Poets Theater, Caffe Cino, the Open Theatre, and Café La MaMa, which is still a thriving experimental theatre to this day.[100]

Hair

Most Broadway composers in the 1960s were trying to ignore rock and roll. Those that did attempt their hand at the genre typically did so in a mocking fashion. *Hair* was the first musical to play Broadway that had a rock sound.

Hair was born from the off and off-off-Broadway scene. The show was created by two actors, James Rado and Gerome Ragni, who were drawn to the off-off-Broadway scene because of the experimental approaches to storytelling. Ragni was in a show called *Viet Rock* in 1966, which premiered at the popular Café La MaMa. *Viet Rock* revolved around a group of men who serve in Vietnam and was improvisational in nature. The show also featured songs that were influenced by the political folk-rock of the day. Rado and Ragni were inspired by *Viet Rock*, so they began spending time observing hippies in the Village to craft a narrative that would eventually become *Hair*. Rado and Ragni set out to write *Hair* for Broadway from the beginning. They loved the experimental, political nature of off-off-Broadway, but they wanted to write a piece of musical theatre that would be authentically "downtown" but would play uptown for commercial audiences. Unfortunately, no Broadway producers were willing to produce the show. *Hair* found a life thanks to Joseph Papp and the Public Theatre. Papp selected *Hair*, even though it was not completely written, for the inaugural season for his off-Broadway theatre company.

Rado and Ragni still needed a composer for the show. They made the choice to not hire a theatre composer for the project because they wanted a more "downtown" sound. Composer Galt McDermot had experience writing jazz, rock and roll, and rhythm and blues, and wrote the score to *Hair* in two weeks. The show's music included various genres of popular music, all with a "rock" point of view. The show played off Broadway at The Public before being moved to a discotheque called The Cheetah Club.[101] Once the creative team found a home at the Biltmore Theater, they officially opened on Broadway in 1968.

The show not only ushered in rock music on Broadway, but pushed the boundaries of storytelling for commercial musical theatre.[102] Director Tom O'Horgan repeatedly had the actors break the fourth wall and address the audience directly, which was a common approach in off-off-Broadway theatre, but rarely seen on Broadway.[103] Structurally, *Hair* had a thin plot and is typically considered to be a concept musical, with a heavy focus on themes and ideas over linear storytelling. Both the concept musical and rock music would play a huge role in musical theatre in the coming decades.

Black Representation during the 1960s and 1970s

Every decade since 1900 had seen highly successful all-Black productions on Broadway until the 1960's. Despite the country being in the middle of the Civil Rights Movement, Broadway maintained its predominately White productions and audiences.[104] There were few new, all-Black productions happening. *Hallelujah, Baby!* was the most successful attempt, in 1967, with its mixed-race cast and all-White creative team. It was also 1967 that saw the recasting of *Hello, Dolly!* with an all-Black cast. Pearl Bailey was in the title role of Dolly Levi and Cab Calloway played Horace Vandergelder. The recasting was met with varied reactions from critics and the Black community and closed shortly after opening.[105]

Purlie opened in 1970 and had a score that was a mixture of gospel, blues, and soul. *Purlie* was followed by *Don't Bother Me, I Can't Cope* in 1972. Micki Grant, the first Black woman to write the music and lyrics to a Broadway musical, crafted the score with sounds of gospel, jazz, funk, soul, calypso, and soft rock.[106] *Raisin*, based on the Pulitzer Prize winning play *A Raisin in the Sun*, opened on Broadway in 1973 and was a huge success. A mixed-race revival of *The Pajama Game* also arrived in 1973 and an all-Black rendition of *Guys and Dolls* in 1976. *The Wiz* was one of the most successful musicals of the 1970s, winning seven Tony Awards for the predominately Black creative team and all-Black cast. The score was Motown inspired and showed the staying power of musicals written by Black writers, starring Black actors, for Black audiences. The 1970s also saw multiple all-Black reviews such as *Bubbling Brown Sugar*, *Ain't Misbehavin'*, and *Eubie!*

Rock Music

Rock music cemented itself as a mainstay on Broadway during the 1970s. *Hair* was followed on Broadway by *Promises, Promises*, which had a pop score penned by songwriter Burt Bacharach. Andrew Lloyd Webber and Tim Rice's rock musical *Jesus Christ Superstar* was released as a concept album in 1970. The album was so successful that it was staged for Broadway in 1971 and became one of the longest-running shows of the 1970s. Stephen Schwartz saw his first off-Broadway hit in 1971 with *Godspell*, the pop-inspired musical based on biblical parables. He followed that success with *Pippin* and *The Magic Show*. *Grease* opened on Broadway in 1972 and was one of the biggest hits of the decade. The show featured rock music of the 1950s, which hit the right nostalgic chord for Broadway theatregoers. *Shenandoah*, *The Robber Bridegroom*, and *The Best Little Whorehouse in Texas* all brought country music to Broadway in the 1970s. The decade ended with another Lloyd Webber and Rice rock collaboration with the rock musical *Evita* as well as the Marvin Hamlisch and Carole Bayer Sager pop musical *They're Playing Our Song*.

One of the major changes rock musicals brought to Broadway was the use of electric instruments and microphones. *Hair* and *Jesus Christ Superstar* both used electric instruments in their shows, as well as hand-held microphones on stage for their actors. *Promises, Promises* was the first musical to use microphones in the orchestra in the late 1960s.[107] By the 1970s and 1980s, performers were wearing body mics and being amplified over the orchestra at all times. Rock music, and its related genres, were here to stay.

Stephen Sondheim

Sondheim, an apprentice to Oscar Hammerstein II, began his Broadway career by writing lyrics for *West Side Story* in 1957 and *Gypsy* in 1959. Although Hal Prince was a producer on *West Side Story*, Sondheim and Prince really began their legendary partnership in 1970 with *Company*, a risky concept musical that centered around the idea of committed relationships. The show challenged American audiences in ways that musical theatre had not done in the past, which became a common theme in Sondheim's work.[108] Prince and Sondheim went on to collaborate on some of the most groundbreaking musicals of the 1970s and early 1980s. *Follies*, *A Little Night Music*, *Pacific Overtures*, and *Merrily We Roll Along* were all financial disappointments at the time, although a few of the shows had decent runs. *Sweeney Todd* opened in 1979 and was the most financially and critically successful of the Prince and Sondheim collaborations.

Dance in the 1970s

Bob Fosse hit his stride in the 1970s as a director and choreographer. In 1972, his unique style of direction and choreography brought him two Tony Awards for *Pippin*, an Oscar for best director for the film version of *Cabaret*, and an Emmy for best direction of Liza Minnelli's TV special, *Liza with a Z*.[109] In 1975, he directed and choreographed the new Kander and Ebb musical *Chicago* and created the all-dance show *Dancin'* in 1979. In 1999, a tribute to Fosse entitled *Fosse*, ran on Broadway for over a year and a half.

Michael Bennett was a Broadway performer turned choreographer and director. His first directing credit was as codirector of *Follies* with Hal Prince, but it was *A Chorus Line* that put Bennett on the map. The show was a concept musical that centered around the audition process for Broadway dancers. The stories in the show were based on the real-life experiences of dancers, many of whom were in the show playing themselves. *A Chorus Line* began at the Public Theatre through a series of workshops, but then ran for fifteen years on Broadway and was financially a massive success. Bennett's next, and final, hit before passing away was *Dreamgirls*, which opened on Broadway in 1982.

One of the most successful traditional book musicals of the 1970s was *Annie*, by Martin Charnin, Charles Strouse, and Thomas Meehan. The show was for families and showed that there was a profit to be made from shows that appealed to the entire family.

A RETURN TO SPECTACLE

The 1980s saw a major shift in the business model of Broadway. It was becoming increasingly more expensive to mount a Broadway production. The 1980s saw the end of the single producer and instead, saw shows being coproduced by multiple entities. There was also a big push toward unionization in the 1980s, so the cost of hiring union actors, stagehands, musicians, front-of-house employees, and so on, increased the weekly running costs of a show substantially. Additionally, in the 1970s and 1980s, three major organizations bought all the theatres on Broadway: the Shubert Organization, the Nederlander Organization, and Jujamcyn Theatres. In the 1980s, these theatre owners began to take on the role of coproducer in the shows that ran in their spaces. This meant that these organizations were not only making rent money from the productions but were now financially invested in the long-term success of the shows. These three organizations became the gatekeepers of Broadway. As a result of all these factors, ticket prices began to skyrocket. In 1970, the average ticket price for an orchestra seat was ten dollars. By 1980, the average price per ticket was between fifty-five and sixty-five dollars. This was a 600 percent increase in just ten years.[110]

To make a profit on a commercial Broadway run, you now had to have a long-running hit. Broadway began to return to its roots of extravaganza with lavish sets and special effects, and even saw an influx of sung-through shows, somewhat like the musical form of operetta. Enter the megamusical.

The Megamusical

Cats was the first megamusical to make its way to Broadway. Cameron Mackintosh was the sole producer on *Cats* and decided to open the show in London first, then transfer the production to Broadway. This helped lower costs as well as give the show plenty of time to build interest through marketing. The *Cats* logo was splattered all over New York City in the months leading up to opening. The show's set was lavish, the score was sung through, and the show appealed to the many tourists who visit New York City. *Cats* became a hit and ran for eighteen years on Broadway. *Cats* paved the way for other British imports such as *Les Misérables*, *Miss Saigon*, and *Phantom of the Opera*, all of which were financially successful on Broadway. *Chess*, *Aspects of Love*, *Starlight Express*, and *Sunset Boulevard* were other British shows that played Broadway but found less financial success.[111]

American Musicals

There were plenty of American musicals that opened on Broadway in the 1980s, despite the influx of British megamusicals. They included *Baby*, *Sunday in the Park with George*, *Into the Woods*, *The Rink*, *La Cage aux Folles*, *Big River*, *The Mystery of Edwin Drood*, *Grand Hotel*, *City of Angels*, *Nine*, *42nd Street*, and *Jerome Robbins' Broadway*, a revue celebrating the work of Jerome Robbins. *Little Shop of Horrors* began off-off-Broadway, but quickly moved off-Broadway where it ran for over two thousand performances. While some of these shows did win awards, and many are considered classics in the musical theatre cannon, none came close to the financial success of the British megamusicals.

THE INCORPORATION OF BROADWAY

Times Square had been in decline during the 1970s and 1980s. The area was filled with strip clubs, porn houses, and seedy massage parlors, not to mention a rise in crime. Although attempts had been made to clean up the area in the 1980s, no plans included the theatres as part of this revitalization. That began to change in the 1990s when the city of New York was able to convince corporations that investing in Times Square and the theatre industry would be financially viable.[112]

Disney

The Walt Disney Company's first foray into Broadway was with *Beauty and the Beast* in 1993. As production costs rose throughout the 1980s, it was nearly impossible to mount new, full-scale productions on Broadway without some serious financial help. The Walt Disney Corporation had money to spare and was able to foot the bill for the stage adaptation of their beloved animated film. The family-friendly model that started with *Annie* in the 1970s was adopted by Disney to overwhelming success. The show not only made money through ticket sales, but the merchandising for the show brought in substantial additional revenue.

Next, Disney invested six million dollars into the renovation of the New Amsterdam Theatre, which had fallen into disrepair after years of neglect. They would retain use of the space for their own properties, which is still in effect today. The New Amsterdam was the original home of *The Lion King* and now houses *Aladdin*.

Other corporations took note and began purchasing property and investing in theatrical properties. Companies like Cablevision, News Corp., Hallmark, and SFX-Entertainment, which later became part of Clear Channel Communications, all had a presence on Broadway in the 1990s and into the new century.[113] By the end of the 1990s, Times Square had been cleaned up and was a safe, family-friendly tourist destination.

Broadway and Beyond

The 1990s saw the rise of some new writers who were finding notoriety through other means than having a hit show on Broadway. William

Finn was one of the most influential writers of the 1990s and early 2000s. With *In Trousers, March of the Falsettos, Falsettoland, Falsettos,* and *A New Brain,* Finn was able to use traditional musical theatre structure with a more contemporary musical sound. Composers like Michael John LaChiusa, Andrew Lippa, Adam Guettel, Jeanine Tesori, and Jason Robert Brown were other important voices of the era. At one point in time, both LaChiusa and Lippa had a musical adaptation of *The Wild Party* playing in NYC. Lippa's version played off-Broadway, while LaChiusa's played on Broadway. Many of these writer's shows were written for smaller theatres, like regional theatres or off-Broadway, and were not aimed for the commercial landscape of Broadway. This meant they could push the boundaries of storytelling, a risky move for Broadway. Many of their shows also became licensed, which allowed productions to be done by regional and educational theatres nationwide. Licensing was the new model for musical theatre. Producers no longer expected to make their money back during the commercial run, but rather, would make royalties throughout the life of the property.[114] This allowed off-Broadway and regional theatres to become major players in the development of new musicals. Shows that were not meant for Broadway could still be successful.

On Broadway, another composer was finding success. Frank Wildhorn burst onto the scene with his adaptation of *Jekyll and Hyde* in 1997. He followed that with *The Scarlet Pimpernel* and *The Civil War.* At one point, all three shows were running on Broadway at the same time. Wildhorn would go on to write other Broadway shows, such as *Dracula, Bonnie and Clyde,* and *Wonderland.* Other shows that opened on Broadway in the 1990s were *Ragtime, Kiss of the Spiderwoman, Passion* (which won the Tony Award for best musical over *Beauty and the Beast*), *Victor/Victoria, Titanic,* and a revival of *Chicago* that is still running as of this writing.

Rent

Rent began off-Broadway, as many groundbreaking musicals do. The show was written by Jonathan Larson, who tragically died of an aortic aneurysm right before the show opened. The musical was based on Puccini's *La bohème,* was almost completely sung through, and brought a new generation of rock singers to Broadway. *The Who's Tommy* had opened in the early 1990s with its rock score, but *Rent*'s success brought a whole new generation of young people to the theatre. To make the show accessible to people in their twenties and thirties, the producers of *Rent* sold what they called "rush" tickets to anyone who was willing to stand outside and wait for a last-minute ticket. These twenty-dollar, front-row tickets were sold two hours before the show.[115] The show was a massive hit, winning the Pulitzer Prize for Drama in 1996.

Jonathan Larson was one of the strongest musical theatre voices of the 1990s, and his untimely death was a tragedy. In 1997, his family created the Jonathan Larson Grant, which is awarded yearly to a musical theatre writer to help fund their work. In 2018, theatre historian Jennifer Ashley Tepper put together a tribute album entitled *The Jonathan Larson Project*, which featured sixteen songs written by Larson that had not been heard since his death.

A NEW CENTURY (AGAIN)

Broadway struggled financially in the 1990s, mainly due to the high production costs. Off-Broadway and regional theatre were finding more success because of their ability to focus on the long-term life of a property rather than recoupment. When the attack on the World Trade Center happened on September 11, 2001, Broadway was halted for two days. The tourist industry was shattered and had to be rebuilt, but New Yorkers were insistent on gathering and showing their support of their city and country.[116]

Jukebox Musicals

Unsurprisingly, shows that were entertaining and provided escapism were the most successful in the years following 9/11. Jukebox musicals, which began appearing in the 1990s, became a mainstay on Broadway in the new millennium. Jukebox musicals can take two forms. The first is a revue type show such as *Smokey Joe's Café*, and the second is a plot-driven show that weaves the songs of an artist or era into the show, such as *Mamma Mia!* These shows became increasingly popular and successful, oftentimes due to the nostalgia that they offered. Shows like *Jersey Boys*, *The Boy from Oz*, or the later successful *Ain't Too Proud* offer audiences a look into the life of their favorite artist, all while hearing their songs on stage.

Movies into Musicals

Another trend that took hold in the 2000s was the prevalence of adapting movies into stage musicals. This trend began in the 1990s and was advantageous, given the high cost of mounting a Broadway musical. Selecting a property that was already known to the public was a smart financial decision. Movies that graced the Broadway stage included *Thoroughly Modern Millie*, *Urban Cowboy*, *Saturday Night Fever*, *The Full Monty*, *Dirty Rotten Scoundrels*, *Spamalot*, *Chitty Chitty Bang Bang*, *Mary Poppins*, *Xanadu*, *High Fidelity*, *Billy Elliot the Musical*, *9 to 5*, and the list goes on.

Comedies

Theatre goers were also seeking laughs in the 2000s. *Urinetown* opened nine days after the attack on the World Trade Center. The show poked fun at the seriousness of musicals and provided a much needed opportunity to laugh.[117] *The Producers*, which was based on the Mel Brooks movie, took home more Tony Awards in 2001 than any other musical had before. The show was a huge hit and tickets were hard to come by. It was the first show to offer "premium" tickets at a very premium price of $480 per orchestra seat.[118] *Avenue Q* was another sleeper hit that used Jim Henson inspired puppetry to tell an adult-themed story. The show, surprising everyone, beat the new Stephen Schwartz musical *Wicked* for the 2003 Tony Award for best musical. *Spamalot* was based on the film *Monty Python and the Search for the Holy Grail* and ran for just over four years throughout the new decade. *The 25th Annual Putnam County Spelling Bee* was penned by William Finn and was a small show that played Circle in the Square Theatre, which is Broadway's only theatre in the round. The show followed a common trajectory of musicals in this new century. It began in a regional theatre, moved to off-Broadway, then finally made its way to Broadway where it enjoyed a successful run. As the 2000s progressed, we began to see some shows alter this trajectory by moving back off-Broadway after a successful Broadway run. Both *Avenue Q* and *Jersey Boys* enjoyed long off-Broadway runs after closing on Broadway.

THE "NEW" GOLDEN AGE

In the 2010's, musical theatre became more mainstream than it had been in decades. Popular artists Dolly Parton, Cindy Lauper, Sting, Bono, David Bowie, and Sara Bareilles all penned original musicals. Musicals also began showing up on the big and small screen. Original musical television shows, live televised musicals, animated movie musicals, and feature musical films have all become part of American popular culture.

Hamilton rolled onto the scene in 2015 and was a cultural phenomenon. The show used rap, R&B, hip-hop, and pop genres in its storytelling. Not to mention the directorial vision of casting actors of color to play the historically White founding fathers. The cast album hit number one on the *Billboard* rap charts, something that was unprecedented for a musical.[119] In 2016, Lin-Manuel Miranda, the show's writer, released the *Hamilton Mixtape*, a collection of covers of the show's songs sung by popular recording artists of various musical genres. *Hamilton* had officially crossed over into mainstream music and culture. Musicals had not been this popular since the 1950s.

FINAL THOUGHTS: THE FUTURE

Broadway was coming off one of its most profitable seasons when the COVID-19 pandemic hit the world in 2020. Unlike the pandemic of 1918, this time New York theatres did close—for eighteen months. Despite being shuttered, theatre showed its resiliency. Gathering for storytelling has been part of human nature since the beginning of time, and this did not stop during the pandemic. New, innovative, digital formats of musical theatre began to emerge. Theatres began streaming performances to audiences across the globe, making musicals more accessible than ever before. Humans found a way to gather for storytelling, despite not being in the same physical location. The future of musical theatre looks bright, as it will be one of innovation and resilience.

NOTES

1. Jason Lipshutz. "Songs That Defined the Decade: Idina Menzel's 'Let It Go.'" *Billboard*, November 24, 2019, https://www.billboard.com/articles/columns/pop/8543911/idina-menzel-let-it-go-songs-that-defined-the-decade.

2. Michael Paulson, "Broadway's Box Office Keeps Booming. Now Attendance Is Surging Too," *New York Times*, May 29, 2019, https://www.nytimes.com/2019/05/29/theatre/broadway-box-office.html.

3. Jennifer Ashley Tepper, "Are We Living in a New Golden Age of Musical Theatre?," *Playbill*, August 28, 2018, https://www.playbill.com/article/are-we-living-in-a-new-golden-age-of-musical-theatre.

4. Nathan Hurwitz, *A History of the American Musical Theatre: No Business Like It* (New York: Routledge, 2014), 3.

5. Daniel J. Levitin, *This Is Your Brain on Music: The Science of a Human Obsession* (New York: Dutton, 2006), 250.

6. Sharrell D. Luckett and Tia M. Shaffer, *Black Acting Methods: Critical Approaches* (New York: Routledge, 2017), 1–2.

7. Hurwitz, *A History*, 3.

8. Gordon Heller, *The Voice in Song and Speech*, fourth edition (London: K. Paul, Trench, Trubner & Co., Ltd., ca. 1917), 3.

9. Hurwitz, *A History*, 7.

10. "Florentine Camerata," Wikipedia, Accessed October 24, 2021. https://en.wikipedia.org/wiki/Florentine_Camerata.

11. "Monteverdi's L'Orfeo," Lumen Learning, Accessed October 24, 2021. https://courses.lumenlearning.com/suny-musicapp-medieval-modern/chapter/monteverdis-lorfeo/.

12. Hurwitz,. *A History*, 9–11.

13. John Kenrick, *Musical Theatre: A History* (New York: Continuum, 2008), 33–34.

14. John Bush Jones, *Our Musicals, Ourselves: A Social History of the American Musical Theatre* (Waltham MA: Brandeis University Press, 2003), 1.

15. John Kenrick, "1700–1865: Musical Pioneers," Musicals 101, Revised 2020, http://www.musicals101.com/1700bway.htm.

16. Kenrick, "1700–1865."
17. Hurwitz, *A History*, 16.
18. Hurwitz, *A History*, 20.
19. Bernard L. Peterson, *The African American Theatre Directory, 1816–1960* (Westport, CT: Greenwood Press,1997), 3–4.
20. Peterson, *African American Theatre*, 3–4.
21. Krystyna Kujawinska Courtney, "Ira Aldridge, Shakespeare, and Color-Conscious Performance in Nineteenth-Century Europe," in *Colorblind Shakespeare*, edited by Ayanna Thompson (New York: Routledge, 2006), 103.
22. Robert Hornback, *Racism and Early Blackface Comic Traditions* (Cham, Switzerland: Palgrave, 2018), 215.
23. Hurwitz. *A History*, 22.
24. Hornback, *Racism*, 215.
25. Hornback, *Racism*, 219.
26. Kenrick, "Minstrel Shows," Musicals 101, Revised 2003, http://www.musicals101.com/minstrel.htm.
27. Hornback, *Racism*, 122.
28. Samuel A. Hay, *African American Theatre: An Historical and Critical Analysis* (Cambridge: Cambridge University Press, 1994), 19.
29. Kenrick, "Minstrel Shows."
30. Jones, *Our Musicals*, 28.
31. Jones, *Our Musicals*, 28.
32. Hurwitz. *A History*, 25.
33. Victoria Sherrow, "Keene, Laura," in *A to Z of Women: American Women Business Leaders and Entrepreneurs*, second edition, 2016. http://ezproxy.cul.columbia.edu/login?qurl=https%3A%2F%2Fsearch.credoreference.com%2Fcontent%2Fentry%2Ffofwblaese%2Fkeene_laura%2F0%3FinstitutionId%3D1878.
34. Katherine K. Preston, "American Musical Theatre before the Twentieth Century," in *The Cambridge Companion to the Musical*, ed. William A. Everett and Paul R. Laird, third edition (Cambridge: Cambridge University Press, 2017), 19–20.
35. Kenrick, *Musical Theatre*, 62.
36. Sherrow, Keene, Laura.
37. Hurwitz. *A History*, 28.
38. Preston, *American Musical Theatre*, 46.
39. Kenrick, *Musical Theatre*, 97.
40. Emily Castelow, "Pantomime," Historic UK, accessed May 2, 2021. https://www.historic-uk.com/CultureUK/Pantomime/.
41. Hurwitz. *A History*, 37–38.

42. Michael Kantor and Laurence Maslon, *Broadway: The American Musical* (New York: Applause, 2010), 42.

43. While we use the term operetta today, at the time these operas were referred to by their specific subgenres such as opéras bouffes or comic operas. Musicologists still make these distinctions.

44. Jones, *Our Musicals*, 7.

45. Hurwitz. *A History*, 42.

46. Jones, *Our Musicals*, 6.

47. Hurwitz. *A History*, 43.

48. Hurwitz. *A History*, 56.

49. Jones, *Our Musicals*, 25–26.

50. Jones, *Our Musicals*, 25.

51. Hurwitz. *A History*, 60.

52. "About Us," The Shubert Organization, accessed May 2, 2021. https://shubert.nyc/.

53. Hurwitz, *A History*, 64.

54. Hurwitz, *A History*, 64.

55. John Graziano, "The Early Life and Career of the 'Black Patti': The Odyssey of an African American Singer in the Late Nineteenth Century," *Journal of the American Musicological Society* 53, no. 3 (2000): 543–96.

56. Jones, *Our Musicals*, 34.

57. Hurwitz, *A History*, 63.

58. Kantor and Maslon, *Broadway*, 10.

59. Hurwitz, *A History*, 76–77.

60. Edward A. Berlin, "Ragtime before Scott Joplin," in *King of Ragtime: Scott Joplin and His Era*. second edition (New York: Oxford University Press, 2016).

61. Hurwitz, *A History*, 55.

62. Hurwitz, *A History*, 79.

63. Kantor and Maslon, *Broadway*, 12.

64. Kantor and Maslon, *Broadway*, 38.

65. "History," Actor's Equity Association, accessed May 2, 2021, https://www.actorsequity.org/aboutequity/history/.

66. Charlotte M. Canning, "Theatre and the Last Pandemic," *American Theatre*, March 24, 2020, https://www.americantheatre.org/2020/03/24/theatre-and-the-last-pandemic/.

67. Francesco Aimone, "The 1918 Influenza Epidemic in New York City: A Review of the Public Health Response," *Public Health Reports*, supplement 3, 125 (2010), 77.

68. Geoffrey Block, "The Melody (and the Words) Linger On: American Musical Comedies of the 1920s and 1930s," in *The Cambridge Companion to the Musical*, edited by William A. Everett and Paul R. Laird, third edition (Cambridge: Cambridge University Press, 2017), 132.
69. Hurwitz, *A History*, 94.
70. Kenrick, *Musical Theatre*, 169.
71. Hurwitz, *A History*, 100–101.
72. Hurwitz, *A History*, 131.
73. Kenrick, *Musical Theatre*, 189.
74. Hurwitz, *A History*, 110.
75. Kenrick, *Musical Theatre*, 190.
76. Hurwitz, *A History*, 113.
77. Warren Hoffman, *The Great White Way: Race and the Broadway Musical*, second edition (New Brunswick, NJ: Rutgers University Press, 2020), 32.
78. Hoffman, *Great White Way*, 34.
79. Hurwitz, *A History*, 119–20.
80. Hurwitz, *A History*, 132.
81. Kenrick, *Musical Theatre*, 232.
82. Hurwitz, *A History*, 133.
83. Jones, *Our Musicals*, 126.
84. Jones, *Our Musicals*, 128–29.
85. "Notes on Cabin in the Sky," The Library of Congress, accessed March 20, 2021. https://memory.loc.gov/diglib/ihas/html/dunham/dunham-notes-cabininthesky.html.
86. Hurwitz, *A History*, 141.
87. Kenrick, *Musical Theatre*, 238.
88. "An Award for Excellence," Tony Awards, accessed March 20, 2021, https://www.tonyawards.com/history/our-history/.
89. "The Uncompromising World of Jerome Robbins," BBC World Service, accessed March 20, 2021. https://www.bbc.co.uk/worldservice/arts/highlights/001004_robbins.shtml.
90. Hurwitz, *A History*, 153–55.
91. Thomas L. Riis and Ann Sears, "The Successors of Rodgers and Hammerstein from the 1940s to 1960s," in *The Cambridge Companion to the Musical*, edited by William A. Everett and Paul R. Laird, third edition (Cambridge: Cambridge University Press, 2017), 223.
92. Hurwitz, *A History*, 157–58.
93. Hurwitz, *A History*, 161–62.
94. Elizabeth L. Wollman, *The Theatre Will Rock* (Ann Arbor: University of Michigan Press, 2009), 16.

95. Hurwitz, *A History*, 159.

96. Howard Kissel, *David Merrick: The Abominable Showman* (New York: Applause, 1993), 293.

97. Hurwitz, *A History*, 172.

98. "Off-Broadway." Wikipedia. Accessed May 3, 2021. https://en.wikipedia.org/wiki/Off-Broadway.

99. Stephen J. Bottoms, *Playing Underground: A Critical History of the 1960's Off-Off-Broadway Movement* (Ann Arbor: University of Michigan Press, 2009), 2.

100. Visit https://www.lamama.org/ to learn more about LaMaMa and their work.

101. Wollman, *Theatre Will Rock*, 43–46.

102. Sarah Browne, "'Dedicated to the Proposition . . .' Raising Cultural Consciousness in the Musical *Hair* (1967)," in *Reframing the Musical: Race, Culture, and Identity*, edited by Sarah Whitfield (London: Red Globe Press, 2019), 170.

103. Wollman, *Theatre Will Rock*, 48.

104. Jones, *Our Musicals*, 203–4.

105. To learn more about the complexities of the Black productions in the 1960s and 1970s, see Hoffman, *The Great White Way*.

106. "Don't Bother Me, I Can't Cope," Wikipedia, accessed May 3, 2021. https://en.wikipedia.org/wiki/Don%27t_Bother_Me,_I_Can%27t_Cope.

107. Wollman, *Theatre Will Rock*, 126.

108. Hurwitz, *A History*, 191.

109. Hurwitz, *A History*, 196.

110. Hurwitz, *A History*, 202–5.

111. Hurwitz, *A History*, 208–11.

112. Wollman, *Theatre Will Rock*, 142–43.

113. Wollman, *Theatre Will Rock*, 143.

114. Hurwitz, *A History,* 220.

115. Logan Culwell-Block, "From Sleeping on the Streets to Swiping on a Screen: The Evolution of Rush Tickets From *Rent* to Digital Lotteries," *Playbill*, September 7, 2015, https://playbill.com/news/article/from-sleeping-on-the-streets-to-swiping-on-a-screen-the-evolution-of-rush-tickets-from-rent-to-digital-lotteries-361078.

116. Hurwitz, *A History*, 235.

117. Hurwitz, *A History*, 237.

118. Hurwitz, *A History*, 228.

119. Jennifer Ashley Tepper, "Are We Living in a New Golden Age of Musical Theatre?," *Playbill*, August 28, 2018, https://www.playbill.com/article/are-we-living-in-a-new-golden-age-of-musical-theatre.

2

MUSICAL GENRES

There is no one sound that defines musical theatre. There are enough musical genres represented in the musical theatre canon that it would be impossible to define Broadway as a singular musical genre or sound. The musical theatre singer needs to have fluency between these various genres. It is not uncommon for singers to move from one genre of music to another, sometimes in the same audition. Understanding the various genres will help singers navigate styles more easily, in addition to aiding in selecting repertoire for auditions or performance.[1]

If you think back to musical theatre history, you will recall that the music of Broadway from the 1920s to the 1950s typically became the popular music of the day. Popular Broadway songs would be played on the radio and folks would purchase sheet music of musical theatre hits to play at home. This began to shift when rock music became popular in American culture. Eventually, Broadway caught up and started using rock music in its storytelling. The musical genres represented on Broadway began to grow and expand as rock, blues, gospel, funk, and country started showing up on stages in the 1960s and 1970s. The genres have expanded even further to include rap, EDM, folk, indie/alternative, and punk. While it is not a requirement for every musical theatre singer to master *all* genres of music represented in musical theatre, facility across multiple genres is what is typically asked of the musical theatre singer in the current Broadway climate.

WHY GENRE IS IMPORTANT

The musical theatre industry often uses the umbrella term "pop/rock" to indicate songs that are not from a musical, although this term typically encompasses *all* non–musical theatre genres, not just pop and not just rock. In order to select material that is appropriate for an audition, especially a pop/rock song, you need to have a thorough understanding of the show, which includes the musical genres used.

For instance, when auditioning for *Mean Girls*, you might be asked to prepare a pop song in the style of the show. To find the right song, you would first need to identify what character you felt you were the most right for, and then recognize what genre of music their songs were written in. In contemporary musical theatre, composers often incorporate multiple genres within one show. Thinking specifically about genre gets you ruminating on what artists, composers, or bands sound similar to the role you're auditioning for. This brainstorming can help you pick an audition song. For *Mean Girls*, the role of Regina has a more R&B, rock, and pop sound, while Cady has more of a straightforward pop sound. The same pop song might not work for both roles.[2]

Sometimes the divide between genres in a show is even more vast than the above example. For instance, consider Orpheus and Hades in *Hadestown*. Not only do they sing in different ranges and parts of their voice, but each of their songs utilize different musical genres. Orpheus's music is more in line with indie/alternative and is especially reminiscent of the artist Jeff Buckley, while Hades's music is more blues, beckoning to the music of Tom Waits. It would not make sense to sing the same song for Orpheus that you would for Hades. It is important to dig as deep as you can when exploring genres, especially when subgenres come into play. Every musical genre has subgenres and variations within. Voice teacher and author Melissa Foster gives an example by saying that:

> Rap (and Hip-Hop, the broader cultural movement to which it belongs) has existed for over 50 years. In that time, Rap has evolved considerably and now encompasses over a dozen subgenres under its umbrella. Under-

standing and performing in this genre requires intentional thought, listening, and specified rehearsal to perform appropriately and well. An auditioner for the musical *Fame* might do well to listen to Kurtis Blow's 1980, *The Breaks*, which requires reasonably straight-ahead rhythmic speech. Auditioning for the role of Plankton in *The Spongebob Squarepants Musical* (2016), however, requires some facility with Rap's rhythmically complex, Southern born "Trap" subgenre. The breadth and depth of Rap music requires performers to be studied and practiced in its "genre within the genre" intricacies.[3]

Some shows are written in a specific time period and draw musical influences from the music of the day. For instance, *Memphis* takes place in the 1950s. Some of the music feels like 1950s pop music, such as "Someday" and "Stand Up," while other songs, like "Colored Women" and "The Music of My Soul," take on more of a blues feel.[4]

Many contemporary musicals draw influences from a multitude of genres as well. *Hadestown* has songs that run the gamut from the New Orleans jazz sounding "Road to Hell," to more 1970s folk-inspired "Epic I," to the contemporary indie/alternative "All I've Ever Known." *The Lightning Thief* is another example of using a variety of musical genres. Some songs are rock, like "Good Kid" and "Bring on the Monsters," while "Drive" is country/bluegrass. There is a soul and funk inspired song called "D.O.A.," and a pop tune called "My Grand Plan." Musical genre has become an integral aspect of storytelling with composers moving from genre to genre as their story unfolds.

MUSICAL THEATRE VERSUS POP/ROCK

As we dive further into genre, it is helpful to understand some of the musical and vocal differences between pop/rock music and theatre music, as well as understand how pop/rock music has influenced theatre music over the years.

Rhythm

The roots of rock rhythm can be traced back to African music, which emphasized backbeats and syncopation.[5] This rhythmic structure was used in early jazz and blues, which were predecessors to rock and roll. This rhythm leads to the music accentuating beats 2 and 4 instead of 1 and 3, which is common in classical music.[6] This also leads to pop/rock songs having what we call a "groove." The groove is a combination of a rhythmic pattern with a "feel," which leads to an obvious style, pace, intensity, and mood.[7] Some theatre songs could also be said to incorporate a groove, but its importance in interpreting pop/rock music cannot be understated. Pop/rock songs are also often loud, energized, drum and bass heavy, with rhythms that make people want to dance.[8]

Hooks

The "hook" of a song is a catchy lyric or melodic pattern that the song is built upon.[9] It's essentially the part of the song that is meant to "hook" in the listener.[10] Pop/rock songs are not the only songs to have hooks. Plenty of musical theatre songs have hooks, and one could even argue that classical music has musical hooks. The difference is that pop/rock songs tend to be built upon the hooks and typically require a catchy hook to become a successful, commercial, radio hit.

Simplicity

Pop/rock songs tend to be short in length, typically three to five minutes. This helps them to be "radio ready" and makes them more palatable to the average listener. Pop/rock songs also tend to follow a predictable format composed of verses, choruses, and a bridge, and are often repetitive.[11] This simplicity of predictable structure, coupled with the hook, makes pop/rock songs accessible and memorable to the listener. Theatre songs might adhere to this simplicity as well, but sometimes involve more complicated structure and storytelling.

Universality

Since pop/rock music is meant to be accessible, it tends to deal with universal ideas, themes, and experiences. This helps pop/rock songs appeal to the masses, increasing commercial success.[12] While some pop/rock songs can be quite complex and narrative in nature, they are often reactive or emotive. Theatre songs tend to deal with specific moments in the context of dramatic storytelling, so the lyrics are focused on revealing character or furthering plot.

Improvisation

Pop/rock songs weren't meant to be written down in the same way that theatre songs were.[13] Many pop/rock songs were created through improvisation, which often remains a major part of delivering a pop/rock song. Pop/rock songs are also often passed through oral traditions, which keep them from being written down. Theatre songs are almost always written down and the definitive version of what the composer wants is typically reflected on the page. Pop/rock songs are often interpreted in a multitude of ways, with no single, definitive version.

Individuality

This leads us to the individuality of pop/rock music and artists. No two artists will interpret the same song in the same fashion.[14] Pop/rock artists are seeking uniqueness and individuality, and these qualities are often what make pop/rock music so diverse. Sometimes the goal in pop/rock singing is to purposefully not sound "trained," but rather to sound unique, interesting, and spontaneous. We hear a wide variety of vocal styles such as breathiness, glottals, straight tone, and a variety of vocal colors and vowels, including manufactured diphthongs.[15] We also hear purposeful distortions such as growls, gravel, scooping, sliding, and shouting.[16] Many of these elements show up in contemporary musical theatre as well, depending on the genre of music and the composer's intention.

Lyrics and Phrasing

Pop/rock song lyrics might rhyme or they might not. This approach is different than most theatre songs, where rhyming is considered to be a crucial aspect of the storytelling, helping with lyric comprehension.[17] Additionally, in theatre songs, the lyrics are typically delivered with similar prosody and scansion to speech in order for the audience to understand them.[18] This leads to phrasing that lines up with complete thoughts, which is crucial for clarity. This also leads to singers typically using clear, precise articulation and vowels for the audience to understand the lyrics. However, in pop/rock songs, this is not always the case. Sometimes the lyrics line up with speech emphasis, but sometimes they don't. "Mis-accents" are often chosen on purpose in pop songs. Sometimes singers even breathe in the middle of words or phrases or purposefully incorporate mumbled diction.[19] The phrasing of pop/rock songs is more varied and less about conveying complete thoughts, and more about conveying emotion.

ARRANGEMENT AND ORCHESTRATION

Another important consideration for genre is the arrangement and orchestration of the music. Arrangement refers to adapting music to fit the medium. For instance, taking a melody of a song and fleshing it out to fit an ensemble, or taking a song that was written for one instrument and adapting it for a new instrument.[20] Orchestration refers to fleshing out the melodic line with instrumentation.[21] The orchestrator often decides what instruments will be included in the band or orchestra, which plays a huge role in genre. Orchestrators and arrangers are essential to crafting the sound of a musical.

An example of the importance of orchestration is *Oklahoma!* Typically, it is a golden age musical that features a full, twenty-eight-piece orchestra, with legit and traditional musical theatre singing. However, in the 2019 revival, the show was reorchestrated for a seven-piece band, with a focus on folk instruments like the mandolin and steel guitar.[22] This changed the genre of music, and subsequently, the singing. There were more county/pop vocal elements used like a twangy accent, belting, scoops, and straight tone. The show went from sounding like a golden age musical to sounding like a contemporary country show. This change stemmed from the arrangements and orchestrations.

Orchestrators can also make shows sound more pop/rock by carefully crafting the orchestrations. A song that might sound more contemporary musical theatre on the piano might sound like a rock song with the band due to the orchestrations. Arrangers and orchestrators also play a huge

MUSICAL GENRES

role in crafting jukebox musicals. These shows typically incorporate the canon of an artist or band and require carefully crafted arrangements and orchestrations to fit the vocal and musical demands of a musical. Some songs might need to become group numbers that require ensemble singing and others might need to be rearranged to feel more stage worthy and dramatic. As you explore genre in this chapter, keep in mind the importance of orchestration and arrangement.

MUSICAL THEATRE AS A GENRE

The musical theatre canon now includes a variety of genres. Music that sounds older, like more traditional musical theatre, is still being sung and written. In addition, we have pop/rock songs from the commercial music canon that are inserted into dramatic contexts in the form of jukebox musicals. And finally, what we see most frequently, are new musical theatre songs that are influenced by pop/rock music. Let's begin by looking at the variety of musical theatre genres that exist in musical theatre today, before diving into the pop/rock genres. The line between these categories is *thin*, and many of these categories overlap with each other. These categories are not definitive, nor are they mutually exclusive. There are plenty of songs and shows that defy category or could be placed in multiple categories. These are simply here to help you begin to understand the variety of musical theatre songs that exist in the canon today.

Jazz Standards and the Great American Songbook

Before the book musical took us into the golden age of Broadway, most musical comedies were compilations of songs, skits, and dance numbers. Some of these shows had thin plots, but many were plotless. The shows featured the popular music of the day, which included jazz standards and other popular songs that became part of the Great American Songbook. Musically, we might hear full orchestras, with lots of blue notes and jazz chords. Vocally, we might hear brighter, brassier, speechlike singing, including crooning. Musicals with jazz standards or Great American Songbook material would include *Ain't Misbehavin*,

Sophisticated Ladies, Babes in Arms, Crazy for You, Nice Work If You Can Get It, An American in Paris, Shuffle Along, 42nd Street, and *Eubie!*

Traditional Musical Theatre

Traditional musical theatre could include jazz standards and songs from the Great American Songbook, but it could also extend into the golden age era and all the way today.[23] Traditional musical theatre is typically what people think of when they think of "showtunes" or "Broadway songs." Musically, we might hear full orchestras. Vocally, we might hear brighter, brassier, speechlike singing. Adelaide and Nathan in *Guys and Dolls*, or Annie Oakley and Frank Butler in *Annie Get Your Gun* would be examples of characters whose songs are traditional musical theatre. Many Jerry Herman shows, like *Mame, La Cage aux Folles,* and *Hello, Dolly!* have traditional musical theatre sounds in both the orchestrations and the singing. More contemporary shows with a similar genre would be *Thoroughly Modern Millie, War Paint,* and *Grand Hotel*. Much of the music in these contemporary shows feel like a throwback to the more traditional musicals of the 1920s, 1930s, and 1940s.

Legit Musical Theatre

The legit genre is also found in the same time period as the traditional musical theatre genre. The golden age was particularly fond of the legit musical theatre sound. Legit musical theatre would encompass music that leans more classical in nature.[24] This might mean more lush orchestrations and singers would choose rounded, purer vowels, instead of the brighter, more speechlike sounds found in the "non-legit" traditional musical theatre shows. Shows like *Carousel, The Music Man, She Loves Me, Flower Drum Song,* and *West Side Story* all have some element of legit music and legit vocalism.

Legit musical theatre is not solely found in the golden age. There are contemporary writers who have written entire shows or songs in shows with a legit sound. *The Light in the Piazza, A Gentleman's Guide to Love and Murder, Death Takes a Holiday,* and *Grey Gardens* are examples of shows with legit elements written after the year 2000. It should also be

MUSICAL GENRES

noted that in revivals of older legit musicals and in new legit musicals, singers often employ more contemporary sounds, such as straight tone and brighter vowels. While legit musical theatre leans more classical, it is not the same genre as classical singing.[25]

1960s/1970s/1980s Musical Theatre (Transitional)

Once we get past *Hair* in 1968, categorizing musical theatre genres becomes a bit tricky. Pop/rock genres began to show up in musicals, yet many writers were still writing music that felt more like musical theatre songs and showtunes. Even today we have shows that are being written that sound very theatrical with very little pop style, and we have shows that are heavily influenced by specific pop/rock genres. For many years, people considered anything post-*Hair* to be contemporary musical theatre. This worked throughout the 1980s and 1990s, but by current standards doesn't quite cut it. Musical theatre has evolved substantially in the last fifty years since *Hair* debuted on Broadway, so considering everything post-1968 to be contemporary is a bit of an outdated system.

As musical theatre moved into the 1960s–1980s, we get a sound that could be called "transitional musical theatre."[26] These are shows that have a musical theatre sound that does not quite fit into the sounds of the golden age but does not quite feel at home with modern day musical theatre. These are songs that might have some light pop influence, but still feel like theatre songs. These shows will typically have an orchestra, with the occasional electric instrument added. Vocally you tend to hear traditional musical theatre sounds, with the occasional flavor of pop styling. Belting was not yet the default sound in musical theatre, so cast recordings from this time period might feature more mixing, head voice, and legit qualities, although that is often not the case when these shows are revived. Shows like *Cabaret*, *Pippin*, *Baby*, *Big*, *Company*, and *Falsettos* might be said to fall into this category.

1980s/1990s Musical Theatre (The Pop Opera)

The 1980s and 1990s saw the megamusical rise to fame on Broadway, in addition to more and more pop influences in the music. This gave way to something that is sometimes referred to as the "pop opera." Shows like *Les Misérables, Miss Saigon, Evita, Cats, Joseph and the Amazing Technicolor Dreamcoat, Jekyll and Hyde, Chess,* and *The Scarlet Pimpernel* were all musicals that had pop-inspired scores, with elements of legit musical theatre thrown in. These shows would have full orchestras, with some also using electronic instruments. Vocally, we hear more belting, as it was starting to become more of the default sound. You also hear pop elements like straight tone and some occasional riffing. However, many of these shows also use a legit vocalism for some characters where you might hear rounded vowels with more vibrato. These types of shows really combined the new pop sounds that were becoming popular with the more traditional vocal and musical elements that had been heard on Broadway for years.

1990s/2000s Musical Theatre (Early Contemporary)

In the 1990s and early 2000s, many musical theatre writers were inspired by the popular music they had grown up with, especially the piano rock music that had gained popularity since the 1970s. Popular artists like Ben Folds, Tori Amos, Elton John, and Billy Joel all wrote story songs on the piano that inspired a generation of musical theatre writers. Jonathan Larson helped usher in this musical trend, with his piano rock music in the early to mid-1990s. Jason Robert Brown, Andrew Lippa, and Laurence O'Keefe all followed in this trend in the later years with shows like *The Last Five Years, John and Jen,* and *Bat Boy.* The musicals of the 1990s and early 2000s still have a contemporary sound, but many might not quite have the same feel as what you hear on Broadway today. In these shows you might hear bands with electric instruments, and sometimes orchestras. Vocally, you'll hear sounds that begin to move more toward contemporary pop sounds, such as straight tone. Belting was also becoming more of the default sound found in musicals during the time period.

Contemporary Musical Theatre

Contemporary means "existing or happening now."[27] Contemporary musical theatre is *always* evolving, because writers are constantly reinventing the art form. What is contemporary as of the printing of this book might cease to be contemporary in a few years' time. Pop/rock music has been on Broadway for over fifty years, which means that it has been part of the book musical longer than it hasn't. This has changed the sound of musical theatre. There is a wide spectrum of contemporary musical theatre. On one end, there are shows like *Sweet Smell of Success*, *Queen of the Mist*, *Little Women*, *The Glorious Ones*, and *Anastasia* that all have roots in traditional and/or legit musical theatre, while incorporating more contemporary musical and vocal elements. You might hear more contemporary vocal styles such as straight tone, brighter vowels, glottals, scoops, and higher belting. The other end of the spectrum are shows that lean more heavily on pop/rock genres. These shows will typically have electronic instruments in their bands, and vocally you hear more genre-specific styles in the singing. This might include higher belting, cries, calls, growls, gravel, breathiness, straight tone, glottals, and scoops. Shows like *A Strange Loop*, *Soft Power*, *Amélie*, *Dear Evan Hanson*, *High Fidelity*, and *Be More Chill* might fall into this end of the spectrum.

POP/ROCK GENRES

We will now begin an exploration of the multiple pop/rock genres that are found in musical theatre, especially contemporary musical theatre. You'll see examples of shows and songs that use a particular genre, as well as artists in those genres for comparison and research. The list of artists is by no means complete. The best way to learn about pop/rock music is to listen to artists outside of theatre who write and perform music in the genre. As a reminder, it takes "intentional thought, listening, and specified rehearsal" to be prepared to understand and perform in various popular genres.[28] Note that many shows today incorporate a multitude of genres or span multiple decades, so you may see a show under a variety of categories. Some of the shows listed are original musicals with songs written in a particular pop/rock style, and some of the shows are jukebox musicals where the songs come from a particular genre, decade, or artist.

It should also be noted that the line between these genres is, once again, *thin* and *overlapping*. As popular music evolved, subgenres began appearing, and the lines between genre became even blurrier. The difference between subgenres can sometimes be slight, and more contemporary artists often make music that combines genres. You'll see this reflected as we journey toward contemporary pop/rock music. Additionally, this list of pop/rock genres is *not* exhaustive, it simply reflects the genres most commonly found in the musical theatre canon.

1950s Pop/Rock

Pop music typically refers to popular music that is commercial and accessible.[29] While rhythm and blues and rock and roll were gaining popularity among young people in the 1950s, music that had more of a mass appeal was still considered the popular music of the day.

Some examples of 1950s pop musicals are *Forever Plaid* and the first act of *Marvelous Wonderettes*, which are both jukebox musicals featuring pop songs of the 1950s. Both of these shows incorporate a bit of doo-wop, which is a subgenre of pop music that emphasizes harmonies and group singing.[30] Many of the pop artists of the day were an evolution of the big band and jazz bands of the 1940s, which you can hear in their lush orchestrations. Some artists of both the popular music of the 1950s and doo-wop include the Chordettes, Bobby Darin, Mel Carter, Connie Francis, the Four Aces, Harry Belafonte, the Everly Brothers, Nat "King" Cole, Peggy Lee, Frank Sinatra, Dean Martin, and Perry Como.

In the 1950s, the line between rock, rhythm and blues, and even country, was blurry as they were all born from the blues. Blues music incorporates syncopated rhythms in addition to other African musical elements, such as call-and-response.[31] Blues music typically uses basic chord structures with the addition of blue notes. These flattened third and seventh notes are reflective of pitch inflections that were common in many West African languages and music.[32] Many Southern musicians took blues and added their own musical styles, which led to country or "hillbilly" music.[33] When blues met jazz in the 1940s, rhythm and blues was born.[34] This music evolved even further with Wynonie Harris—one of the founding fathers of rock and roll—whose hit, "Good Rockin' Tonight," was one of the first rock-and-roll songs to appeal to both Black and White audiences. Bill Haley was one of the first White artists to sing rock and roll, which was a style that was created—and should always be attributed to—Black Americans.

Jukebox musicals with 1950s rock and roll and/or rhythm and blues include *All Shook Up* and *Buddy: The Buddy Holly Story*. *Cry Baby* and *Grease* are original musicals with 1950s-inspired rock and roll scores. Jukebox musicals like *Million Dollar Quartet*, *Memphis*, and *Always . . . Patsy Cline* reflect both rhythm and blues and the country music of the 1950s. Artists who made music through these blurred lines include Big Mama Thornton, Chuck Berry, Elvis Presley, Patsy Cline, Loretta Lynn, Johnny Cash, Sam Cooke, Ray Charles, B.B. King, Carl Perkins, Jerry Lee Lewis, Buddy Holly, Fats Domino, and Little Richard.

1960s Pop/Rock

By the 1960s, many people declared that rock and roll was dead, mainly due to the rise of White, clean-cut crooners like Frankie Avalon and Pat Boone. However, this decade saw three major influences on rock and roll: Motown, the British Invasion, and roots rock (or folk rock).[35]

The music of Motown—a combination of rhythm and blues, soul, and pop music—is heard quite often in the musical theatre canon. Jukebox musicals with this type of music include *Baby It's You!*, *Ain't Too Proud*, *Motown*, and *Beehive*. *Hairspray* and *Little Shop of Horrors* are original musicals that have 1960s-inspired Motown music as well. Motown artists that inspired these sounds include the Four Tops, Marvin Gaye, Gladys Knight and the Pips, the Supremes, Aretha Franklin, and the Temptations.

In 1964, the Beatles made their American television debut, and Beatlemania was officially underway.[36] The Beatles became a defining sound of 1960s rock and roll. They paved the way for other British bands, like the Rolling Stones, who used more blues influences in their rock and roll. There are multiple reviews based on the Beatles' music including *Let It Be*, *Beatlemania*, and *Rain*. *Across the Universe* is a movie musical that incorporates the Beatles canon as well. The musical *Lennon* played Broadway and focuses on the music and life of John Lennon, but does not include any music from the Beatles era, instead, focusing on Lennon's solo career.

The Beach Boys were another popular band of the 1960s. While not a musical, their album *Pet Sounds* is a concept album that is consistently ranked as one of the most influential albums of all time.[37] *Good Vibrations* is a jukebox musical based on the entire canon of the Beach Boys. Other rock artists of the 1960s include the Monkees, Herman's Hermits, Jimi Hendrix, Jefferson Airplane, James Brown, the Velvet Underground, and Sly and the Family Stone.

Roots rock and folk rock also took hold in the 1960s with artists like the Band and Bob Dylan becoming popular. A show like *Violet* has 1960s roots rock as the main genre, while *Hair* uses multiple rock genres of the 1960s, including R&B, folk rock, and the newly popular protest song. *The Girl from the North Country* and *The Times They Are a-Changin'* are two musicals that are based on the musical canon of Bob Dylan.

Lots of other musicals include a variety of 1960s pop music. *A Bronx Tale*, *Jersey Boys*, *Dusty: The Dusty Springfield Musical*, *Your Own Thing*, *Forever Dusty*, *Sympathy Jones*, and *Beautiful: The Carole King Musical* all include various 1960s pop music. Pop artists of the 60s include Frankie Valli and the Four Seasons, Dusty Springfield, Carole King, Nancy Sinatra, Chubby Checker, and Lesley Gore.

1970s Pop/Rock

The 1970s brought about an array of pop subgenres including disco. Disco gained popularity on the airwaves as many radio stations were leaning toward playing more conservative music, rather than the politically charged rock music that was prevalent early in the decade.[38] Jukebox musicals that feature disco music include *Donna: The Donna Summer Musical*, *Saturday Night Fever*, *The Donkey Show*, *Xanadu*, *Disaster!*, and *Priscilla, Queen of the Desert*. Original musicals with some disco music as part of their storytelling include *They're Playing Our Song*, *Sister Act*, *The Wiz*, and *Rachael Lily Rosenbloom (And Don't You Ever Forget It!)*, which was written by Paul Jabara, one of the most famous disco writers of the era. Disco artists include Donna Summer, the Bee Gees, Gloria Gaynor, Sister Sledge, KC and the Sunshine Band, the Village People, the Pointer Sisters, and Kool and the Gang. Even Broadway star Ethel Merman jumped on the disco trend with *The*

Ethel Merman Disco Album in 1979, which features her Broadway hits set to a disco beat.

Additional subgenres like Afrobeat and funk began to appear in the 1970s. Artists also began creating music that combined the genres of pop, funk, and R&B. The musical *Fela!* tells the story of Fela Kuti, the Nigerian pioneer of Afrobeat. The band Earth, Wind, and Fire rose to fame in the 1970s with their music that spanned the multiple genres of pop, R&B, disco, and funk. The band consisted of Lamont Dozier, Eddie Holland, and Brian Holland, who were the writing team behind many of the Motown hits of the 1960s and 1970s. The musical *Hot Feet* includes their popular hits. The musicals *Fortress of Solitude* and *Broadway Bounty Hunter* also combine multiple subgenres of the 1970s such as pop, funk, and R&B.

Some jukebox musicals with 1970s pop music are *Mamma Mia*, *Beautiful: The Carole King Musical*, and *The Cher Show*. Those musicals feature the music of ABBA, Carole King, and Cher, respectively. *Promises, Promises* was an original musical written by Burt Bacharach, which included 1970s pop music.

Just as rock music was making its way to the Broadway stage in the late 1960s and early 1970s, rock music was becoming increasingly theatrical. The Rolling Stones took the stage with an inherent theatricality, with lead singer Mick Jagger's unpredictability and mesmerizing stage presence.[39] The Kinks experimented with theatrical storytelling through concept albums, some of which include *The Kinks Are the Village Green Preservation Society*, *Arthur (or the Decline and Fall of the British Empire)*, *Lola Versus Powerman and the Moneygoround*, *Soap Opera*, and *Schoolboys in Disgrace*. Artists like Frank Zappa continued to push rock music toward theatricality with concept albums like *Freak Out* and *Joe's Garage*.

The Who was one of the most popular and creative rock bands of the 1960s and 1970s.[40] Pete Townshend, the band's guitarist and main writer, was looking for ways to elevate rock music. After encouragement from their manager, Kit Lambert, Townshend began working on a "rock opera," which was a fully sung through, rock album. The rock opera went even further than the concept album, with a fully fleshed out storyline, complete with characters' points of view. *The Who's Tommy* was released by The Who in 1969 and was eventually adapted for the Broadway stage in 1993. The Who's second fully realized rock opera, *Quadrophenia*, was released in 1973, made into a film adaptation featuring the music from the album in 1979, and has appeared in stage adaptations since. Despite never reaching the commercial stage success of *Tommy*, *Quadrophenia* is one of Pete Townshend's favorite albums he's ever written.[41]

The theatricality of rock extended into a new subgenre: glam rock. Glam rockers frequently donned costumes, makeup, and wild hairstyles, while also engaging in overly theatrical performances on stage. David Bowie's *The Rise and Fall of Ziggy Stardust and the Spiders from Mars* was a concept album with a central character that Bowie would embody on stage. Much of Bowie's music was theatrical in nature, as were his live performances. Bowie wrote a musical, *Lazarus*, that debuted in 2016, shortly before his death. Glam rock would influence artists like Elton John, who incorporated glam elements into his live performances. John would go on to write musicals such as *Aida*, *Billy Elliott*, *Lestat*, and *The Lion King*.

Other musicals that have 1970s rock music are *Lennon*, *A Night with Janis Joplin*, and *Love, Janis*. These jukebox musicals incorporate the music of John Lennon's solo career, with the latter two using the music of Janis Joplin. Shows like *Jesus Christ Superstar*, *Rocky Horror Picture Show*, *Runaways*, and *Dude* were original musicals written in the 1970s that have pop and rock sounds of the era. The song "Where Did the Rock Go" from *School of Rock* is written in the style of Fleetwood Mac, especially reminiscent of their iconic 1977 album *Rumours*. Other artists who made rock music in the 1970s were Ike and Tina Turner, the Rolling Stones, the Isley Brothers, Pink Floyd, Led Zeppelin, AC/DC, the Eagles, and Funkadelic.

Country music made its way onto the Broadway stage in the 1970s as well. Musicals with 1970s country and roots rock are *The Best Little Whorehouse in Texas*, *Pump Boys and Dinettes*, *The Robber Bridegroom*, and *Shenandoah*. Artists of this genre include the Allman Brothers Band, Charley Pride, Dolly Parton, Creedence Clearwater Revival, the Band, Linda Rondstadt, Crystal Gayle, and Crosby, Stills, Nash, and Young.

1980s Pop/Rock

The 1980s were a huge decade for music, including pop music. New wave and dance music began to take the place of disco.[42] Jukebox musicals with 1980s pop music are *Head over Heels*, *On Your Feet!*, *Back to the Future*, *MJ*, and *The Cher Show*. Original musicals with 1980s-inspired pop music are *American Psycho*, *Footloose*, *Carrie*, *Chess*, and *Taboo*. Pop artists of the 1980s include Madonna, George Michael, Devo, Michael Jackson, Culture Club, the Bangles, Huey Lewis and the News, Cher, Whitney Houston, and Cyndi Lauper.

The 1980s also saw the rise of multiple subgenres of rock including hair metal, goth rock, soft rock, and heavy metal. Jukebox musicals with 1980s rock music include *Rock of Ages*, *Bat Out of Hell*, and *We Will Rock You*. Some rock artists from the 1980s include Blondie, Pat Benatar, Tina Turner, Guns N' Roses, Aerosmith, Heart, Bon Jovi, the Police, Prince, Bruce Springsteen, Queen, and Kiss.

Musicals like *Kinky Boots* and *The Wedding Singer* have both 1980s pop and rock styles throughout their music, and musicals like *MJ*, *Tina*, and *The Cher Show* include Michael Jackson, Tina Turner, and Cher's music, respectively, which means they feature music that spans multiple decades.

1990s Pop/Rock

The popular music of the 1990s was eclectic. One of the major reasons for this was a technological shift in how record sales were tabulated. In 1991, *SoundScan* was introduced, which was a digital tracking system of record sales. *Billboard* began using the sales data from *SoundScan* to calculate their music charts. Before 1991, *Billboard* would call record store managers across the country each week and ask about their sales. This method was error-prone with plenty of room for personal bias. The charts immediately became more genre diverse with *SoundScan*, with artists beginning to cross over from one genre to another. This paved the way for country, rap, and R&B artists to start charting on the pop charts.[43]

Clueless is a jukebox musical that features music of the 1990s, much of which is pop. *Bare* is billed as a pop opera that has original music with a nineties-inspired pop feel, as does *Spring Awakening*, which is reminiscent of 1990s pop and alternative. Artists from the 1990s include Duncan Sheik, Mariah Carey, Madonna, Celine Dion, TLC, No Doubt, and the Fugees.

Rent is one of the most popular original 1990s rock musicals. *Hedwig and the Angry Inch* was also written in the 1990s, but the music was inspired by the glam rock and early punk of the 70s.[44] *Jagged Little Pill* is a jukebox musical based on the music of Alanis Morrisette's 1995 album of the same name. *Spiderman Turn Off the Dark* is not a jukebox musical, but it was written by Bono of the band U2, which was one of the most popular bands in the world in the late 1980s and 1990s. Much of the music is reminiscent of that era. Some artists of the 1990s rock scene were U2, Sinéad O'Connor, Oasis, Pearl Jam, 4 Non Blondes, REM, Hole, Nirvana, Bon Jovi, Smashing Pumpkins, Bruce Springsteen, Radiohead, Red Hot Chili Peppers, and Weezer.

Early 2000s Pop/Rock

The early 2000s pop scene saw the rise of the boy band with groups like NSYNC, Backstreet Boys, and 98 Degrees. The musical *Altar Boyz* has early 2000s inspired, boy band–esque music, and the song "One Knight" from *Wonderland* is also written as a boy band number. Britney Spears was called the "Princess of Pop"[45] during the early 2000s, and her music is the basis of the musical, *Once Upon a One More Time*. The West End musical *& Juliet* is a jukebox musical that features early 2000s pop hits. Other early 2000 pop artists include Christina Aguilera, Jennifer Lopez, Pink, Janet Jackson, Mariah Carey, Avril Lavigne, Destiny's Child, and Fefe Dobson.

Contemporary Pop/Rock

As we start to get into musicals from the last decade or so, we start to see writers using various musical genres for their storytelling. This is not a new trend, but it is something that has become more and more popular. Some shows are hard to classify as one overarching genre because they include a multitude of musical genres within the confines of one show.

Contemporary pop encompasses musicals like *Six, Everybody's Talking about Jamie, Dear Evan Hanson, Ghost, Waitress,* and *Mean Girls*.

MUSICAL GENRES

Some contemporary pop artists from 2010 onward include Katy Perry, Beyoncé, Ariana Grande, The Weeknd, Miley Cyrus, John Legend, Ed Sheeran, Sam Smith, Taylor Swift, Sara Bareilles, Lady Gaga, Bruno Mars, Olivia Rodrigo, Billie Eilish, and Sammy Rae.

Musicals with contemporary rock sounds are *School of Rock*, *The Lightning Thief*, *Passing Strange*, *Alice by Heart*, *Next to Normal*, *Murder Ballad*, and *Bloody, Bloody, Andrew Jackson*. Some contemporary rock singers and bands from 2010 on include Maroon 5, Green Day, Band of Skulls, Mitski, Greta Van Fleet, Lake Street Dive, Miley Cyrus, Vampire Weekend, and Kelly Clarkson.

Indie/Alt Rock

American folk music was closely tied to bluegrass, country, and blues in the early twentieth century. In the 1960s, folk music had a revival with artists like Bob Dylan, Pete Seeger, Woody Guthrie, Joan Baez, Joni Mitchell, the Byrds, and Peter, Paul and Mary. *Violet*, *The Girl from the North Country*, and *The Times They Are a Changin'* have already been mentioned as musicals with this 1960s folk rock music.

In the 1990s, indie folk/alt rock became a popular subgenre of rock. This genre is influenced by rock and traditional folk music. Musicals with indie folk music are *Hadestown*, *Whisper House*, and *Spring Awakening*. *Once* and *The Last Ship* both have contemporary folk sounds of Ireland and Northern England, respectively. Indie/alt rock artists include Anaïs Mitchell, Ani DiFranco, Bon Iver, Tallest Man on Earth, Phoebe Bridgers, the Lumineers, Maggie Rogers, Middle Kids, and Elliott Smith.

Punk

Punk is another subgenre of rock that appeared in the 1970s. It was born out of a push against the commercialism of rock, and it often has political, antiestablishment lyrics.[46] The American band Green Day released a punk rock concept album in 2004 titled *American Idiot*, which made its way to Broadway in 2010. Other musicals with punk music include *Agent 355*, *Punk Rock Girl*, and *Home Street Home*.

Punk bands through the decades include Sex Pistols, Black Flag, Dead Kennedy's, the Ramones, Bikini Kill, Sleater-Kinney, Death, Green Day, Fall Out Boy, Siouxsie and the Banshees, New York Dolls, and the later punk pop bands My Chemical Romance and Paramour.

Latin Pop

Latin pop is a fusion of US-style music production with Latin music genres. It typically combines Latin beats with American pop music and has appeared in a few musicals. The jukebox musical *On Your Feet!* features the music of Gloria Estefan, who was one of the most successful pop artists of the 1980s and 1990s. *In the Heights* is an original musical that also features Latin pop sounds throughout the show. Some Latin pop artists through the years are Enrique Iglesias, Thalía, Ricky Martin, Shakira, Jon Secada, Jennifer Lopez, Marc Anthony, Selena, and Leslie Grace.

Indi-Pop and Hindi Film Music

Indi-pop music is a genre of pop music that came about as a competition to the popular Hindi film music.[47] These genres have shown up in musicals like *Bombay Dreams*, *Bend It Like Beckham*, and *Monsoon Wedding*. Indi-pop and Hindi film music artists include Lucky Ali, Alisha Chinai, Sonu Nigam, A. R. Rahman, Shreya Ghoshal, and Shweta Shetty.

K-Pop

K-pop is short for Korean popular music and is music that originated from South Korea. This music draws its influence from many genres including pop, R&B, hip hop, jazz, rock, and traditional Korean music.[48] K-pop artists are also known for their intricate choreography. K-pop music was the basis for the original musical *K-Pop*, and some artists include H.O.T., BTS, Blackpink, TVXG, and BoA.

Gospel

The precursor to gospel was the African American spiritual.[49] Gospel music typically encompasses harmonies sung by a group or choir, with superb, often challenging, lead vocals. In the 1960s, gospel became more mainstream and still influences much of the pop music of today. Musicals that incorporate gospel music in their storytelling include *Born for This*, *Leap of Faith*, *Sister Act*, *Tambourines to Glory*, *Your Arm's Too Short to Box with God*, *Violet*, and *The Color Purple*. Gospel artists include Sister Rosetta Tharpe, Mahalia Jackson, Kirk Franklin, Cece Winans, Tamela Mann, Yolanda Adams, the Fisk Jubilee Singers, and the Hampton Singers.

R&B

Rhythm and blues is a distinctly African American genre of music that combines elements of jump blues, big band, gospel, and jazz.[50] As we've already discussed, rock and roll was heavily influenced by R&B in the 1950s. As R&B evolved, it began to incorporate elements of pop, soul, funk, and electronic music. The biggest shift in R&B was in the 1990s when R&B, soul, and rap began to cross-over into new R&B subgenres.[51] *Hamilton*, *Hair*, *Dreamgirls*, *Memphis*, *The Wiz*, *Motown*, *Ain't Too Proud*, *Brooklyn*, and *Baby It's You!* all have elements of R&B in their music. R&B artists through the years include Ruth Brown, the Temptations, the Supremes, Barry White, Ray Charles, Stevie Wonder, Aretha Franklin, Boyz II Men, Vanessa Williams, Mary J. Blige, TLC, Mariah Carey, En Vogue, Toni Braxton, John Legend, D'Angelo, Amy Winehouse, and Brian McKnight.

Rap

Rap music began at block parties in New York City in the 1970s. DJs would extend the percussion breaks of funk, soul, and disco music, and eventually began talking in time over the musical breaks.[52] By the 1990s, rap was part of the popular music lexicon, with rappers charting on the pop charts.[53] Rap has been in musicals such as *Holler If You Hear Me*, which is a jukebox musical based on the work of Tupac Shakur, *Hamilton*, *In the Heights*, *BASH'd: A Gay Rap Opera*, and *Spamilton*. Some rap artists include the Sugarhill Gang, Run-D.M.C., Public Enemy, N.W.A., the Beastie Boys, Salt-N-Pepa, DJ Jazzy Jeff and the Fresh Prince, Snoop Dogg, Jay-Z, Missy Elliott, Queen Latifah, Wu Tang Clan, Sean Combs, Cardi B, Method Man, Lauryn Hill, 50 Cent, Nicki Minaj, and Lil' Kim.

Country

Country music appeared on Broadway in the 1970s with *The Best Little Whorehouse in Texas* and *Pump Boys and Dinettes*. Both shows had a country roots rock feel, which is heavily inspired by blues and rock and roll. Other shows with country inspired music include *Bonnie and Clyde, Cowgirls, Debbie Does Dallas, Bridges of Madison County, The Great American Trailer Park Musical, Giant, Hands on a Hardbody, The Spitfire Grill, Urban Cowboy,* and *Always . . . Patsy Cline*. Country artists through the years include Patsy Cline, Waylon Jennings, Willie Nelson, Charley Pride, Dolly Parton, The Judds, George Strait, Shania Twain, Faith Hill, The Chicks, Reba McEntire, Mickey Guyton, Carrie Underwood, Miko Marks, Keith Urban, and Darius Rucker.

Bluegrass

Bluegrass began in the 1940s in the Appalachian region of the United States. Bluegrass has roots in traditional English, Irish, and Scottish music, as well as jazz and blues. You typically hear acoustic instruments such as the banjo and mandolin in the orchestrations.[54] Musicals with bluegrass music are *Bright Star, Floyd Collins, Robber Bridegroom,* and *Burnt Part Boys*. Bluegrass artists include Lester Flatt and Earl Scruggs, Bill Monroe, the Carolina Chocolate Drops, Alison Krauss and Union Station, Kaia Kater, and Nickel Creek.

Electronic and Electronic Dance Music

Electronic music began to gain popularity in the 1960s and 1970s with the invention of the Moog Synthesizer. Composer Wendy Carlos was a pioneer in bringing electronic sounds to the mainstream with her

MUSICAL GENRES

compositions for the movies *The Shining*, *A Clockwork Orange*, and *Tron*.[55] Electronic music became the basis for synth pop, which gained popularity in the 1980s with bands like Sparks, Pet Shop Boys, Devo, and the Buggles.

While electronic sounds have been heard on stage for a while, electronic dance music (EDM) is a newer genre of music to make its way into musical theatre. EDM is typically percussive and leans heavily on electronic sounds. Musicals with some elements of EDM and electronic music include *Here Lies Love*, *Nikola Tesla Drops the Beat*, *American Psycho*, and *Natasha, Pierre, and the Great Comet of 1812*. Some current EDM artists include David Byrne, Fatboy Slim, and deadmau5.

Acapella

There are musicals that have been written to be sung completely acapella, drawing on the tradition of acapella groups. A cappella musicals include *In Transit*, *Octet*, *Choir Boy*, and *Avenue X*. Some acapella groups include Pentatonix, Straight No Chaser, the Persuasions, and the Filharmonic.

FINAL THOUGHTS

While an entire book could be written on each genre listed in this chapter, my hope is that this overview gives you a basic understanding of the wide array of musical genres found in musical theatre. Gone are the days of a homogenous show tune representing the sound of Broadway. Also gone are the days of having one pop/rock song in your audition book that encompasses all pop/rock shows. The genres represented in the musical theatre canon are vast. This chapter has given an overview of many of the genres represented, as well as a list of artists for reference. The best way to familiarize yourself with these musical genres is to listen to the recording artists, then refer to the musicals to see if you can recognize what artists or songs the musicals are inspired by. Pay attention to the orchestrations, arrangements, and vocal choices to begin to understand the elements of creating a pop/rock musical.

NOTES

1. Thank you to Melissa Foster for contributing feedback on this chapter.
2. In addition, both characters are vastly different in personality and intentions. More details about picking repertoire for auditions will be discussed in the chapter on auditioning.
3. Melissa Foster, *Hip-Hop and Rap: A Performer's Guide* (London: Rowman & Littlefield, forthcoming).
4. Many of these songs are pastiche songs, which will be discussed more thoroughly in a later chapter.
5. Stuart A. Kallen, *The History of Rock and Roll* (Farmington Hills, MI: Gale, Cengage Learning, 2012), 10.
6. Matthew Edwards, *So You Want to Sing Rock and Roll* (London: Rowman & Littlefield, 2014), 149.
7. Joseph Church, *Rock in the Musical Theatre* (New York: Oxford University Press, 2019), 11.
8. Church, *Rock*, 19; Kallen, *Rock and Roll*, 10.
9. Church, *Rock*, 19.
10. Tom Cole, "You Ask We Answer: What's a Hook?" October 15, 2010, NPR. https://www.npr.org/sections/therecord/2010/10/15/130588663/you-ask-we-answer-what-s-a-hook.
11. Church, *Rock*, 19.
12. Church, *Rock*, 20.
13. Church, *Rock*, 19–20.
14. Edwards, *Rock and Roll*, 86.
15. Edwards, *Rock and Roll*, 147; Kelly Hoppenjans, "The Indie Pop Voice Phenomenon, Part 1," Singing in Popular Musics, August 12, 2018, https://singinginpopularmusics.com/2018/08/12/the-indie-pop-voice-phenomenon-part-1/.
16. Edwards, *Rock and Roll*, 152.
17. Church, *Rock*, 27.
18. Church, *Rock*, 26.
19. Laura Donahue, "Is It Truly Pop or Musical Theater?," February 8, 2021, Singing in Popular Musics, https://singinginpopularmusics.com/2021/02/08/is-it-truly-pop-or-is-it-musical-theater-laura-donohue/.
20. "Arrangement," *Britannica Online*. Accessed July 21, 2021, https://www.britannica.com/art/arrangement.
21. Dominic Symonds, "Orchestration and Arrangement: Creating the Broadway Sound," in *The Oxford Handbook of the American Musical*, ed. Raymond Knapp, Mitchell Morris, and Stacy Wolf (New York: Oxford, 2018), 267.

22. Logan Culwell-Block, "Stripping Down *Oklahoma!* with a Brand New Sound for the Broadway Revival," *Playbill*, March 14, 2019, https://www.playbill.com/article/stripping-down-oklahoma-with-a-brand-new-sound-for-the-broadway-revival.

23. As a reminder, the golden age of Broadway ran from approximately 1943 to the early 1960s.

24. A further explanation of the term *legit* and what it means for vocal function awaits you in the pedagogy chapter.

25. A more detailed explanation of the differences between legit musical theatre singing and classical singing will be found in the pedagogy chapter.

26. This term is one that is used in the curriculum at CAP21 musical theatre conservatory, and I find it useful to identify this unique time in musical theatre history.

27. "Contemporary," *Cambridge Dictionary*, Accessed July 21, 2021. https://dictionary.cambridge.org/us/dictionary/english/contemporary.

28. Foster, *Hip Hop and Rap*.

29. "Pop Music," Wikipedia, Accessed July 21, 2021, https://en.wikipedia.org/wiki/Pop_music.

30. Frank Hoffmann, "Doo Wop," in *Survey of American Popular Music* (modified for the web by Robert Birkline), accessed July 21, 2021, https://www.shsu.edu/~lis_fwh/book/roots_of_rock/Doo-Wop2.htm.

31. Kallen, *Rock and Roll*, 10.

32. "Jazz," *Britannica*, Accessed July 21, 2021, https://www.britannica.com/art/jazz#ref395907.

33. Kallen, *Rock and Roll*, 12.

34. Kallen, *Rock and Roll*, 12.

35. Kallen, *Rock and Roll*, 28.

36. Kallen, *Rock and Roll*, 32.

37. "The Beach Boys: *Pet Sounds*," This Day in Music, accessed July 21, 2021, https://www.thisdayinmusic.com/classic-albums/the-beach-boys-pet-sounds.

38. Kallen, *Rock and Roll*, 62.

39. Robert Somma, "Rock Theatricality," *The Drama Review*, 14, no. 1 (Autumn 1969): 132.

40. Kallen, *Rock and Roll*, 58.

41. Chris Heath, "Pete Townshend: The *'Rolling Stone'* Interview," *Rolling Stone*, August 8, 2002, 61–62, 64, 66.

42. "The 1980s," Rock Archive, accessed July 21, 2021, https://www.rockarchive.com/music-eras/the-1980s.

43. Nisha Gopalan, "The 90s: The Decade That Doesn't Fit?," February 5, 2021, UDiscoverMusic. https://www.udiscovermusic.com/stories/90s-music/.

44. "Hedwig and the Angry Inch (musical)," Wikipedia, accessed July 21, 2021. https://en.wikipedia.org/wiki/Hedwig_and_the_Angry_Inch_(musical).

45. Leah McLaren, "Britney Spears: Will the Princess of Pop Finally Find Freedom?," *The Guardian*, February 13, 2021, https://www.theguardian.com/music/2021/feb/13/britney-spears-will-the-princess-of-pop-finally-find-freedom.

46. "Punk Rock," Wikipedia, accessed July 21, 2021, https://en.wikipedia.org/wiki/Punk_rock.

47. Devarsi Gosh, "Press Play (and wipe away the tears): The Ultimate 1990s Indipop Songlist," Scroll.in, December 31, 2019, https://scroll.in/reel/942185/press-play-and-wipe-away-the-tears-the-ultimate-1990s-indipop-songlist.

48. "K-Pop," Wikipedia, accessed July 21, 2021, https://en.wikipedia.org/wiki/K-pop.

49. "African American Gospel," Library of Congress, accessed July 21, 2021, https://www.loc.gov/collections/songs-of-america/articles-and-essays/musical-styles/ritual-and-worship/african-american-gospel.

50. Mark Puryear, "Tell It Like It Is: A History of Rhythm and Blues," Folklife, September 30, 2016, https://folklife.si.edu/magazine/freedom-sounds-tell-it-like-it-is-a-history-of-rhythm-and-blues.

51. Gopalan, "The 90s."

52. David Dye, "The Birth of Rap: A Look Back, NPR, February 27, 2007, https://www.npr.org/templates/story/story.php?storyId=7550286.

53. Gopalan, "The 90s."

54. "Bluegrass Music," Wikipedia, https://en.wikipedia.org/wiki/Bluegrass_music.

55. Karen Iris Tucker, "Wendy Carlos, the Electronic Music Pioneer Who Happens to Be Transgender," *Washington Post*, October 23, 2021, https://www.washingtonpost.com/outlook/wendy-carlos-the-electronic-music-pioneer-who-happens-to-be-transgender/2020/10/22/fa4f511e-d5ac-11ea-930e-d88518c57dcc_story.html.

❸
SINGING AND VOICE SCIENCE

Scott McCoy

This chapter presents a concise overview of how the voice functions as a biomechanical, acoustic instrument. We will be dealing with elements of anatomy, physiology, acoustics, and resonance. But don't panic: the things you need to know are easily accessible, even if it has been many years since you last set foot in a science or math class!

All musical instruments, including the human voice, have at least four things in common, consisting of a power source, sound source (vibrator), resonator, and a system for articulation. In most cases, the person who plays the instrument provides power by pressing a key, plucking a string, or blowing into a horn. This power is used to set the sound source in motion, which creates vibrations in the air that we perceive as sound. Musical vibrators come in many forms, including strings, reeds, and human lips. The sound produced by the vibrator, however, needs a lot of help before it becomes beautiful music—we might think of it as raw material, like a lump of clay that a potter turns into a vase. Musical instruments use resonance to enhance and strengthen the sound of the vibrator, transforming it into sounds we identify as a piano, trumpet, or guitar. Finally, instruments must have a means of articulation to create the nuanced sounds of music. Let's see how these four elements are used to create the sounds of singing.

PULMONARY SYSTEM: THE POWER SOURCE OF YOUR VOICE

The human voice has a lot in common with a trumpet: both use flaps of tissue as a sound source, both use hollow tubes as resonators, and both rely on the respiratory (pulmonary) system for power. If you stop to think about it, you quickly realize why breathing is so important for singing. First and foremost, it keeps us alive through the exchange of blood gases—oxygen in, carbon dioxide out. But it also serves as the storage depot for the air we use to produce sound. Most singers rarely encounter situations in which these two functions are in conflict, but if you are required to sustain an extremely long phrase, you could find yourself in need of fresh oxygen before your lungs are totally empty.

Misconceptions about breathing for singing are rampant. Fortunately, most are easily dispelled. We must start with a brief foray into the world of physics in the guise of Boyle's Law. Some of you no doubt remember this principle: the pressure of a gas within a container changes inversely with changes of volume. If the quantity of a gas is constant and its container is made smaller, pressure rises. But if we make the container get bigger, pressure goes down. Boyle's law explains everything that happens when we breathe, especially when we combine it with another physical law: nature abhors a vacuum. If one location has reduced pressure, air flows from an area of higher pressure to equalize the two, and vice versa. So if we can create a zone of reduced air pressure by expanding our lungs, air automatically flows in to restore balance. When air pressure in the lungs is increased, it has no choice but to flow outward.

As we all know, the air we breathe goes in and out of our lungs. Each lung contains millions and millions of tiny air sacs called alveoli, where gases are exchanged. The alveoli also function like ultra-miniature versions of the bladder for a bagpipe, storing the air that will be used to set the vocal folds into vibration. To get the air in and out of them, all we need to do is make the lungs larger for inhalation and smaller for exhalation. Always remember this relationship between cause and effect during breathing: we inhale because we make ourselves large; we exhale because we make ourselves smaller. Unfortunately, the lungs are organs, not muscles, and have no ability on their own to accomplish this feat. For this reason, your bodies came from the factory with special

SINGING AND VOICE SCIENCE

muscles designed to enlarge and compress your entire thorax (rib cage), while simultaneously moving your lungs. We can classify these muscles in two main categories: any muscle that has the ability to increase the volume capacity of the thorax serves an inspiratory function; any muscle that has the ability to decrease the volume capacity of the thorax serves an expiratory function.

Your largest muscle of inspiration is called the diaphragm (figure 3.1). This dome-shaped muscle originates from the bottom of your sternum (breastbone) and completely fills the area from that point around your ribs to your spine. It's the second-largest muscle in your body, but you probably have no conscious awareness of it or ability to directly control it. When we take a deep breath, the diaphragm contracts and the

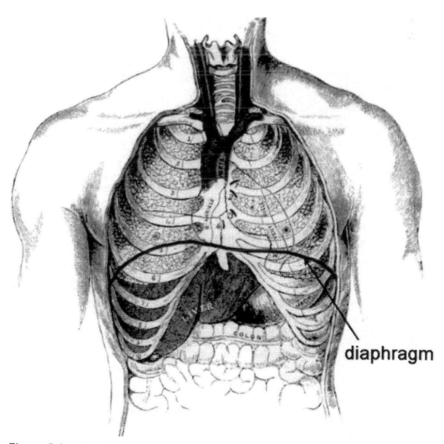

Figure 3.1. Location of Diaphragm. *Courtesy of Scott McCoy*

central portion flattens out and drops downward a couple inches into your abdomen, pressing against all of your internal organs. If you release tension from your abdominal muscles as you inhale, you will feel a gentle bulge in your upper or lower belly, or perhaps in your back, resulting from the displacement of your innards by the diaphragm. This is a good thing and can be used to let you know you have taken a good inhalation.

The diaphragm is important, but we must remember that it cannot function in isolation. After you inhale, it relaxes and gently returns to its resting position through an action called elastic recoil. This movement, however, is entirely passive and makes no significant contribution to generating the pressure required to sustain phonation. Therefore, it makes no sense at all to try to "sing from your diaphragm"—unless you intend to sing while you inhale, not exhale!

Eleven pairs of muscles assist the diaphragm in its inhalatory efforts, which are called the external intercostal muscles (figure 3.2). These muscles start from ribs one through eleven and connect at a slight angle downward to ribs two through twelve. When they contract, the entire thorax moves up and out, somewhat like moving a bucket handle. With the diaphragm and intercostals working together, you are able to increase the capacity of your lungs by about three to six liters, depending on your gender and overall physical stature; thus, we have quite a lot of air available to power our voices.

Eleven additional pairs of muscles are located directly under the external intercostals, which, not surprisingly, are called the internal intercostals (figure 3.2). These muscles start from ribs two through twelve and connect upward to ribs one through eleven. When they contract, they induce the opposite action of their external partners: the thorax is made smaller, inducing exhalation. Four additional pairs of expiratory muscles are located in the abdomen, beginning with the rectus (figure 3.2). The two rectus abdominis muscles run from your pubic bone to your sternum and are divided into four separate portions, called bellies of the muscle (lots of muscles have multiple bellies; it is coincidental that the bellies of the rectus are found in the location we colloquially refer to as our belly). Definition of these bellies results in the so-called ripped abdomen or six-pack of body builders and others who are especially fit.

The largest muscles of the abdomen are called the external obliques (figure 3.3), which run at a downward angle from the sides of the rec-

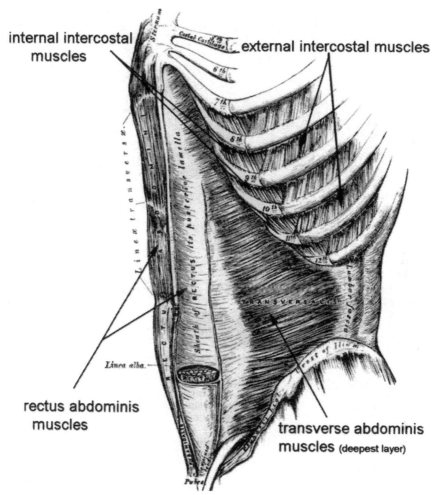

Figure 3.2. Intercostal and Abdominal Muscles. *Courtesy of Scott McCoy*

tus, covering the lower portion of the thorax, and extend all the way to the spine. The internal obliques lie immediately below, oriented at an angle that crisscrosses the external muscles. They are slightly smaller, beginning at the bottom of the thorax, rather than extending over it. The deepest muscle layer is the transverse abdominis (figure 3.3), which is oriented with fibers that run horizontally. These four muscle pairs completely encase the abdominal region, holding your organs and digestive system in place while simultaneously helping you breathe.

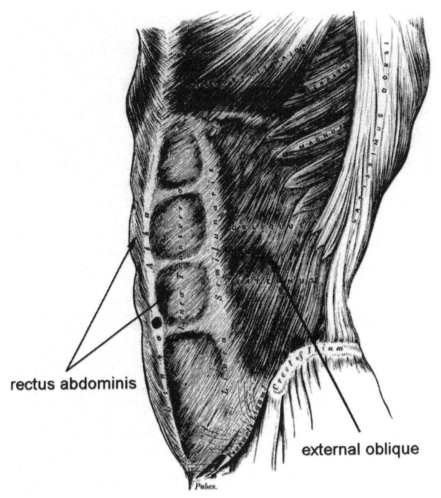

Figure 3.3. External Oblique and Rectus Abdominus Muscles. *Courtesy of Scott McCoy*

Your expiratory muscles are quite large and can produce a great deal of pulmonary or air pressure. In fact, they easily can overpower the larynx. Healthy adults generally can generate more than twice the pressure that is required to produce even the loudest sounds; therefore, singers must develop a system for moderating and controlling airflow and breath pressure. This practice goes by many names, including breath support, breath control, and breath management, all of which rely on the principle of muscular antagonism. Muscles are said to have an antagonistic relationship when they work in opposing directions, usually pulling on a common point of attachment, for the sake of increasing stability or motor control. You can see a clear example of muscular antagonism in the relationship between your biceps (flexors) and triceps (extensors) when you hold out your arm. In breathing for singing, we activate inspiratory muscles (e.g., diaphragm and external intercostals) during exhalation to help control respiratory pressure and the rate at which air is expelled from the lungs.

One of the things you will notice when watching a variety of singers is that they tend to breathe in many different ways. You might think that voice teachers and scientists, who have been teaching and studying singing for hundreds, if not thousands of years, would have come to agreement on the best possible breathing technique. But for many reasons, this is not the case. For one, different musical and vocal styles place varying demands on breathing. For another, humans have a huge variety of body types, sizes, and morphologies. A breathing strategy that is successful for a tall, slender woman might be completely ineffective in a short, robust man. Our bodies actually contain a large number of muscles beyond those we've already discussed that are capable of assisting with respiration. For an example, consider your latissimi dorsi muscles. These large muscles of the arm enable us to do pull-ups (or pull-downs, depending on which exercise you perform) at the fitness center. But because they wrap around a large portion of the thorax, they also exert an expiratory force. We have at least two dozen such muscles that have secondary respiratory functions, some for exhalation and some for inhalation. When we consider all these possibilities, it is no surprise at all that there are many ways to breathe that can produce beautiful singing. Just remember to practice some muscular antagonism—maintaining a degree of inhalation posture during exhalation—and you should do well.

LARYNX: THE VIBRATOR OF YOUR VOICE

The larynx, sometimes known as the voice box or Adam's apple, is a complex physiologic structure made of cartilage, muscle, and tissue. Biologically, it serves as a sphincter valve, closing off the airway to prevent foreign objects from entering the lungs. When firmly closed, it also is used to increase abdominal pressure to assist with lifting heavy objects, childbirth, and defecation. But if we gently close this valve while we exhale, tissue in the larynx begins to vibrate and produce the sounds that become speech and singing.

The human larynx is a remarkably small instrument, typically ranging from the size of a pecan to a walnut for women and men, respectively. Sound is produced at a location called the glottis, which is formed by two flaps of tissue called the vocal folds (aka vocal cords). In women, the glottis is about the size of a dime; in men, it can approach the diameter of a quarter. The two folds are always attached together at their front point but open in the shape of the letter V during normal breathing, an action called abduction. To phonate, we must close the V while we exhale, an action called adduction (just like the machines you use at the fitness center to exercise your thigh and chest muscles).

Phonation only is possible because of the unique multilayer structure of the vocal folds (figure 3.4). The core of each fold is formed by muscle, which is surrounded by a layer of gelatinous material called the lamina propria. The vocal ligament also runs through the lamina propria, which

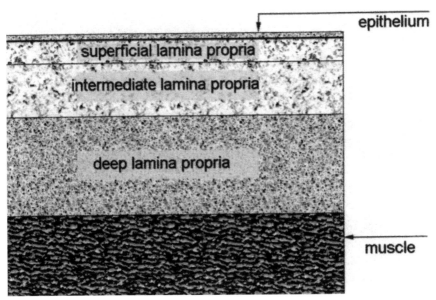

Figure 3.4. Layered Structure of the Vocal Fold. *Courtesy of Scott McCoy*

helps to prevent injury by limiting how far the folds can be stretched for high pitches. A thin, hairless epithelial layer that is constantly kept moist with mucus secreted by the throat, larynx, and trachea surrounds all of this. During phonation, the outer layer of the fold glides independently over the inner layer in a wavelike motion, without which phonation is impossible.

We can use a simple demonstration to better understand the independence of the inner and outer portions of the folds. Explore the palm of your hand with your other index finger. Note that the skin is attached quite firmly to the flesh beneath it. If you poke at your palm, that flesh acts as padding, protecting the underlying bone. Now explore the back of your hand. You will observe that the skin is attached quite loosely—you easily can move it around with your finger. And if you poke at the back of your hand, it is likely to hurt; there is very little padding between the skin and your bones. Your vocal folds combine the best attributes of both sides of your hand. They provide sufficient padding to help reduce impact stress, while permitting the outer layer to slip like the skin on the back of your hand, enabling phonation to occur. When you are sick with laryngitis and lose your voice (a condition called aphonia), inflammation in the vocal folds couples the layers of the folds tightly together. The outer layer no longer can move independently over the inner, and phonation becomes difficult or impossible.

The vocal folds are located within the five cartilaginous structures of the larynx (figure 3.5). The largest is called the thyroid cartilage, which is shaped like a small shield. The thyroid connects to the cricoid cartilage below it, which is shaped like a signet ring—broad in the back and narrow in the front. Two cartilages that are shaped like squashed pyramids sit atop the cricoid, called the arytenoids. Each vocal fold runs from the thyroid cartilage in front to one of the arytenoids at the back. Finally, the epiglottis is located at the top of the larynx, flipping backward each time we swallow to prevent food and liquid from entering our lungs. Muscles connect between the various cartilages to open and close the glottis and to lengthen and shorten the vocal folds for ascending and descending pitch, respectively. Because they sometimes are used to identify vocal function, it is a good idea to know the names of the muscles that control the length of the folds. We've already mentioned that a muscle forms the core of each fold. Because it runs between the

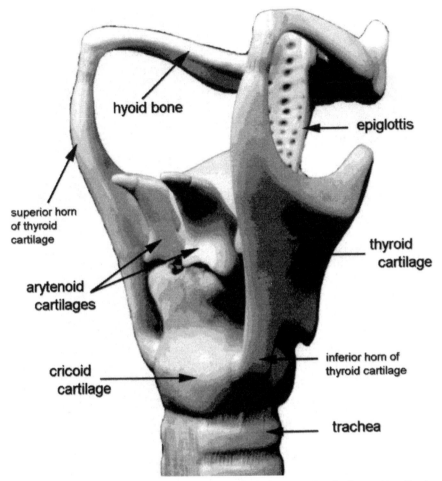

Figure 3.5. Cartilages of the Larynx, Viewed at an Angle from the Back.
Courtesy of Scott McCoy

thyroid cartilage and an arytenoid, it is named the thyroarytenoid muscle (formerly known as the vocalis muscle). When the thyroarytenoid, or TA muscle, contracts, the fold is shortened and pitch goes down. The folds are elongated through the action of the cricothyroid, or CT muscles, which run from the thyroid to cricoid cartilage.

Vocal color (timbre) is created by the combined effects of the sound produced by the vocal folds and the resonance provided by the vocal tract. While these elements can never be completely separated, it is

SINGING AND VOICE SCIENCE

useful to consider the two primary modes of vocal fold vibration and their resulting sound qualities. The main differences are related to the relative thickness of the folds and their cross-sectional shape (figure 3.6). The first option depends on short, thick folds that come together with nearly square-shaped edges. Vibration in this configuration is given a variety of names, including mode 1, thyroarytenoid (TA) dominant, chest mode, or modal voice. The alternate configuration uses longer, thinner folds that only make contact at their upper margins. Common names include mode 2, cricothyroid (CT) dominant, falsetto mode, or loft voice. Singers vary the vibrational mode of the folds according to the quality of sound they wish to produce.

Before we move on to a discussion of resonance, we must consider the quality of the sound that is produced by the larynx. At the level of the glottis, we create a sound not unlike the annoying buzz of a duck call. That buzz, however, contains all the raw material we need to create speech and singing. Vocal or glottal sound is considered to be complex, meaning it consists of many simultaneously sounding frequencies (pitches). The lowest frequency within any tone is called the fundamental, which corresponds to its named pitch in the musical scale. Orchestras tune to a pitch called A-440, which means it has a frequency of 440 vibrations per second, or 440 Hertz (abbreviated Hz). Additional frequencies are included above the fundamental, which are called overtones. Overtones in the glottal sound are quieter than the fundamental. In voices, the overtones usually are whole number multiples of the fundamental, creating a pattern called the harmonic series (e.g., 100 Hz, 200 Hz, 300 Hz, 400 Hz, 500 Hz, etc. or G2, G3, D4, G4, B4—note that pitches are named by the international system in which the lowest C of

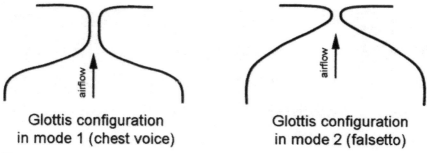

Figure 3.6. Primary Modes of Vocal Fold Vibration. *Courtesy of Scott McCoy*

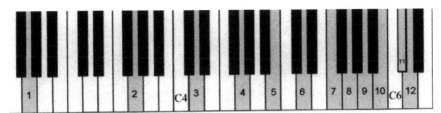

Figure 3.7. Natural Harmonic Series, Beginning at G2. *Courtesy of Scott McCoy*

the piano keyboard is C1; middle C therefore becomes C4, the fourth C of the keyboard) (figure 3.7).

Singers who choose to make coarse or rough sounds as might be appropriate for rock or blues often add overtones that are inharmonic, or not part of the standard numerical sequence. Inharmonic overtones also are common in singers with damaged or pathological voices.

Under most circumstances, we are completely unaware of the presence of overtones—they simply contribute to the overall timbre of a voice. In some vocal styles, however, harmonics become a dominant feature. This is especially true in throat singing or overtone singing, as is found in places like Tuva. Throat singers tune their vocal tracts so precisely that single harmonics are highlighted within the harmonic spectrum as a separate, whistle-like tone. These singers sustain a low-pitched drone and then create a melody by moving from tone to tone within the natural harmonic series. You can learn to do this too. Sustain a comfortable pitch in your range and slowly morph between the vowels /i/ and /u/. If you listen carefully, you will hear individual harmonics pop out of your sound.

The mode of vocal fold vibration has a strong impact on the overtones that are produced. In mode 1, high-frequency harmonics are relatively strong; in mode 2, they are much weaker. As a result, mode 1 tends to yield a much brighter, brassier sound.

VOCAL TRACT: YOUR SOURCE OF RESONANCE

Resonance typically is defined as the amplification and enhancement (or enrichment) of musical sound through supplemental vibration. What does this really mean? In layman's terms, we could say that resonance makes instruments louder and more beautiful by reinforcing the original vibrations of the sound source. This enhancement occurs in two primary ways, which are known as forced and free resonance (there is nothing pejorative in these terms: free resonance is not superior to forced resonance). Any object that is physically connected to a vibrator can serve as a forced resonator. For a piano, the resonator is the soundboard (on the underside of a grand or on the back of an upright); the vibrations of the strings are transmitted directly to the soundboard through a structure known as the bridge, which also is found on violins and guitars. Forced resonance also plays a role in voice production. Place your hand on your chest and say /a/ at a low pitch. You almost certainly felt the vibrations of forced resonance. In singing, this might best be considered your private resonance; you can feel it and it might impact your self-perception of sound, but nobody else can hear it. To understand why this is true, imagine what a violin would sound like if it were encased in a thick layer of foam rubber. The vibrations of the string would be damped out, muting the instrument. Your skin, muscles, and other tissues do the same thing to the vibrations of your vocal folds.

By contrast, free resonance occurs when sound travels through a hollow space, such as the inside of a trumpet, an organ pipe, or your vocal tract, which consists of the pharynx (throat), oral cavity (mouth), and nasal cavity (nose). As sound travels through these regions, a complex pattern of echoes is created; every time sound encounters a change in the shape of the vocal tract, some of its energy is reflected backward, much like an echo in a canyon. If these echoes arrive back at the glottis at the precise moment a new pulse of sound is created, the two elements synchronize, resulting in a significant increase in intensity. All of this happens very quickly—remember that sound is traveling through your vocal tract at more than seven hundred miles per hour.

Whenever this synchronization of the vocal tract and sound source occurs, we say that the system is in resonance. The phenomenon occurs at specific frequencies (pitches), which can be varied by changing the position of the tongue, lips, jaw, palate, and larynx. These resonant frequencies, or areas in which strong amplification occurs, are called formants. Formants provide the specific amplification that changes the raw, buzzing sound produced by your vocal folds into speech and singing. The vocal tract is capable of producing many formants, which are labeled sequentially by ascending pitch. The first two, F1 and F2, are used to create vowels; higher formants contribute to the overall timbre and individual characteristics of a voice. In some singers, especially those who train to sing in opera, formants three through five are clustered together to form a super formant, eponymously called the singer's formant, which creates a ringing sound and enables a voice to be heard in a large theater without electronic amplification.

Formants are vitally important in singing, but they can be a bit intimidating to understand. An analogy that works really well for me is to think of formants like the wind. You cannot see the wind, but you know it is present when you see leaves rustling in a tree or feel a breeze on your face. Formants work in the same manner. They are completely invisible and directly inaudible. But just as we see the rustling leaf, we can hear, and perhaps even feel, the action of formants through how they change our sound. Try a little experiment. Sing an ascending scale beginning at B♭3, sustaining the vowel /i/. As you approach the D♮ or E♭ of the scale, you likely will feel (and hear) that your sound becomes a bit stronger and easier to produce. This occurs because the scale tone and formant are on the same pitch, providing additional amplification. If you change to an /u/ vowel, you will feel the same thing at about the same place in the scale. If you sing to an /o/ or /e/ and continue up the scale, you'll feel a bloom in the sound somewhere around C5 (an octave above middle C); /a/ is likely to come into its best focus at about G5.

To remember the approximate pitches of the first formants for the main vowels, /i–e–a–o–u/, just think of a C-major triad in first inversion, open position, starting at E4: /i/ = E4, /e/ = C5, /a/ = G5, /o/ = C5, and /u/ = E4 (figure 3.8). If your music theory isn't strong, you could use the mnemonic "every child gets candy eagerly." These pitches might vary by as much as a minor third higher and lower but no farther: once a formant changes by more than that interval, the vowel that is produced must change.

Formants have absolutely no preference for what they amplify—they are indiscriminate lovers, just as happy to bond with the first harmonic as the fifth. When men or women sing low pitches, there almost always will be at least one harmonic that comes close enough to a formant to produce a clear vowel sound. The same is not true for women with high

SINGING AND VOICE SCIENCE

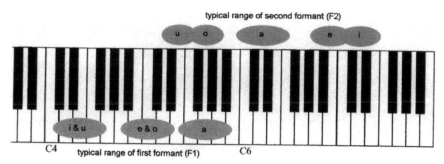

Figure 3.8. Typical Range of First and Second Formants for Primary Vowels. *Courtesy of Scott McCoy*

voices, especially sopranos, who routinely must sing pitches that have a fundamental frequency higher than the first formant of many vowels. Imagine what happens if she must sing the phrase "and I'll leave you forever," with the word "leave" set on a very high, climactic note. The audience won't be able to tell if she is singing leave or love; the two will sound identical. This happens because the formant that is required to identify the vowel /i/ is too far below the pitch being sung. Even if she tries to sing leave, the sound that comes out of her mouth will be heard as some variation of /a/.

Fortunately, this kind of mismatch between formants and musical pitches rarely causes problems for anyone but opera singers, choir sopranos, and perhaps ingenues in classic music theater shows. Almost everyone else generally sings low enough in their respective voice ranges to produce easily identifiable vowels.

Second formants also can be important, but more so for opera singers than everyone else. They are much higher in pitch, tracking the pattern /u/ = E5, /o/ = G5, /a/ = D6, /e/ = B6, /i/ = D7 (you can use the mnemonic "every good dad buys diapers" to remember these pitches) (figure 3.8). Because they can extend so high, into the top octave of the piano keyboard for /i/, they interact primarily with higher tones in the natural harmonic series. Unless you are striving to produce the loudest unamplified sound possible, you probably never need to worry about the second formant; it will steadfastly do its job of helping to produce vowel sounds without any conscious thought or manipulation on your part.

If you are interested in discovering more about resonance and how it impacts your voice, you might want to install a spectrum analyzer on your computer. Free (or inexpensive) programs are readily available for download over the internet that will work with either a PC or Mac computer. You don't need any specialized hardware—if you can use Skype or FaceTime, you already have everything you need. Once you've installed something, simply start playing with it. Experiment with your voice to see exactly how the analysis signal changes when you change the way your voice sounds. You'll be able to see how harmonics change in intensity as they interact with your formants. If you sing with vibrato, you'll see how consistently you produce your variations in pitch and amplitude. You'll even be able to see if your tone is excessively nasal for the kind of singing you want to do. Other programs are available that will help you improve your intonation (how well you sing in tune) or enhance your basic musicianship skills. Technology truly has advanced sufficiently to help us sing more beautifully.

MOUTH, LIPS, AND TONGUE: YOUR ARTICULATORS

The articulatory life of a singer is not easy, especially when compared to the demands placed on other musicians. Like a pianist or brass player, we must be able to produce the entire spectrum of musical articulation, including dynamic levels from hushed pianissimos to thunderous fortes, short notes, long notes, accents, crescendos, diminuendos, and so on. We produce most of these articulations the same way instrumentalists do, which is by varying our power supply. But singers have another layer of articulation that makes everything much more complicated; we must produce these musical gestures while simultaneously singing words.

As we learned in our brief examination of formants, altering the resonance characteristics of the vocal tract creates the vowel sounds of language. We do this by changing the position of our tongue, jaw, lips, and sometimes palate. Slowly say the vowel pattern /i–e–a–o–u/. Can you feel how your tongue moves in your mouth? For /i/, it is high in the front and low in the back, but it takes the opposite position for /u/. Now slowly say the word Tuesday, noting all the places your tongue comes into contact with your teeth and palate and how it changes shape as you produce the vowels and diphthongs. There is a lot going on in there—no wonder it takes so long for babies to learn to speak!

Our articulatory anatomy is extraordinarily complex, in large part because our bodies use the same passageway for food, water, air, and sound. As a result, our tongue, larynx, throat, jaw, and palate are all interconnected with common physical and neurologic points of attachment. Our anatomical Union Station in this regard is a small structure called the hyoid bone. The hyoid is one of only three bones in your entire body that do not connect to other bones via a joint (the other two are your patellae, or kneecaps). This little bone is suspended below your jaw, freely floating up and down every time your swallow. It is a busy place, serving as the upper suspension point for the larynx, the connection for the root of the tongue, and the primary location of the muscles that open your mouth by dropping your jaw.

Good singing—in any genre—requires a high degree of independence in all these articulatory structures. Unfortunately, nature conspires against us to make this difficult to accomplish. From the time we were born, our bodies have relied on a reflex reaction to elevate the palate and raise the larynx each time we swallow. This action becomes habitual: palate goes up, larynx also lifts. But depending on the style of music we are singing, we might need to keep the larynx down while the palate goes up (opera and classical) or palate down with the larynx up (country and bluegrass). As we all know, habits can be very hard to change, which is one of the reasons that it can take a lot of study and practice to become an excellent singer. Understanding your body's natural reflexive habits can make some of this work a bit easier.

There is one more significant pitfall to the close proximity of all these articulators: tension in one area is easily passed along to another. If your jaw muscles are too tight while you sing, that hyperactivity will likely be transferred to the larynx and tongue—remember, they all are interconnected through the hyoid bone. It can be tricky to determine the primary offender in this kind of chain reaction of tension. A tight tongue could just as easily be making your jaw stiff, or an elevated, rigid larynx could make both tongue and jaw suffer.

Neurology complicates matters even further. You have sixteen muscles in your tongue, fourteen in your larynx, twenty-two in your throat and palate, and another sixteen that control your jaw. Many of these are very small and lie directly adjacent to each other, and you often are required to contract one quite strongly while its next-door neighbor must remain totally relaxed. Our brains need to develop laser-like control, sending signals at the right moment with the right intensity to the precise spot where they are needed. When we first start singing, these brain signals come more like a blast from a shotgun, spreading the neurologic impulse over a broad area to multiple muscles, not all of which are the intended target. Again, with practice and training, we learn to refine our control, enabling us to use only those muscles that will help, while disengaging those that would get in the way of our best singing.

FINAL THOUGHTS

This brief chapter has only scratched the surface of the huge field of voice science. To learn more, you might visit the websites of the National Association of Teachers of Singing (NATS), the Voice Foundation (TVF), or the National Center for Voice and Speech (NCVS). You can easily locate the appropriate addresses through any Internet search engine. Remember: knowledge is power. Occasionally, people are afraid that if they know more about the science of how they sing, they will become so analytical that all spontaneity will be lost or they will become paralyzed by too much information and thought. In my forty-plus years as a singer and teacher, I've never encountered somebody who actually suffered this fate. To the contrary, the more we know, the easier—and more joyful—singing becomes. ♪

4

VOCAL HEALTH FOR SINGERS

Wendy LeBorgne

GENERAL PHYSICAL WELLBEING

All singers, regardless of genre, should consider themselves as "vocal athletes." The physical, emotional, and performance demands necessary for optimal output require that the artist consider training and maintaining their instrument as an athlete trains for an event. With increased vocal and performance demands, it is unlikely that a vocal athlete will have an entire performing career completely injury free. This may not be the fault of the singer, as many injuries occur due to circumstances beyond the singer's control such as singing through an illness or being on a new medication seemingly unrelated to the voice. ♪

Vocal injury has often been considered taboo to talk about in the performing world as it has been considered to be the result of faulty technique or poor vocal habits. In actuality, the majority of vocal injuries presenting in the elite performing population tend to be overuse and/or acute injury. From a clinical perspective over the past seventeen years, younger, less experienced singers with fewer years of training (who tend to be quite talented) generally are the ones who present with issues related to technique or phonotrauma (nodules, edema, contact ulcers), while more mature singers with professional performing careers tend to present with acute injuries (hemorrhage) or overuse and misuse injuries (muscle tension dysphonia, edema, GERD) or injuries following an illness. There are no current studies documenting use and training in correlation to laryngeal pathologies. However, there are studies that document that somewhere between 35 percent and 100 percent of professional vocal athletes have abnormal vocal fold findings on stroboscopic evaluation. Many times these "abnormalities" are in singers who have no vocal complaints or symptoms of vocal problems. From a performance perspective, uniqueness in vocal quality often gets hired and perhaps a slight aberration in the way a given larynx functions may become quite marketable. Regardless of what the vocal folds may look like, the most integral part of performance is that the singer must maintain agility, flexibility, stamina, power, and inherent beauty (genre appropriate) for their current level of performance taking into account physical, vocal, and emotional demands.

Unlike sports medicine and the exercise physiology literature where much is known about the types and nature of given sports injuries, there is no common parallel for the vocal athlete model. However, because the vocal athlete utilizes the body systems of alignment, respiration, phonation, and resonance with some similarities to physical athletes, a parallel protocol for vocal wellness may be implemented/considered for vocal athletes to maximize injury prevention knowledge for both the singer and teacher. This chapter aims to provide information on vocal wellness and injury prevention for the vocal athlete.

CONSIDERATIONS FOR WHOLE BODY WELLNESS

Nutrition

You have no doubt heard the saying "You are what you eat." Eating is a social and psychological event. For many people, food associations and eating have an emotional basis resulting in either overeating or being malnourished. Eating disorders in performers and body image issues may have major implications and consequences for the performer on both ends of the spectrum (obesity and anorexia). Singers should be encouraged to reprogram the brain and body to consider food as fuel. You want to use high-octane gas in your engine, as pouring water in your car's gas tank won't get you very far. Eating a poor diet or a diet that lacks appropriate nutritional value will have negative physical and vocal effects on the singer. Effects of poor dietary choices for the vocal athlete may result in physical and vocal effects ranging from fatigue to life-threatening disease over the course of a lifetime. Encouraging and engaging in healthy eating habits from a young age will potentially prevent long-term negative effects from poor nutritional choices. It is beyond the scope of this chapter to provide a complete overview of all the dietary guidelines for pediatrics, adolescents, adults, and the mature adult; however, a listing of additional references to help guide your food and beverage choices for making good nutritional choices can be found online at websites such as Dietary Guidelines for Americans, Nutrition. gov Guidelines for Tweens and Teens, and Fruits and Veggies Matter. See the online companion web page on the NATS website for links to these and other resources. ♪

Hydration

"Sing wet, pee pale." This phrase was echoed in the studio of Van Lawrence regarding how his students would know if they were well hydrated. Generally, this rule of pale urine during your waking hours is a good indicator that you are well hydrated. Medications, vitamins, and certain foods may alter urine color despite adequate hydration. Due to the varying levels of physical and vocal activity of many performers, in order to maintain adequate oral hydration, the use of a hydration calculator based on activity level may be a better choice. These hydration calculators are easily accessible online and take into account the amount and level of activity the performer engages in on a daily basis. In a recent study of the vocal habits of musical theater performers, one of the findings indicated a significantly underhydrated group of performers.[1]

Laryngeal and pharyngeal dryness as well as "thick, sticky mucus" are often complaints of singers. Combating these concerns and maintaining an adequate viscosity of mucus for performance has resulted in some research. As a reminder of laryngeal and swallowing anatomy, nothing that is swallowed (or gargled) goes over or touches the vocal folds directly (or one would choke). Therefore, nothing that a singer eats or drinks ever touches the vocal folds, and in order to adequately hydrate the mucous membranes of the vocal folds, one must consume enough fluids for the body to produce a thin mucus. Therefore, any "vocal" effects from swallowed products are limited to potential pharyngeal and oral changes, not the vocal folds themselves.

The effects of systemic hydration are well documented in the literature. There is evidence to suggest that adequate hydration will provide some protection of the laryngeal mucosal membranes when they are placed under increased collision forces as well as reducing the amount of effort (phonation threshold pressure) to produce voice. This is important for the singer because it means that with adequate hydration and consistency of mucus, the effort to produce voice is less and your vocal folds are better protected from injury. Imagine the friction and heat produced when two dry hands rub together and then what happens if you put lotion on your hands. The mechanisms in the larynx to provide appropriate mucus production are not fully understood, but there is enough evidence at this time to support oral hydration as a vital component of every singer's vocal health regime to maintain appropriate mucosal viscosity.

Although very rare, overhydration (hyperhidrosis) can result in dehydration and even illness or death. An overindulgence of fluids essentially makes the kidneys work "overtime" and flushes too much water out of the body. This excessive fluid loss in a rapid manner can be detrimental to the body.

In addition to drinking water to systemically monitor hydration, there are many nonregulated products on the market for performers that lay claim to improving the laryngeal environment (e.g., Entertainer's Secret, Throat Coat, Grether's Pastilles, slippery elm, etc.). Although there may be little detriment in using these products, quantitative research documenting change in laryngeal mucosa is sparse. One study suggests that the use of Throat Coat when compared to a placebo treatment for pharyngitis did show a significant difference in decreasing the perception of sore throat.[2] Another study compared the use of Entertainer's Secret to two other nebulized agents and its effect on phonation threshold pressure (PTP).[3] There was no positive benefit in decreasing PTP with Entertainer's Secret.

Many singers use personal steam inhalers and/or room humidification to supplement oral hydration and aid in combating laryngeal dryness.

There are several considerations for singers who choose to use external means of adding moisture to the air they breathe. Personal steam inhalers are portable and can often be used backstage or in the hotel room for the traveling performer. Typically, water is placed in the steamer and the face is placed over the steam for inhalation. Because the mucus membranes of the larynx are composed of a saltwater solution, one study looked at the use of nebulized saline in comparison to plain water and its potential effects on effort or ease to sound production in classically trained sopranos.[4] Data suggested that perceived effort to produce voice was less in the saline group than the plain water group. This indicated that the singers who used the saltwater solution reported less effort to sing after breathing in the saltwater than singers who used plain water. The researchers hypothesized that because the body's mucus is not plain water (rather it is a saltwater—think about your tears), when you use plain water for steam inhalation, it may actually draw the salt from your own saliva, resulting in a dehydrating effect.

In addition to personal steamers, other options for air humidification come in varying sizes of humidifiers from room size to whole house humidifiers. When choosing between a warm air or cool mist humidifier, considerations include both personal preference and needs. One of the primary reasons warm mist humidifiers are not recommended for young children is due to the risk of burns from the heating element. Both the warm mist and cool air humidifiers act similarly in adding moisture to the environmental air. External air humidification may be beneficial and provide a level of comfort for many singers. Regular cleaning of the humidifier is vital to prevent bacteria and mold buildup. Also, depending on the hardness of the water, it is important to avoid mineral buildup on the device and distilled water may be recommended for some humidifiers.

For traveling performers who often stay in hotels, fly on airplanes, or are generally exposed to other dry-air environments, there are products on the market designed to help minimize drying effects. One such device is called a Humidflyer, which is a face mask designed with a filter to recycle the moisture of a person's own breath and replenish moisture on each breath cycle.

For dry nasal passages or to clear sinuses, many singers use Neti pots. Many singers use this homeopathic flushing of the nasal passages regularly. Research supports the use of a Neti pot as a part of allergy relief and chronic rhinosinusitis control when utilized properly, sometimes in combination with medical management.[5] Conversely, long-term use of nasal irrigation (without taking intermittent breaks from daily use) may result in washing out the "good" mucus of the nasal passages, which naturally help to rid the nose of infections. A study presented at the 2009 American College of Allergy, Asthma, and Immunology (ACAAI) annual scientific meeting reported that when a group of individuals who were using twice-daily nasal irrigation for one year discontinued using it, they had an increase in acute rhinosinusitis.[6]

Tea, Honey, and Gargle to Keep the Throat Healthy

Regarding the use of general teas (which many singers combine with honey or lemon), there is likely no harm in the use of decaffeinated tea (caffeine may cause systemic dryness). The warmth of the tea may provide a soothing sensation to the pharynx and the act of swallowing can be relaxing for the muscles of the throat. Honey has shown promising results as an effective cough suppressant in the pediatric population.[7] The dose of honey given to the children in the study was two teaspoons. Gargling with salt or apple cider vinegar and water are also popular home remedies for many singers with the uses being from soothing the throat to curing reflux. Gargling plain water has been shown to be efficacious in reducing the risk of contracting upper respiratory infections. I suggest that when gargling, the singer only "bubble" the water with air and avoid engaging the vocal folds in sound production. Saltwater as a gargle has long been touted as a sore throat remedy and can be traced back to 2700 BCE in China for treating gum disease. The science behind a saltwater rinse for everything from oral hygiene to sore throat is that salt (sodium chloride) may act as a natural analgesic (pain killer) and may also kill bacteria. Similar to the effects that not enough salt in the water may have on drawing the salt out of the tissue in the steam inhalation, if you oversaturate the water solution with excess salt and gargle it, it may act to draw water out of the oral mucosa, thus reducing inflammation.

Another popular home remedy reported by singers is the use of apple cider vinegar to help with everything from acid reflux to sore throats. Dating back to 3300 BCE, apple cider vinegar was reported as a medicinal remedy, and it became popular in the 1970s as a weight loss diet cocktail. Popular media reports apple cider vinegar can improve conditions from acne and arthritis to nosebleeds and varicose veins. Specific efficacy data regarding the beneficial nature of apple cider vinegar for the purpose of sore throat, pharyngeal inflammation, and/or reflux has not been reported in the literature at this time. Of the peer-reviewed studies found in the literature, one discussed possible esophageal erosion and inconsistency of actual product in tablet form.[8] Therefore, at this time, strong evidence supporting the use of apple cider vinegar is not published.

Medications and the Voice

Medications (over the counter, prescription, and herbal) may have resultant drying effects on the body and often the laryngeal mucosa. General classes of drugs with potential drying effects include: antidepressants, antihypertensives, diuretics, ADD/ADHD medications, some oral acne medications, hormones, allergy drugs, and vitamin C in high doses. The National Center for Voice and Speech (NCVS) provides a listing of some common medications with potential voice side effects including laryngeal dryness. This listing does not take into account all medications, so singers should always ask their pharmacist of the potential side effects of a given medication. Due to the significant number of drugs on the market, it is safe to say that most pharmacists will not be acutely aware of "vocal side effects," but if dryness is listed as a potential side effect of the drug, you may assume that all body systems could be affected. Under no circumstances should you stop taking a prescribed medication without consulting your physician first. As every person has a different body chemistry and reaction to medication, just because a medication lists dryness as a potential side effect, it does not necessarily mean you will experience that side effect. Conversely, if you begin a new medication and notice physical or vocal changes that are unexpected, you should consult with your physician. Ultimately, the goal of medical management for any condition is to achieve the most benefits with the least side effects. Please see the companion page on the NATS website for a list of possible resources for the singer regarding prescription drugs and herbs. ♪

In contrast to medications that tend to dry, there are medications formulated to increase saliva production or alter the viscosity of mucus. Medically, these drugs are often used to treat patients who have had a loss of saliva production due to surgery or radiation. Mucolytic agents are used to thin secretions as needed. As a singer, if you feel that you need to use a mucolytic agent on a consistent basis, it may be worth considering getting to the root of the laryngeal dryness symptom and seeking a professional opinion from an otolaryngologist.

Reflux and the Voice

Gastroesophageal reflux (GERD) and/or laryngopharyngeal reflux (LPR) can have a devastating impact on the singer if not recognized and treated appropriately. Although GERD and LPR are related, they are considered as slightly different diseases. GERD (Latin root meaning "flowing back") is the reflux of digestive enzymes, acids, and other stomach contents into the esophagus (food pipe). If this backflow is propelled through the upper esophagus and into the throat (larynx and pharynx), it is referred to as LPR. It is not uncommon to have both GERD and LPR, but they can occur independently.

More frequently, people with GERD have decreased esophageal clearing. Esophagitis, or inflammation of the esophagus, is also associated with GERD. People with GERD often feel heartburn. LPR symptoms are often "silent" and do not include heartburn. Specific symptoms of LPR may include some or all of the following: lump in the throat sensation, feeling of constant need to clear the throat/postnasal drip, longer vocal warm-up time, quicker vocal fatigue, loss of high frequency range, worse voice in the morning, sore throat, and bitter/raw/brackish taste in the mouth. If you experience these symptoms on a regular basis, it is advised that you consider a medical consultation for your symptoms. Prolonged, untreated GERD or LPR can lead to permanent changes in both the esophagus and/or larynx. Untreated LPR also provides a laryngeal environment that is conducive for vocal fold lesions to occur as it inhibits normal healing mechanisms.

Treatments of LPR and GERD generally include both dietary and lifestyle modifications in addition to medical management. Some of the dietary recommendations include: elimination of caffeinated and carbonated beverages, smoking cessation, no alcohol use, and limiting tomatoes, acidic foods and drinks, and raw onions or peppers, to name a few. Also, avoidance of high-fat foods is recommended. From a lifestyle perspective, suggested changes include not eating within three hours of lying down, eating small meals frequently (instead of large meals), elevating the head of your bed, avoiding tight clothing around the belly, and not bending over or exercising too soon after you eat.

Reflux medications fall in three general categories: antacids, H2 blockers, and proton pump inhibitors (PPI). There are now combination drugs that include both an H2 blocker and proton pump inhibitor. Every medication has both associated risks and benefits, and singers should be aware of the possible benefits and side effects of the medications they take. In general terms, antacids (e.g., Tums, Mylanta, Gaviscon) neutralize stomach acid. H2 (histamine) blockers, such as Axid (nizatidine), Tagamet (cimetidine), Pepcid (famotidine), and Zantac (ranitidine), work to decrease acid production in the stomach by preventing histamine from triggering the H2 receptors to produce more acid. Then there are the PPIs: Nexium (esomeprazole), Prevacid (lansoprazole), Protonix (pantoprazole), AcipHex (rabeprazole), Prilosec (omeprazole), and Dexilant (dexlansoprazole). PPIs act as a last line of defense to decrease acid production by blocking the last step in gastric juice secretion. Some of the most recent drugs to combat GERD/LPR are combination drugs (e.g., Zegrid [sodium bicarbonate plus omeprazole]), which provide a short-acting response (sodium bicarbonate) and a long release (omeprazole). Because some singers prefer a holistic approach to reflux management, strict dietary and lifestyle compliance is recommended and consultation with both your primary care physician and naturopath are warranted in that situation. Efficacy data on non-regulated herbs, vitamins, and supplements is limited, but some data does exist.

Physical Exercise

Vocal athletes, like other physical athletes, should consider how and what they do to maintain both cardiovascular fitness and muscular strength. In today's performance culture, it is rare that a performer stands still and sings, unless in a recital or choral setting. The range of physical activity can vary from light movement to high-intensity choreography with acrobatics. As performers are being required to increase their on-stage physical activity level from the operatic stage to the pop-star arena, overall physical fitness is imperative to avoid compromise in the vocal system. Breathlessness will result in compensation by the larynx, which is now attempting to regulate the air. Compensatory vocal behaviors over time may result in a change in vocal performance. The health benefits of both cardiovascular training and strength training are well documented for physical athletes but relatively rare in the literature for vocal performers.

Mental Wellness

Vocal performers must maintain a mental focus during performance and a mental toughness during auditioning and training. Rarely during vocal performance training programs is this important aspect of performance addressed, and it is often left to the individual performer to develop their own strategy or coping mechanism. Yet, many performers are on antianxiety or antidepressant drugs (which may be the direct result of performance-related issues). If the sports world is again used as a parallel for mental toughness, there are no elite-level athletes (and few junior-level athletes) who don't utilize the services of a performance/sports psychologist to maximize focus and performance. I recommend that performers consider the potential benefits of a performance psychologist to help maximize vocal performance. Several references that may be of interest to the singer include the audio recording *Visualization for Singers* (1992) and the classic voice pedagogy book *Power Performance for Singers: Transcending the Barriers* (1998).[9] ♪

Unlike instrumentalists, whose performance is dependent on accurate playing of an external musical instrument, the singer's instrument is uniquely intact and subject to the emotional confines of the brain and body in which it is housed. Music performance anxiety (MPA) can be career threatening for all musicians, but perhaps the vocal athlete is more severely impacted. The majority of literature on MPA is dedicated to instrumentalists, but the basis of definition, performance effects, and treatment options can be considered for vocal athletes. Fear is a natural reaction to a stressful situation, and there is a fine line between emotional excitation and perceived threat (real or imagined). The job of a performer is to convey to an audience through vocal production, physical gestures, and facial expression a most heightened state of emotion. Otherwise, why would audience members pay top dollar to sit for two or three hours for a mundane experience? Not only is there the emotional conveyance of the performance but also the internal turmoil often experienced by the singers themselves in preparation for elite performance. It is well documented in the literature that even the most elite performers have experienced debilitating performance anxiety. MPA is defined on a continuum with anxiety levels ranging from low to high and has been reported to comprise four distinct components: affect, cognition, behavior, and physiology. Affect comprises feelings (e.g., doom, panic, anxiety). Affected cognition will result in altered levels of concentration, while the behavior component results in postural shifts, quivering, and trembling. Finally physiologically the body's autonomic nervous system (ANS) will activate, resulting in the "fight or flight" response.

In recent years, researchers have been able to define two distinct neurological pathways for MPA. The first pathway happens quickly and without conscious input (ANS), resulting in the same fear stimulus as if a person were put into an emergent, life-threatening situation. In those situations, the brain releases adrenaline, resulting in physical changes of increased heart rate, increased respiration, shaking, pale skin, dilated pupils, slowed digestion, bladder relaxation, dry mouth, and dry eyes, all of which severely affect vocal performance. The second pathway that has been identified results in a conscious identification of the fear/threat and a much slower physiologic response. With the second neuromotor response, the performer has a chance to recognize the fear, process how to deal with the fear, and respond accordingly.

Treatment modalities to address MPA include psycho-behavioral therapy (including biofeedback) and drug therapies. Elite physical performance athletes have been shown to benefit from visualization techniques and psychological readiness training, yet within the performing arts community, stage fright may be considered a weakness or character flaw precluding readiness for professional performance. On the contrary, vocal athletes, like physical athletes, should mentally prepare themselves for optimal competition (auditions) and performance. Learning to convey emotion without eliciting an internal emotional response by the vocal athlete may take the skill of an experienced psychologist to help change ingrained neural pathways. Ultimately, control and understanding of MPA will enhance performance and prepare the vocal athlete for the most intense performance demands without vocal compromise.

VOCAL WELLNESS: INJURY PREVENTION

In order to prevent vocal injury and understand vocal wellness in the singer, general knowledge of common causes of voice disorders is imperative. One common cause of voice disorders is vocally abusive behaviors or misuse of the voice to include phonotraumatic behaviors such as yelling, screaming, loud talking, talking over noise, throat clearing, coughing, harsh sneezing, and boisterous laughing. Chronic or less than optimal vocal properties such as poor breathing techniques, inappropriate phonatory habits during conversational speech (glottal fry, hard glottal attacks), inapt pitch, loudness, rate of speech, and/or hyperfunctional laryngeal-area muscle tone may also negatively impact vocal function. Medically related etiologies, which also have the potential to impact vocal function, range from untreated chronic allergies and sinusitis to endocrine dysfunction and hormonal imbalance. Direct trauma, such as a blow to the neck or the risk of vocal fold damage during intubation, can impact optimal performance in vocal athletes depending on the nature and extent of the trauma. Finally, external irritants ranging from cigarette smoke to reflux directly impact the laryngeal mucosa and ultimately can lead to laryngeal pathology.

Vocal hygiene education and compliance may be one of the primary essential components for maintaining the voice throughout a career. This section will provide the singer with information on prevention of vocal injury. However, just like a professional sports athlete, it is unlikely that a professional vocal athlete will go through an entire career without some compromise in vocal function. This may be a common upper respiratory infection that creates vocal fold swelling for a short time, or it may be a "vocal accident" that is career threatening. Regardless, the knowledge of how to take care of your voice is essential for any vocal athlete.

Train Like an Athlete for Vocal Longevity

Performers seek instant gratification in performance sometimes at the cost of gradual vocal building for a lifetime of healthy singing. Historically, voice pedagogues required their students to perform vocalises exclusively for up to two years before beginning any song literature. Singers gradually built their voices by ingraining appropriate muscle memory and neuromotor patterns through development of aesthetically pleasing tones, onsets, breath management, and support. There was an intensive master-apprentice relationship and rigorous vocal guidelines to maintain a place within a given studio. Time off was taken if a vocal injury ensued or careers potentially were ended, and students were asked to leave a given singing studio if their voices were unable to withstand the rigors of training. Training vocal athletes today has evolved and appears driven to create a "product" quickly, perhaps at the expense of the longevity of the singer. Pop stars emerging well before puberty are doing international concert tours, yet many young artist programs in the classical arena do not consider singers for their programs until they are in their mid- to late twenties.

Each vocal genre presents with different standards and vocal demands. Therefore, the amount and degree of vocal training are varied. Some would argue that performing extensively without adequate vocal training and development is ill-advised, yet singers today are thrust onto the stage at very young ages. Dancers, instrumentalists, and physical athletes all spend many hours per day developing muscle strength, memory, and proper technique for their craft. The more advanced the artist or athlete, generally the more specific the training protocol becomes. Consideration of training vocal athletes in this same fashion is recommended. One would generally not begin a young, inexperienced singer on a Richard Wagner (1813–1883) aria without previous vocal training. Similarly, in non-classical vocal music, there are easy, moderate, and difficult pieces to consider pending level of vocal development and training.

Basic pedagogical training of alignment, breathing, voice production, and resonance are essential building blocks for development of good voice production. Muscle memory and development of appropriate muscle patterns happen slowly over time with appropriate repetitive practice. Doing too much, too soon for any athlete (physical or vocal) will result in an increased risk for injury. When the singer is being asked to do "vocal gymnastics," they must be sure to have a solid basis of strength and stamina in the appropriate muscle groups to perform consistently with minimal risk of injury.

Vocal Fitness Program

One generally does not get out of bed first thing in the morning and try to do a split. Yet many singers go directly into a practice session or audition without proper warm-up. Think of your larynx like your knee, made up of cartilages, ligaments, and muscles. Vocal health is dependent upon appropriate warm-ups (to get things moving), drills for technique, and then cooldowns (at the end of your day). Consider vocal warm-ups a "gentle stretch." Depending on the needs of the singer, warm-ups should include physical stretching; postural alignment self-checks; breathing exercises to promote rib cage, abdominal, and back expansion; vocal stretches (glides up to stretch the vocal folds and glides down to contract the vocal folds); articulatory stretches (yawning, facial stretches); and mental warm-ups (to provide focus for the task at hand). Vocalises, in my opinion, are designed as exercises to go beyond warm-ups and prepare the body and voice for the technical and vocal challenges of the music they sing. They are varied and address the technical level and genre of the singer to maximize performance and vocal growth. Cooldowns are a part of most athletes' workouts. However, singers often do not use cooldowns (physical, mental, and vocal) at the end of a performance. A recent study looked specifically at the benefits of vocal cooldowns in singers and found that singers who used a vocal cooldown had decreased effort to produce voice the next day.[10]

Systemic hydration as a means to keep the vocal folds adequately lubricated for the amount of impact and friction that they will undergo has been previously discussed in this chapter. Compliance with adequate oral hydration recommendations is important and subsequently so is the minimization of agents that could potentially dry the membranes (e.g., caffeine, medications, dry air). The body produces approximately two quarts of mucus per day. If not adequately hydrated, the mucus tends to be thick and sticky. Poor hydration is similar to not putting enough oil in the car engine. Frankly, if the gears do not work as well, there is increased friction and heat, and the engine is not efficient.

Speak Well, Sing Well

Optimize the speaking voice utilizing ideal frequency range, breath, intensity, rate, and resonance. Singers generally are vocally enthusiastic individuals who talk a lot and often talk loudly. During typical conversation, the average fundamental speaking frequency (times per second the vocal folds are impacting) for a male varies from 100 to 150 Hz and 180 to 230 Hz for women. Because of the delicate structure of the vocal folds and the importance of the layered microstructure vibrating efficiently and effectively to produce voice, vocal behaviors or outside factors that compromise the integrity of the vibration patterns of the vocal folds may be considered phonotrauma.

Phonotraumatic behaviors can include yelling, screaming, loud talking, harsh sneezing, and harsh laughing. Elimination of phonotraumatic behaviors is essential for good vocal health. The louder one speaks, the farther apart the vocal folds move from midline, the harder they impact, and the longer they stay closed. A tangible example would be to take your hands, move them only six inches apart, and clap as hard and as loudly as you can for ten seconds. Now, move your hands two feet apart and clap as hard, loudly, and quickly as possible for ten seconds. The farther apart your hands are, the more air you move and the louder the clap, and the skin on the hands becomes red and ultimately swollen (if you do it long enough and hard enough). This is what happens to the vocal folds with repeated impact at increased vocal intensities. The vocal folds are approximately 17 mm in length and vibrate at 220 times per second on A3, 440 on A4, 880 on A5, and more than 1,000 per second when singing a high C. That is a lot of impact for little muscles. Consider this fact when singing loudly or in a high tessitura for prolonged periods of time. It becomes easy to see why women are more prone than men to laryngeal impact injuries due to the frequency range of the voice alone.

In addition to the amount of cycles per second (cps) the vocal folds are impacting, singers need to be aware of their vocal intensity (volume). One should be aware of the volume of the speaking and singing voice and consider using a distance of three to five feet (about an arms-length distance) as a gauge for how loud to be in general conversation. Using cell phones and speaking on a Bluetooth device in a car generally results in greater vocal intensity than normal and singers are advised to minimize unnecessary use of these devices.

Singers should be encouraged to take "vocal naps" during their day. A vocal nap would be a short period of time (five minutes to an hour) of complete silence. Although the vocal folds are rarely completely still (because they move when you swallow and breathe), a vocal nap minimizes impact and vibration for a short window of time. A physical nap can also be refreshing for the singer mentally and physically.

Avoid Environmental Irritants: Alcohol, Smoking, Drugs

Arming singers with information on the actual effects of environmental irritants so that they can make informed choices on engaging in exposure to these potential toxins is essential. The glamour that continues to be associated with smoking, drinking, and drugs can be tempered with the deaths of popular stars such as Amy Winehouse (1983–2011) and Cory Monteith (1982–2013) who engaged in life-ending choices. There is extensive documentation about the long-term effects of toxic and carcinogenic substances, but here are a few key facts to consider when choosing whether to partake.

Alcohol, although it does not go over the vocal folds directly, does have a systemic drying effect. Due to the acidity in alcohol, it may increase the likelihood of reflux, resulting in hoarseness and other laryngeal pathologies. Consuming alcohol generally decreases one's inhibitions, and therefore you are more likely to sing and do things that you would not typically do under the influence of alcohol.

Beyond the carcinogens in nicotine and tobacco, the heat at which a cigarette burns is well above the boiling temperature of water (water boils at 212 degrees Fahrenheit; cigarettes burn at over 1400 degrees Fahrenheit). No one would consider pouring a pot of boiling water on their hand, and yet the burning temperature for a cigarette results in significant heat over the oral mucosa and vocal folds. The heat alone can create a deterioration in the lining, resulting in polypoid degeneration.

Obviously, cigarette smoking has been well documented as a cause for laryngeal cancer.

Marijuana and other street drugs are not only addictive but can cause permanent mucosal lining changes depending on the drug used and the method of delivery. If you or one of your singer colleagues is experiencing a drug or alcohol problem, research or provide information and support on getting appropriate counseling and help.

SMART PRACTICE STRATEGIES FOR SKILL DEVELOPMENT AND VOICE CONSERVATION

Daily practice and drills for skill acquisition are an important part of any singer's training. However, overpracticing or inefficient practicing may be detrimental to the voice. Consider practice sessions of athletes: they may practice four to eight hours per day broken into one- to two-hour training sessions with a period of rest and recovery in between sessions. Although we cannot parallel the sports model without adequate evidence in the vocal athlete, the premise of short, intense, focused practice sessions is logical for the singer. Similar to physical exercise, it is suggested that practice sessions do not have to be all "singing." Rather, structuring sessions so that one-third of the session is spent on warm-up; one-third on vocalises, text work, rhythms, character development, and so on; and one-third on repertoire will allow the singer to function in a more efficient vocal manner. Building the amount of time per practice session—increasing duration by five minutes per week, building to sixty to ninety minutes—may be effective (e.g., Week 1: twenty minutes three times per day; Week 2: twenty-five minutes three times per day, etc.).

Vary the "vocal workout" during your week. For example, if you do the same physical exercise in the same way day after day with the same intensity and pattern, you will likely experience repetitive strain–type injuries. However, cross-training or varying the type and level of exercise aids in injury prevention. So when planning your practice sessions for a given week (or rehearsal process for a given role), consider varying your vocal intensity, tessitura, and exercises to maximize your training sessions, building stamina, muscle memory, and skill acquisition.

For example, one day you may spend more time on learning rhythms and translation and the next day you spend thirty minutes performing coloratura exercises to prepare for a specific role. Take one day a week off from vocal training and give your voice a break. This does not mean complete vocal rest (although some singers find this beneficial), but rather a day without singing and limited talking.

Practice Your Mental Focus

Mental wellness and stress management are equally as important as vocal training for vocal athletes. Addressing any mental health issues is paramount to developing the vocal artist. This may include anything from daily mental exercises/meditation/focus to overcoming performance anxiety to more serious mental health issues/illness. Every person can benefit from improved focus and mental acuity.

ADDITIONAL VOCAL WELLNESS TIPS

When working with singers across all genres, the most common presentation in my voice clinic relates to vocal fatigue, acute vocal injury, and loss of high frequency range. Vocal fatigue complaints are generally related to the duration of their rehearsals, recording sessions, "meet and greets," performances, vocal gymnastics, general lack of sleep, and the vocal requirements to traverse their entire range (and occasionally outside of physiological comfort range). Depending on the genre performed, singing includes a high vocal load with the associated risk of repetitive strain and increased collision force injuries. Acute vocal injuries within this population include phonotraumtic lesions (hemorrhages, vocal fold polyps, vocal fold nodules, reflux, and general vocal fold edema/erythema). Often these are not injuries related to problematic vocal technique, but rather due to "vocal accidents" and/or overuse (due to required performance/contract demands). Virtually all singers are required to connect with the audience from a vocal and emotional standpoint. Physical performance demands may be extreme and at times highly cardiovascular and/or acrobatic. Both physical and vocal fitness should be foremost in the minds of any vocal performer, and these singers should be physically and vocally in shape to meet the necessary performance demands.

The advanced and professional singer must possess an flexible, agile, and dynamic instruments and have appropriate stamina. The singer must have a good command of their instrument as well as exceptional underlying intention to what they are singing as it is about relaying a message, characteristic sound, and connecting with the audience. Singers must reflect the mood and intent of the composer requiring dynamic control, vocal control/power, and an emotional connection to the text.

Commercial music singers use microphones and personal amplification to their maximal capacity. If used correctly, amplification can be used to maximize vocal health by allowing the singer to produce voice in an efficient manner while the sound engineer is effectively able to mix, amplify, and add effects to the voice. Understanding both the utility and limits of a given microphone and sound system is essential for the singer both for live and studio performances. Using an appropriate microphone can not only enhance the singer's performance, but can also reduce vocal load. Emotional extremes (intimacy and exultation) can be enhanced by appropriate microphone choice, placement, and acoustical mixing; thus, saving the singer's voice.

Not everything a singer does is "vocally healthy," sometimes because the emotional expression may be so intense it results in vocal collision forces that are extreme. Even if the singer does not have formal vocal training, the concept of "vocal cross-training"—which can mean singing in both high and low registers with varying intensities and resonance options—before and after practice sessions and services is likely a vital component to minimizing vocal injury.

FINAL THOUGHTS

Ultimately, the singer must learn to provide the most output with the least "cost" to the system. Taking care of the physical instrument through daily physical exercise, adequate nutrition and hydration, and focused attention on performance will provide a necessary basis for vocal health during performance. Small doses of high-intensity singing (or speaking) will limit impact stress on the vocal folds. Finally, attention to the mind, body, and voice will provide the singer with an awareness when something is wrong. This awareness and knowledge of when to rest or seek help will promote vocal wellbeing for the singer throughout his or her career.

NOTES

1. Wendy LeBorgne et al., "Prevalence of Vocal Pathology in Incoming Freshman Musical Theatre Majors: A 10-year Retrospective Study," Fall Voice Conference, New York, 2012.

2. Josef Brinckmann et al., "Safety and Efficacy of a Traditional Herbal Medicine (Throat Coat) in Symptomatic Temporary Relief of Pain in Patients with Acute Pharyngitis: A Multicenter, Prospective, Randomized, Double-Blinded, Placebo-Controlled Study," *Journal of Alternative and Complementary Medicine* 9, no. 2 (2003): 285–98.

3. Nelson Roy et al., "An Evaluation of the Effects of Three Laryngeal Lubricants on Phonation Threshold Pressure (PTP)," *Journal of Voice* 17, no. 3 (2003): 331–42.

4. Kristine Tanner et al., "Nebulized Isotonic Saline versus Water Following a Laryngeal Desiccation Challenge in Classically Trained Sopranos," *Journal of Speech Language and Hearing Research* 53, no. 6 (2010): 1555–66.

5. Cristopher L. Brown and Scott M. Graham, "Nasal Irrigations: Good or Bad?" *Current Opinion in Otolaryngology, Head and Neck Surgery* 12, no. 1 (2004): 9–13.

6. Talal N. Nsouli, "Long-Term Use of Nasal Saline Irrigation: Harmful or Helpful?" American College of Allergy, Asthma and Immunology Annual Scientific Meeting, Abstract 32, 2009.

7. Mahmoud Norri Shadkam et al. "A Comparison of the Effect of Honey, Dextromethorphan, and Diphenhydramine on Nightly Cough and Sleep Quality in Children and Their Parents," *Journal of Alternative and Complementary Medicine* 16, no. 7 (2010): 787–93.

8. Laura L. Hill et al., "Esophageal Injury by Apple Cider Vinegar Tablets and Subsequent Evaluation of Products," *Journal of the American Dietetic Association* 105, no. 7 (2005): 1141–44.

9. Joanna Cazden, *Visualizations for Singers* (Burbank, CA: Voice of Your Life, 1992); Shirlee Emmons and Alma Thomas, *Power Performance for Singers: Transcending the Barriers* (New York: Oxford University Press, 1998).

10. Renee Gottliebson, "The Efficacy of Cool-Down Exercises in the Practice Regimen of Elite Singers," PhD dissertation, University of Cincinnati, 2011.

USING AUDIO ENHANCEMENT TECHNOLOGY

Matthew Edwards

In the early days of popular music, musicians performed without electronic amplification. Singers learned to project their voices in the tradition of vaudeville performers with a technique similar to operatic and operetta performers who had been singing unamplified for centuries. When microphones began appearing on stage in the 1930s, vocal performance changed forever since the loudness of a voice was no longer a factor in the success of a performer. In order to be successful, all a singer needed was an interesting vocal quality and an emotional connection to what he or she was singing. The microphone would take care of projection.[1]

Vocal qualities that may sound weak without a microphone can sound strong and projected when sung with one. At the same time, a singer with a voice that is acoustically beautiful and powerful can sound harsh and pushed if he or she lacks microphone technique. Understanding how to use audio equipment to get the sounds a singer desires without harming the voice is crucial. The information in this chapter will help the reader gain a basic knowledge of terminology and equipment commonly used when amplifying or recording a vocalist as well as providing tips for singing with a microphone.

THE FUNDAMENTALS OF SOUND

In order to understand how to manipulate an audio signal, you must first understand a few basics of sound including frequency, amplitude, harmonics, and resonance.

Frequency

Sound travels in waves of compression and rarefaction within a medium, which for our purposes is air (see figure 5.1). These waves travel through the air and into our inner ears via the ear canal. There they are converted via the eardrums into nerve impulses that are transmitted to the brain and interpreted as sound. The number of waves per second is measured in Hertz (Hz), which gives us the frequency of the sound that we have learned to perceive as pitch. For example, we hear 440 Hz (440 cycles of compression and rarefaction per second) as A4, the pitch A above middle C.

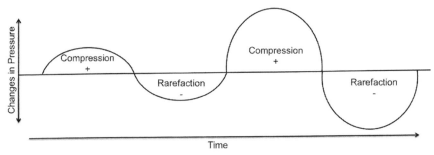

Figure 5.1. Compression and Rarefaction. *Creative Commons* **(CC BY-SA 4.0)**

Amplitude

The magnitude of the waves of compression and rarefaction determines the amplitude of the sound, which we call its "volume." The larger the waves of compression and rarefaction, the louder we perceive the sound to be. Measured in decibels (dB), amplitude represents changes in air pressure from the baseline. Decibel measurements range from zero decibels (0 dB), the threshold of human hearing, to 130 dB, the upper edge of the threshold of pain.

Harmonics

The vibrating mechanism of an instrument produces the vibrations necessary to establish pitch (the fundamental frequency). The vibrating mechanism for a singer is the vocal folds. If an acoustic instrument, such as the voice, were to produce a note with the fundamental frequency alone, the sound would be strident and mechanical like the emergency alert signal used on television. Pitches played on acoustic instruments consist of multiple frequencies, called overtones, which are emitted from the vibrator along with the fundamental frequency. For the purposes of this chapter, the overtones that we are interested in are called harmonics. Harmonics are whole number multiples of the fundamental frequency. For example, if the fundamental is 220 Hz (A3), the harmonic overtone series would be 220 Hz, 440 Hz (fundamental frequency times two), 660 Hz (fundamental frequency times three), 880 Hz (fundamental frequency times four), and so on. Every musical note contains both the fundamental frequency and a predictable series of harmonics, each of which can be measured and identified as a specific frequency. This series of frequencies then travels through a hollow cavity (the vocal tract) where they are attenuated or amplified by the resonating frequencies of the cavity, which is how resonance occurs.

Resonance

The complex waveform created by the vocal folds travels through the vocal tract, where it is enhanced by the tract's unique resonance characteristics. Depending on the resonator's shape, some harmonics are amplified and some are attenuated. Each singer has a unique vocal tract shape with unique resonance characteristics. This is why two singers of the same voice type can sing the same pitch and yet sound very different. We can analyze these changes with a tool called a spectrum analyzer as seen in figure 5.2. The slope from left to right is called the spectral slope. The peaks and valleys along the slope indicate amplitude variations of the corresponding overtones. The difference in spectral

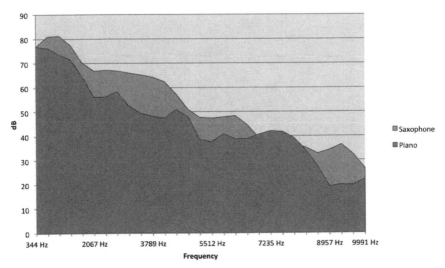

Figure 5.2. The figure above shows two instruments playing the same pitch. The peak at the far left is the fundamental frequency and the peaks to the right are harmonics that have been amplified and attenuated by the instrument's resonator, resulting in a specific timbre. *Courtesy of Matthew Edwards*

slope between instruments (or voices) is what enables a listener to aurally distinguish the difference between two instruments playing or singing the same note.

Because the throat and mouth act as the resonating tube in acoustic singing, changing their size and shape is the only option for making adjustments to timbre for those who perform without microphones. In electronically amplified singing, the sound engineer can make adjustments to boost or attenuate specific frequency ranges, thus changing the singer's timbre. For this and many other reasons discussed in this chapter, it is vitally important for singers to know how audio technology can affect the quality of their voice.

SIGNAL CHAIN

The signal chain is the path an audio signal travels from the input to the output of a sound system. A voice enters the signal chain through a microphone, which transforms acoustic energy into electrical impulses.

The electrical pulses generated by the microphone are transmitted through a series of components that modify the signal before the speakers transform it back into acoustic energy. Audio engineers and producers understand the intricacies of these systems and are able to make an infinite variety of alterations to the vocal signal. While some engineers strive to replicate the original sound source as accurately as possible, others use the capabilities of the system to alter the sound for artistic effect. Since more components and variations exist than can be discussed in just a few pages, this chapter will discuss only basic components and variations found in most systems.

Microphones

Microphones transform the acoustic sound waves of the voice into electrical impulses. The component of the microphone that is responsible for receiving the acoustic information is the diaphragm. The two most common diaphragm types that singers will encounter are dynamic and condenser. Each offers advantages and disadvantages depending on how the microphone is to be used.

Dynamic Dynamic microphones consist of a dome-shaped Mylar diaphragm attached to a free-moving copper wire coil that is positioned between the two poles of a magnet. The Mylar diaphragm moves in response to air pressure changes caused by sound waves. When the diaphragm moves, the magnetic coil that is attached to it also moves. As the magnetic coil moves up and down between the magnetic poles, it produces an electrical current that corresponds to the sound waves produced by the singer's voice. That signal is then sent to the soundboard via the microphone cable. The Shure SM58 dynamic microphone is the industry standard for live performance because it is affordable, nearly indestructible, and easy to use. Dynamic microphones such as the Shure SM58 have a lower sensitivity than condenser microphones, which makes them more successful at avoiding feedback. Because of their reduced tendency to feedback, dynamic microphones are the best choice for artists who use handheld microphones when performing. ♪

Condenser Condenser microphones are constructed with two parallel plates: a rigid posterior plate and a thin, flexible anterior plate. The anterior plate is constructed of either a thin sheet of metal or a piece of

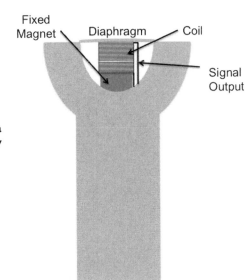

Figure 5.3. Basic Design of a Dynamic Microphone. *Courtesy of Matthew Edwards*

Mylar that is coated with a conductive metal. The plates are separated by air, which acts as a layer of insulation. In order to use a condenser microphone, it must be connected to a soundboard that supplies "phantom power." A component of the soundboard, phantom power sends a 48-volt power supply through the microphone cable to the microphone's plates. When the plates are charged by phantom power, they form a capacitor. As acoustic vibrations send the anterior plate into motion, the distance between the two plates varies, which causes the capacitor to release a small electric current. This current, which corresponds with the acoustic signal of the voice, travels through the microphone cable to the soundboard where it can be enhanced and amplified.

Electret condenser microphones are similar to condenser microphones, but they are designed to work without phantom power. The anterior plate of an electret microphone is made of a plastic film coated with a conductive metal that is electrically charged before being set into place opposite the posterior plate. The charge applied to the anterior plate will last for ten or more years and therefore eliminates the need for an exterior power source. Electret condenser microphones are often used in head-mounted and lapel microphones, laptop computers, and smartphones.

Recording engineers prefer condenser microphones for recording applications due to their high level of sensitivity. Using a condenser

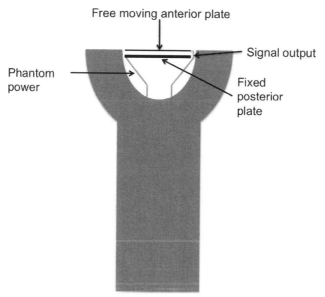

Figure 5.4. Basic Design of a Condenser Microphone.
Courtesy of Matthew Edwards

microphone, performers can sing at nearly inaudible acoustic levels and obtain a final recording that is intimate and earthy. While the same vocal effects can be recorded with a dynamic microphone, they will not have the same clarity as those produced with a condenser microphone.

Frequency Response Frequency response is a term used to define how accurately a microphone captures the tone quality of the signal. A "flat response" microphone captures the original signal with little to no signal alteration. Microphones that are not designated as "flat" have some type of amplification or attenuation of specific frequencies, also known as cut or boost, within the audio spectrum. For instance, the Shure SM58 microphone drastically attenuates the signal below 300 Hz and amplifies the signal in the 3 kHz range by 6 dB, the 5 kHz range by nearly 8 dB, and the 10 kHz range by approximately 6 dB. The Oktava 319 microphone cuts the frequencies below 200 Hz while boosting everything above 300 Hz with nearly 5 dB between 7 kHz and 10k Hz (see figure 5.5). In practical terms, recording a bass singer with the Shure SM58 would drastically reduce the amplitude of the fundamental frequency while the Oktava 319 would produce a slightly more consistent

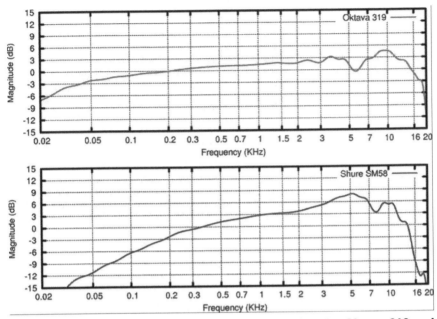

Figure 5.5. Example Frequency Response Graphs for the Oktava 319 and the Shure SM58. *Creative Commons* **(CC BY-SA 4.0)**

boost in the range of the singer's formant. Either of these options could be acceptable depending on the situation, but the frequency response must be considered before making a recording or performing live.

Amplitude Response The amplitude response of a microphone varies depending on the angle at which the singer is positioned in relation to the axis of the microphone. In order to visualize the amplitude response of a microphone at various angles, microphone manufacturers publish polar pattern diagrams (also sometimes called a directional pattern or a pickup pattern). Polar pattern diagrams usually consist of six concentric circles divided into twelve equal sections. The center point of the microphone's diaphragm is labeled 0° and is referred to as "on-axis" while the opposite side of the diagram is labeled 180° and is described as "off-axis."

Although polar pattern diagrams appear in two dimensions, they actually represent a three-dimensional response to acoustic energy. You can use a round balloon as a physical example to help you visualize a three-dimensional polar pattern diagram. Position the tied end of the balloon away from your mouth and the inflated end directly in front of your lips. In this position, you are singing on-axis at 0° with the tied end of the balloon being 180°, or off-axis. If you were to split the balloon in half vertically and horizontally (in relationship to your lips), the point at which those lines intersect would be the center point of the balloon. That imaginary center represents the diaphragm of the microphone. If you were to extend a 45-degree angle in any direction from the imaginary center and then drew a circle around the inside of the balloon following that angle, you would have a visualization of the three-dimensional application of the two-dimensional polar pattern drawing.

The outermost circle of the diagram indicates that the sound pressure level (SPL) of the signal is transferred without any amplitude reduction, indicated in decibels (dB). Each of the inner circles represents a –5 dB reduction in the amplitude of the signal up to –25 dB. Figure 5.7 below is an example. Figures 14.8, 14.9, and 14.10 show the most commonly encountered polar patterns.

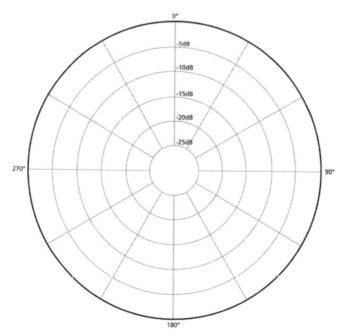

Figure 5.6. Example of a Microphone Polar Pattern Diagram. *Creative Commons* **(CC BY-SA 4.0)**

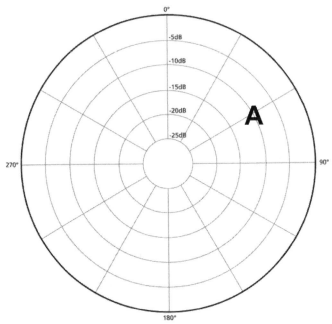

Figure 5.7. If the amplitude response curve intersected with point A, there would be a −10-dB reduction in the amplitude of frequencies received by the microphone's diaphragm at that angle. *Creative Commons* **(CC BY-SA 4.0)**

When you are using a microphone with a polar pattern other than omnidirectional (a pattern that responds to sound equally from all directions), you may encounter frequency response fluctuations in addition to amplitude fluctuations. Cardioid microphones in particular are known for their tendency to boost lower frequencies at close proximity to the sound source while attenuating those same frequencies as the distance between the sound source and the microphone increases. This is known as the "proximity effect." Some manufacturers will notate these frequency response changes on their polar pattern diagrams by using a combination of various lines and dashes alongside the amplitude response curve.

Sensitivity While sensitivity can be difficult to explain in technical terms without going into an in-depth discussion of electricity and electrical terminology, a simplified explanation should suffice for most readers. Manufacturers test microphones with a standardized 1 kHz tone at

USING AUDIO ENHANCEMENT TECHNOLOGY

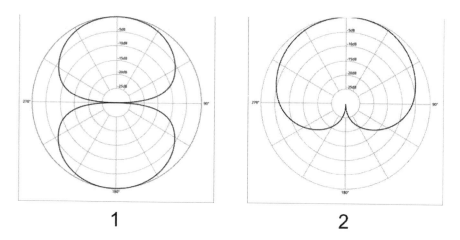

Figure 5.8. Diagram one represents a bidirectional pattern; diagram two represents a cardioid pattern. *Creative Commons* **(CC BY-SA 4.0)**

94 dB in order to determine how sensitive the microphone's diaphragm will be to acoustic energy. Microphones with greater sensitivity can be placed farther from the sound source without adding excessive noise to the signal. Microphones with lower sensitivity will need to be placed closer to the sound source in order to keep excess noise at a minimum. When shopping for a microphone, the performer should audition sev-

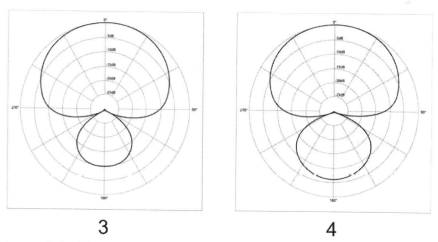

Figure 5.9. Diagram three represents a supercardioid pattern; diagram four represents a hypercardioid pattern. *Creative Commons* **(CC BY-SA 4.0)**

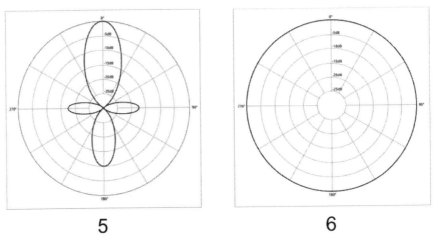

Figure 5.10. Diagram five represents a shotgun pattern, and diagram six represents an omnidirectional pattern. *Creative Commons* (CC BY-SA 4.0)

eral ext to each other, plugged into the same soundboard, with the same volume level for each. When singing on each microphone, at the same distance, the performer will notice that some models replicate the voice louder than others. This change in output level is due to differences in each microphone's sensitivity. If a performer has a loud voice, they may prefer a microphone with lower sensitivity (one that requires more acoustic energy to respond). If a performer has a lighter voice, they may prefer a microphone with higher sensitivity (one that responds well to softer signals).

Equalization (EQ)

Equalizers enable the audio engineer to alter the audio spectrum of the sound source and make tone adjustments with a simple electronic interface. Equalizers come in three main types: shelf, parametric, and graphic.

Shelf Shelf equalizers cut or boost the uppermost and lowermost frequencies of an audio signal in a straight line (see figure 5.11). While this style of equalization is not very useful for fine-tuning a singer's tone quality, it can be very effective in removing room noise. For example, if an air conditioner creates a 60-Hz hum in the recording studio, the shelf can be set at 65 Hz, with a steep slope. This setting eliminates

USING AUDIO ENHANCEMENT TECHNOLOGY

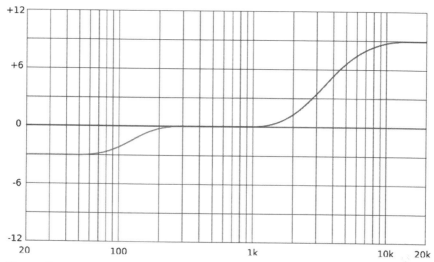

Figure 5.11. The frequency amplitude curves above show the effect of applying a shelf EQ to an audio signal. *Creative Commons* (CC BY-SA 4.0)

frequencies below 65 Hz and effectively removes the hum from the microphone signal.

Parametric Parametric units simultaneously adjust multiple frequencies of the audio spectrum that fall within a defined parameter. The engineer selects a center frequency and adjusts the width of the bell curve surrounding that frequency by adjusting the "Q" (see figure 5.12). He or she then boosts or cuts the frequencies within the bell curve to alter the audio spectrum. Parametric controls take up minimal space on a soundboard and offer sufficient control for most situations. Therefore, most live performance soundboards have parametric EQs on each individual channel. With the advent of digital workstations, engineers can now use computer software to fine-tune the audio quality of each individual channel using a more complex graphic equalizer in both live and recording studio settings without taking up any additional physical space on the board. However, many engineers still prefer to use parametric controls during a live performance since they are usually sufficient and are easier to adjust mid-performance.

Parametric adjustments on a soundboard are made with rotary knobs similar to those in figure 5.13 below. In some cases, you will find a button labeled "low cut" or "high pass" that will automatically apply a shelf

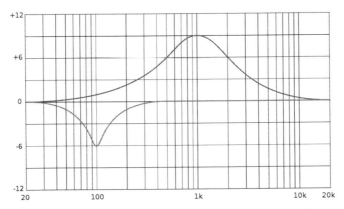

Figure 5.12. The frequency amplitude curves above display two parametric EQ settings. The top curve represents a boost of +8 dB set at 1 kHz with a relatively large bell curve—a low Q. The lower curve represents a high Q set at 100 Hz with a cut of –6 dB. *Creative Commons* (**CC BY-SA 4.0**)

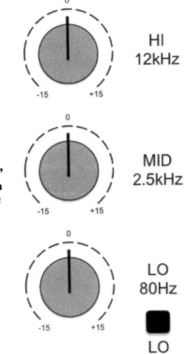

Figure 5.13. This is an example of a parametric EQ interface. The "**LO CUT**" button applies a shelf EQ at 80 Hz when depressed. *Courtesy of Matthew Edwards*

filter to the bottom of the audio spectrum at a specified frequency. On higher-end boards, you may also find a knob that enables you to select the high pass frequency.

Graphic Graphic equalizers enable engineers to identify a specific frequency for boost or cut with a fixed frequency bandwidth. For example, a ten-band equalizer enables the audio engineer to adjust ten specific frequencies (in Hz): 31, 63, 125, 250, 500, 1K, 2K, 4K, 8K, and 16K. Graphic equalizers are often one of the final elements of the signal chain, preceding only the amplifier and speakers. In this position, they can be used to adjust the overall tonal quality of the entire mix.

Utilizing Equalization Opinions on the usage of equalization vary among engineers. Some prefer to only use equalization to remove or reduce frequencies that were not a part of the original sound signal. Others will use EQ if adjusting microphone placement fails to yield acceptable results. Some engineers prefer a more processed sound and may use equalization liberally to intentionally change the vocal quality of the singer. For instance, if the singer's voice sounds dull, the engineer could add "ring" or "presence" to the voice by boosting the equalizer in the 2–10 kHz range.

Compression

Many singers are capable of producing vocal extremes in both frequency and amplitude levels that can prove problematic for the sound team. To help solve this problem, engineers often use compression.

Compressors limit the output of a sound source by a specified ratio. The user sets the maximum acceptable amplitude level for the output, called the "threshold," and then sets a ratio to reduce the output once it surpasses the threshold. The typical ratio for a singer is usually between 3:1 and 5:1. A 4:1 ratio indicates that for every 4 dB beyond the threshold level, the output will only increase by 1 dB. For example, if the singer went 24 dB beyond the threshold with a 4:1 ratio, the output would only be 6 dB beyond the threshold level (see figure 4.15).

Adjusting the sound via microphone technique can provide some of the same results as compression and is preferable for the experienced artist. However, compression tends to be more consistent and also gives the singer freedom to focus on performing and telling a story. The addi

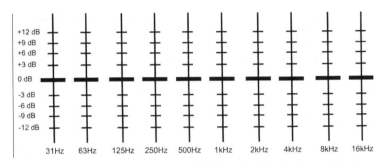

Figure 5.14. Example of a Graphic Equalizer Interface. *Courtesy of Matthew Edwards*

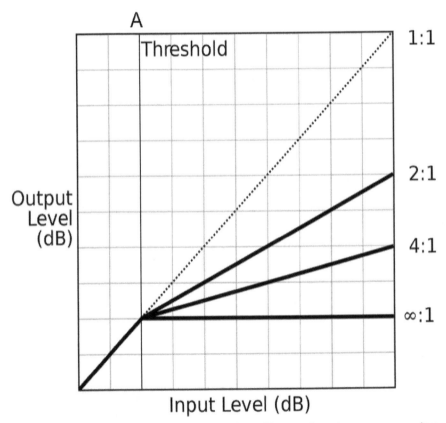

Figure 5.15. This graph represents the effects of various compression ratios applied to a signal. The 1:1 angle represents no compression. The other ratios represent the effect of compression on an input signal with the threshold set at line A. *Creative Commons* **(CC BY-SA 4.0)**

tional artistic freedom provided by compression is especially beneficial to singers who use head-mounted microphones, performers who switch between vocal extremes such as falsetto and chest voice, and those who are new to performing with a microphone. Compression can also be helpful for classical singers whose dynamic abilities, while impressive live, are often difficult to record in a manner that allows for consistent listening levels through a stereo system.

If a standard compressor causes unacceptable alterations to the tone quality, engineers can turn to a multiband compressor. Rather than affecting the entire spectrum of sound, multiband compressors allow the engineer to isolate a specific frequency range within the audio signal and then set an individual compression setting for that frequency range. For example, if a singer creates a dramatic boost in the 4-kHz range every time they sing above an A4, a multiband compressor can be used to limit the amplitude of the signal in only that part of the voice. By setting a 3:1 ratio in the 4-kHz range at a threshold that corresponds to the amplitude peaks that appear when the performer sings above A4, the engineer can eliminate vocal "ring" from the sound on only the offending notes while leaving the rest of the signal untouched. These units are available for both live and studio use and can be a great alternative to compressing the entire signal.

Reverb

Reverb is one of the easier effects for singers to identify; it is the effect you experience when singing in a cathedral. An audience experiences natural reverberation when they hear the direct signal from the singer and then, milliseconds later, they hear multiple reflections as the acoustical waves of the voice bounce off the side walls, floor, and ceiling of the performance hall.

Many performance venues and recording studios are designed to inhibit natural reverb. Without at least a little reverb added to the sound, even the best singer can sound harsh and even amateurish. Early reverb units transmitted the audio signal through a metal spring, which added supplementary vibrations to the signal. While some engineers still use spring reverb to obtain a specific effect, most now use digital units. Common settings on digital reverb units include wet/dry, bright/dark, and options for delay time. The wet/dry control adjusts the amount of direct signal (dry) and the amount of reverberated signal (wet). The bright/dark control helps simulate the effects of various surfaces within a natural space. For instance, harder surfaces such as stone reflect high frequencies and create a brighter tone quality while softer surfaces such as wood reflect lower frequencies and create a darker tone quality. The delay time, which is usually adjustable from milliseconds to seconds, adjusts the amount of time between when the dry signal and wet signals reach the ear. Engineers can transform almost any room into a chamber music hall or concert stadium simply by adjusting these settings.

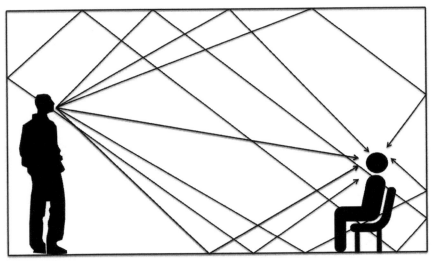

Figure 5.16. This diagram illustrates the multiple lines of reflection that create reverb. *Courtesy of Matthew Edwards*

Delay

Whereas reverb blends multiple wet signals with the dry signal to replicate a natural space, delay purposefully separates a single wet signal from the dry signal to create repetitions of the voice. With delay, you will hear the original note first and then a digitally produced repeat of the note several milliseconds to seconds later. The delayed note may be heard one time or multiple times and the timing of those repeats can be adjusted to match the tempo of the song.

USING AUDIO ENHANCEMENT TECHNOLOGY 127

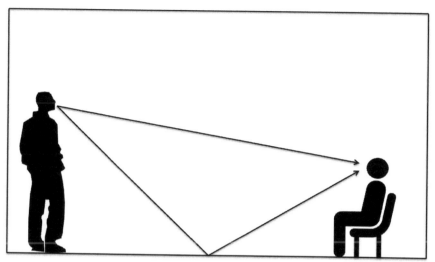

Figure 5.17. This diagram illustrates how a direct line of sound followed by a reflected line of sound creates delay. *Courtesy of Matthew Edwards*

Auto-Tune

Auto-Tune was first used in studios as a useful way to clean up minor imperfections in otherwise perfect performances. Auto-Tune is now an industry standard that many artists use, even if they are not willing to admit it. Auto-Tune has gained a bad reputation in the past few years, and whether or not you agree with its use, it is a reality in today's market. If you do not understand how to use it properly, you could end up sounding like T-Pain (b. 1985).[2]

Both Antares and Melodyne have developed Auto-Tune technology in both "auto" and "graphical" formats. "Auto" Auto-Tune allows the engineer to set specific parameters for pitch correction that are then computer controlled. "Graphical" Auto-Tune tracks the pitch in the selected area of a recording and plots the fundamental frequency on a linear graph. The engineer can then select specific notes for pitch correction. They can also drag selected pitches to a different frequency, add or reduce vibrato, and change formant frequencies above the fundamental. To simplify, the "auto" function makes general corrections while the "graphic" function makes specific corrections. The "auto" setting is usually used to achieve a specific effect—for instance, "Believe"

(1998) by Cher (b. 1946)—while the "graphic" setting is used to correct small imperfections in a recorded performance.

Digital Voice Processors

Digital voice processors are still relatively new to the market and have yet to gain widespread usage among singers. While there are several brands of vocal effects processors available, the industry leader as of this printing is a company called TC-Helicon. TC-Helicon manufactures several different units that span from consumer to professional grade. TC-Helicon's premier performer-controlled unit is called the VoiceLive 3. The VoiceLive 3 incorporates more than twelve vocal effects, eleven guitar effects, and a multi-track looper with 250 factory presets and 250 memory slots for user presets. The VoiceLive 3 puts the effects at the singer's feet in a programmable stomp box that also includes phantom power, MIDI in/out, a USB connection, guitar input, and monitor out. Onboard vocal effects include equalization, compression, reverb, and "auto" Auto-Tune. The unit also offers μMod (an adjustable voice modulator), a doubler (for thickening the lead vocal), echo, delay, reverb, and several other specialized effects.[3] ♪

One of the most impressive features of digital voice processors is the ability to add computer-generated harmonies to the lead vocal. After the user sets the musical key, the processor identifies the fundamental frequency of each sung note. The computer then adds digitized voices at designated intervals above and below the lead singer. The unit also offers the option to program each individual song, with multiple settings for every verse, chorus, and bridge.

THE BASICS OF LIVE SOUND SYSTEMS

Live sound systems come in a variety of sizes from small practice units to state-of-the-art stadium rigs. Most singers only need a basic knowledge of the components commonly found in systems that have one to eight inputs. Units beyond that size usually require an independent sound engineer and are beyond the scope of this chapter.

USING AUDIO ENHANCEMENT TECHNOLOGY

Following the microphone, the first element in the live signal chain is usually the mixer. Basic portable mixers provide controls for equalization, volume level, auxiliary (usually used for effects such as reverb and compression), and, on some units, controls for built-in digital effects processors. Powered mixers combine an amplifier with a basic mixer, providing a compact solution for those who do not need a complex system. Since unpowered mixers do not provide amplification, you will need to add a separate amplifier to power this system.

The powered mixer or amplifier connects to speaker cabinets, which contain a "woofer" and a "tweeter." The woofer is a large round speaker that handles the bass frequencies while the tweeter is a horn-shaped speaker that handles the treble frequencies. The crossover, a component built into the speaker cabinet, separates high and low frequencies and sends them to the appropriate speaker (woofer or tweeter). Speaker cabinets can be either active or passive. Passive cabinets require a powered mixer or an amplifier in order to operate. Active cabinets have an amplifier built-in and do not require an external amplifier.

If you do not already own a microphone and amplification system, you can purchase a simple setup at relatively low cost through online vendors such as Sweetwater.com and MusiciansFriend.com. A dynamic microphone and a powered monitor are enough to get started. If you would like to add a digital voice processor, Digitech and TC-Helicon both sell entry-level models that will significantly improve the tonal quality of a sound system.

Monitors are arguably the most important element in a live sound system. The monitor is a speaker that faces the performers and allows them to hear themselves and/or the other instruments on stage. On-stage volume levels can vary considerably, with drummers often producing sound levels as high as 120 dB. Those volume levels make it nearly impossible for singers to receive natural acoustic feedback while performing. Monitors can improve aural feedback and help reduce the temptation to oversing. Powered monitors offer the same advantages as powered speaker cabinets and can be a great option for amplification when practicing. They are also good to have around as a backup plan in case you arrive at a venue and discover they do not supply monitors. In-ear monitors offer another option for performers and are especially useful for those who frequently move around the stage.

MICROPHONE TECHNIQUE

The microphone is an inseparable part of the contemporary commercial music singer's instrument. Just as there are techniques that improve singing, there are also techniques that will improve microphone use. Understanding what a microphone does is only the first step to using it successfully. Once you understand how a microphone works, you need hands-on experience.

The best way to learn microphone technique is to experiment. Try the following exercises to gain a better understanding of how to use a microphone when singing:

1. Hold a dynamic microphone with a cardioid pattern directly in front of your mouth, no farther than one centimeter away. Sustain a comfortable pitch and slowly move the microphone away from your lips. Listen to how the vocal quality changes. When the microphone is close to the lips, you should notice that the sound is louder and has more bass response. As you move the microphone away from your mouth, there will be a noticeable loss in volume and the tone will become brighter.
2. Next, sustain a pitch while rotating the handle down. The sound quality will change in a similar fashion as when you moved the microphone away from your lips.
3. Now try singing breathy with the microphone close to your lips. How little effort can you get away with while producing a marketable sound?
4. Try singing bright vowels and dark vowels and notice how the microphone affects the tone quality.
5. Also experiment with adapting your diction to the microphone. Because the microphone amplifies everything, you may need to under-pronounce certain consonants when singing. You will especially want to reduce the power of the consonant sounds /t/, /s/, /p/, and /b/.

FINAL THOUGHTS

Since this is primarily an overview, you can greatly improve your comprehension of the material by seeking other resources to deepen your knowledge. There are many great resources available that may help clarify some of these difficult concepts. Most important, you must experiment. The more you play around with sound equipment on your own, the better you will understand it and the more comfortable you will feel when performing or recording with audio technology.

NOTES

1. Paula Lockheart, "A History of Early Microphone Singing, 1925–1939: American Mainstream Popular Singing at the Advent of Electronic Amplification," *Popular Music and Society* 26, no. 3 (2003): 367–85.

2. For example, listen to T-Pain's track "Buy You a Drank (Shawty Snappin')."

3. "VoiceLive 3," TC-Helicon, www.tc-helicon.com/products/voicelive-3/ (accessed May 2, 2016).

6

HOW LEARNING WORKS

An Introduction to Motor Learning Theory
Lynn Helding

Voice science has influenced voice pedagogy since the famous Spanish voice teacher Manuel García II (1805–1906) procured two dental mirrors, slid one into his mouth, and aimed the other at just the right angle to catch a ray of sunlight, revealing the marvel of the human vocal folds.[1] Thus, voice *physiology* (the way in which body parts function) was established as the first pillar of voice science. This view held sway until the 1970s, when Swedish voice scientist Johan Sundberg (b. 1936) published research on the acoustics of the singing voice that revealed a special resonance cluster that male opera singers exhibit that allows them to be heard over an orchestra.[2] Dubbed the "singer's formant," Sundberg's discovery firmly established voice acoustics as the second pillar of voice science, creating a firm foundation for the field of voice *pedagogy*, defined as the art and science of teaching. This fact, that pedagogy is about teaching—or more pointedly as professor of education Deborah Loewenberg Ball (b. 1954) once commented, "Teaching depends on what other people think"—makes it all the more ironic that what has been missing from voice pedagogy until very recently is both the delivery system and the receptacle for voice science information: the human mind.

The fund of voice science knowledge that has accumulated since García's time is rich with insight about the human voice. This bounty inspired pedagogue Richard Miller (1926–2009) to admonish singers to take advantage not only of everything that was known two hundred years ago but also of everything that is known today. The most urgent questions for those who rise to this challenge are "How might I gain this knowledge?" and—more important—"How might I apply it to singing?" Answering these questions requires an understanding of how humans learn.

Learning is the vital question of *cognitive science*, an interdisciplinary science that arose when the cognitive revolution of the 1950s swept aside *behaviorism* as the dominant field in psychology. Learning itself is not a single entity but a complex activity comprised of many interrelated processes. Cognitive science, built upon the foundation of psychology, reflects this complexity by including neuroscience, artificial intelligence, linguistics, anthropology, sociology, and philosophy to study human perception, thinking, and learning. We may now turn to cognitive science as the third pillar in the field of voice pedagogy.

TWO BASIC MODES OF LEARNING

The ancient Greek philosophers identified two primary sources of human knowledge: knowledge that is gained by exercising the human attribute of reason, or *rationalism*, and knowledge gained through sensory experience, known as *empiricism*. This dichotomy is still reflected in standard modern learning theories, despite the terms used to describe them. Two of the most accepted are *declarative learning* and *procedural learning*; in philosophy, these two modes are identified as "know-that" and "know-how." Declarative learning ("know-that") is information about which one can speak, or "declare." The construction "know-that" refers to knowledge of facts, as in "I know that a formant is a resonance of the vocal tract." This kind of knowledge is not innate; it has to be "declared" to the learner and is best elucidated by an expert teacher as a guide. Declarative learning typically takes place over a time period of days, weeks, or months. Memory for words and life episodes also fall under declarative learning.

Procedural learning ("know-how") refers to learning physical skills (procedures) by doing and is inclusive of both those innate movements with which we are born, like crawling, as well as advanced skills, such as learning to ride a bicycle or learning to play a musical instrument.[3] The field of study dedicated to research in procedural learning is called *motor learning*, wherein "motor" refers both to motion and to the *motor neurons* (brain cells) that create movement.

Procedural learning in humans begins almost from birth. We are, one might say, preprogrammed to learn to grasp and crawl, and walk all on our own as toddlers, which we do by trying, falling, and trying again—no teacher is necessary. Acquisition of the physical movements needed for survival advances relatively quickly, usually in a matter of hours. Thus, a crucial difference between declarative learning and procedural learning is the speed with which each adheres.

However, advanced skills—also called *higher-order* skills, such as those on display in a concert pianist—do not come preinstalled in humans. These skills must be learned via a combination of declarative and procedural learning. Singing displays this dual nature: We explore the range and extent of our own voices by wailing, giggling, and cooing as babies. As we mature, we can easily find our own singing voice, particularly if our surrounding culture provides for it and supports it; family sing-alongs and community singing in religious services provide these opportunities. Many singers of popular styles report these experiences as formative and rightfully claim to be self-taught.

However, those wishing to learn the Western, classical tradition of singing—which is distinguished by a large pitch range, sustained breathing, natural amplification, seamless register shifts, and agile execution of rapid scale passages—must first be led by a master teacher as their guide, and then must practice with regularity and discipline. Similarly, singers of contemporary commercial styles (CCM) who wish to extend their vocal range, stamina, and control should consult a voice teacher if they wish to excel.

These kinds of singing styles are considered to be higher-order tasks, more complex and refined than generic voicing. Higher-order and complex muscular tasks all have one attribute in common: They all require practice over time. The amount of practice time required to become an expert is estimated to be about ten thousand hours. This number was arrived at by combining over a century's worth of studies by multiple researchers. K. Anders Ericsson (b. 1947), a founder of the field of expertise studies, further identified that the quality of practice required to become an expert is even more crucial than simply logging practice hours. He dubbed this high-quality type of practice *deliberate practice*, defined as "an effortful activity designed to improve individual target performance."[4] Higher-order muscular tasks are situated at the nexus of declarative and procedural learning: we must first "know that" in order to "know how." Table 10.1 illustrates the standard synonyms in use for declarative and procedural learning, as well as their attributes.

Table 6.1. The Two Basic Modes of Human Information Processing and Their Attributes

DECLARATIVE LEARNING or MEMORY	PROCEDURAL LEARNING or MEMORY
Propositional	Tacit
Explicit	Implicit
Controlled	Automatic
Learned	Inherent
Slow	Fast
Demands attention	Can multitask
Avoidable	Unavoidable
Volitional	Not volitional
Know-that	Know-how
Top-down (refers to the *executive control center* of the brain)	Bottom-up (the intuitive responses of our *autonomic nervous system*)

LEARNING DEFINED

Learning has been the most assiduously studied topic in psychology, from its inception as a field in the early nineteenth century throughout the twentieth. Schools of thought and their resultant vocabularies sprang up around the world, yet in the face of the subject's enormity, and without the connective power of the internet, the creation of a commonly accepted definition of learning was nearly impossible. In the twenty-first century, the ability to view the brain's inner workings in real time via *functional magnetic resonance imaging* (fMRI) and the rapid dissemination of digital information have generated only more information, not more clarity toward a definition of learning.

Nevertheless, we will need a working definition if we are to understand some fundamental properties of learning. Therefore, two simple definitions for each of the modes of learning are offered here, based on the most common elements found in accepted learning theories.

- Declarative Learning: A process that results in a permanent change in behavior as a result of *experience*.
- Procedural Learning: A process that results in a permanent change in behavior as a result of *practice*.

Notice that both definitions are exactly the same except for the crucial factor that causes each type of learning to adhere, or "cause a permanent change in behavior." In the case of *declarative learning*, if the information presented is easily understood, it is enough to simply be introduced to a topic to be able to claim it as learned. For example, in chapter 2 of this book ("Singing and Voice Science"), it may have surprised you that the diaphragm muscle is attached to the bottom of the sternum and is therefore more highly situated in the body than many people imagine. If that information held particular meaning for you, you are not likely to forget it. However, other types of declarative information contained in this book, such as the names, locations, and functions of all the other respiratory muscles, must be studied in order to be truly learned. And as any student knows, studying facts to the extent that they can be successfully recalled for an exam requires motivation and diligence. Thus, a key attribute of declarative learning that distinguishes it from procedural learning is volition—the learner must want to learn.

Conversely, procedural learning requires doing. No substitutions are viable. Procedural learning of basic human skills occurs concurrently with the development of *proprioception*, the body's own sense of its movements, positions, balance, and *spatial orientation* (where it is in relation to other people and objects). Learning these most fundamental human physical skills is largely nonvolitional; we learn them by experiencing the world, thus the learning will occur whether we wish it to or not, as a matter of survival. Procedural learning and declarative learning exhibit significant differences regarding speed of acquisition and volition. But both types of learning share certain commonalities. We will now consider these commonalities before returning to focusing on their differences.

HOW LEARNING WORKS: THE TRIUMVIRATE OF ATTENTION, LEARNING, AND MEMORY

The human brain is perhaps the most complex system in the known universe. Exactly how humans learn is still not completely understood, but at present, it is accepted that learning is not one discrete entity but rather a three-step process of *attention, learning itself,* and *memory*. These three phases display their own attributes while attending to both declarative and procedural learning. The box below offers a very simplified scheme of these phases for reference as we consider both the psychological and the neurobiological processes that underpin our most fundamental and complex activity: learning.

ATTENTION, LEARNING ITSELF, AND LONG-TERM MEMORY

- Step 1: Attention. This is the prerequisite condition for learning. Learning cannot happen until and unless one first pays attention. Note: Attention has a limited capacity in the human brain.
  - Brain Activity: Biochemical changes, specifically the release of the chemical messengers called *neurotransmitters*. In the early stages of learning, the *synapses* (the gaps between brain cells where chemical messages are exchanged) are temporarily destabilized.
- Step 2: Learning Itself. The dynamic process whereby new information is first absorbed (called *short-term memory*) and then sorted (called *working memory*) and manipulated, which features the act of *constructive memory*.

- Brain Activity: More release of neurotransmitters. With repetition, the number of synaptic connections in the brain begins to stabilize. This process is called *memory consolidation*.
- Step 3: Long-Term Memory. Once a thing is learned (past tense), it has exited the realm of learning (*short-term* and *working memory*) and exists in the realm of *long-term memory*. Long-term memory is like a treasure chest where things of value are stored and from which they can be retrieved. The evidence that a thing is learned is its repeatability; in the motor realm, this is called *automaticity*.
  - Brain Activity: Anatomical changes in brain tissue are observed. The brain has reorganized itself.

Step 1: Attention

Attention is the prerequisite condition for learning, but what is it exactly? Attention is a complex neurological system distributed throughout the brain via a connected neural network as opposed to a single entity. The attention network is best understood as an attentional filtering system, called the *autonomic nervous system* (ANS), which incessantly sifts the information that bombards our senses every second, parsing the important from the trivial. The *autonomic nervous system* is essentially distributed between two systems: the *sympathetic nervous system* (SNS) and the *parasympathetic nervous system* (PNS).

The SNS, borne from the "bottom up" or *intuitive response*, is primed to alert in the presence of danger or excitement, such as sexual arousal. This alerting operates rapidly, and largely outside our awareness and control. Some typical body signs that the SNS is fired up are increased heart rate, shortness of breath, weak knees, loss of appetite, and sweaty palms. The SNS is linked to the *fight-or-flight* response, which is the impulse to either stand one's ground in the presence of danger or flee.

Unfortunately, the SNS is also operational in times of purely psychological stress, such as the disorienting experience of *music performance anxiety*, or MPA. Apparently, the SNS does not always differentiate between a hungry animal bearing down on you in the wilderness and a full house in a concert hall. A vexing question regarding MPA is whether it is a condition unique to music performance per se or rather a manifestation of a broader psychopathology. At present, MPA remains vastly understudied (especially in comparison to anxiety in sport performance), as does the efficacy of certain treatment methods.

The *parasympathetic nervous system* (PNS) operates from the "top down" or *executive control center* of the brain and works to calm the body—after fear, flight, or arousal—and restore it to a resting state. Executive attention governs conscious control of attention (also called *selective attention*), which is what allows us to filter out the most important bits from the wealth of stimuli that assaults our senses from moment to moment. We can choose attention by exerting the human parameter of free will, but only when desire and motivation inspire us do so. Thus, a subgenre of attention research is a condition called *preattentive processing*, which is a particularly significant component of voluntary attention. Committed learners will want to know how they might prime their attention for success before they enter a learning situation.

Desire and Motivation Learners must first want to pay attention before they truly can. Desire and its twin, motivation, are both the simplest and yet the most elusive of conditions for learning, as anyone who has tried to commit to a study schedule, exercise routine, or diet can attest. Before we consider what does work to ignite motivation, let us quickly dispense with a popular yet ultimately counterproductive method: the use of rewards, such as candy, praise, or money. Research has shown that such rewards are not the primary forces that stimulate human endeavor and creativity. Rather, so-called intrinsic rewards are the best motivation—for example, the joy found in pursuing the endeavor itself, the excitement of discovery, and the freedom of charting one's own course.

One of the best techniques shown to ignite motivation is *goal setting*, the conscious act of listing one or several goals one wishes to reach. Goal setting stimulates motivation and, when applied consistently, can actually increase achievement. Goal setting concretizes vague notions of achievement and also promotes focus, cultivates self-regulation by aiding impulse control, and helps calibrate efficient use of time and financial resources. These various benefits accrue to promote positive feelings, which in turn feed more motivation.

Four of the most important parameters to consider if using this technique are *specificity, format, difficulty*, and *process*. In order, goals must (1) be very specific rather than general; (2) be written down, not merely kept in mind; (3) be challenging, not easy—note that this factor echoes Ericsson's definition of deliberate practice; and (4) answer the question "How?"

Students who answer this last question by listing exactly how they intend to achieve their goals are more likely to succeed.

Emotion We have considered desire and motivation as the twin ignition systems of attention. But once attention is fired up, how does it keep going? One simple answer is "emotion." But as with everything else having to do with the human condition, emotion is far from simple. It is a vast and complex topic, as well as an age-old conundrum. Emotion has bedeviled human beings for as long as we have been sentient.

Pathé is a term for emotion developed by Aristotle (384 BCE–322 BCE). *Pathé* is variously translated as "desires" or "appetites." During the seventeenth century, René Descartes (1596–1650) recognized the physiological upheavals generated by these appetites as "passions of the soul" and attributed this agitation to the pineal gland in the brain, which he believed to be home base for the human soul. Eighteenth-century beliefs about emotion were particularly influenced by romantic thought, which regarded emotion as a natural and raw human attribute that was enchained by propriety and longed to escape its fetters. This take on emotion persisted throughout the nineteenth and early twentieth centuries and is still present in popular culture today.

In the early twentieth century, emotion experienced a kind of banishment at the hands of behaviorist psychologists, who eschewed emotion as far too frivolous for serious scientific study. The cognitive revolution chipped away at behaviorism and eventually displaced it by ushering in the current era of brain science, but the pioneers of cognitivism in the 1950s had as much interest in emotion as their predecessors, which is to say almost none.

Throughout most of the twentieth century, rational thought was exalted as the pinnacle of human wisdom while emotion was not only deemed worthless as a serious research topic but also branded as downright seditious: emotion bewitched and muddled rational thought. Emotion is still commonly viewed as an element that one must tame, silence, or outgrow.

The very newest research on emotion from the field of neuroscience reveals that emotion—rather than being rationality's polar, frivolous opposite—is actually fundamentally entwined with human reason. Neuroscientists like Jaak Panskepp (1942–2017), Antonio Damasio (b. 1944), and Joseph LeDoux (b. 1949) have worked to repair the mind-body split that Descartes proposed by plucking emotion from the ephemeral realm of the spirit and grounding it within the physical functions of the body. LeDoux defines emotions as "biological functions of the nervous system."[5] Damasio, through his now-famous *somatic marker hypothesis*, has advanced emotion as a critical component of human decision-making and thus an assistant to reason—a far cry from its centuries-old characterization as a fickle temptress.[6] "Emotion," Damasio notes, "is not a luxury."[7]

Emotion plays a critical role in sustaining attention during learning, for emotion necessarily attends motivation and desire. Unless people care enough to expend some effort, they will not learn because they will not have "attended." Emotion also assists encoding our experiences into long-term memory—a process called *memory consolidation*—particularly if the emotions were strong ones. Joyful life episodes, such as one's wedding day or elation at the birth of a child, become permanently fixed in our memory. It is perhaps for this reason that extreme technical breakthroughs in a voice lesson, or superlative achievements reached in performance, are deeply remembered.

On the other end of the emotion spectrum, extremely frightening or humiliating events can become so encoded in memory that certain stimuli, especially smells and sounds, can activate the "alerting network" of the autonomic nervous system. Harmless sounds like fireworks can recall a returning war veteran's memory of enemy fire with devastating consequences for mental health, as is seen in posttraumatic stress disorder (PTSD). Even the scent of a certain aftershave or a personal ringtone on a cell phone, if they are entangled with memories of particularly brutal or humiliating events, can engender symptoms of PTSD. Please note, however, that emotion's role in attention, learning, and memory has been qualified as necessarily "strong" in order to assist. Tripping during a stage entrance, or enduring the tirade of a nasty conductor, as unpleasant or unwarranted as such events might be, do not encode themselves in the long-term memories of most people, nor to such a degree as to cause long-term damage.

Sleep Along with desire, motivation, and emotion, a final parameter to consider in regard to attention is sleep. Sleep is understood by researchers as a complex set of brain processes, not a single state of being. It is well established in science research that lack of sleep impairs brain function, damages learning, weakens performance in cognitive tests, and slows reaction time for physical tasks that require alertness, such as driving and operating heavy machinery. Yet the underlying, biological reasons sleep deprivation is so damaging, and conversely why abundant sleep is so restorative, are still something of a mystery. Several studies offer some clues.

An important sleep study in 2013 revealed that sleep may be critical for what amounts to brain cleaning. According to these researchers, the brain lacks the conventional version of the *lymphatic system*, which clears cellular debris out of the body. Therefore, it evolved its own metabolic system, the *glymphatic system*, which operates during sleep to flush away waste products accumulated during wakefulness that are toxic to brain cells. According to this theory, the uncluttered and detoxified brain should rise from sleep refreshed and more able to pay attention.

Another theory concerns *synaptic pruning*, the processes by which *synapses* that are weak (due to lack of attention and practice) wither away with no trace in the brain, leaving only the strongest synaptic connections behind. It is believed that sleep is the state most conducive to this pruning process, because the brain is least subject to interference from incoming stimuli. A related theory is that the purpose of sleeping and dreaming is to replay short-term memories gathered throughout the previous day and, in so doing, strengthen the neural pathways of those memories and send them along their journey to long-term memory consolidation, which we will revisit below in depth in "Step 2: Learning Itself." But before we leave the topic of attention, we must consider a relatively recent cultural phenomenon known to be toxic to attention: *multitasking*.

Attention and Multitasking The term "multitask" first appeared in the nascent computer technology of the 1960s, but since the advent of the World Wide Web in the 1990s, the word was absorbed into the popular lexicon. While multitasking per se has been a part of human activity for millennia, the current manifestation of the term "multitasking" refers to the mingling of one or more technology-based tasks: reading email while listening to music, texting while watching television, or driving a car while following a GPS. Research on human multitasking in the digital environment has zeroed in on the following parameters listed in the box below.

> **PARAMETERS OF MULTITASKING**
>
> - Attentional filtering: The ability to successfully filter relevant from irrelevant information.
> - Task-switching: Shifting from task to task and/or returning to an important task after distraction by a task of lesser importance.
> - Organization of thoughts: Keeping cognitive results organized for later retrieval. (Note: This is a hallmark of learning; a thing is not truly learned if it cannot be retrieved and repeated.)

Multiple studies have shown that the vast majority of people manage all these parameters extremely poorly when faced with digital distractions. This is due to our limited attentional capacity. Stated simply, it is very difficult for people to pay deep attention to more than one thing at a time.

Because multitasking is toxic to attention, it also degrades learning itself. Multitaskers demonstrate decrements in their ability to engage in higher levels of thinking, such as analytical reasoning. And even if a learner is able to muster some attention while still multitasking, the learned thing acquired in this fraught state has been shown to be less flexible, making later retrieval more difficult. As we shall see, retrieval is proof that a thing is learned.

Worse, habitual multitasking makes our attentional abilities degrade over time. An influential series of studies conducted at Stanford University showed that the more chronic a person's multitasking habit, the less possible it was for them to ignore irrelevant distractions. The terms "acquired attention deficit disorder" and "attention deficit trait" have been introduced by two psychiatrists—John Ratey (b. 1948) and Edward Hallowell (b. 1949), respectively—who posit that heavy technology use may be actually creating attention deficit disorders in people not otherwise disposed toward them. It appears that we can remodel our brains both for good and for ill.

Step 2: Learning Itself

As the ancient Greek philosopher Aristotle wrote in his treatise *Metaphysics*, "If you are learning, you have not at the same time learned." This simple statement perfectly captures two important facets of learning: first, its essence, which is its dynamic nature. That is, learning is marked by change, even instability. Learning is messy. If approached with a no-holds-barred spirit of adventure, learning can be fun. But learning can also be challenging to the point of joylessness, distress, or even humiliation. Nevertheless, learning is a fundamental—some say *the* fundamental—activity of life.

Yet given learning's dynamic nature, we cannot always be in a state of upheaval and transition. Learned items must be stowed, in order to make way for new experiences and ideas, and also for later retrieval. Thus, once learning has progressed from the transitive to the past tense (as in "I have learned"), one is no longer actively learning. The second facet of Aristotle's astute observation is realized; the learned thing is a fait accompli, stored in *long-term memory*. This process—from "learning" to "have learned"—is called *memory consolidation*.

Much research is devoted to this storage process, from the moment new information is absorbed and held in mind for a period of seconds, called *short-term memory*, to how this information is then sorted and manipulated while actively learning, called *working memory*. Some researchers refer to this process as *maintenance*, and maintenance plus *manipulation*, respectively. For our purposes, let us think of short-term memory as a "brain pad" of "sticky notes"—a place to temporarily jot down impressions or facts. And just like a collection of those small bits of paper, they may be easily misplaced if we are not attentive to them.

Working memory may be thought of as learning itself: that process whereby we are able to hold several bits of information in mind (and that includes sensory information in motor learning) as we toss those bits about, consider or try them from different angles, and recombine them with facts we already know—and experiences we have already had—in order to make sense of them. Here is this last sentence restated in more compressed fashion to allow in one new piece of information:

> **DEFINITION OF WORKING MEMORY**
>
> *Learning itself* is that *process*
> whereby we hold about seven *bits*, or four *chunks* of information in mind,
> *manipulate* those bits or chunks,
> and *recombine* them with facts or experiences we already know.

Working memory, or *learning*, is a process that starts as we consider a few *bits* of information—"seven (plus or minus two)," the compound number George Miller (1920–2012), a founder of cognitive psychology, famously posited in 1956—and more recently understood as *chunks* of information, of which we seem to be able to manage around four. Let us consider how this works.

Working memory is what is allowing you to read this chapter and hopefully learn from it. As your reading progresses, your success is partially dependent upon the ability to maintain the information from the previous paragraphs in your mind; each successive paragraph can build on the next only by your understanding of the former. For example, if you have been reading with attention, you know that we are now considering step number 2 of the learning process, learning itself. Step 1 was the topic of attention with side trips featuring bits of information that were all related to the main topic. Therefore, we may call the topic of attention a *chunk*, made up of minicomponents. Researchers have invented a new verb—"chunking"—to describe this process. Chunking itself is the subject of much research and seems to be a key talent that people with superior memories possess. However, all of us can learn to use chunking to improve learning and develop superior memory techniques.

One final component of learning from the last line of our definition in the box above deserves mention: the notion of *recombination*. As we have already seen, learning begins with attention, followed by absorbing new bits of information into our short-term memory, then using working attention to manipulate those bits, and finally storing those bits in long-term memory. But no learner is a blank slate, and our individual slates become more populated with ideas and experiences as we navigate our lives. We call these ideas and experiences *memories*.

Any process of absorbing new information will necessarily collide with our previous memories. Therefore, in order to calm the collision and make sense of it all, we recombine the new information with the memories we already own. This dynamic moment in the learning process is called *constructive memory*. The main benefit of constructive memory is its cumulative quality: we use past experiences to change our actions in the present and also to imagine the future. We learn from our mistakes. But detriments due to constructive memory abound, chief among them being memory's fallibility. It is now known that human memory is enormously prone to distortion and outright error. Since what we encode in memory is always mixed up with what we already know (or think we know), our memories are never completely pure. As our memories pile up, our minds create frameworks to keep them organized. These frameworks are called *schemas*. A schema may be defined as a cognitive structure for representing, organizing, and retrieving related information. Schemas (also called *schemata*) are particularly important in motor learning.

STEP 3: LONG-TERM MEMORY

The complex neurobiological process of learning itself is encoded in the well-known maxim called Hebb's rule: "Neurons (nerve cells) that fire together, wire together."[8] Recall that learning begins when a thought or a sensation excites the synapses (the gap between neurons).**[Au: Change OK?]** With the addition of attention, emotion, and desire, short-term memory rapidly progresses to working memory—otherwise known as learning. As this nascent memory is manipulated, the already-excited neural pathways are reactivated. Repeated reactivation of the same neurons (through repetition or practice) is what creates a neural pathway—a memory. The process of encoding working memory to long-term memory is called memory consolidation; thus, memory may be considered synonymous with the term "learned."

Neuroscientist Eric Kandel (b. 1929) was awarded a Nobel Prize in 2000 for his groundbreaking discoveries about the biological bases of this process. Kandel realized that short-term memory is not a diminutive version of long-term memory, as was previously believed, but is altogether biologically distinct. Short-term memories cause biochemical changes in the brain, indeed, by the release of neurotransmitters. Long-term memories, however, cause anatomical changes in brain tissue by increasing the number of synaptic connections. Kandel's discoveries, which occurred in tandem with other significant brain research at the very end of the previous century, led to the astounding realization that the brain continually remodels itself. Before the 1990s, it was believed that the adult brain could not change much past childhood and was, by all accounts, fixed. But it is now accepted wisdom that brain cells (neurons) can regenerate (*neurogenesis*) and the brain changes continually in response to experience. This process is called *neuroplasticity*.

We have now considered what declarative and procedural learning share in common. To understand their differences, and specifically what cognitive processes undergird the attributes needed for mastering performance art, we can now turn to research in the field of motor performance and learning.

MOTOR LEARNING AND PERFORMANCE

As noted in the simple definitions in the second box, the crucial factor that distinguishes declarative from procedural learning is practice. More motor learning occurs with more practice. Two leaders in motor learning research, Richard Schmidt (1941–2017) and Tim Lee (b. 1955), dubbed this concept the "Power Law of Practice" while also conceding that this law is so obvious it should not have to be mentioned.[9] This is true until one considers an astounding finding from motor learning research: Performance improvements generally accelerate rapidly for novices, and generally decelerate the more experienced one becomes. In other words, the rate of growth slows as motor performance improves. To make sense of this and other key findings from the field of motor learning research, let us start by considering a more complex definition of motor learning:

> **DEFINITION OF MOTOR LEARNING**
>
> Motor learning is a *process*,
> which is *inferred* rather than directly observed,
> which leads to *permanent changes* in *habit*
> as the result of *experience* or *practice*.

There are many variations of this definition, but the most prominent ones accepted by researchers contain the six italicized components. The term *process* underscores the dimension of time. The acquisition and retention of physical skills occur along a continuum. Temporary breakthroughs notwithstanding, progress happens not all at once but over a period of time.

That this process is *inferred* refers to learning's dynamism, for learning itself can never be directly observed; we can only assume it is happening and wait for proof that the learned thing has adhered. This proof shows up in two guises: the first being the relatively *permanent changes* that distinguish procedural from declarative learning; the second is that these changes are stable enough to be called physical *habits*, even under variable conditions. Finally, these conclusions are all based upon the supposition that students will continue to *experience* sensations that they will then repeatedly *practice*.

Now that we have made one pass through the complex definition of motor learning, the following components from this definition are worth even deeper inspection: *permanent changes*, *practice*, and *habit*, respectively. As we do so, it is important to note the essential difference between learning and performance.

Learning is the process by which one acquires skill or knowledge. Remember: Learning is dynamic, unstable, and messy. *Performance* refers to the manner or quality with which someone functions. Performance is like the freeze frame button on a video projector—it captures where the learner stands at that point in time along the learning continuum. Because of this frozen quality, most of us want our performances to be as polished as we can manage, which is the opposite of unstable and messy. In other words, the goals of learning and performance are—and should be—not just different but diametrically opposed to one another. When these goals are conflated, both learning and performance may suffer.

PERFORMANCE SHIFTS: MASTER CLASS SYNDROME

The evidence that a motor skill is truly learned is its repeatability, especially under many different conditions. These two parameters are called *retention* and *transfer*, respectively. Without proof that the learning has been retained, we can only say that the learner was merely exposed to the information. What about changes observed during training that are not permanent? Motor learning researchers call these changes *performance shifts*, and they can be both positive and negative. Motor learners can absorb powerful lessons from both. Let us begin with positive performance shifts.

Most singers are familiar with the phenomenon of instant success upon a first or second trial, which may occur in the midst of a voice lesson or solo practice session but then vaporize moments or hours later. This phenomenon may occur in weekly singing lessons, especially if the students feel they never sing as well in their own practice or performance as they do in their lessons. This phenomenon is particularly common in a onetime master class setting, in which a guest master teacher is able to evoke a positive vocal response from the singer on display, but only in that moment. The student is at a loss to recapture that magical moment later in his or her own practice. These are prime examples of positive performance shifts. While these positive experiences may have been significant moments for the student, real learning has not occurred due to the lack of proof that there were retrievable and permanent changes. I have dubbed this phenomenon "master class syndrome" and counsel students to run, not walk, to the practice room immediately following a successful experience. There is some evidence that by doing so, it is possible to re-create the experience for oneself.

What is revelatory, and perhaps even shocking, is that habitual manipulations by coaches or teachers that improve performance in the moment may actually stifle long-term learning. Why is this? Part of the answer lies with one factor we have already considered in tandem with practice: *effort*. Research into the biochemistry of the brain reveals that the more difficult a task is, the more "neuronal firing" from our brains is required; in essence, we must dig deeper for more complicated tasks. Repeated firing of the neurons from this deeper place creates a neural pathway that becomes stronger each time it is activated during learning. As we have seen, this is the explanation of what happens during working memory and the neuroscientific definition of practice. With enough practice, difficult tasks become easier and eventually, if mastered, are stored in long-term memory.

Cognitive psychologist Robert A. Bjork (b. 1939) labeled such tasks "desirable difficulties," because obstacles must form the foundation of any viable teaching method, especially if the goal is true learning and not simply improved performance in the short term. Researchers have concluded that the solutions learners discover for themselves, through effort, are truly learned and are thus retained and retrievable. This conclusion explains why withholding "desirable difficulties" may actually damage learning.

Performance shifts can also be negative, brought on by illness, depression, or injury. But negative performance shifts may also signal the phenomenon of *unlearning*. This theory holds that when someone is attempting to learn a new motor skill, there may be a simultaneous destabilization of the previous, habitual motor pattern. This is both good news and bad news. The bad news is that unlearning can cause psychological distress. In addition, musicians should note that multitasking and task-switch cost may be particularly toxic to motor learning, due to unlearning. If distractions are allowed to poison attention during this crucial phase of learning, the learner may wind up in a lose-lose situation: the new task attempted is certainly not gained, but the old, comfortable habit may become damaged as well. For example, a baritone who transitions to tenor may wager he has nothing to lose in the attempt; he assumes the familiar voice will always be there, just like an old pair of jeans—or Colline's old coat in *La bohème*! Such singers may be distressed to find that, after a time, the old habit no longer "fits"; however, the new technique does not fit either, for it has not yet stabilized. Therefore, this particular juncture in motor skill learning appears to be particularly vulnerable. Musicians would do well to ban distraction from the practice room and pay total and complete attention to the task before them.

On the whole though, negative performance shifts can be seen as positive signs that a new, learned skill is actively destabilizing an old, ingrained habit. Exactly how the destabilized habit becomes a stable new skill occurs via the last component of our complex definition of motor learning: practice.

THE PATH TO CARNEGIE HALL

"How do I get to Carnegie Hall?" the hapless New York City tourist asks. "Practice!" goes the punch line. This maxim is Schmidt and Lee's "Power Law of Practice," which was introduced above. We must add to this power law that quantity and quality matter: Specifically, ten thousand hours of high-quality, deliberate practice—marked by effortful engagement with desirable difficulties—are required to become an expert. Motor learning researchers study many discrete parameters of practice, and while the results are numerous, the following three essential rules of effective practice for motor learning can be gleaned from them.

Distributed Practice Is More Effective than *Massed Practice*

People whose regular practice sessions alternate with periods of rest retain more than piling information on all at once in long mega-practice sessions. Even more compelling is the finding that the longer the rest session is in between practice sessions, the better the learning, as evidenced by both retention and transfer in later performance. This phenomenon could be at least partly due to the cognitive benefits of sleep, as previously noted. What this means for musicians is this: Practicing every day for one hour proves to be much more beneficial than practicing twice a week for three and a half hours per each session, even though the total number of hours per week are the same.

An added benefit of *distributed practice*—or *spaced practice*—is protection from injury. Athletes studied in motor learning research are more at risk for injury during massed practice. Why is this? The answer is quite simple: massed practice without rest leads to muscle fatigue, and tired muscles are more vulnerable to injury.

A side note here is that too little practice also makes musicians and athletes vulnerable to injury, due to lack of fitness. Musician guilt over lack of preparation may feed prerehearsal panic that in turn fuels the desire to mass practice. Therefore, distributed practice is not only cognitively beneficial for learning; it is a sensible strategy for developing a safe and healthy vocal training regimen and has the added potential for keeping anxiety levels in check.

Varied Practice Is More Effective than *Constant Practice*

This rule of practice is about conditions of practice and is somewhat dependent upon whether the skill one is practicing already displays an inherent amount of variability (an *open-skill task*) versus one that does not (a *closed-skill task*). Examples are downhill skiing (an open-skill task), in which conditions are constantly varied, versus bowling (a closed-skill task), in which the setting is fairly predictable.

Learning to sing is an inherently open-skill task; variability is "built in" to the endeavor. Consider the trajectory involved with learning a singing role from beginning to opening night: There are vocal technique lessons with a teacher, coachings with a pianist for style and diction, staging rehearsals with a director, and dress rehearsals with a conductor and an orchestra. All of these carefully rehearsed parameters may yet be varied again by costumes, makeup, and jitters in front of a live audience. Clearly, honing one's craft as a performer involves doing so under a lot of variable conditions.

How does this relate to the second rule of effective practice? Recall that the evidence that a thing is learned is its repeatability, and that a goal of motor learning is that the task remains repeatable even under variable conditions. Therefore, the second rule of practice means that variation in practice, while potentially unnerving, is actually quite good for learning—so good, in fact, that it not only strengthens the task at hand but also has been shown to positively boost other related skills. This latter effect is called *generalizability* in motor learning research. The next time you feel thrown off by a change in venue—or you encounter new timbres when hearing orchestral rather than piano accompaniment—embrace these variations as vitamin packs for learning that boost both the target skill itself and the many related skills needed for performance. This type of multitasking is anything but toxic to learning!

Randomly Ordered Practice Is More Effective than *Blocked Practice*

Blocked practice focuses on training one movement over and over again until mastery is gained. The use of blocked practice is a popular method for inculcating discrete skills that make up complex activities, particularly when training beginners. For example, singers may be required to practice vocal onset exercises over and over again in middle voice range until glottal onsets disappear. While this method may seem to make common sense, *randomly ordered practice* has been shown over decades of motor learning research to be more effective for long-term learning than blocked practice. That is, singers will ultimately be more successful at clean onsets if they practice vowel onsets interspersed with onsets featuring voiced and unvoiced consonants—and onsets at variable pitch levels—than if they were to practice each of these components in repetitive isolation.

Note the use of the phrase "long-term learning," which highlights an interesting twist regarding this rule of practice: blocked practice actually boosts performance in the short term, that is, during the skill-acquisition phase. This explains the one condition in which blocked practice is preferable, and that is for rank beginners. But if testing the viability of such boosts in real-world performance venues is delayed or avoided altogether, blocked practice can eventually lead to a false sense of accomplishment, for both student and trainer. Such musicians make excellent "practicers," but they tend to fall apart in performance. The salient point here is that while both *randomly ordered practice* and *varied practice* may degrade immediate performance, they boost long-term learning as evidenced by superior retention (memory) and transfer because they hold up in many different situations.

CONTROLLED VERSUS AUTOMATIC PROCESSES

An ancient distinction has existed between things we do with conscious attention and those things we do automatically. In motor learning, these modes are called controlled versus automatic processing, respectively, and these modes have received quite a lot of attention over the past two decades. The resulting research has painted a mixed picture, with strongly held views on both sides. A similarly mixed picture, with equally strongly held opinions, can be seen in the field of voice pedagogy, between those who promote a technical, or science-based approach, and those who prefer more intuitive methods.

Teaching methods that employ specific, frank instructions, such as "lift your soft palate as you ascend in pitch" or "engage your abdominal muscles as you crescendo," are examples of directives that evoke controlled processing. In contrast, automatic processing does not call attention to these mechanics. Teachers who use a combination of emotion (for example, a "stifled sob"), imagery ("imagine an inflatable swimming ring around your middle"), or allusion to common physical gestures ("inhale through a yawn") are evoking automatic processing.

Many voice teachers use a combination of controlled and automatic directives. Regardless of which directives are used, in a typical voice lesson singers are being showered with feedback, simply defined as any and all information available to the learner. Feedback is therefore an essential part of motor learning. There are two main types of feedback: inherent feedback—what the learners themselves perceive or feel—and augmented feedback, which is information delivered from an external source (like a coach or teacher). Augmented feedback also includes auditory and visual information delivered through a device such as a mirror, a video camera, an audio recording, or computer voice analysis. Augmented feedback in the form of verbal instruction given from teacher to student exerts such a powerful influence on motor learning that it is second only to practice itself. Due to this power, augmented feedback has received a lot of scrutiny in motor learning research. We shall consider a few facets of feedback before we return to the controlled versus automatic processing controversy.

Feedback frequency (how often a voice coach should provide augmented feedback) is one of several parameters studied by scientists. A commonsense approach, backed up by scientific research, is for teachers to provide frequent feedback in the early stages of vocal study, and as mastery increases, this feedback should decrease, especially in light of what we now know about how immediate performance gains depress long-term learning.

Another consideration is timing. Is augmented feedback best used by the student terminally—after the lesson—or concurrently, while the singer is engaged in singing? This question is especially important when considering computer-aided display devices, such as VoceVista, which operates in real time; in fact, it is this feature that its proponents tout as an advantage for use in the voice studio. Results from studies in motor learning have yielded varied results on the question of timing, but the following seem to be the most effective forms of feedback, in ranked order.

Immediate augmented feedback—verbal commentary from teacher to student provided during the lesson—appears to be the most effective feedback timing, but after a short time delay (short meaning a few seconds). Terminal feedback is also effective; this is feedback given after a period of time has elapsed, for example, several days. Also, learners can provide their own terminal feedback, for example, by self-evaluation through journaling. This kind of feedback can receive a boost if paired with goal setting.

Concurrent augmented feedback—a stream of verbal coaching while the student is singing, or an overdependence on spectrographic feedback—should be used sparingly. Besides distracting learners from the ability to receive their own sensory information (biofeedback), concurrent augmented feedback also displays the troublesome characteristic of potentially boosting short-term performance but depressing real learning. Note that spectrographic feedback used for research, or to target specific vocal phenomena, do not bear this caution.

A cautious note is in order regarding the physical feedback known as manipulation. This is literally the "hands-on" teaching approach in which the teacher touches a student's body in order to elicit a physical or tonal response. Ethical and legal considerations aside for the moment, the evidence suggests that manipulative correction sometimes follows the same outcome as controlled processing and concurrent augmented feedback: such solutions may temporarily benefit performance but ultimately may not take root in the singer's long-term memory. Nevertheless, anecdotal evidence does suggest that the immediate benefit from manipulation techniques may be retained if learners can encode the desired sensations in their own memory banks.

Regarding the ethical and legal considerations of teacher-to-student touching: The potential for misunderstanding, misuse, or outright abuse among both parties is high, particularly if there are no witnesses present. This is often the case in one-on-one studio teaching, where student and teacher are alone, behind closed doors. Teachers should be aware that simply asking permission to touch a student may not be enough, due to the asymmetrical power dynamic inherent in the teacher-student relationship; students may not feel free to say no. For their part, students should know they have the fundamental human right to forbid touching—even if doing so creates awkwardness or anxiety. Yet despite these significant concerns, physical guidance or manipulation remains a very useful tool for motor learning. Therefore, a simple and sensible solution to these dilemmas is for the teacher to demonstrate upon his or her own body, never directly touching the student but instead guiding the student acting in mirror imitation upon his or her own body. Another solution is for the teacher to give written instructions for what to do as homework—literally "put your hands here"—followed by what the learner should seek: "Notice when the spine is aligned that the jaw tends to relax."

THE THEORY OF ATTENTIONAL FOCUS

Expert athletes, dancers, instrumentalists, and singers all share the central objective of muscular efficiency, the ability to enact fine movement with the least amount of energy necessary for the task. Other common motor learning goals are accuracy, speed, consistency, and especially automaticity. The mark of the expert is said to be that their performances are achieved automatically, outside of their conscious awareness, and this view has gone unchallenged until very recently.

How to achieve automaticity revolves around the question of where the performer should place his attention: on the target, or on the mechanics of achieving that target? In motor learning research, the theory of attentional focus holds that motor skills are best accomplished when the performer focuses on an external goal rather than on internal mental processes. For example, in a dart task, people are much more likely to achieve success if they focus on landing the dart in the center of the bull's-eye than if they turn their attention inward to the mechanics of their movements, such as the best angle to hold the arm or the degree of flexion to rotate their wrist. An external focus of attention for motor tasks (the target), rather than an internal focus of attention (the mechanics), has shown strong positive results in lab studies, particularly athletic pursuits that feature balance, and those that feature manipulation of objects, such as balls, clubs, darts, and rackets.

As further evidence for the superiority of an external focus of attention, many studies have revealed that an internal focus of attention has been shown to actually harm motor learning and performance. When this occurs as a performance gaffe in front of an audience (like missing a putt in golf), it is known in both scientific and popular sports literature as choking. To explain the choking phenomenon, motor learning researcher Gabriele Wulf (b. ca. 1960) developed the constrained action hypothesis, which holds that an internal focus of attention interferes with automatic control processes. Her hypothesis is based on the observation that automatic responses are accomplished much more rapidly than consciously controlled ones.[10] Since processing speed has been positively correlated with all of the goals of motor learning, the constrained action hypothesis holds that all of these parameters are harmed when performers slow down their own motor system by, in popular parlance, "thinking too much." Antidotes for choking are reflected in such popular sayings as "don't overthink," "stay out of your own head," and "go with the flow."

The constrained action hypothesis has been expanded to include the observation that when performers are induced to think of their bodies during performance, this triggers an internal focus of attention that begets a rapid spiral of self-evaluation, self-consciousness, negative emotion, and paradoxical attempts to stop all such thinking. Wulf has dubbed these spirals "micro-choking."[11]

It is important to note that choking of any type is directly proportional to ability: the more expert the performer, the more spectacular the mistake. In popular parlance, the higher you climb, the harder you fall. Experts choke, but beginners simply fail. Why is this? The answer lies in the performer's abilities at the time of performance. Researcher Sian Beilock (b. 1975), an expert in motor learning research and the choking phenomenon, notes that beginners have no fund of procedural knowledge; we might say they have no flow with which to go. Because of this, Beilock notes that the early stages of learning may actually require an internal focus of attention, with a step-by-step approach to the mechanics of movement until learners have established the necessary motor patterns that allow them to put those learned skills on "automatic pilot," thus freeing up the brain for other cognitive tasks.[12]

Yet questions remain concerning attentional focus. At what stage in the learner's journey might he or she abandon an internal focus for an external one? Do all advanced performers use an external focus of attention, and under all conditions? Have all motor pursuits been put to the test to determine whether an external focus of attention applies to all motor skills?

On this last question, prominent researchers like Wulf are so confident of the superior effectiveness of an external focus of attention that they claim this principle is generalizable to virtually every skilled motor pursuit, including music. This confidence is so ubiquitous that the dancer and philosopher Barbara Gail Montero (b. ca. 1971) dubbed it "the Maxim."

> Both in the ivory tower and on the football field, it is widely thought that focusing on highly skilled movements while performing them hinders their execution. Once you have developed the ability to tee off in golf, play an arpeggio on the piano, or perform a pirouette in ballet, attention to your bodily movement is thought to lead to inaccuracies, blunders, and sometimes even utter paralysis. At the pinnacle of achievement, such skills, it is urged, should proceed without conscious interference. . . . Let me call the view that bodily awareness tends to hinder highly accomplished bodily skills "the Maxim."[13]

Recently, Wulf conducted a review of the extant research and concluded that in her overview of eighty different studies, "in no case was an internal focus advantageous."[14] In addition to Wulf's constrained action hypothesis, several more hypotheses were offered in support of the superiority of an external focus of attention.

One suggests that directing attention to mechanical movement actually causes existing muscular patterns to stabilize, thus working in opposition to the positive benefits of unlearning. A related theory involves the degree of freedom with which the body operates most efficiently and observes that an internal focus of attention seems to exert a "freezing" effect on the joints. Another theory holds that analytical thinking, the province of the brain's executive control center, processes information more slowly than the intuitive responses of our autonomic nervous system, and this slow pace impedes motor learning and performance.

Finally, the limitations of language have been noted as a barrier to motor learning, because of the difficulty in describing physical sensations in words. It is reasoned that poorly described sensations are, in essence, tracked into the nonmotor regions of the brain where they are essentially "lost in translation."

CHALLENGES TO "THE MAXIM"

Recent challengers to "the Maxim" question whether all performers use an external focus in all situations, whether automaticity always attends higher order motor tasks, and if automaticity is even a goal valued by all expert performers in all domains.[15] Their research is based in part on firsthand accounts of what expert instrumentalists, dancers, and athletes actually think about in real performance situations. This is in stark contrast to previous research that has largely been carried out with nonexperts, using simple motor tasks, and conducted under laboratory, not real-world, conditions.

New research is finding that many experts do exert executive control by issuing mechanical directives to themselves when engaged in high-skill activity. This is quite the opposite from operating automatically. Thus, challenges to "the Maxim" are based on three key criticisms: (1) that research subjects are generally not experts, nor even very high-skilled performers; (2) that lab studies do not (and cannot) study complex motor skills; and (3) that studies conducted in a lab rather than on a court, on a mountainside, or in a theater are not "ecologically valid."

An additional note is that very little motor learning research has been carried out on performance artists. This makes the automaticity account especially troubling, for the fundamental reason that automaticity may be desired in athletics, but absolutely not in performance art. In other words, taking risks in athletic performance may have dire consequences, from losing a championship match to broken bones. However, a goal for many artists is anything but automaticity; this is a particularly salient point for expert musicians, most of whom strive to keep their performances fresh and exciting and may even introduce an element of risk or improvisation to prevent well-worn repertoire from becoming stale. Yet a reasonable argument in favor of automaticity in performance art persists: firsthand accounts by successful performers indeed describe an automatic response to the nimble fingering required for executing rapid scale passages, and decrements are ascribed to overthinking in this scenario.

A second challenge to automaticity as a valued goal involves performers' reactions to changed or changing conditions. For example, downhill skiers report the necessity and benefits of issuing technical commands to themselves (using an internal focus) during performance when changed snow conditions force them to be more strategic and less automatic. No one could argue that performance artists like singers, actors, and dancers do not also face constantly changing performance conditions, from daily internal fluctuations like muscle fatigue and hoarse voice to external changes such as humidity levels and performance space acoustics.

A third challenge to automaticity is the observation that the mark of an expert is the continual quest for improvement; the only way to improve is to counteract automaticity through deliberate practice. If we match this observation with the powerful finding from motor learning research mentioned at the beginning of this section (the rate of growth slows as motor performance improves), then we must conclude that the only way to improve after one has achieved an excellent level of ability is to design deliberate practice regimens featuring tasks of greater and more varied difficulty; until learned, these tasks would seem to require an attentional focus on mechanics. Critics of "the Maxim" cite this last reason when noting that an internal focus of attention is required when experts decide to radically alter ingrained habits in order to learn new techniques.

Current research on attentional focus in high-level performers is offering powerful evidence that attention itself is trainable. A recent theory is the "AIR" approach—Applying Intelligence to Reflexes—defined as training that aims to develop "dynamic repertoires of potential action sequences which can be accessed, redeployed, and transformed" in response to changing performance conditions.[16] Exactly how this might be accomplished is also being scrutinized. Among the various techniques proposed are (1) contrast drills, in which the learner in training toggles back and forth between correct and incorrect movement; and (2) developing a repertoire of cue words that operate as linguistic nudges intended to evoke desired action—the latter is related to chunking. This process builds and accesses flexible links between knowing and doing, thus building bridges between declarative and procedural learning. Motor learning research on musicians is still in its infancy; practically none to date have used singers. Therefore, singers are encouraged to experiment with both internal and external foci.

FINAL THOUGHTS

Voice pedagogy is a dance between science and art. Since García first opened the possibility of using voice science to advance vocal art, voice science has influenced and even defined voice pedagogy. In doing so, García unwittingly unleashed a historic schism between science and art in cultivated singing, between those who feel that science drains the mystery out of artistic singing and those who believe science can inform quality teaching methods based on physiological and acoustic facts. For singers and teachers who seek to practice a flexible and balanced approach between the two, the multidisciplinary field of cognitive science is proposed as the best arena for performing this dynamic dance between voice science and vocal art.

NOTES

1. This chapter was adapted from the my chapter "Brain" in Scott McCoy's *Your Voice: An Inside View*, 3rd ed. (Gahanna, OH: Inside View Press, 2019). Portions of this chapter also appear in my book *The Musician's Mind: Teaching, Learning, and Performance in the Age of Brain Science* (Lanham, MD: Rowman & Littlefield, 2020).

2. Johan Sundberg, *The Science of the Singing Voice* (DeKalb, IL: Northern Illinois University Press, 1987).

3. Although the average age at which babies typically begin to crawl is nine months, no one teaches them how do it; absent any frank physical disorders, all that is necessary is the opportunity to do so. Babies know how to crawl on their own because this knowledge is encoded in their DNA. In other words, they are born with this knowledge "preinstalled."

4. K. Anders Ericsson, Ralf T. Krampe, and Clemens Tesch-Römer, "The Role of Deliberate Practice in the Acquisition of Expert Performance," *Psychological Review* 100, no. 3 (1993): 363–406.

5. Joseph LeDoux, *The Emotional Brain: The Mysterious Underpinnings of Emotional Life* (New York: Simon & Schuster, 1996), preface.

6. The somatic marker hypothesis proposes that emotional processes guide (or bias) behavior, particularly decision-making. Somatic markers are feelings in the body that are associated with emotions, such as the association of rapid heartbeat with anxiety or of nausea with disgust. According to the hypothesis, somatic markers strongly influence subsequent decision-making. Within the brain, somatic markers are thought to be processed in the ventromedial prefrontal cortex (VMPFC) and the amygdala.

7. Antonio Damasio, *Descartes' Error: Emotion, Reason and the Human Brain* (New York: G. P. Putnam's Sons, 1994), 130.

8. Hebb's rule—also called Hebb's postulate, Hebbian theory, or cell assembly theory—was developed by the Canadian psychologist Donald O. Hebb (1904–1985), who introduced the concept in his 1949 book *The Organization of Behavior: A Neuropsychological Theory*.

9. Richard A. Schmidt and Timothy A. Lee, *Motor Control and Learning: A Behavioral Emphasis*, 4th ed. (Champaign, IL: Human Kinetics, 2005), 322.

10. Refer back to the first box and note that declarative learning is generally slow while procedural learning is relatively fast.

11. Gabriele Wulf, "Attentional Focus and Motor Learning: A Review of Fifteen Years," *International Review of Sport and Exercise Psychology* 6, no. 1 (2013): 77–104.

12. Sian Beilock, Thomas Carr, Clare MacMahon, and Janet Starkes, "When Paying Attention Becomes Counter-Productive: Impact of Divided Versus Skill-Focused Attention on Novice and Experienced Performance of Sensorimotor Skills," *Journal of Experimental Psychology: Applied* 8, no. 1 (March 2002): 6–16; Sian Beilock, Bennett Bertenthal, Annette McCoy, and Thomas Carr, "Haste Does Not Always Make Waste: Expertise, Direction of Attention, and Speed versus Accuracy in Performing Sensorimotor Skills," *Psychonomic Bulletin and Review* 11, no. 2 (April 2004): 373–79.

13. Barbara Gail Montero, "Does Bodily Awareness Interfere with Highly Skilled Movement?" *Inquiry: An Interdisciplinary Journal of Philosophy* 53, no. 2 (March 2010): 105–6.

14. Gabriele Wulf, "Attentional Focus and Motor Learning: A Review of Fifteen Years," *International Review of Sport and Exercise Psychology* 6, no. 1 (2013): 77.

15. Barbara Gail Montero, *Thought in Action: Expertise and the Conscious Mind* (New York: Oxford University Press, 2017); John Toner, Barbara Gail Montero, and Aidan Moran, "Considering the Role of Cognitive Control in Expert Performance," *Phenomenology and the Cognitive Sciences* 14, no. 4

(December 2014): 1127–44; John Sutton, Doris Mcilwain, Wayne Christensen, and Andrew Geeves, "Applying Intelligence to the Reflexes: Embodied Skills and Habits Between Dreyfus and Descartes," *Journal of the British Society for Phenomenology* 42, no. 1 (January 2011): 78–103.

16. John Sutton, Doris Mcilwain, Wayne Christensen, and Andrew Geeves, "Applying Intelligence to the Reflexes: Embodied Skills and Habits between Dreyfus and Descartes," *Journal of the British Society for Phenomenology* 42, no. 1 (January 2011).

7

MUSICAL THEATRE VOCAL PEDAGOGY

One of the key ingredients for successful musical theatre singing is flexibility and the ability to sing in a multitude of styles.[1] As we've already explored in the chapter on genre, there are many sounds heard on the musical theatre stage. It is not uncommon for performers to be asked to sing in a variety of styles, genres, and vocal functions. Not to mention the need for accents and character voices, depending on the show. This is one of the things that makes musical theatre singing unique from other CCM (contemporary commercial music) genres. It is less common for a singer studying a genre of CCM singing to be seeking the flexibility to sing in a variety of opposing styles. They may need some adaptability across a few related genres, but they typically do not need the wide breadth of genre mastery that musical theatre singers seek. It can be challenging to learn how to use your voice in this manner, but luckily there are strategies to help explore all areas of the voice.

Before we dive into a discussion of various aspects of singing function, it's important to briefly discuss terminology. Many of the words and definitions that we use in singing are *not* agreed upon in the voice community, despite being used frequently and with certainty in voice studios across the globe.[2] People spend a lot of time arguing over the exact definition of a belt, or whether a certain sound is a mix or not.

There is no way to satisfy all parties when it comes to terminology. As we proceed, I will attempt to clearly define the sounds or ideas that we are talking about. I encourage you to focus more on the sounds we're discussing and less on the name of the sound. I will also provide audio samples on the resource page to help acclimate your ear to the sounds that I am describing.

THE BIG THREE

As we begin to talk about how to develop your voice for musical theatre singing, there are three words that will show up frequently—legit, belt, and mix. These words are used constantly not only in musical theatre training, but also in auditions, character breakdowns, and rehearsal rooms. It's important that we take a moment to describe what these words might mean.

Legit Singing

Legit is short for "legitimate" singing. It typically encompasses sounds that fall more in line with classical singing.[3] These are the sounds we might hear from most of the characters in *Carousel* or *The Light in the Piazza*. One of the major differences between classical singing and legit musical theatre singing is the middle range. It is common to hear chest voice and speechlike sounds in legit musical theatre singing in this range. This is typically quite different from many classical approaches. Additionally, in more contemporary legit scores and revivals of older material, we often hear brighter and more open vowel choices, and the use of straight tone in addition to vibrato. It's important to note that legit musical theatre singing is not synonymous with classical singing. ♪

Belting

Belting typically refers to a sound quality that aligns more with a call or shout. This sound can be produced by all humans in various degrees of their speaking voice and is often most easily recognized on open vowels, despite being able to be produced on closed vowels. While belting tends to be louder and more dramatic when looked at contextually, it does not require a loud volume to be produced functionally. These are the sounds we might hear from the character of Anita in *West Side Story*, Elphaba in *Wicked*, or Evan in *Dear Evan Hanson*. ♪

Mixing

In the musical theatre industry, mixing most commonly refers to sounds that cannot be classified as legit or belt. These sounds almost sound as if your head voice and chest voice were "mixed" together, despite that not being physically accurate. Humans can make these sound qualities that sound "mixed" together in both head voice and chest voice and are often most successful when they are able to transition between laryngeal registration seamlessly. These are the sounds we might hear from the character Beth in *Little Women* during "Some Things Are Meant to Be," Gabe in *Next to Normal* when he sings "There's a World," or Telephone Guy in *The Band's Visit* when he sings "Answer Me." ♪

REGISTRATION AND RESONANCE

One component of this flexibility is mastery of registration and resonance. Registration can be defined as a series of notes that are perceived to be made in the same manner.[4] Historically we thought of registration as happening solely at the vocal fold level. We now know that what we perceive as registration involves more than just the vocal folds—we must consider what happens *above* the vocal folds.[5] Registration can be broken into two categories—laryngeal registration and acoustic registration.

Laryngeal Registration

Laryngeal registration is the type of registration that most singers and teachers are familiar with. It refers to the mode of vibration that is enacted by specific muscles engaging at the vocal fold level.[6] This type of registration was discussed in Scott McCoy's chapter. As a refresher, we have one registration that uses short, thick vocal folds that come together robustly in an almost square-shaped fashion. This registration is commonly referred to as chest voice, modal voice, thick mechanism, thyroarytenoid (TA) dominant, or vibrational mode one (M1). The other main registration uses longer, thinner vocal folds that make less contact on the vibrational edge. This registration is commonly referred to as head voice, falsetto, thin mechanism, cricothyroid (CT) dominant, or vibrational mode two (M2). There is also a vibrational mode zero (M0, vocal fry or "pulse" register) and vibrational mode three (M3, whistle, or "flageolet" register), but a full discussion of their function is beyond the scope of this book.

The terms *head voice* and *chest voice* have been used for centuries by voice teachers.[7] There has been a trend in recent years to move toward using the terms TA dominant and CT dominant, but that is not a completely accurate description of what is happening at the laryngeal level. Recent research indicates that the thyroarytenoid and cricothyroid muscles work in tandem, and that CT muscle activation is more related to frequency than laryngeal register.[8] As researchers Sandage and Hoch point out, using the terms CT and TA dominant is not much more scientifically accurate than using head and chest voice.[9] Many people also prefer to use the modes of vibration when referring to laryngeal registration. While this is more accurate than CT and TA, it is not as common outside of voice science circles. Other language such as thick and thin mechanism, modal voice, and falsetto are also frequently used to describe these laryngeal phenomena.

Any of these terms for registration may prove to be effective in the voice studio. In fact, in my teaching, I use all these terms to describe laryngeal registration so that singers understand that there is a flexibility of language out there to describe laryngeal registration events. It also helps to find language that works for each individual singer. One term might work well for one human, and the next person might need different language to understand laryngeal registers. While some of these words may be oversimplifications of mechanics, or not be as evidence-based as we would like, the goal of using these terms is simply for "student cueing."[10] For simplicity, I have chosen to use the terms head and chest voice in this text as we continue to explore vocal function. My rationale for doing so is that these terms are still frequently used in the musical theatre industry. It is not uncommon to see the words head and chest voice used in casting breakdowns, auditions, and rehearsals.

For the remainder of this text, chest voice will refer to sounds that are produced in M1, and commonly called modal voice, full voice, heavy mechanism, thick mechanism, or TA dominant. Head voice will refer to sounds that are produced in M2, and commonly called falsetto, loft voice, light mechanism, thin mechanism, or CT dominant.

Acoustic Registration

While many teachers are familiar with laryngeal registration, some may not be aware of what is sometimes referred to as acoustic registration. This refers to the timbral shifts that happen because of the interaction of harmonics and resonances throughout the range.[11] Ken Bozeman, a voice teacher and acoustics expert, talks about four major acoustic registers—whoop, yell, open timbre, and close timbre. Whoop timbre refers to a harmonic setup that is most commonly heard in head voice and has the sound quality of "whooping" at a sporting event. It can also be called "hoot."[12] Close timbre occurs when the voice "turns over" or "covers." Open timbre occurs lower in the range and is typically heard as bright or forward. Finally, yell timbre—sometimes called "calling voice"[13]—is carrying open timbre higher in one's range. One component of belting requires a skilled adaptation of this acoustic register.[14]

What is important to know about acoustic registration is that it is greatly impacted by the laryngeal registration, the vowel, the dynamic, the pitch, and the anatomy of the singer. While we can conceptualize each of these factors as separate entities on paper, it becomes nearly impossible to separate them in singing. Each of these aspects interacts with each other, causing constant changes and shifts. Every singer feels and experiences these shifts differently. Successful musical theatre singing is about controlling all these factors independent of each other.

One of the most important factors on that list is vowel. Vowels sit on a spectrum ranging from open to close, which is dependent on the distance between the palate and the tongue. When they are further apart, the vowel is said to be more opened, and when they are close together, the vowel is said to be more closed. Vowels can fall anywhere on the spectrum between the most opened and most closed. The ability to control open and close vowels in a functional way is a key ingredient to musical theatre singing.[15]

Resonance and Sensory Feedback

If you recall, resonance is defined as the amplification and enhancement of musical sound through supplemental vibration. For singers, resonance is typically experienced through sensory feedback. As sound passes through the vocal tract, sympathetic vibrations can be felt in the bones and tissues of the neck, mouth, sinuses, and head. The feedback will change depending on the shape of the vocal tract and the singer's ability to interpret the sensations. Singers can experience specific feedback from both laryngeal registration and acoustic registration choices. Singers use this sensory feedback as a way of controlling their singing. This feedback is sometimes referred to as "placement," although you are not actually placing the sound anywhere. For instance, sound is only in your nose and sinuses when the soft palate is down, even though people can feel energy and feedback in those areas when the soft palate is lifted. The term placement might work for some, but for many singers it implies a feeling of being stagnant and can sometimes lead to pushing or a lack of freedom. Using the term *feedback*, or simply taking the time to identify where the singer feels the energy of the sound as it moves through the body, could lead to a more fluid approach to interpreting resonance.

THE E4–E5 RANGE

One of the major differences between musical theatre singing and classical singing occurs in the approximate E4–E5 range for *all* singers, regardless of gender or voice classification.[16] While classical training generally seeks to smooth out this octave and create a cohesive, unified sound, musical theatre training seeks flexibility and the ability to create a multitude of sounds within this range. One must be able to sing legit, belt, and mix in this range, in addition to creating a variety of dynamics and styles.

The musical theatre singer needs a command of laryngeal registration. They must be able to function in chest voice in this range, in addition to being able to transition fluidly into head voice. Both register choices are used and appropriate in musical theatre singing for all singers. The musical theatre singer also needs a command of resonance strategies in this range. All singers must be able to utilize both open and close timbre in chest and head voice, as well as navigate between open and close vowels.

In addition to function, musical theatre singers need to be able to work in a multitude of styles. It is not uncommon for a musical theatre singers' career to take them from *Hamilton* or *Waitress* to *Carousel*, which require different uses of the voice, both in function and style.[17] Singers training in musical theatre should be working on accuracy of style across a multitude of genres.

CONSIDERATIONS FOR VOCAL EXERCISES

As we begin to look at vocal exercises to help singers find this flexibility and balance, it's important to discuss some considerations when crafting exercises for singing. The exercises in this book are simple and designed to give you ideas about how to work on specific parts of the voice. My hope is that each exercise in here sparks an idea for you to create your own exercise. Every exercise out there will only be successful when it is implemented effectively. These considerations are meant to help you understand how to have the most impact from your lessons in the studio.

Every Exercise Needs a Purpose

Make sure you understand the purpose of all exercises. Unfortunately, there are no magic exercises. Vocal exercises are most effective when given a clear, specific target. If you're unsure what purpose an exercise serves, ask your teacher or investigate more deeply to figure out how it is serving you or your singers. Exercises without clear purposes or goals will not fully serve any singer. It is also important to recognize how the purpose of the exercise can easily change with a shift in vowel, range, or tempo. Be sure that every part of the exercise is specific to the goal. It can also be helpful to organize your vocal exercises into categories of ranges or goals. This can help you know what exercises to pull from when there is a need to work something specific in a voice lesson.

Top-Down Singing

Generally speaking, exercises that descend are easier than exercises that ascend. This does not mean that we avoid ascending exercises, it just means that singers need a certain amount of coordination to be successful with ascending exercises. It is helpful to place ascending exercises at the appropriate point in the warm-up.

Pacing, Order, and Range of Exercises

It's important to start in the easiest place for each singer. Oftentimes, this means midtempo and easy, gradually building into harder, faster, more complicated, more sustained, or more ascending exercises. You don't want to expect too much too soon. It is also important to understand what range each singer likes to start in and target the order of your exercises appropriately. Starting in the easiest range for each singer and building from there will typically lead to more successful singing.

Speed of Exercises

Agility exercises or slow, sustained exercises might be more successful once you're more warmed up than right at the beginning. Think about the ideal tempo for each exercise and place it in the warmup accordingly. And remember that it takes a certain amount of coordination to do these types of exercises successfully, so beginning singers might need to build some coordination before attempting.

Accompaniment of Exercises

If you're a teacher, you might find yourself adding in additional notes or chords to accompany the vocal exercises. Always pay attention to whether the singer in front of you needs the additional chords or accompaniment or not. Some might thrive with them, but others might struggle with too much going on musically. Refer back to the goal of the exercise to determine if the added accompaniment is helping or hindering.

Always Return Home

Once you've stretched up or down with an exercise, it's helpful to make your way back to the range where you started the exercise. Oftentimes, more discoveries are made on the way back. This also allows the vocal folds to relax back to a more neutral state. Descending by whole step instead of half step can help save time in a lesson, but still allows for the singer to return to their starting range.

Vowels

Which vowels you select for each exercise is crucial in determining if the exercise will be successful. An exercise might be easy on one vowel, but extremely challenging on another. Vowels can also be individual for each singer. A vowel that is well coordinated for one person might be a struggle for another. Be ready to be flexible with the vowels that you choose to best suit the singer.

A NOTE ON GENDER AND SEX

A larynx is a larynx is a larynx. All healthy larynges have the same parts, no matter what gender identity the human attached to the larynx identifies with.[18] A larynx can be smaller or larger, which can be dependent on the size of the human and the hormones present in the body. Additionally, the respiratory system that helps operate the larynx can vary in size and strength based on the size of the ribcage, which is often dictated by the hormones present. When a testosterone puberty happens organically in the body, as it does in cisgender men or nonbinary people who naturally produce testosterone, the laryngeal cartilages grow, in addition to the muscles and ligaments. This causes a drop in fundamental frequency of speaking and singing.[19] When testosterone therapy is used, such as through an injection, patch, gel or oral administration, the vocal folds increase in mass and the pitch drops, but the size of the cartilages typically do not change much.[20] These masculinizing therapies may be used by trans men, nonbinary folks, or anyone who wish to masculinize their voice and body.

When a larynx goes through an organic estrogen dominant puberty, the laryngeal cartilages, muscles, and ligaments also grow, but not nearly as much as they do with testosterone. This causes the fundamental frequency of speaking and singing to lower, but again, not as much as with testosterone.[21] Femininizing hormone therapy may be administered as estrogen, estrogen with testosterone blockers, estrogen with progesterone and testosterone blockers, or just testosterone blockers.[22] These therapies do cause some changes to the structure of the vocal folds, but do not drastically alter the fundamental frequency of the sound, especially if the larynx has already been exposed to testosterone. These feminizing therapies may be used by trans women, nonbinary folks, or anyone who seeks a more feminine sound and appearance.[23]

I find it helpful to think about the voice as existing on two spectrums. The first is the functional spectrum. One extreme of this spectrum might be the large larynx that produces low frequencies easily such as Paul Robeson, who famously sang "Ol' Man River" in *Show Boat*. The other extreme might be the small larynx that produces high pitches easily, such as Kristen Chenoweth, who easily sang "Glitter and Be Gay" from *Candide*. If these are the extremes of the functional binary, there thousands of options that exist in between, many of which may or may not align with societal gender expectations. It is not fair to assume that a voice that has been through a certain hormonal change will behave in one way only. For instance, Kathleen Turner is a cisgender woman who is known for her low, sultry voice, and Mykal Kilgore is a cisgender man that has a naturally higher speaking and singing voice. Singers may operate fully in one end of the spectrum or may find themselves somewhere in the middle. It is important that singers find where their voice functions on this spectrum, and not put themselves in a box of what they are "supposed" to do.

The second spectrum is the auditory target spectrum. While sound itself has no gender, sound in society has been gendered. We have deemed sounds as being more masculine or feminine. When one sings "I Could Have Danced All Night" from *My Fair Lady*, we expect to hear head voice dominant singing because that is the auditory target, we as a society, have deemed as being feminine and appropriate for the female character. When one sings "Soliloquy" from *Carousel*, we expect to hear chest dominant singing because that is the auditory target we have deemed as being masculine and appropriate for the male character. If these are examples of the extremes of this auditory spectrum, there are plenty of sounds that exist in between what we deem as solely masculine or feminine. Any singer may be seeking to make sounds that fall anywhere on this auditory target spectrum. A cisgender female may wish to make sounds that sound more masculine, and a nonbinary person might want to work on sounds that are perceived to be feminine. *There are no rules about what auditory targets humans can make.*

Musical theatre has historically operated firmly in the gender binary. Most roles that have been written have a gender identity of male or female, and many older shows go as far as to reaffirm traditional gender roles in society. This is, thankfully, starting to change as we are now seeing more roles written for trans and nonbinary characters, many of which are written by trans and nonbinary writers. ♪

As we begin to look at vocal exercises for musical theatre singing, I want to acknowledge the impact the binary has historically had in voice training. Most voice texts only discuss male and female, with no room for anyone who might not identify that way. I believe in gender-neutral training, which is, thankfully, not a new concept.[24] Exercises should be tailored to each individual student based on the function of their larynx and their desired auditory targets. Lumping students into male and female serves no one, and only helps to reinforce "archaic myths, inaccurate definitions, and cultural biases" as voice teacher Robert Edwin boldly states.[25]

To create a more gender-neutral voice training space, the exercises in this book are designed to be used with any and all singers. Each exercise in this book should be tailored to the individual singer based on the function of the voice and their desired auditory targets. When I use the term *higher voice*, I'm including anyone whose voice might fall more on the higher spectrum of function and who might be working on sounds in the treble clef range. When I use the term *lower voice*, I'm including anyone whose voice might fall more on the lower end of the spectrum, and who might be working on sounds in the bass clef range.[26] While some exercises might work better in the higher or lower range, no exercise is off limits for anyone!

THE MIDDLE RANGE

Like with most singing training, the middle range is a great place to start. Singing in this range allows the singer to work on executing technical goals in an easy, manageable range. When working with singers in this range, we are working on coordinating inhale, airflow, resonance, energy, ease of sound, tension, and anything else that might need to be addressed. Every singer's middle range will be slightly different, so it's important to pay attention to where they are comfortable and able to produce easy sound. Below are some exercises for the middle range for all singers to help get the voice lined up and ready for more extended singing.

Lip Trills, Raspberries, and Bubbles

Lip trills, raspberries, or blowing bubbles through a straw in water is one of the best ways to start any voice work. It allows the breath to coordinate with the sound and typically makes for an easy start. You can do these on any pattern, but I typically start with either an eight or five note descending scale as noted in figure 7.1. ♪

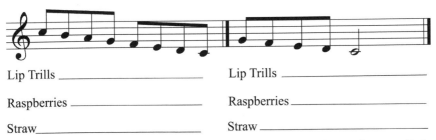

Lip Trills _____   Lip Trills _____

Raspberries _____   Raspberries _____

Straw _____   Straw _____

Figure 7.1. Singers can use a five or eight not scale depending on their comfortability. *Courtesy of the author*

Moving into Vowels

As you move into vowels in the middle range, it's helpful to think about what type of sound quality you are aiming to achieve. For instance, singers with higher voices, especially those working on more feminine auditory targets, might choose to work on balancing laryngeal registration throughout this range. Working head voice in these exercises will prove beneficial. Working top down with descending exercises will help reinforce this head-dominant approach. Singers with lower voices, especially those aiming for more masculine auditory targets, might be more focused on chest-voice singing in these exercises.

You'll see that /u/ and /i/ are common vowels in these exercises. For higher voices aiming for head voice production, /u/ and /i/ vowels provide many benefits. First, they both have lower first resonance frequencies, helping to reinforce the more rounded, legit acoustic output.[27] They are also more closed vowels, which can help reinforce lighter production. Both factors help the singer make sound qualities that acoustically line up with lighter, more head-dominant legit singing, including the "whoop" timbre mentioned earlier. For lower voices aiming for chest-voice production, many of the same benefits exist with the use of /u/ and /i/ vowels. The exercises in figures 7.2–7.3 are appropriate in head voice for all singers, as well as appropriate for lower voices in the middle range chest voice. ♪

Figure 7.2. Descending five or eight note scales on easy vowels are a great way to begin vocalizing. *Courtesy of the author*

Figure 7.3. This exercise is a great way to begin to introduce other vowels than /u/ and /i/. *Courtesy of the author*

MOVING UP

As the middle range becomes more balanced and aligned, singers might be ready to move higher in their range. The exercise in 7.4 is a nice way to work up into the higher range in a more rounded, legit sound quality for all voices. ♪

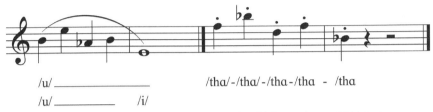

/u/ _____   /tha/-/tha/-/tha-/tha - /tha
/u/ _____ /i/

Figure 7.4. This exercise ascends into the higher range. If it is too complicated for a singer, consider shortening it to the last three notes of the exercise only. Additioanlly, you can use this pattern in a stacatto fashion, especially in one's highest range. *Courtesy of the author*

As singers become more coordinated with these legit sounds, they will be ready to start playing with more challenging vowels, patterns, and length of exercise. The exercises in figure 7.5–7.7 provide slightly more challenging patterns. ♪

/u/ __ /i/ __ /ɑ/ _____
/u/ __ /i/ __ /ɑ/ __ /i/ __ /u/

Figure 7.5. This pattern allows singers to begin working on ascending through their middle range. You can even take this exercise a bit higher if the singer is ready to work on ascending through their passaggio. *Courtesy of the author*

/the/__ /tha/__ /the/__ /tha/__ /the/   /the/__ tha/__ /the/__ /tha/__ /the/ - /ɑ/ - /e/
/thi/__ /thu/__ /thi/__ /thu/__ /thi/   /thi/__ /thu/__ /thi/__ /thu/__ /thi/ - /u/ - /i/

Figure 7.6. This exercises is a great way to introduce a more rapid moving pattern that still feels descending in nature. You can eventually add in an octave jump at the end to make the exercise more advanced. *Courtesy of the author*

MUSICAL THEATRE VOCAL PEDAGOGY 179

Figure 7.7. Simple five note scale runs are a great way to introduce agility. These runs can be implemented as noted, or they could be reversed in pattern to begin on a descend. You can also extend them to eight, nine, or eleven note scales for a more advanced singer. *Courtesy of the author*

RESONANT VOICE

When working on voice production, the target is often resonant voice, which is described as easy voicing that produces oral and facial vibratory sensations.[28] Resonant voice is one tool used in voice therapy to help people gain a clearer, more efficient speaking voice. Aiming for these same sensations when working on chest voice in the speaking range can be valuable. One of the first things to pay attention to when working with a singer are their speaking habits. Do they already exhibit the qualities of resonant voice in their speaking patterns, or do they lack a clear, consistent sound? Either way, as we've already discussed, learning to find the oral and facial sensory feedback in the speaking range will prove valuable to one's singing.

One of the first exercises to try is a hum in chest voice in your speaking range and assess where you feel the energy of the sound. I often refer to this energy as a feeling of buzz or vibration. Can you try humming and feeling it on your teeth? What about in your cheeks? How about the hard palate? The practice of aiming the energy of the sound to various spots in the mouth and face can be a valuable exercise. You want to find the spot that perceptually feels the easiest for the singer and sounds the clearest on the outside.

Once the hum feels consistently in a clear spot, you can take the hum into words, all while trying to maintain the feeling of buzziness and the use of chest voice. The speaking voice should feel light, easy, and buoyant, all while maintaining a connection to chest voice. You can make up your own words and phrases, or try a phrase like "my, my, my." It can be a valuable exercise as well when needing to work on clarity of dialogue from a show. You can easily take the hum into a piece of dialogue. It's important to note that lack of clarity in the speaking or singing voice—in particular a raspy, hoarse, or breathy quality—can be symptoms of a voice injury or medical issue. This is not always the case, but it's important to seek the care of a laryngologist if you or your student are unable to find consistent clarity in the voice. ♪

SPEECH INTO SINGING

Taking the clear, resonant, easy chest voice quality that you found and putting it on sung pitches is the next step. One of the tricks here is to make sure you keep the same quality you found in the humming exercise. It's common for singers to shape or alter the sound differently, or sometimes flip into head voice once pitches become involved. Keep these speechlike exercises as simple as possible as you work through the exercises in figure 7.8. This is an important skill for musical theatre singing where you must move from speech to singing constantly. ♪

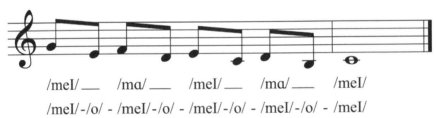

Figure 7.8. Using the hum to impact the lower singing range is a great way to find a connectiong between speaking and singing. Let this exercise feel as speechlike as possible. *Courtesy of the author*

If a singer is struggling with finding chest voice, I might choose to work their lower range with the exercise in figure 7.9. ♪

Figure 7.9. A simple exercise like this can help a singer find their lower, chest voice. I find this exercise particularly helpful for a higher voiced singer who has trouble finding chest voice in their lower range.

Once I know a singer understands chest voice in the lower range, I will move into speechlike exercises as in figure 7.10, where we take the resonant speech quality and use it on pitches. Again, keep these exercises as simple and speechlike as you can. The resonant speaking voice found in these exercises is sometimes called a "speech mix" and it will prove to be valuable when we explore belting later. ♪

Figure 7.10. Taking a spoken phrase and putting it on pitches is a great way for a singer to experience their speaking voice on pitch. It can help them recognize any habits they may have such when pitches come into play such as flipping into head voice, becoming too heavy, or darkening the resonance. *Courtesy of the author*

BACK AND FORTH

Many singers are focused on a smooth transition between chest and head voice, which is understandable, especially in musical theatre singing where that seamless quality is often desirable. Before this laryngeal register transition can happen smoothly, it needs to be able to happen at all. Exercises that require the singer to move from one laryngeal register to another, such as the one in figure 7.11, is a great way to learn to iso-

/meɪ/ - /o/ - /meɪ/ - /o/ - /meɪ/ - /o/ - /meɪ/ - /o/ - /meɪ/ - /u/ - /meɪ/

Figure 7.11. In this exercise, you want the lower notes to use the same clear, resonant speaking voice that has already been practiced, while the octave jump can flip into a lighter, more rounded, head voice. It can be helpful to think of this exericse as an exploration in sounds that might feel "opposite." *Courtesy of the author*

late laryngeal registration. With this exercise, you are initially not aiming for smooth, seamless transitions, but instead you are working on the ability to accurately change laryngeal registers with ease and precision. ♪

MIXING

The word *mix* can come with a lot of confusion and frustration from singers. It can feel like an elusive unicorn that everyone is in search of. Much of the confusion centers around the fact that the mechanics of mixing are not fully understood.[29] Additionally, not all voice teachers and singers agree about what a mix sounds like, nor do they agree about how you achieve the sound. Typically, mixing is a sound that does not sound like belting, nor does is sound like legit singing. It often sounds even and smooth with no discernable breaks or changes. It also tends to maintain a more speechlike pronunciation of the words.

My approach to mixing in the musical theatre world is twofold. The first aspect is the ability to change laryngeal registers seamlessly with what I like to call "shared resonance." Shared resonance is about finding similar feedback in the body between laryngeal registers. We've already explored some aspects of resonant voice in speech, so now it's time to think about this speechlike quality in head voice. Our goal here is to take the shape and articulation used in speech and transfer it to head voice. The goal is to resist the temptation to round or loft the sound into a legit, "whoop" quality.[30]

One exercise is to speak throughout the range. Talk about what you did today and allow your voice to move from the low extremes to the high extremes and everywhere in the middle. This can be a great way to explore what it feels like to use a speechlike approach in both laryngeal registers. It is important that you do not increase the laryngeal pressure or squeeze when talking in head voice. You want to maintain the neutrality of speech. It is common for people to over pressurize this sound. Try repeating the exercise in figure 7.10, but this time in head voice in a higher range. ♪

Once you can find this head voice quality, the goal becomes to move between chest voice and head voice while maintaining the same speech-like shape and articulation, which also introduces the second aspect of mixing: nuance of laryngeal registers. It is important that you can sing in chest voice without it feeling too heavy or weighted down. This requires you to be able to lighten chest voice as you ascend in pitch. This happens by allowing the vocal folds to stretch as you go higher, while maintaining enough vocal fold closure to remain in chest voice and not flip to head voice too soon (see figure 7.12). This is essential for moving, or mixing, between registers. ♪

Figure 7.12. The bottom note of this exercise should always be in chest voice, while the top note should always be in head voice. Each note as you ascend should feel as though it lightens, or thins out, while still maintaining the energy of the sound in the same spot in the body. The tendency is for the sound to either pull back or push more forward as it ascends. *Courtesy of the author*

The exercises in figures 7.13 and 7.14 continue to work laryngeal register shifts but offer the opportunity to work in a more legit, rounded quality instead of a speechlike, brighter quality, should you desire. If you remember, legit musical theatre singing is not the same as classical. There should be more chest voice used in the middle range, potentially with more speechlike qualities. The functional goals are the same here (shared resonance higher throughout the range and moving between head voice and chest voice), but the auditory target can shift into more of a legit quality. ♪

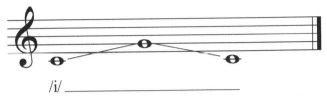

/i/ _____

Figure 7.13. The bottom note should always be chest voice and the top should always be head voice. Try sliding up and down slowly with no regard for tempo. Aiming for a consistent sensation of sound energy will help the transition smooth out. *Courtesy of the author*

/i/ - /u/ - /i/ - /u/ - /i/ - /u/ _____ /i/

Figure 7.14. The bottom note should always be in chest voice with the higher notes lightening up accordingly. *Courtesy of the author*

BELTING

If you've noticed, we have explored a lot of different sounds and skills thus far before we've gotten to belting. It should be noted that while belting is a requisite skill for musical theatre singing, it is not the only skill needed. Most of the singing that we do falls into a combination of all these categories. We rarely do just one thing in a song or show. Before we dive deeper into belting, it is important that we discuss the history and origin of this sound.

A Little History

The origin of the word *belt* to describe singing is a bit tricky to track. From the 1920s to the 1940s, *belt* was a boxing term that meant to knock someone out.[31] By the 1950s, the word had begun being used to describe a style of singing. Many people attributed the word belt to Ethel Merman and even consider her to be the epitome of belting.[32]

What is important to note is that while the word *belt* may have come into use to describe a singing style often found on Broadway stages, the sound was not born there. Humans across the globe have been "calling out" since time began, and it would only make sense that we would use those sounds in our musical communication. No one person created this sound quality that we call belting, and it was most certainly not created by White people in America on Broadway. Indigenous communities across the globe have been belting and using speechlike qualities in their music since time began. ♪

As we start to look at what we know as belting in the current musical theatre world, we cannot underestimate the importance of Black women. They belted before Broadway as we know it even existed. We can look at women like Ma Rainey, Bessie Smith, Ida Cox, and Ethel Waters, to name just a few. These women took speechlike qualities, calls, moans, and cries and imbued them with musicality and artistry. ♪

White women began co-opting this sound on the vaudeville circuit. May Irwin was considered one of the first White women to make these speechlike, call qualities on the vaudeville stage. The sound became popular, and more and more folks began to sing in this style, which led to Ethel Merman famously belting out "I Got Rhythm" in *Girl Crazy* in 1930. ♪

Taking a moment to appreciate the history of this sound is important. Belting is *not* a derivative of Western classical singing and observing it through that lens can be frustrating and confusing. As we explore belting, it is imperative that we understand that it is a natural, organic quality that *all* humans can make.

Exercises

It is important that the earlier speech exercises found in figures 7.8–7.11 are easy, clear, and consistent before working on belting. If a singer has trouble finding chest voice or can't find a resonant quality in the speech exercises, more than likely they will have trouble belting. The same goes for the ability to change registration. There will always be exceptions to this, but—generally speaking—having access to a resonant speech quality in the lower and middle range and the ability to change registration easily are prerequisites for belting.

One of the first ways to explore belting is to practice calling out or projecting your voice. Try calling out for mom, dad, your pet, your sibling, or even calling out "Stop!" to someone who might be in danger. Play with a variety of words and pitches in this projected voice. An important thing to note is that acoustically speaking, we cannot get into this call quality until we reach certain pitches. For higher voices, this call might begin around a G4 or A4, and for lower voices it might begin around an E4 or F#4. For beginners, it can be helpful to begin these exercises below these notes to ensure a connection to chest voice or the speaking voice, but know that the acoustic call quality that we expect from this sound won't kick in until these notes, approximately.

Once the call feels free and easy on a variety of phrases, try putting it on pitches (figures 7.15 and 7.16) to see if you can keep the same feeling. Many people struggle once pitches come into play, so be prepared to alternate between calling with no pitches and calling on pitch. With beginner belters, these exercises might be most successful topping out anywhere around G4–C5, or sometimes even lower. ♪

Figure 7.15. Practice calling out then try putting the call on pitches. *Courtesy of the author*

Figure 7.16. Adding in an ascending pattern can help folks who need a bit more chest connection. *Courtesy of the author*

The Variations of Belting

People sometimes think of belting as being one sound only. The reality is that there are a multitude of sounds that can fall under the umbrella of belting.[33] Most successful belters can produce a variety of sounds within the context of a belt song. This nuance is crucial to successful belting in any genre of music used in the musical theatre cannon.

There are many ways to talk about these variations, and singers will experience them all differently. A flexibility in approach and language can prove to be helpful in exploring the variations found in figure 7.17. In the figure, you'll see a few different categories where singers can play with their belt. The items on the left side of the chart tend to line up together. Subsequently, the items on the right tend to line up as well. This is not a binary, but rather a spectrum of sound that singers can play with. Let's explore each one more in depth.

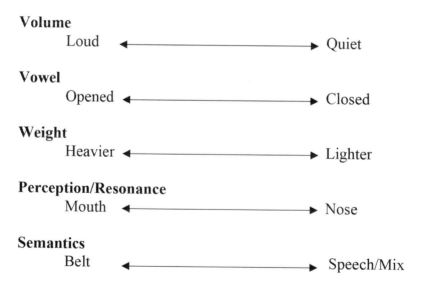

Figure 7.17. This figure shows the various ways singers might explore the variations of belting. There is no one way to explore these spectra, as all singers will experience these shifts differently. *Courtesy of the author*

Volume While belting is almost always loud contextually, it does not have to be loud to be produced functionally. This is an important distinction. Beginning belters will almost always need to be loud to find a belt quality to start, which is perfectly acceptable. As belters become more advanced, they can work on maintaining a stable volume throughout their range. The exercise in figure 7.18 is a great way to work on volume control. As you slide up, try to not let the sound get louder. Either decrescendo some or keep the loudness perceptually the same while staying connected to chest voice. ♪

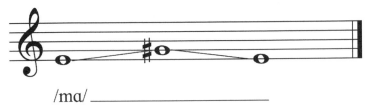

Figure 7.18. Slide higher with no specific tempo while perceptually maintaining the same volume. Many singers will notice their tendency to get louder as they ascend. *Courtesy of the author*

You can also work exercises with the specific goal of being louder and then quieter. Figure 7.19's exercise can be done at a louder volume then repeated at a quieter volume. ♪

Figure 7.19. Try doing this exercise twice in a row with the first time at forte (f) and the second at piano (p). *Courtesy of the author*

Vowel Talking about open and close vowels is a great way to explore the variations of belting. Open vowels are great when working on calling. Calls like "Mom!" in figure 7.15 or Saunders-Barton's famous

"Taxi!"[34] allow you to explore a belt sound on open vowels. These open vowels also tend to be easier for beginning belters to find the call quality that is needed for a belt sound. In fact, it is this open vowel that tends to be the deciding factor in whether a lower voice is belting or not. Lower voices have acoustical registration options in their upper range. They can choose close timbre, or they can choose a more open timbre.[35] The more open timbres align with the call on the left side of figure 7.17, while the more closed timbre aligns more with a legit musical theatre quality. Learning how to navigate these options is crucial for the lower voiced musical theatre singer.

The more closed vowels, in particular /i/ and /u/, tend to be challenging for beginning belters.[36] For higher voices, the tendency on those vowels is to flip into head voice instead of maintaining a connection to chest voice. For lower voices, the tendency to flip into head voice/falsetto is present as well. Additionally, they sometimes want to sing these vowels with a more rounded, legit shape instead of the speechlike quality needed. As belters become more skilled, you can start working on a more closed vowel belt with the exercise in 7.20. ♪

Figure 7.20. Leading with an /i/ or /u/ vowel in a speech like pattern helps singers work on a closed vowel in their belt. This closed vowel often feels more speech like or mixy, which is perfectly accetable, as long as it maintains a chest voice connection. *Courtesy of the author*

It can be helpful to have singers work through a more closed, speechlike vowel and a more open, called vowel back-to-back to help compare the difference. In the exercise in figure 7.21, "why would you do that" should feel like speech, with the first "why" taking on a more closed vowel sound. The second "why" should open to a more opened vowel call. ♪

Figure 7.21. This exercise allows you to practice moving from a speech like quality to a more call like quality. *Courtesy of the author*

For another exercise, try revisiting figure 7.18 with a slightly different intention. Try starting the exercise on /a/ and sliding up to more of an /ʌ/. This helps work on going from a more opened vowel to a more closed vowel as you ascend. ♪

You can also implement a variation on figure 7.19 by adding in an arpeggio on yep. The nope arpeggio will take on a more closed vowel quality, but the yep will almost always want to move more toward a more opened vowel. Singers should attempt to close the /ɛ/ of yep more towards the /oʌ/ of nope.[37] Learning how to close open vowels is essential for mastering the variations of belting and musical theatre singing in general. ♪

Weight The vocal folds create different types of sound waves in chest voice than in head voice, which can lead to feeling a heavier, or weightier, production when singing in chest voice.[38] Some singers are really tuned into this, so recognizing the various weights when belting can be valuable. While you can repeat figure 7.18 and ask for the weight to shift as the singer slides higher, oftentimes a weight shift is a by-product of executing 7.18 well. Recognizing that a more closed, less loud chest voice feels a bit lighter is appropriate to understand that belting is not just one weight.

Perception/Resonance When a singer is belting loudly, on an open vowel, with a heavier sound, they often feel more feedback from the sound in the mouth, hard palate, teeth, gums, or any combination of those structures. Once the belt moves to a less loud, more closed vowel, with a lighter quality, the sound often feels as though it shifts up higher into the cheeks, sinuses, nose, eyes, or any combination thereof.[39] This is also often the perception as one belts higher. None of these things are requirements for singers to feel when belting, and none of these sensations directly impact the sound quality.[40] These are simply common sensations that singers experience when belting. In figure 7.18, as the singer slides higher to a quieter, more closed vowel belt, see if they experience a change in sensation, or resonance, as the sound moves up in pitch.

One way to explore shifting perceptions is to play with various ideas and images that help singers feel these perceptual shifts. One idea is to invite the singer to imagine their face as a bookshelf (or a ladder, a staircase, etc.). Then, identify where the singer feels the sound when they are working on the speech exercise in 7.10. Label that spot as the lowest shelf (or rung, stair, etc.) and instruct them to aim each new starting note in the belt exercise in 7.15 on the next highest shelf (or rung, stair, etc.). This is just one way to play with the shifting sensations that come with the variations of belting.

Semantics We cannot talk about these variations of belting without talking about semantics. Everyone will use a different word to describe these sound qualities. For some, when the belt is more toward the right side of the chart (not as loud, on a more closed vowel, lighter, and resonating higher in the body), they may perceive the sound to be more of a mix, speech mix, or belt/mix. Some will not. Some will use the other labels on this chart to describe the sounds on the right. For instance, some will simply call it a "closed vowel belt." Others might call it a "nasal belt." Some will call it a "lighter belt." Some will say that it's a "quiet belt." And some will call it simply a "mix." Some might even have other ways of talking about these differences. Any of this language is appropriate and could resonate with a singer. The important thing to know is that not all humans will experience these variations in the same way, which is great! It makes it more fun and challenging to figure out how each individual person will perceive their belt. The most important thing is that all the sounds that fall on this chart maintain a connection to chest voice and do not flip into pure head voice. Once that happens, we move away from belting, or a speech quality, and into the sounds that are more in line with what we explored in 7.12–7.14.

The Higher Belt Range

Now this is where things get tricky. As singers ascend in pitch, the sound shifts. This happens in all types of singing. For instance, a higher voiced singer will sing an E5 differently than a B5 when singing in head voice. As the pitches ascend and the vocal folds stretch, the singer will probably use a different mouth shape, different energy and airflow, and use a different acoustic strategy, even if they are singing the same vowel in the same laryngeal register. This can make the B5 feel quite different to the singer than the E5. The same can be said for singers who ascend in pitch while belting–their strategies and perceptions change.

As a belter ascends in pitch, the vocal folds will stretch, just as they do with the higher voice we already mentioned. This means that belting a B4 will feel different than belting an F5. Belters often feel themselves move toward the right side of figure 7.17 as they belt higher. They might feel the sound lighten, the vowels close, and/or the resonance shift higher. This shift can cause quite a bit of confusion for singers and teachers alike.

The Belter Bridge

Before we discuss how to work on this higher belt range, we should discuss what I like to call "the belter bridge." This is my name for the notes that often act as a transition between the higher and lower belt ranges. These are the notes where singers tend to have the most options when it comes to belting. They can swing either to the left or to the right of figure 7.17. The world is their oyster! Once they ascend out of this area, the options become more limited. Most feel as though they must live more on the right side of figure 7.17 when they move out of the belter bridge and into the higher range. A lower voice's belter bridge might fall around A♭4–C5, and a higher voice's belter bridge might fall around B♭5–D5. These are typically the areas of the most instability when working on belting. It is important to work on maintaining a connection to chest voice in this range while working on moving the sounds toward the right of figure 7.17. What often happens when belters try to work on lighter, quieter, more closed vowels in this range, is that they often flip into head voice. This is one of the biggest struggles with mastering the belter bridge, and subsequently, the higher belt range.

Working the Higher Belt Range

One of the most confusing things about the higher belt range is understanding what it actually feels like to produce. It has been noted that successful belters tend to feel a shift as they ascend higher in their belt, but they also agree that belting is different than mixing in their higher belt range.[41] What is so challenging is that most folks do feel a distinct difference between belting lower and higher, which can sometimes even introduce a "break" in their belt. Because of this, some singers feel as though the term "mix-belt" applies to their higher belt range where they adjust strategies but remain connected to chest voice in some manner,[42] while others might use different terminology such as "high belt." The important thing to note is that successful belters can maintain a connection to chest voice throughout their belt range, despite the belt shifting higher. They can resist the "flip" into a lighter, more legit sounding head voice.[43] This is something that newer belters tend to struggle with.

This higher range can be approached a multitude of ways. You can work up into the higher belt from the lower chest voice range or work down into the higher belt from head voice. Both approaches can be valuable and should be utilized, but it is suggested that you almost always start by working up from chest voice and the speech range. This helps singers understand the connection that belting has to the speaking voice.[44] This is an incredibly important connection for singers to make, especially musical theatre singers who go in and out of speaking and singing. The exercises in 7.15 and 7.16 are great gateways into belting. Once they are comfortable up to about an G5 for lower voices and B5 for higher voices, it is a great idea to extend them higher through the bridge and beyond. Just as we did in 7.15 and 7.16, stop and practice calling it out when needed, but make sure you're calling in the higher range. It can help if you add a sense of urgency to the sound. ♪

When a singer is struggling with too much weight in their voice as they ascend into the higher belt range, there are a few ways to approach this. One is to purposefully work from head voice into the belt. Finding a pressurized, more nasal feeling head voice, like that of a witch cackle, can be used to help these heavier belters work on letting go into a lighter quality as they ascend. In this exercise, start by organically finding a witch cackle sound. Then, try the cackle on pitches, with both notes being the head dominant cackle. ♪

Once the singer can feel the resonance and pressure of the witch cackle, you can work on moving from a headier witch cackle on the top note to a chestier witch cackle on the bottom note. Be sure and keep the perception of resonance to be in the same spot between notes. There is a tendency to let the bottom note drop down in the body and not stay locked into the same resonance pocket as the higher note. ♪

With these exercises, it's important to know that this head dominant sound is not a final product belt. Ultimately, this exercise is a means to an end to help the singer feel the feeling of letting go as they ascend higher in their belt. I always let singers know that their higher belt range will ultimately connect to their chest voice more, but it will feel closer to the witch cackle than the heavier version they are attempting. If singers aren't struggling with too much weight higher, this exercise might not be necessary.

An exercise that can be particularly helpful with belting, especially the belter bridge, is a modified version of a messa di voce exercise that targets laryngeal registration. Since the singer will be moving from head voice to chest voice in the exercise, it is essentially a top-down approach to belting, despite only being one note. In this exercise, which I call the "crescendo/decrescendo exercise" with my singers, the singer will begin quietly on one note and slowly crescendo to a loud, fortissimo (*ff*) volume. Once they are there, they will slowly decrescendo back to their initial quiet volume. In the beginning, I only give them the directive to get louder and then return to a quiet sound. What might happen is that some singers get louder in head voice, but never cross over into chest voice. The goal of this exercise is to shift from head to chest, even if it's clunky with a huge break. This exercise is a great way for singers to explore laryngeal registration and gain an understanding of the energy and mechanics needed to shift between head voice and chest voice. It's important that singers know what laryngeal register they are singing in, and this exercise can help them understand this concept more clearly.

You can also think of this exercise (and belting in general) in terms of vocal fold closure. You are shifting from the vocal folds being more open (head voice) to more closed (chest voice). When there is a big break between the two laryngeal registers, it means the vocal folds don't have the coordination needed to smoothly shift from less closure to more. Our goal in this exercise is to help singers develop the coordination needed to evenly shift between these laryngeal registers, or vocal fold closures. Since the higher belt range requires the vocal folds to stretch while remaining more closed than they are in head voice, this exercise can help singers find the right closure to make a belt sound.

There is a hierarchy of things to think about in this exercise that you can implement as you get comfortable. The first is to always *find the break*. Sometimes singers intentionally avoid the laryngeal register shift because they don't like the sound of it, or they feel as though it's a bit effortful to shift. You should feel a shift in this exercise for it to be most effective.[45] Once you've found the break, it's important to *go slow* through the break. Most people can feel the break coming, so they jump the gun and cross over too quickly. Going slowly helps build the coordination from the more open vocal folds to the more closed vocal folds. The next step is to be clear about where you want to *feel the feedback* from the sound, especially once you're in the louder, more chest dominant portion of the exercise. You want to aim the sound in a resonant spot right out of the gate, and you don't want to allow it to move as you cross over to chest voice. Oftentimes singers will feel the sound and will drop down or pull back, which is what you want to avoid. The final step is to make sure that your *vowel stays as similar as possible* when you cross over into chest voice. The tendency is to shift vowels toward /æ/, which is not always helpful. This exercise is great for a singer's belt, but it also works so many other aspects of technique, that it can be beneficial in the voice studio for overall voice development. ♪

More Advanced Belting Exercises

As singers begin to gain an understanding of how to belt throughout their range, you can begin to add in more complicated patterns and exercises. The first skill is sustaining. It is one thing to be able to find a belt sound on a short note, but it is a totally different thing to be able to sustain that sound. Start working on sustaining the belt with figures 7.22–7.23. ♪

Agility in the belt is also crucial, especially for more contemporary musical genres that might ask for runs or riffs. Figures 7.24 and 7.25 target this agility. ♪

Figure 7.22. When attempting the sustained portion of this exercise, be sure and aim for the same resonance and energy of the shorter call. While sustaining, continue to keep the energy and intention moving until you finish singing. *Courtesy of the author*

Figure 7.23. Try to maintain energy and intention through the repeated notes at the beginning. Try to feel the sensation of singing through the consonants instead of restarting the sound for each new note. *Courtesy of the author*

Figure 7.24. The vowels in this exercise are very flexible and should be tailored to each singer, but be sure you are executing these runs in a chest, or speech, dominant laryngeal registration. *Courtesy of the author*

Figure 7.25. Adding in turns on a run are a great way to increase the skill level of the exercise. *Courtesy of the author*

Once singers have started to figure out their belter bridge and higher belt range, you can introduce exercises like figure 7.26 that require them to navigate through the bridge and higher range, all in one exercise. ♪

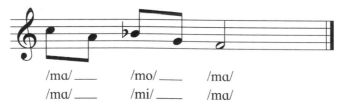

Figure 7.26. This exercise is an excellent way to work through connecting the higher belt range to the lower belt range. This exercise often feels as though it has a "break" as singers move through their higher and lower belt ranges, but that break can be smoothed out over time with exercises like this. *Courtesy of the author*

WORKING STYLE

Flexibility of style is equally important as flexibility of function. The next few exercises help work on a few stylistic elements that are common in musical theatre.

Straight Tone versus Vibrato

Vibrato is a "periodic oscillation of the fundamental frequency (perceived as pitch) and all its harmonics, amplitude (perceived as apparent intensity or volume), timbre (a result of harmonics sweeping through vowel formants), subglottic pressure, closed quotient (the percentage of each vibration cycle the vocal folds are in contact), and formant frequencies."[46] Because musical theatre uses a multitude of musical genres in its canon, learning to control vibrato is paramount in musical theatre singing. Some genres require vibrato all the time and some use next to none.

Vibrato can be produced a few ways. The first is through pulses of subglottic air pressure controlled through the abdominal muscles.[47] This type of vibrato is under voluntary control of the singer, but not typically encouraged. Over-contraction of the abdominal muscles comes with other consequences vocally, so it is encouraged to move away from this abdominal controlled vibrato.[48] One could also create vibrato by actively wobbling the laryngeal structures, including the tongue. This is not common but does happen. This type of vibrato is also not encouraged because of the excess tension it can cause in the larynx and tongue.

The final way vibrato is created is the most desired. This organic vibrato is controlled by the larynx. The modulation of fundamental frequency happens because of a contraction between two antagonistic laryngeal muscles. Vibrato appears when the structures of the larynx are in balance with the breath system.[49] Vibrato requires a mature laryngeal and neuromuscular system to work. This maturity explains why younger singers and more beginner singers may not experience vibrato in their singing.

Working on the ability to utilize vibrato and straight tone in singing can feel like a challenge for some singers. I find that resonance and its sympathetic vibrations play a big role in learning to navigate between straight tone and vibrato. It is also easier to work on these exercises once a more natural vibrato has begun to emerge, although they can be attempted by anyone.

When a singer operates in a vibrato mode most of the time, one of the easiest ways to get them to experience straight tone is through speech. Try having them say "hey!" in their chest voice or speaking range. This will automatically be straight tone with no vibrato. Have them extend the "hey!" even longer and notice the energy required to sustain the tone with no vibrato. You can repeat this exercise in head voice as well but remember to use a speechlike quality and to do it in the speaking range first.

The energy that most people feel when sustaining the "hey!" in a speechlike manner will likely feel a bit different than what they are used to when sustaining vibrato. Sometimes the idea of a laser beam is helpful. A laser is a straight line of focused energy. There is no vibrato, or movement, in a laser. This visual is often helpful for singers when they are attempting to sustain a sung pitch.[50] I like to revisit a simple exercise like 7.2–7.3, but with the intention of straight tone throughout, especially the last note. ♪

Once a singer can use straight tone throughout the previous exercises, they can begin working on releasing into vibrato. Repeat exercises 7.2–

7.3, but this time the last note should be straight tone for a few beats and then the singer can release into vibrato. When they do so, it is helpful if they attempt to keep the sympathetic vibrations the same. Often when vibrato kicks in there is a drop or some sort of shift in where the singer feels the energy of the sound. Attempting to keep the sympathetic vibrations the same can yield a more stable vibrato. This can be arduous for some singers who struggle to find a release into vibrato. The release from straight tone takes time for singers to experience as they continue to coordinate the balance between the laryngeal structures and breathing mechanism. ♪

Blues Scales

Working outside of the diatonic scale is valuable in the musical theatre voice studio. Musical theatre uses a multitude of musical genres, many of which utilize non-diatonic scales. Any of the previous exercises could be adapted to utilize a non-diatonic scale, especially those that are scalar. Using a five-note blues scale (figure 7.27) as a run is a great way to exercise non-diatonic agility. ♪

Figure 7.27. Using a blues scale is a great way for singers to practice moving through a scale that is non-diatonic. *Courtesy of the author*

Riff Exercise

Riffing is a form of improvising on a melody. It can be as simple as changing one note in a melody line, or as complicated as improvising a new melody, including embellished runs. Figures 7.24–7.25 are a great lead into improvisational runs. Riffing can be daunting for some singers, but there are ways to work on riffing, especially runs. There are two major components to improvisational runs. The first is vocal. The voice must be agile and have the ability to move quickly. Working runs on any type of scale is a great way to work on the needed agility. Exercises 7.7, 7.24, 7.25, and 7.27 are a great place to start. Once those exercises feel solid, try the belt exercise in figure 7.28. ♪

Figure 7.28. This exercise allows you to practice sustaining a note and then moving quickly down the scale as if it were a quick run. *Courtesy of the author*

The second component to riffing is musical. You must be able to hear an alteration to the melody within the chord structure of the song. This musical skill can be developed. One way to do this is to play a chord on the piano and then sing a scale with a variety of improvised rhythms. ♪

Once this feels easy, you can then play a chord and create your own improvised melody within the chord. You can always give yourself parameters such as improvising a descending run on an /u/ vowel. The parameters can get more and more challenging, such as beginning with a descend on an /u/, but then moving up and end on a yeah. You can also work with no parameters. ♪

Onsets and Phonation

We use a variety of onsets in musical theatre. The actor playing Orpheus in *Hadestown* might find breathy onsets and phonation to be valuable when singing "Epic I." The actor playing Tracy in *Hairspray* would have a hard time singing "Good Morning Baltimore" without glottals. Having the ability to use different types of onsets helps with flexibility of style within musical genres.

Onset is all about coordination of vocal fold closure and breath. A simple exercise such as what is noted in figure 7.29 can be helpful for exploring this coordination. Try adding an /h/ in before the vowel to explore leading the onset with breath to feel a breathy, or aspirate onset.

Try timing the breath with the onset to have a balanced onset. To work on a glottal onset that feels in control and consistent, take a moment to inhale as if you were going to say something, but then you stop at the last second before speaking. You should feel your vocal folds close without making sound. Try the exercise in figure 7.29 coming from this place of gentle vocal fold closure. Exploring these onsets will help you dive into various genres more genuinely. ♪

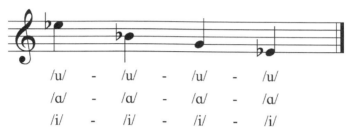

Figure 7.29. This exercise can be used to work on clean, breathy, or glottal onsets. Be sure each note gets its own onset. It's important that musical theatre singers know how to use all onset options effectively. *Courtesy of the author*

An alternative to this exercise is shown in figure 7.30, an easy staccato on an arpeggio. You can choose an /u/ vowel, or even a neutral, hooty vowel that comes when your tongue is out of your mouth.[51] ♪

Figure 7.30. When the tongue is out, this exercise can help with onset as well as a general feeling of pharyngeal release. *Courtesy of the author*

Cries, Whines, and Twang, Oh My!

Adding a cry, whine, or what some might call twang, into your singing is helpful for many genres of music found in musicals. The word twang is controversial in some circles, so some might refer to this sound quality as a whine or cry.[52] With this sound quality, the singer is narrowing the epilarynx, or space just above the vocal folds, which increases the ring in the acoustic output. This ring can help add a brightness and edge to the sound that is appropriate in some music. One way to find this sound quality is to repeat figure 7.15, but this time add in a whine, like a bratty kid who is really annoyed. In fact, alternate between a call and a cry in figure 7.15 to feel the difference between the two sounds. ♪

SEMI-OCCLUDED VOCAL TRACT POSITIONS

No chapter on musical theatre pedagogy would be complete without a discussion on semi-occluded vocal tract, or SOVT, positions. SOVT positions are a sophisticated way of saying that the vocal tract is partially closed off, or semi-occluded. This occlusion most commonly happens by partially closing the mouth off in some way. When you do this, you increase the back pressure in the vocal tract, which leads to a change in how the vocal folds vibrate. There are three main changes that happen with the vocal folds—the vocal folds use a lower phonation threshold pressure, the vibrational amplitude and collision force of the vocal folds reduces allowing more efficient vibration, and there is an acoustic boost due to the vocal tract inertance being amplified.[53] SOVT positions also lead to a perceptual change in the voice, with most singers feeling more ease and efficiency.[54]

We've already included some SOVT positions in this chapter when we discussed beginning your vocal exercises with lip trills, raspberries, or a straw in water. All of these are SOVT positions that can be used on just about any exercise in this book. To implement SOVT work into your singing, it is helpful to understand the variety of SOVT options and their potential impacts.

Each semi-occlusion creates a different amount of back pressure in the vocal tract. Using a small, 3–4 mm diameter straw, like those used as a coffee or cocktail stirrer, create a high level of back pressure. This is beneficial when you are looking for a large change in the vocal folds. I find the small straw especially helpful in figures 7.2–7.7 in higher voices. It can help a singer find head voice in the middle and upper range if they are over pressurizing or utilizing too much vocal fold closure. Additionally, it can also help achieve better vocal fold closure when the sound is breathy. In lower voices, the small straw (figure 7.31) can be helpful when working on head voice, or falsetto, but might not be as effective in their chest voice range.[55] A normal-sized, straw of 6 mm in diameter (figure 7.32), however, can be incredibly beneficial for lower voices. The resistance from the normal drinking straw is less than that from the smaller, coffee stirrer straw, which better aligns with the subglottic pressure created in the lower-voiced larynx.[56] The same can be said for higher voices when working on their chest-voice range. The small straw might not be exactly right, but the larger straw might work perfectly to help find more efficient vocal fold closure in their chest voice.

Figure 7.31. The singer is singing into a small straw. Notice the complete closure around the lips. The sound should only be coming out the straw, with no sound leaking out the nose. *Courtesy of the author*

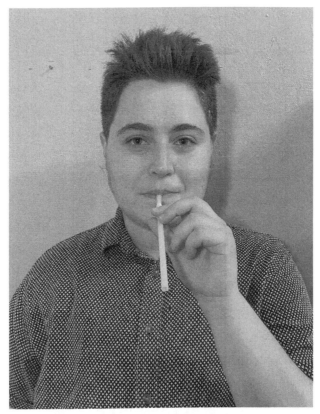

Figure 7.32. The regular sized straw can be used throughout the entire range. *Courtesy of the author*

The 6 mm straw can also be used in water, as can larger straws or small tubes. Place the straw about one–two inches in the water and blow bubbles while singing. The water creates more resistance than using the straw alone and can feel particularly therapeutic. It is also a great way to visualize the airflow used when singing. Blowing bubbles can be particularly effective for singers who need to work on a steady use of airflow. When working with musical theatre performers who are in a show, I recommend that they keep a straw in their water bottle off stage. This allows them to blow bubbles on breaks between songs, which helps them fight fatigue.

Cups and manual occlusions provide less occlusion than straw work, but they allow for tongue and/or lip movement. A paper, Styrofoam, or plastic cup with a small hole cut in the bottom provides a semi-occlusion while allowing for articulation (figure 7.33). Closing the mouth off with the palm or back of the hand (figure 7.34) and humming with the nares open is another semi-occlusion. One might call it a manual occlusion. This exercise is similar to the "open-mouthed hum" used by voice pedagogue Berton Coffin. This position allows for vowel movement behind the hand.[57] Both the cup and manual occlusion can be beneficial as a stepping-stone from the straw to the words on the song or exercise.

Bilabial and labiodental fricatives, such as /f/, /v/, and /θ/, come next in the list of SOVT positions. These fricatives can be used in almost any exercise to help find the benefits of SOVT work. Adding a /v/ or similar into a simple exercise can help the singer feel more ease in their

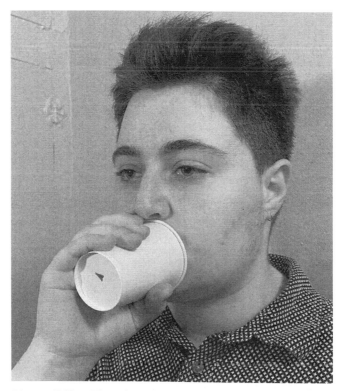

Figure 7.33. The singer is creating a seal around the mouth with the cup that has a small hole in the bottom. This allows articulation while singing or speaking, which still receiving the benefits of SOVT work. *Courtesy of the author*

Figure 7.34. The singer is closing off their mouth with the back of their hand to help increase the back pressure. It can be helpful to feel buzziness, or sound energy, where the lips meet than hand. *Courtesy of the author*

singing. Likewise, lip trills and raspberries are SOVT positions that can be utilized in almost any exercise to feel more efficiency. Lip trills and raspberries also provide an element of airflow that is beneficial to many singers.

Nasal consonants, such as /n/, /ŋ/, or /m/, come next in this hierarchy of SOVT positions.[58] They provide some back pressure, while often increasing the sympathetic vibrations or feedback that the singer feels. This feedback can prove to be valuable in learning to control one's voice, which is why nasal consonants are a favorite of many singers and teachers.

The least occluded position is vowels. More closed vowels like /u/ and /i/ provide some occlusion, which is why they tend to be efficient vowels for working in the middle range. More opened vowels like /a/ provide little to no back pressure, often making it a more challenging vowel in the middle range.

SOVT positions can be utilized in any exercise in this book. It often takes a bit of trial and error to find the position that works best for each singer in each part of their voice. While suggestions have been made in how to utilize them in the studio, everyone will benefit from something a little different. Flexibility is key in finding the right position for you.

FINAL THOUGHTS

Musical theatre singing requires a flexible voice across many parameters. This chapter has provided some insights into how you might work this flexibility in the voice studio. It's important to remember that there are no magic exercises out there. Always set a specific goal for each exercise you partake in to achieve maximum benefits. My hope is that the exercises in this book are a starting point for you to create your own exercises that help work the vocal functions needed in musical theatre.

NOTES

1. Norman Spivey and Mary Saunders-Barton, *Cross-Training in the Voice Studio* (San Diego, CA: Plural, 2018), 28.

2. Mary J. Sandage and Matthew Hoch, "Working toward a Common Vocabulary: Reconciling the Terminology of Teachers of Singing, Voice Scientists, and Speech-Language Pathologists," *Journal of Voice* 31, no. 6 (2017): 647.

3. Robert Edwin, "A Broader Broadway," *Journal of Singing*, 55, no. 5 (2003): 431–32.

4. Scott McCoy, *Your Voice: An Inside View* (Columbus, OH: Inside View Press, 2019), 229.

5. Kari Ragan, *A Systematic Approach to Voice: The Art of Studio Application* (San Diego, CA: Plural, 2020), 116.

6. Kenneth Bozeman, *Practical Vocal Acoustics: Pedagogic Applications for Teachers and Singers* (Sheffield, MA: Pendragon, 2013), 6.

7. Sandage and Hoch, "Working toward a Common Vocabulary," 648.

8. Karen Ann Kochis-Jennings, Eileen M. Finnegan, Henry T. Hoffman, Sanyukta Jaiswal, "Laryngeal Muscle Activity and Vocal Fold Adduction during Chest, Chestmix, Headmix, and Head Registers in Females," *Journal of Voice* 26, no. 2 (2012): 182–93.

9. Sandage and Hoch, "Working toward a Common Vocabulary," 648.

10. Ragan, *A Systematic Approach*, 122.

11. Bozeman, *Practical Vocal Acoustics*, 15.

12. Bozeman, *Practical Vocal Acoustics*, 147.

13. Spivey and Saunders-Barton, *Cross-Training*, 48.

14. This is an oversimplification of these acoustic registers. For a more in depth understanding of the acoustic underpinnings of these timbres, please refer to Kenneth Bozeman's work.

15. Please visit https://en.wikipedia.org/wiki/IPA_vowel_chart_with_audio for a complete vowel chart including audio samples.

16. This range can shift with individual voices. E4–E5 is an approximation but know that this might be lower or higher in certain voices.

17. Joshua Henry played Aaron Burr in *Hamilton*, which has an R&B/pop style, and then played Billy Bigelow in *Carousel*, which is legit material from the golden age. Likewise, Jessie Mueller played Jenna in *Waitress*, which has an indie/alt/pop style, and then played Julie Jordan, opposite Henry, in the legit-sounding *Carousel*.

18. This is assuming there has been no injury or is no abnormality present in the larynx.

19. Timothy D. Anderson, Dawn D. Anderson, and Robert Thayer Sataloff, "Endocrine Function," in *Vocal Health and Pedagogy: Science, Assessment, and Treatment*, ed. R. T. Sataloff, (San Diego, CA: Plural, 2017), 377–80.

20. Liz Jackson Hearns and Brian Kremer, *The Singing Teacher's Guide to Transgender Voices*, (San Diego, CA: Plural, 2018), 90.

21. Anderson, Anderson, and Sataloff, "Endocrine Function," 379.

22. Hearns and Kremer, *Transgender Voices*, 98.

23. It should be noted that there are other reasons folks might be on hormone therapy besides gender affirming therapies. Estrogen or testosterone are sometimes used in menopausal therapies, aging therapies, fertility treatments, or other conditions.

24. See Spivey and Saunders-Barton, *Cross-Training*, for their approach to gender neutral training.

25. Robert Edwin, "Culture vs. Science and Voice Pedagogy," *Journal of Singing*, 77, no. 1 (2020): 81–83.

26. A special thanks to Sandy Sahar Gooen for his valuable feedback on this section.

27. John Nix, "Closing Your Mouth to 'Open' Your Sound," *Journal of Singing* 73, no. 1 (2016): 35–41.

28. Katherine Verdolini, David G. Druker, Phyllis M. Palmer, and Hani Samawi, "Laryngeal Adduction in Resonant Voice, *Journal of Voice* 12, no. 3 (1998): 315–27.

29. Into Titze, "Mixed Registration," *Journal of Singing* 75, no. 1 (2018): 49–50.

30. We are essentially resisting the urge to go into a whoop timbre and trying to maintain more of an open timbre, but in head voice. This increases the auditory roughness, which makes head voice sound more like speech.

31. *Historical Dictionary of American Slang*, vol. 1 (New York: Penguin Random House). s.v. "belt out."

32. Troy Dargin, "Compared with Ethel: Analyzing the Singing Styles of Reba McEntyre and Bernadette Peters with Ethel Merman in *Annie Get Your Gun*," *Voice and Speech Review* 11, no. 3 (2017): 296–307.

33. Lisa Popeil, "The Multiplicity of Belting," *Journal of Singing* 64, no. 1 (2007), 77–80.

34. Spivey and Saunders-Barton, *Cross-Training*, 133.

35. For a more detailed exploration of these acoustical registers, please see the work of Kenneth Bozeman.

36. Know that there will always be exceptions to this. I once had a singer who could only access her belt on an /u/ vowel. Go figure! Just know that that is the exception to the rule.

37. Singers tend to end up somewhere around /ʌ/, although there is individuality in where each singer might head when attempting to close and open vowel.

38. McCoy, *Your Voice*, 235.

39. This idea is what Bozeman calls The Epsilon Image and The Capital C Image. See Kenneth Bozeman, *Kinesthetic Voice Pedagogy 2* (Columbus, OH: Inside View Press, 2018), 60–61.

40. For more of an understanding of how the sensations singers feel impact the actual sound, please refer to McCoy, *Your Voice*, 48–50, where he discusses free and forced resonance.

41. Amanda Flynn, Jared Trudeau, and Aaron M. Johnson, "Acoustic Comparison of Lower and Higher Belt Ranges in Professional Broadway Actresses," *Journal of Voice*, 34, no. 3 (2020): P410–P414.

42. Christianne Roll, "The Female Broadway Belt Voice: The Singer's Perspective," *Journal of Singing* 76, no. 2 (2019): 155–62.

43. Roll, "Female Broadway Belt," 155–62.

44. Norman Spivey, "Music Theater Singing . . . Let's Talk, Part 1: On the Relationship of Speech and Singing," *Journal of Singing*, 64, no. 4 (2008),

483–89; "Music Theater Singing . . . Let's Talk, Part 2: Examining the Debate on Belting," *Journal of Singing* 64, no. 5 (2008): 607–14; Roll, "Female Broadway Belt," P639.E1–P639-E1.

45. Note that some singers can do this exercise flawlessly where you hear no discernable shift. The goal is to shift no matter what, but we don't always hear that shift happen and that's OK!

46. John Nix, "Shaken, Not Stirred: Practical Ideas for Addressing Vibrato and Nonvibrato Singing in the Studio and the Choral Rehearsal," *Journal of Singing* 70, no. 4 (2014): 411.

47. Nix, "Shaken Not Stirred," 412.

48. The upcoming chapter on the musical theatre athlete will address this in more depth.

49. Nix, "Shaken not Stirred," 412.

50. The most important thing with any visualization is that it connects to the singer. If the idea of a laser is not helpful, the singer should identify their own visual or metaphor for what they experience when using straight tone. This goes for all visuals in singing, not just straight tone. What the singer experiences is far more valuable than anything a teacher might suggest.

51. Thank you to Dr. Jeanne Goffi-Fynn for introducing me to this exercise.

52. For many folks, twang refers to an accent that is used in many parts of the United States, not necessarily a narrowing of the epilarynx. For this reason, many people avoid the word in singing training. Likewise, for some, a cry requires a low larynx with no narrowing of the epilarynx, which would make it different than twang. There is not one word that will suit all when it comes to this sound quality!

53. Ragan, *Systematic Approach*, 75–76.

54. Lynn Maxfield, Ingo Titze, Eric Hunter, and Mara Kapsner-Smith, "Intraoral Pressures Produced by Thirteen Semi-Occluded Vocal Tract Gestures," *Logopedics Phoniatrics Vocology* 40, no. 2 (2014): 86–92.

55. Maxfield et al., "Intraoral Pressures."

56. Maxfield et al., "Intraoral Pressures."

57. Berton Coffin, *The Mechanism and the Technic* (New York: Carl Fisher, 1967), 216.

58. Ingo Titze, "Voice Training and Therapy with a Semi-Occluded Vocal Tract: Rationale and Scientific Underpinnings," *Journal of Speech, Language, and Hearing Research* 49, no. 2. (2006): 448–59.

8

MUSICAL THEATRE DEVELOPMENTAL REPERTOIRE

Musical theatre is an artform that is constantly evolving, which means that the repertoire is also ever changing. As was evident in the previous chapter, new genres of music are appearing in musicals every year, and writers are getting more and more creative in how they tell stories. Additionally, the vocal demands of musical theatre are intensifying, with singers being asked to belt higher and skillfully navigate between a multitude of musical and vocal styles.[1] This variety can make selecting repertoire challenging. How can we decipher between a beginning belt song and an intermediate belt song? How do we select material that will help build vocal skills for ourselves or our students? This chapter will focus on how to select musical theatre repertoire with developmental concerns in mind.[2]

PEDAGOGICAL CONCERNS

When selecting material for yourself or your students, it's helpful to recognize what aspects of a song can make them more or less challenging. These considerations are important for all song assignments, whether they will be heard outside of a voice lesson or not. Voice teacher John Nix said it beautifully: "Few singers can overcome the difficulties caused by repertoire that is not suited for their voice."³ He goes on to say that as teachers, we can even "hamper" or "tear down" the technique that we have so carefully built during exercises by assigning inappropriate repertoire.⁴ Songs can be challenging dramatically, functionally, musically, or stylistically, and many songs are challenging in more than one category. Let's look at what this might mean when selecting musical theatre repertoire.

Dramatic Concerns

Context of the Song The first thing to note when selecting repertoire is the context. Is the song being used only in the voice studio to help achieve technical goals, or is it going to be used in an audition or performance setting? Not all songs that work for skill acquisition work well for auditions or performances, and vice versa. It's important to note the context when deciding on repertoire because that will inform your material selection.

Dramatic Content Some songs in the musical theatre canon come with challenging acting objectives. It is important to note whether the dramatic demands of the song will help the singer with their vocal goals, or if the dramatic demands will hinder the singer. For instance, "Daddy's Son" from *Ragtime* comes with mature acting objectives that not all singers will be prepared to tackle. A singer might fare better with communicating challenging acting objectives when they are well-coordinated vocally.

Lyrical Content Lyrical content is important when selecting repertoire. Ideally, lyrics should be age appropriate, especially if you're working with a young singer. Oftentimes musicals have characters that are teenagers but are played by adult actors. Sometimes these songs might have lyrics that are appropriate for an adult playing a teen but might not be appropriate for all teens to sing. For instance, a song like "Dead Girl Walking" from *Heathers* might be a favorite among teenagers, but the mature lyrical content might not be appropriate for all teens. It's also important to look at the pronouns used in a song and make sure that the singer is comfortable with them. Oftentimes pronouns can be altered without changing the intention of the song, but sometimes songs feel gendered beyond just the pronouns as is the case with "How Lovely to Be a Woman" from *Bye*

Bye Birdie and "Man" from *The Full Monty*. Lastly, it is helpful if the singer has a personal connection to the lyrics. This makes working on the song more enjoyable, even if it's just for the voice studio.

Racial and Ethnic Identity Is the singer's race and/or ethnicity sensitive to the song they have chosen to sing? If a song was written for a character with a specific race or ethnicity, a singer should bring great thought and care into deciding whether it is appropriate for them to sing this song. Furthermore, it is not appropriate for a White singer to sing a song written for characters who are Black, Indigenous, or other people of color. For every song that was written for a character that is a person of color, there are hundreds that were written for White singers, or singers of no specific racial or ethnic identity that do similar things vocally. For instance, "Breathe" from *In the Heights* is written for a Latina character and is best suited to be sung by singers who identify in that way. Instead of assigning this song to a White singer, consider other songs like "Anywhere but Here" from *Honeymoon in Vegas*, "My Grand Plan" from *The Lightning Thief*, or "One Perfect Moment" from *Bring It On*. These are three suggestions that are appropriate for singers of any racial and/or ethnic identity that all have a similar dramatic and vocal objective. When determining whether a character's race or ethnicity is aligned with how a singer identifies, it is important to make your decisions based on how the character is written, as opposed to basing your decision on the actors who have historically played the role in the past. For example, there are numerous characters in the golden age canon of musical theatre that have been historically played by White actors, but many of the roles were written without an assigned race or ethnicity and therefore any actor should be able to sing the material.

Gender Expression and Identity Just as songs can be written for singers of specific racial and/or ethnic identities, the same can be said for gender. If a song is written for a trans or non-binary character, it is important that a cisgender singer not sing the song. For instance, the role of Pythio in the musical *Head over Heels* is a nonbinary character, and their songs, in show context, should be sung by singers who identify that way. Songs written in the binary are occasionally gender swapped, which is a somewhat standard practice. For instance, in 2018, the Oregon Shakespeare Festival produced *Oklahoma!* with a female Curly and a male Ado Annie.[5]

Functional Concerns

Range Always look at the range of the song. How high and low does it go? Can you, or your student, comfortably hit the notes in the song? When singers are just starting out, or when they are working on a new skill, a smaller range will be beneficial. Singing songs that extend past your comfortable range is not the most effective way to work on range extension.

Tessitura Sometimes tessitura is even more important than range. Tessitura refers to where the majority of the notes of the melody sit on the staff. Songs that spend too much time in areas of the voice that are less stable will have an increased difficulty level. An example of this might be a song where most of the notes sit right in the passaggio, or break. This can make songs feel extremely challenging and often elicit frustration, especially when the song is lower than other songs that you, or your student, might sing easily.

When comparing two advanced musical theatre songs, "Michael in the Bathroom" and "Waving through a Window," you'll notice that range and tessitura play a huge role in making these songs challenging for different reasons. "Waving through a Window" has a range of A3 to B♭5, while "Michael in the Bathroom" has a range of B3 to A4. "Waving through a Window" has a wider range between the two songs. However, "Michael in the Bathroom" has over sixty notes in the A♭4 to A4 range, while "Waving through a Window" has around twenty notes in the A♭4 to B♭4 range. Although "Michael in the Bathroom" does not go as high at "Waving through a Window," the tessitura clearly makes it just as, if not more, challenging of a song.

Melodic Pattern Just as with vocal exercises, songs that have descending melodic patterns will typically be easier to navigate. This is especially true for singers who are still coordinating their middle range. This does not mean you should avoid songs with ascending melodies. What it does mean is that you should make sure you, or your student, are coordinated enough before tackling a challenging ascending line. It's also helpful to identify if the song uses a predominately scalar pattern or if there are mostly intervals in the melody. Larger, more challenging intervals require a certain amount of coordination, so you want to make sure one is coordinated enough before working on that type of repertoire.

Tempo How fast or slow the song goes plays a role in how challenging it will be. Songs that are slower require sustained breath control, and a sense of legato line. Songs that are fast require a different understanding of breath control, and a fluency in agility. Make sure the coordination for various tempi are in place before working on this type of material. If those are skills that you, or your student, do not have coordinated yet, you want to avoid songs that are written with extreme tempi.

Dynamics Just as with tempo, dynamic extremes can be challenging. For singers who are working on coordination, look for songs with middle-of-the-road dynamics, such as mezzo forte (*mf*) or mezzo piano (*mp*), or make a point to purposefully ignore the dynamics and focus on a comfortable level of loudness. Dynamics such as fortississimo (*fff*) or pianississimo (*ppp*) require skilled coordination, so you want to make sure that is in place before tackling those dynamics in a song.

Breaths It can be helpful to identify how frequently a singer can breathe in a song. Do they get to breathe every two to four measures, or does the song require longer breaths? Are you, or your student, coordinated enough to make it through the phrases without needing a breath? In addition to how often a singer gets to breathe, it's helpful to look at what type of breaths are allowed in the song. Are there short catch breaths, or is there adequate time to breath between phrases? Any singer in the process of coordinating their breath system will benefit from taking breaths every two to four measures, with adequate time for each inhale.

Length of Song Long songs require stamina, and so younger singers and singers who are working on coordination will benefit from shorter songs. You may also choose to work on a section of a longer song that feels more manageable. This is particularly pertinent for kids who want to sing songs written for adults. Children do not have the stamina that adults have, so looking for shorter songs or working with cuts with this demographic can be helpful.[6]

Word-to-Note Ratio It can be challenging for younger and less coordinated singers to sing multiple notes on one vowel, especially singers who are working on their tuning ability. These singers tend to have better tuning and note accuracy when each note lines up with a word or syllable.

Registration Requirements Musical theatre singing requires flexibility of registration, so it's helpful to identify if you or your student can handle the registration requirements of the song. For instance, much of Frankie Valli's music in *Jersey Boys* requires a mastery of head voice/falsetto, just as most of Elphaba's music in *Wicked* requires a mastery of belting. It is important to understand the registration requirements of the song and have the skill set to tackle them. Ultimately, there is no shortage of musical theatre songs, so assigning a belt song and allowing it to be sung in head voice, or a legit manner, might cause confusion. Instead, find a legit song that allows you to flourish in the style you are comfortable in.

Vowel Location Where vowels sit on the staff plays a major role in how challenging the song will be. The first step is identifying what the desired sound is for the song. Is it a belt song? Legit? That will determine which vowels will be helpful and which vowels will be challenging. For instance, /i/ and /u/ vowels tend to be harder to belt, so a song like "No Good Deed" from *Wicked* or "Good for You" from *Dear Evan Hanson* tend to be more challenging because of the vowels. Songs like "Shy" from *Once Upon a Mattress* or "I'm Alive" from *Next to Normal* have vowels that typically lend themselves to belting more easily. Musical theatre singers must learn how to belt all vowels but starting the learning process with helpful vowels will typically be easier.

Musical Concerns

Musical Ability The musical requirements of a song play a role in how challenging it will be. It can be helpful to look at the chromatic movements of the melody, the musical mode, and time signatures. You want to make sure that you or your student have the musical skills to adequately tackle the song. It will be hard to tackle vocal function and technique if the singer is constantly fixated on the notes, rhythms, or complex meter shifts.

Accompaniment Accompaniments can change from edition to edition. Vocal selections also often have a different arrangement than the piano/conductor score. Be sure and observe the accompaniment when selecting a song. Does the accompaniment play along with the melody line? Does the accompaniment contradict the melody line? Are there moments of the singer being on their own with no accompaniment? Just as with musical ability, you want to make sure you or your student have the musical skills and singing experience to work with the accompaniment in the song.

Stylistic Concerns

Style Requirements Does the song have a style requirement that you or your student are ready to execute? "You Oughta Know" from *Jagged Little Pill* asks for a rock sound, which might include growls, screams, glottals, and other stylistic elements. Likewise, "Will He Like Me?" from *She Loves Me* requires a more legit style, which might include rounded vowels, vibrato, and clean onsets. Making sure you or your student is ready to execute the style requirements for the song is an important consideration.

Silent Obligation Singers often give themselves silent obligations. They may think that they must sound a certain way, or that they have to copy the riffs and style choices of the original artist. Sometimes they think this subconsciously without realizing it. Singers compare themselves to others and come up with ideas about what they are "supposed" to sound like. It's helpful for singers and singing teachers to remember this when selecting repertoire. Sometimes it's beneficial to select repertoire that is either new and does not have a cast recording or is old and has so many recordings that there is no one definitive version. It is important to listen to professional singers to learn style, and mimicking can be a helpful way to explore sound. But, we must make sure every singer sets realistic goals about their sound and does not get lost in trying to copy someone else.

SELECTING REPERTOIRE

As already mentioned, the context of the song is important. Songs that work well developmentally sometimes don't work in auditions, and vice versa. Let's dive a bit more into picking songs for vocal development. Below are some questions you can ask yourself as you're picking repertoire for yourself or your students.

What Is the Singer Good at Right Now?

Before picking material, it is always valuable to assess the singers' strengths. Are they a great belter? Is their legit voice amazing? Are they successful on the /a/ vowel? This will help you understand what a song might need in order to be successful.

What Is the Singer Struggling with Right Now?

It's equally valuable to assess what the current vocal struggles are. Is the /i/ vowel a challenge? Is the middle range uncoordinated? Is there a struggle with dynamic control? These specific struggles will help you understand what types of songs might present challenges.

What Does the Singer Need from a Song Right Now?

Life is a journey, and it's important that we recognize where we, or our students, are mentally, emotionally, and spiritually when assigning repertoire. If you, or a student, is struggling, a "vocal win" might be what they need. Selecting a more manageable song might help boost confidence and increase motivation. Sometimes people are already feeling inspired and up for a challenge, so a harder song might be more appropriate.

What about This Song Will Help the Singer Achieve Their Goals?

What goals do you have for yourself, or your student, right now? Goals should always be written down with a plan formulated for how to achieve them.[7] The act of writing makes them feel more tangible and attainable to the singer. Refer to that list when looking for a new song. Repertoire, in conjunction with exercises, can be used to achieve vocal goals and acquire new vocal skills. If the goal has been to successfully belt a C5, then once a C5 is successful in exercises, it's time to try it out on a piece of repertoire. Goals provide tangible markers in the studio as well as guidelines for selecting repertoire.

What about This Song Will Get the Singer to the Next Level?

Repertoire can be valuable in helping singers get to the next level of vocal achievement. When picking songs, look for songs that introduce something new or slightly more challenging than past songs. For instance, a song that has a half step higher top note than your previous song, or a song that introduces a more challenging vowel, or a more sustained note. This is a way to keep progress happening on all fronts while goals are being tackled.

What Vocal Assignments Could Come Along with This Song?

Specific vocal assignments are incredibly valuable when assigning a song. Allowing your student, or yourself, to freely interpret a song within the confines of an assignment can be helpful. For instance, you may decide that a certain phrase should be belted because that is the skill you are working on. This doesn't mean that the phrase must stay that way forever, especially if the singer has a different interpretation for performance, but setting this parameter can be helpful when working on the new skill.

STUDENT-SELECTED REPERTOIRE

Some voice teachers are reluctant to allow their students to select their own repertoire for voice lessons. Allowing singers a say in their repertoire is important. Singers should be able to select material that they connect with or feel represented by, even when working solely on skill acquisition in the studio. Many teachers are nervous about this for fear that a singer will bring in material that is ill suited for their voice, or that they will bring in material that they themselves are unfamiliar with. However, student-selected repertoire can be an eye-opening experience that is rewarding for both the student and teacher. Consider the following when implementing student-selected repertoire in the studio.

Be Clear with Assignments and Goals

When assigning songs in the studio, be clear about the goals and assignments of the song. This specificity allows the singer to understand the goals of repertoire more thoroughly. They begin to see how repertoire helps them achieve their goals, as well as understand what can make songs challenging. When you ask a singer to bring in something on their own, consider setting similar technical parameters for them to consider. For instance, ask them to find a song that belts an A4, sustains an /i/ vowel, or has a more legato line. This makes the singer think about the repertoire more specifically, all while being able to choose their own song.

Present Options

Presenting singers with a list of songs and allowing them to make one selection is a great way for singers to have more of a say in their repertoire. This list allows the teacher to curate songs that help fulfill goals, but still gives an element of choice for the singer. Conversely, the singer can prepare a list of potential songs they'd like to work on, and the teacher can pick the song that is most in line with their goals and current skill level.

Alternating Selections

Getting into a routine of alternating repertoire between a student-selected piece and a teacher-selected piece is a great way to keep the repertoire selections balanced. Alternating can be helpful when a singer brings in a song that is more challenging that might need some time to tackle. This can also be a great way to keep students motivated in lessons. Sometimes singers are more committed to working on the teacher-selected song when they know they get to move to their own selection next.

Adapting

If a student does bring in a song that is beyond their current skill set, consider adapting the song as needed for the studio. This could include working only on a small selection of the song, changing the key of the song, altering the melody of the song to exclude notes that might be challenging, and any other adjustments that help make the song manageable. It is important to note that some of these adjustments would be inappropriate for performance or audition settings but would work well in the studio for skill acquisition.

SONGS FOR SKILL BUILDING

Below you will see the ideas already mentioned in action. The repertoire listed below is organized with vocal function in mind. You'll see a skill set listed and organized into the categories of beginner, intermediate, and advanced, with the occasional advanced beginner category. These skill levels should be thought of as existing on a spectrum. This spectrum means that there will still be variability of difficulty within one skill level category. Also, there is substantial fluctuation in repertoire on an individual voice. A song that might be easy to one singer, could be challenging to another. These categories are *subjective in nature* and will vary from singer to singer. The idea here is to give you a lens with which to look at musical theatre repertoire developmentally.

It's also helpful to remember that singers can be advanced in certain categories of function, while being a beginner in others. Functional ability does not always correlate to age, year in school, or years of training. Moreover, being highly skilled in one area does not always translate to other areas. For instance, a singer might need more advanced songs when working on legit singing, but a more beginning song when working on belting.

The skill sets listed here are by no means complete and many of these songs could be included in multiple categories with a simple change of assignment. A song could be assigned with the goal of staying in head voice through the middle range or with the assignment of navigating between head voice and chest voice in the middle range. A shift in goal might change what difficulty category the song will end up in. These suggestions are simply one idea on how to categorize songs.

When selecting repertoire, remember to consider *everything* that was mentioned previously in this chapter to select the song that is best suited for the singer. This includes researching the show and the character who sings the song to ensure the identity of the character is appropriately matched with the singers' identity.

Below you will see three songs listed with an explanation as to why that song is in a specific category. You'll then see a list of additional songs that could be included in the category as well. You'll see that the key of the edition is notated as well, because changing keys to a song can drastically change the difficulty level.

HIGHER VOICES

Head Voice/Legit

These are songs that can be assigned with the goals of working on head voice development, with a focus on more legit, rounded vowels.

More Beginner Head Voice/Legit
Title: "How about Me?"
Composer/Lyricist: Berlin
Show: N/A
Year: 1928
Key: E♭

This song is more beginner because: it has a small, middle voice range with a mainly descending melody. There are many sustained /ʊ/ vowels to help promote head voice and breaths can be taken every two measures. There is minor chromaticism in the song that could be tricky to a less developed ear. In most editions, the accompaniment plays the melody on the top line, which helps guide the singer.

Title: "Look to the Rainbow"
Composer/Lyricist: Harburg and Lane
Show: *Finian's Rainbow*
Year: 1947
Key: E♭

This song is more beginner because: of the easy, middle voice range with a mainly descending melody. The sustained /ʊ/ helps promote head voice and breaths can be taken every two measures. In most editions, the accompaniment plays the melody on the top line, which helps guide the singer.

Title:	"Do, Do, Do"
Composer/Lyricist:	Gershwin and Gershwin
Show:	*Oh, Kay!*
Year:	1926
Key:	E♭

This song is more beginner because: the up-tempo movement can help encourage a lighter sound production for most, although not all. The song also has /u/ and /i/ vowels that encourage head voice with a mainly descending melody. Breaths can be taken every two measures, but with the faster tempo, catch breaths are required. In most editions, the accompaniment plays the melody on the top line, which helps guide the singer.

Additional songs in this category could include:

"Do It Again" by Gershwin and DeSylva
"Far from the Home I Love" from *Fiddler on the Roof* by Bock and Harnick
"I Wish I Didn't Love You So" from *The Perils of Pauline* by Loesser
"The Song Is Ended" by Berlin
"Where, Oh Where" from *Out of This World* by Porter

More Advanced Beginner Head Voice/Legit

Title:	"Just Imagine"
Composer/Lyricist:	DeSylva, Brown, and Henderson
Show:	*Good News*
Year:	1927
Key:	F

This song is more advanced beginner because: there are multiple sustained F5s that could be challenging. However, the descending melody in the refrain, especially moving from the second passaggio down is good for working head voice into the middle and lower range. The vowels in the second passaggio are also good for promoting head voice. Breaths can be every two to four measures to work on longer phrases. In most editions, the accompaniment plays the melody on the top line, which helps guide the singer.

Title:	"Memories of You"
Composer/Lyricist:	Blake and Razaf
Show:	*Lew Leslie's Blackbirds of 1930* (and then again in *Shuffle Along, or the Making of the Musical Sensation of 1921 and All That Followed*)
Year:	1930 (2016)
Key:	E♭

This song is more advanced beginner because: there are sustained F5s that come from an ascending melody, but they are all on /u/ vowels, which helps with the legit quality. The descending phrases allow the singer to work on bringing head voice down into the middle range. Breaths are every four measures.

Title:	"Lover, Come Back to Me"
Composer/Lyricist:	Hammerstein and Romberg
Show:	*The New Moon*
Year:	1928
Key:	G

This song is more advanced beginner because: the melody is balanced between descending and ascending melody with sustained /u/ and /i/ vowels. Breaths can also be every two to four measures to work on longer phrases. There is chromaticism that can be more challenging to the less developed ear with more sustained /i/ vowels in the higher range that can be challenging. The accompaniment plays with the singer in some parts, but not through the entire song.

Additional songs in this category could include:

"A Little Bit in Love" from *Wonderful Town* by Bernstein, Comden, and Green
"A Sleepin' Bee" from *House of Flowers* by Arlen and Capote
"All Alone" by Berlin
"Before I Gaze at You Again" from *Camelot* by Lerner and Loewe
"Come Home" from *Allegro* by Rodgers and Hammerstein
"Distant Melody" from *Peter Pan* by Styne, Comden, and Green
"He Was Too Good to Me" from *Simple Simon* by Rodgers and Hart
"How Are Things in Glocca Morra?" from *Finian's Rainbow* by Harburg and Lane
"Is It Really Me?" from *110 in the Shade* by Jones and Schmidt
"Mira" from *Carnival* by Merrill
"What's the Use of Wond'rin'" from *Carousel* by Rodgers and Hammerstein

More Intermediate Head Voice/Legit
Title: "I'll Know"
Composer/Lyricist: Loesser
Show: *Guys and Dolls*
Year: 1950
Key: A

This song is more intermediate because: there is a descending melody to promote bringing head voice down with sustained /a/ vowels on the G5. The G5 is approached from a slow ascend through the passaggio and many phrases start on F#5, both of which could be challenging. There are also multiple ascending phrases on triplets in the middle voice that require a more coordinated voice. The song also has bigger jumps melodically.

Title: "Gideon Briggs, I Love You"
Composer/Lyricist: Loesser
Show: *Greenwillow*
Year: 1960
Key: G

This song is more intermediate because: the 3/4 time signature give this song a lilt that is helpful for finding a lighter sound. There are repeated jumps from C5–F5, but the vowels are friendly for head voice. There are two A5s, one sustained on a fermata and the other in a moving passage, but with a head voice friendly vowel. Breaths can be taken every two to four measures and although the accompaniment does not play along with the melody, the piano is helpful.

Title:	"All the Things You Are"
Composer/Lyricist:	Kern
Show:	*Very Warm for May*
Year:	1939
Key:	G

This song is more intermediate because: the range extends lower with ascending phrases through the middle voice. Without the A♭5 at the end, the song is more advanced beginner. Most phrases are four-measure phrases, but at a slower tempo with sustained notes that make the breathing more challenging. Most versions have the melody in the top note of the accompaniment, but the chords are denser.

Additional songs in this category could include:

"Dear Friend" from *She Loves Me* by Bock and Harnick
"I Could Have Danced All Night" from *My Fair Lady* by Lerner and Loewe
"I Have to Tell You" from *Fanny* by Rome
"I Wish It So" from *Juno* by Blitzstein
"Love Look Away" from *Flower Drum Song* by Rodgers and Hammerstein
"Moonfall" from *Mystery of Edwin Drood* by Holmes
"My White Knight" from *Music Man* by Willson
"Patience" from *Illyria* by Mills
"Please, Let's Not Even Say Hello" from *December Songs* by Yeston
"So in Love" from *Kiss Me, Kate* by Porter
"Waitin' for My Dearie" from *Brigadoon* by Lerner and Loewe
"Warm All Over" from *Most Happy Fella* by Loesser
"What Good Would the Moon Be" from *Street Scene* by Weill and Hughes

"When Did I Fall in Love" from *Fiorello!* by Bock and Harnick
"Will He Like Me" from *She Loves Me* by Bock and Harnick

More Advanced Head Voice/Legit

Title: "The Beauty Is"
Composer/Lyricist: Guettel
Show: *The Light in the Piazza*
Year: 2003
Key: G

This song is more advanced because: musically, it has multiple tonality shifts. The accompaniment does not aid the singer. In fact, the accompaniment often goes against the singer's melody. There are lots of accidentals, a mostly ascending melody, and large leaps. Most of the higher notes are approached with an ascending pattern.

Title: "Two Little Words"
Composer/Lyricist: Kander and Ebb
Show: *Steel Pier*
Year: 1997
Key: F

This song is more advanced because: there are multiple coloratura runs that ascend through the middle voice through the second passaggio. Many of the runs are on an /a/ vowel, which is helpful, but the range extends to an E6 with multiple sustained notes A♭5 and above.

Title: "Inside Out"
Composer/Lyricist: Lutvak
Show: *Gentleman's Guide to Love and Murder*
Year: 2012
Key: G♭

This song is more advanced because of the mostly ascending melody through the middle voice and large octave jumps. There are multiple A♭5s, some sustained and some not, with a coloratura run ending on a B♭5 (optional E♭6). The phrase lengths vary, but catch breaths are needed often in the song.

Additional songs in this category could include:

"And This Is My Beloved" from *Kismet* by Wright and Forrest
"Glitter and Be Gay" from *Candide* by Bernstein and Wilbur
"If It Is True" from *My Life with Albertine* by Gordon
"My Man's Gone Now" from *Porgy and Bess* by Gershwin, Gershwin, and Heyward
"Poor Wandering One" from *Pirates of Penzance* by Gilbert and Sullivan
"Steps of the Palace" from *Into the Woods* by Sondheim
"Vanilla Ice Cream" from *She Loves Me* by Lerner and Loewe
"What Will It Be for Me?" from *Juno* by Blitzstein

Registration Work/Mixing

The next group of songs presents the opportunity to work on both laryngeal and acoustic registration changes. These songs are great for working on moving between head voice and chest voice seamlessly with the shared resonance discussed in the pedagogy chapter.

More Beginner Registration Work/Mixing

Title:	"Goodbye, Little Dream, Goodbye"
Composer/Lyricist:	Porter
Show:	*Anything Goes*
Year:	1934
Key:	F

This song is more beginner because: when beginning from the refrain, the song allows for octave jumps from A3–A4 and C4–C5, where you can easily focus on registration changes. Breaths can be taken every two to four measures and the accompaniment has the melody in the top line. The melodic texture follows the texture of the exercises in 7.12 and 7.13 in the pedagogy chapter, which makes for an easier transition from exercise to song.

Title:	"I Got It Bad (And That Ain't Good)"
Composer/Lyricist:	Ellington and Webster

Show: N/A
Year: 1941
Key: G

This song is more beginner because: when starting from the refrain, there are large jumps from chest voice to head voice, as well as arpeggio-like motion in the melody, which also allows for more isolated registration changes. Again, this is similar to figures 7.12 and 7.13 in the previous chapter. Breaths are every two to four measures.

Title: "Don't Get Around Much Anymore"
Composer/Lyricist: Russell and Ellington
Show: N/A
Year: 1942
Key: C

This song is more beginner because: the descending melody of the refrain allows the singer to work on bringing head voice down and transitioning into chest for the lower notes. Breaths happen every two to four measures

Additional songs in this category could include:

"Another Suitcase in Another Hall" by Webber and Rice
"Hurry Up, It's Lovely Here" from *On a Clear Day You Can See Forever* by Lerner and Lane
"I Let a Song Go Out of My Heart" by Ellington, Mills, Nemo, and Redmond
"My Fate Is in Your Hands" by Waller and Razaf
"Raining in My Heart" from *Dames at Sea* by Wise, Haimsohn, and Miller
"Some Things Are Meant to Be" from *Little Women* by Howland and Dickstein
"Sleepy Man" from *Robber Bridegroom* by Uhry and Waldman
"Ten Minutes Ago" from *Cinderella* by Rodgers and Hammerstein
"The Secret of Happiness" from *Daddy Long Legs* by Caird and Gordon

More Intermediate Registration Work/Mixing

Title:	"Happy Working Song"
Composer/Lyricist:	Schwartz and Menken
Show:	*Enchanted*
Year:	2007
Key:	D

This song is more intermediate because: the quicker tempo makes for faster registration shifts, but the octave jumps allow for definite shifts in registration. The contemporary nature of the song sometimes encourages belting from young singers, so many must work on maintaining a mix.

Title:	"That's Him"
Composer/Lyricist:	Weill and Nash
Show:	*One Touch of Venus*
Year:	1943
Key:	C

This song is more intermediate because: the jumps allow for registrations shifts, as in figures 7.12 and 7.13 in the previous chapter. The song spends more time in the middle G4–A4 range, which can be challenging for singers learning to navigate registration through the middle range.

Title:	"A Quiet Thing"
Composer/Lyricist:	Kander and Ebb
Show:	*Flora, The Red Menace*
Year:	1965
Key:	B♭

This song is more intermediate because: in this key that is higher than the show key, singers can work on seamless laryngeal registration changes. The melody ascends mostly in an arpeggio fashion, which is reminiscent of the exercise in figure 7.12 in the previous chapter. There are higher phrases that take on a speechlike feel, which is reminiscent of doing the exercise in figure 7.10 in head voice.

Additional songs in the category could include:

"Another Life" from *Bridges of Madison County* by Brown
"Before It's Over" from *Dogfight* by Pasek and Paul
"Dancing" from *Lavender Girl* by Bucchino
"Isn't It" from *Saturday Night* by Sondheim
"Lion Tamer" from *The Magic Show* by Schwartz
"Lovely" from *A Funny Thing Happened on the Way to the Forum*
"Princess" from *A Man of No Importance* by Flaherty and Ahrens
"Someday" from *The Wedding Singer* by Sklar and Beguelin
"Where or When" from *Babes in Arms* by Rodgers and Hart

More Advanced Registration Work/Mixing

Title: "For the First Time in Forever"
Composer/Lyricist: Lopez and Anderson-Lopez
Show: *Frozen*
Year: 2013
Key: F

This song is more advanced because: the tempo is quick, making for fast registration changes. There is a key change that makes for a sustained D. This can be a challenge for a beginning mixer.

Title: "Thank Goodness"
Composer/Lyricist: Schwartz
Show: *Wicked*
Year: 2003
Key: E♭

This song is more advanced because: there are constant meter shifts that make the song more complicated musically. There are multiple opportunities to work on changing laryngeal registration, with a belted B♭ in the song and a legit A5 at the end.

Title: "Infinite Joys"
Composer/Lyricist: Finn
Show: *Elegies*
Year: 2003
Key: F♯ minor

This song is more advanced because: the slower tempo means more sustained notes in the midrange, where you are changing registration constantly. When focusing on a full, but not belted sound, the song can be challenging.

Additional songs in this category could include:

"Dancing All the Time" from *Big* by Maltby and Shire
"Days and Days" from *Fun Home* by Tesori
"No One Else" from *Natasha, Pierre, and the Great Comet of 1812* by Malloy
"Tell Me Why" from *Amazing Grace* by Smith and Giron
"Up Here" from *Royal Fables* by Luckenbaugh
"Watch What Happens" from *Newsies* by Menken
"Your Texas" from *Giant* by LaChiusa

Midrange/Traditional Belt

The next group of songs focus on belting in the midrange (about A4–D5), with a more traditional belt sound. These songs utilize both a speechlike quality in the midrange as well an open vowel, more call-like belt at some points in the song.

More Beginner Midrange Belt/Traditional Belt
Title: "I'm Not at All in Love"
Composer/Lyricist: Adler and Ross
Show: *The Pajama Game*
Year: 1954
Key: D

This song is more beginner because: the recitative in the beginning allows for the singer to use their speaking voice on pitch. The middle section of the song allows for sustained A4s on belt-friendly vowels, the ending has a B4, and finishes with a series of sustained A4s. All the sustained notes have a "call" quality that helps encourage a belt. There are frequent opportunities to breathe.

Title: "He's Here"
Composer/Lyricist: Bernstein and Leigh

Show: *How Now, Dow Jones*
Year: 1968
Key: G

This song is more beginner because: the tempo and range encourage a speechlike approach to the music. The song does note sustain much and the highest note is a C5. The only sustained notes at the end are friendly belt vowels. There are frequent opportunities to breath. There are a handful of more challenging vowels, but they are short and manageable for most beginning singers.

Title: "Thank Heaven for You"
Composer/Lyricist: Grant
Show: *Don't Bother Me, I Can't Cope*
Year: 1971
Key: C

This song is more beginner because: most of the song sits in a speech range and there are quite a few belted notes in the A4–B4 range. The highest note is a C5 and there are a two belted /u/ vowels on a G4, which could be challenging, but it is low enough that most will be able to navigate. There are frequent breaths.

Additional songs in this category could include:

"Adelaide's Lament" from *Guys and Dolls* by Loesser
"Better" from *Little Women* by Dickstein and Howland
"I Resolve" from *She Loves Me* by Bock and Harnick
"Ooh! My Feet" from *The Most Happy Fella* by Loesser
"Shopping Around" from *Wish You Were Here* by Rome
"Take Back Your Mink" from *Guys and Dolls* by Loesser

More Intermediate Midrange Belt/Traditional Belt

Title: "On the Other Side of the Tracks"
Composer/Lyricist: Coleman and Leigh
Show: *Little Me*
Year: 1962
Key: G

This song is more intermediate because: the tempo and range encourage a speechlike quality, but the range extends higher briefly into the C#5–D5 range. There is no sustaining in that range, but the range is slightly higher than a beginning belt song.

Title: "Hold On"
Composer/Lyricist: Simon and Norman
Show: *The Secret Garden*
Year: 1991
Key: E

This song is more intermediate because: the range is low, with much of the tessitura residing below C4. The song only belts to a B4, with a variety of easy and challenging vowels. Most notably, there are short sustained /i/ and /u/ vowels toward the end of the song. This would be a great song to introduce belted /i/ and /u/ vowels, though, if that is the goal.

Title: "Wherever He Ain't"
Composer/Lyricist: Herman
Show: *Mack and Mabel*
Year: 1974
Key: A minor

This song is more intermediate because: the tempo and range encourage a speechlike quality, but there are multiple sustained C#5s that require an intermediate level belter. The sustained notes are on belt-friendly vowels.

Additional songs in this category could include:

"Don Juan" from *Smokey Joe's Café* by Leiber and Stoller
"I Cain't Say No" from *Oklahoma!* by Rodgers and Hammerstein
"I'm Going Back" from *Bells Are Ringing* by Comden, Green, and Styne
"Shy" from *Once Upon a Mattress* by Rodgers
"Times Like This" from *Lucky Stiff* by Flaherty and Ahrens

"We Deserve Each Other" from *Me and Juliet* by Rodgers and Hammerstein

"Where Is the Warmth" from *The Baker's Wife* by Schwartz

"You Can't Get a Man with a Gun" from *Annie Get Your Gun* by Berlin

More Advanced Midrange Belt/Traditional Belt

Title: "The Music That Makes Me Dance"
Composer/Lyricist: Styne and Merrill
Show: *Funny Girl*
Year: 1963
Key: B

This song is more advanced because: the slower tempo requires more skill in sustaining a belt quality. The song also ranges from a G♯3–E5. There is a sustained C♯5, with a melody line that then extends into the D♯5–E5 range. The sustained notes are on belt-friendly vowels.

Title: "Gimme Gimme"
Composer/Lyricist: Tesori and Scanlan
Show: *Thoroughly Modern Millie*
Year: 2001
Key: G♭

This song is more advanced because: there are multiple tempo and feel changes in the song. The ending has a "big ending" feel with a huge ascending pattern with multiple sustained notes in the B♭5–C5 range. The highest note is a D5, although that note is not sustained. The ending C5 is on a belt-friendly vowel, but there is a sustained C5 on an /i/ vowel that requires more skill to execute.

Title: "The Very Next Man"
Composer/Lyricist: Bock and Harnick
Show: *Fiorello!*
Year: 1959
Key: G

This song is more advanced because: the tempo is not slow, but there is a sustained quality to the melody. The range extends from an A3 to D5. Much of the song lives in the B4–D5 range with multiple sustained notes in that range. There are multiple sustained /i/ vowels, as well as some more friendly belt vowels.

Additional songs in this category could include:

"A Piece of Sky" from *Yentl* by Bergman, Bergman, and LeGrand
"Astonishing" from *Little Women* by Dickstein and Howland
"I Wanted to Change Him" from *Hallelujah, Baby!* by Comden, Green, and Styne
"Meadowlark" from *The Baker's Wife* by Schwartz
"Sing Happy" from *Flora, the Red Menace* by Kander and Ebb
"You've Got Possibilities" from *It's a Bird, It's a Plane, It's Superman* by Strouse and Adams

High Belt/Contemporary Belt

This final group of songs focus on belting in the higher range (D5 and above), with a more contemporary sound. Most of these songs will call for an open vowel, more call-like belt, in addition to the ability to utilize the more closed, speechlike, narrowed belt that occurs higher in the range.

More Beginner High Belt/Contemporary Belt

Title:	"Joey Is a Punkrocker"
Composer/Lyricist:	Iconis
Show:	*The Black Suits*
Year:	2008
Key:	F

This song is more beginner because: there is a speechlike, storytelling quality to the melody. The song ascends into D5 and D♯5s on the chorus, but in a short, relatively easy ascending melody line that can help singers feel the closing, or narrowing, of the higher belt range easily. The groove of the chorus is more in line with a pop/punk song, helping the singer find a more contemporary style. Breaths are every two measures, and the accompaniment is helpful to the singer.

Title: "Captain of the Team"
Composer/Lyricist: Allen
Show: *We Are the Tigers*
Year: 2017
Key: F

This song is more beginner because: the song asks mostly for a speech-like quality up to a C5, with the option to hold a C5 and ad lib higher. The song has a contemporary pop feel, which is helpful for working on contemporary musical theatre style.

Title: "Holding Me Down"
Composer/Lyricist: Li and Yan
Show: *Interstate*
Year: 2020
Key: D

This song is more beginner because: of the speechlike quality in an accessible range, especially for a contemporary song. There is not much of a sustained quality, and the few sustained notes are in the F♯–A range. The highest belted note is a B♭, and there is a moment in the song that allows for some improvisation. There are some sustained /i/ vowels that could be challenging, but they are low enough to be manageable in most voices.

Additional songs in this category could include:

"Asheville" from *Bright Star* by Brickell and Martin
"Blue Horizon" from *Island Song* by Carner and Gregor
"Come to Your Senses" from *Tick, Tick . . . Boom!* by Larson
"If You Ever See Me Talking to a Sailor" from *The Last Ship* by Sting
"Lead Singer" from *11:11* by Rokicki
"Sundays" from *Miss You Like Hell* by Hudes and McKeown

More Intermediate High Belt/Contemporary Belt

Title:	"Breathe"
Composer/Lyricist:	Miranda
Show:	*In the Heights*
Year:	2009
Key:	B♭

This song is more intermediate because: the song has a speechlike quality with moments for head voice. Most of the belted notes are in the B♭4–D5 range, with the occasional pop higher to and E♭ and F. The song also has a driving pop feel.

Title:	"Love Me, Love Me Not"
Composer/Lyricist:	Contreras
Show:	N/A
Year:	2010
Key:	C

This song is more intermediate because: there are numerous belted /i/ vowels on C5s, and one sustained belted /u/ vowel on a C5, both of which are more challenging belt vowels. The range is manageable, as the song only goes to a C5, but the vowels make the song more intermediate.

Title:	"Higher"
Composer/Lyricist:	Kuo
Show:	*Allegiance*
Year:	2015
Key:	E♭

This song is more intermediate because: this song ranges from an A♭3 to D5. There is a speech quality used throughout a lot of the song, but there are sustained notes in the B♭4–D5 range. The song has a more musical theatre feel with less pop/rock stylings.

Additional songs in this category could include:

"A Summer in Ohio" from *The Last Five Years* by Brown
"Always Starting Over" from *If/Then* by Kitt and Yorkey

"And I Will Follow" by Brown
"Betsy's Getting Married" from *Honeymoon in Vegas* by Brown
"Cute Boys with Short Haircuts" from *Vanities* by Kirshenbaum
"Fly, Fly Away" from *Catch Me If You Can* by Shaiman and Wittman
"I'd Rather Be Me" from *Mean Girls* by Richmond and Benjamin
"I'm Not" from *Little Me* by Ross and Greenfield
"It Roars" from *Mean Girls* by Richmond and Benjamin
"Love's a Gun" from *Love's Labour's Lost* by Friedman
"My Grand Plan" from *The Lightning Thief* by Rokicki
"Out of My Head" by Kooman and Dimond
"Safer" from *First Date* by Zachary and Weiner
"Sonya Alone" from *Natasha, Pierre, and the Great Comet of 1812* by Malloy
"The Waiting" from *11:11* by Rokicki

More Advanced High Belt/Contemporary Belt
Title: "Get Out and Stay Out"
Composer/Lyricist: Parton
Show: *9 to 5*
Year: 2008
Key: A♭

This song is more advanced because: there are basically two songs here: before the key change and after. Before, we get lots of sustained B♭4s and C5s, with the occasional D5. After the key change, we have multiple D♯5s and F♯5s, some of which have a slight sustained feel. There is even a belted /u/ vowel into an /i/ twice on a D♯5 and B4. There is a big, sustained B4, then D♯5, then B4 again at the end of the song.

Title: "No Good Deed"
Composer/Lyricist: Schwartz
Show: *Wicked*
Year: 2003
Key: E♭

This song is more advanced because: there are multiple sustained /i/ vowels, with the highest being on a D5. There is a sustained D♭5, in addition to many sustained notes lower. There is the freedom to add riffs to this driving song, which can take you higher than the notes that were written, most notably to an F5.

Title:	"Put You in Your Place"
Composer/Lyricist:	Rokicki
Show:	*The Lightning Thief*
Year:	2018
Key:	A

This song is more advanced because: the song calls for a rock sound, a la Pat Benatar. There are multiple sustained E5s and D5s, with multiple descending phrases starting on G5. This song is a group song, so for solo purposes, there would need to be some cutting to find the through line of the melody.

Additional songs in this category could include:

"I Got Love" from *Purlie* by Geld and Udell
"Say Goodbye" from *Monstersongs* by Rokicki
"The Acid Queen" from *The Who's Tommy* by Townshend
"Ready to Be Loved" from *Edges* by Pasek and Paul
"Sodom and Gomorrah" from *HerSound* by Carlson
"The Wizard and I" from *Wicked* by Schwartz
"Three Failed Escape Attempts of Sheila Nail" from *Love in Hate Nation* by Iconis
"Where Am I Now?" from *Lysistrata Jones* by Flinn

LOWER VOICES

Legit/Traditional Sounds

This category of songs can be assigned to help work on more legit and traditional musical theatre sounds. The more beginner songs focus on middle range alignment, with the more intermediate and advanced songs working into the upper range.

More Beginner Legit/Traditional Sounds (Middle Range Focus)

Title: "You Have Cast Your Shadow on the Sea"
Composer/Lyricist: Rodgers and Hammerstein
Show: *The Boys from Syracuse*
Year: 1938
Key: A♭

This song is more beginner because: it stays in the middle and lower range. The highest note is an E♭4 and much of the melody descends. There are multiple sustained /i/ vowels, which can be helpful for the legit quality. There is some chromaticism that could be tricky to the less developed ear, but the melody is typically in the accompaniment.

Title: "My Romance"
Composer/Lyricist: Rodgers and Hart
Show: *Jumbo*
Year: 1935
Key: C

This song is more beginner because: the range allows for middle-range work, with the top note being an E4. Breaths can be taken every two measures. In most editions, the accompaniment plays the melody on the top line, which helps guide the singer. There is an ascending melody that could be challenging to some voices.

Title: "Solitude"
Composer/Lyricist: deLange, Mills, and Ellington
Show: N/A
Year: 1934
Key: E♭

This song is more beginner because: the song tops out at an E♭4 with lots of sustained /u/ vowels. The tessitura is mostly in the C4–E♭4 range, so this song is excellent for working on stabilizing the upper-middle voice. Breaths are every two to four measures.

Additional songs in this category could include:

"Almost Like Being in Love" from *Brigadoon* by Lerner and Loewe
"Blue Skies" by Berlin
"Don't Fence Me In" by Porter
"If Ever I Would Leave You" from *Camelot* by Lerner and Loewe
"Impossible Dream" from *Man of La Mancha* by Darion and Leigh
"I've Just Seen Her" from *All American* by Adams and Strouse
"Johanna" from *Sweeney Todd* by Sondheim
"Let's Have Another Cup of Coffee" from *Face the Music* by Berlin
"Love, I Hear" from *A Funny Thing Happened on the Way to the Forum* by Sondheim
"Lucky to be Me" from *On the Town* by Bernstein, Comden, and Green
"Sometimes a Day Goes By" from *Woman of the Year* by Kander and Ebb
"The Day Before Spring" from *The Day Before Spring* by Lerner and Loewe
"Where Is the Life That Late I Led?" from *Kiss Me, Kate* by Porter
"Why Can't I Walk Away" from *Maggie Flynn* by Creatore, Peretti, and Weiss

More Intermediate Legit/Traditional Sounds
Title: "Caravan"
Composer/Lyricist: Ellington, Mills, and Tizol
Show: N/A
Year: 1937
Key: A♭

This song is more intermediate because: there are quite a few sustained notes in the upper-middle and upper range. Some of the vowels, like the sustained /u/, are friendly for legit sounds, while some are more challenging. The singer needs to be able to sustain an F4 and needs more intermediate breath control to handle the sustained notes.

Title: "The Song Is You"
Composer/Lyricist: Kern and Hammerstein

MUSICAL THEATRE DEVELOPMENTAL REPERTOIRE 243

Show: *Music in the Air*
Year: 1932
Key: C

This song is more intermediate because: breaths are every two to four measures, although there are sustained notes in almost every phrase. The bridge of the song has intervals that are tricky, and there is a sustained F4. The sustained F4 is on an /i/ vowel, which helps to close the vowel. In most editions, the accompaniment plays the melody on the top line, which helps guide the singer.

Title: "I Like Everybody"
Composer/Lyricist: Bock and Harnick
Show: *The Most Happy Fella*
Year: 1956
Key: C

This song is more intermediate because: the song has a sustained G4 on an /u/ vowel. There are multiple G4s, but the melody is mainly descending, with an up-tempo lilt, helping to encourage a light sound. Breaths are mostly every two measures, with some longer phrases.

Additional songs in this category could include:

"A Bit of Earth" from *The Secret Garden* by Norman and Simon
"Barrett's Song" from *Titanic* by Yeston
"Being Alive" from *Company* by Sondheim
"Giants in the Sky" from *Into the Woods* by Sondheim
"Hey There" from *The Pajama Game*
"I Miss the Music" from *Curtains* by Kander and Ebb
"If I Can't Love Her" from *Beauty and the Beast* by Ashman, Menken, and Rice
"If I Sing" from *Closer Than Ever* by Maltby and Shire
"Sibella" from *Gentleman's Guide to Love and Murder* by Lutvak
"The Only Home I Know" from *Shenandoah* by Geld and Udell
"Younger Than Springtime" from *South Pacific* by Rodgers and Hammerstein

More Advanced Legit/Traditional Sounds

Title: "Soliloquy"
Composer/Lyricist: Rodgers and Hammerstein
Show: *Carousel*
Year: 1945
Key: D

This song is more advanced because: of the sheer length of the song. It runs about eight minutes long. There are multiple tempo and feel shifts throughout the song. Most of the song lives in the middle voice before ending on multiple F4s, a sustained G4, and then a final sustained F4.

Title: "In a Sentimental Mood"
Composer/Lyricist: Ellington, Mills, Kurt
Show: N/A
Year: 1935
Key: F

This song is more advanced because: there are repeated sustained G4s on closed vowels that are approached from ascending phrases. There is also a lot of chromaticism in the song that might require a stronger musical ear.

Title: "Love to Me"
Composer/Lyricist: Guettel
Show: *Light in the Piazza*
Year: 2003
Key: D

This song is more advanced because: this song is written in a 5/8 + 4/8 time signature that often switches into 4/4, making it incredibly challenging to count. The range is not too challenging, topping at an F♯4, but there are some long phrases held out on an /o/ vowel, not allowing for frequent breaths. This song presents the challenge of a slightly operatic sound, but still within the realm of musical theatre.

Additional songs in this category could include:

- "Finishing the Hat" from *Sunday in the Park with George* by Sondheim
- "Later" from *A Little Night Music* by Sondheim
- "Music of the Night" from *The Phantom of the Opera* by Webber and Hart
- "'Til I Hear You Sing" from *Love Never Dies* by Webber and Slater
- "When Love Comes" from *Grand Hotel* by Yeston

Head Voice (Falsetto)

The songs in this section work on incorporating head voice, or falsetto, into material, working on a coordination of laryngeal registration. You'll see a delineation between legit material and contemporary material that all have a falsetto component somewhere in the song.

More Legit Head Voice (Falsetto)

Title: "Come to Me, Bend to Me"
Composer/Lyricist: Lerner and Loewe
Show: *Brigadoon*
Year: 1947
Key: G

This song is more beginner legit falsetto because: the switches to falsetto begin on an /u/ vowel. The move to falsetto happens on every chorus. There is a full voice G5 twice in the song, and then a few falsetto G5s.

Title: "No Moon"
Composer/Lyricist: Yeston
Show: *Titanic*
Year: 1997
Key: C

This song is more beginner legit falsetto because: even though it is a group song, the opening Fleet line has a descending line in falsetto beginning on a G5 on an /o/ vowel. The song calls for a light sound, even when in full voice, so it is good to work on blending from falsetto into the middle range.

Title:	"Bring Him Home"
Composer/Lyricist:	Boublil and Schoenberg
Show:	*Les Misérables*
Year:	1980
Key:	A

This song is more advanced legit falsetto because: the song uses falsetto throughout, as the singer constantly shifts between falsetto and full voice, finally ending back in falsetto on an A4. The song has a more contemporary-legit sound and not a more traditional legit sound. It should be noted that there is a vocal selection version that is in a lower key and might be a good option for some voices.

Additional songs in this category could include:

"Lonely House" from *Street Scene* by Weill and Hughes
"Something's Coming" from *West Side Story* by Bernstein and Sondheim
"Maria" from *West Side Story* by Bernstein and Sondheim

Contemporary Head Voice (Falsetto)

Title:	"I'd Rather Be Sailing"
Composer/Lyricist:	Finn
Show:	*A New Brain*
Year:	1998
Key:	F

This song is more beginner contemporary falsetto because: the last phrase of the song is falsetto on an /u/ vowel on an E♭4 and F4. The rest of the song sits below the E♭ in the middle voice with a soft pop feel.

Title:	"Squip Song"
Composer/Lyricist:	Iconis
Show:	*Be More Chill*
Year:	2015
Key:	E

MUSICAL THEATRE DEVELOPMENTAL REPERTOIRE

This song is more advanced contemporary falsetto because: the tessitura of the song is high, with multiple full-voice G4s. There are two sustained G4s and A4s on /u/ vowels, which are challenging for the rock sound. There are three E5s in a rock falsetto sound, with encouraged growls. There's also a section that allows for riffing in the G4–A4 area.

Title: "I'm Sorry"
Composer/Lyricist: Rokicki
Show: *Monstersongs*
Year: 2018
Key: A

This song is more advanced contemporary falsetto because: most of the verse sits in the middle range, with a full range of A2–C5. There are full voice A4s, including some sustained notes, as well as a full, rock-style falsetto in the A4–C5 range.

Additional songs in this category could include:

"Alone at the Drive-In Movie" from *Grease* by Casey and Jacobs
"Answer Me" from *The Band's Visit* by Yazbek
"Breeze off the River" from *The Full Monty* by Yazbek
"Don't Do Sadness" from *Spring Awakening* by Sheik
"Epic I," "Epic II," and Epic III" from *Hadestown* by Mitchell
"Stay with Me" sung by Sam Smith
"Walk Like a Man" from *Jersey Boys* by Crewe and Gaudio

Belt/Contemporary Sounds

This final group of sounds focus on the more speechlike approach in the middle and upper range, as well as open vowel, call-like qualities.

More Beginner Belt/Contemporary Sounds
Title: "I Want to Go Home"
Composer/Lyricist: Maltby and Shire
Show: *Big*
Year: 1996
Key: C

This song is more beginner because: the range is C3–E4 and breaths can be taken every two to four measures. The texture of the melody encourages a speechlike quality and there is a little bit of sustaining, but most of the melody moves rhythmically. The song ends on a sustained /o/ vowel, which is helpful for working on opening the vowel to a belt sound.

Title:	"Beautiful City"
Composer/Lyricist:	Schwartz
Show:	*Godspell*
Year:	1972
Key:	G♭

This song is more beginner because: the revival key ranges from a D♭3–E♭4, which is an approachable range for most beginner singers. The song has a pop feel and style, and vowels that are helpful when learning to open to a belt sound. Breaths are also every two to four measures.

Title:	"Alone in the Universe"
Composer/Lyricist:	Flaherty and Ahrens
Show:	*Seussical*
Year:	2003
Key:	E

This song is more beginner because: the range is E3–E4, with mostly a descending melody. Breaths can be taken every two to four measures and the song has a slight pop feel.

Additional songs in this category could include:

"Free at Last" from *Big River* by Miller
"Hushabye Mountain" from *Chitty Chitty Bang Bang* by Sherman and Sherman
"I'll Get Up Tomorrow Morning" from *Closer Than Ever* by Maltby and Shire
"Larger Than Life" from *My Favorite Year* by Flaherty and Ahrens
"The Cuddles Mary Gave" from *A Man of No Importance* by Flaherty and Ahrens

"Go Back Home" from *The Scottsboro Boys* by Kander and Ebb
"Where's the Girl?" from *The Scarlet Pimpernel* by Wildhorn

More Advanced Beginner Belt/Contemporary Sounds

Title:	"It Took Me a While"
Composer/Lyricist:	Lippa and Greenwald
Show:	*John and Jen*
Year:	2003
Key:	G

This song is more advanced beginner because: the melody is mostly ascending with a speechlike feel. There are sustained notes in the D4–E4 range on belt-friendly vowels. There are two F♯4s and a few phrases that live in the passaggio, which can be challenging. Breaths can be every two to four measures.

Title:	"I Don't Care Much"
Composer/Lyricist:	Kander and Ebb
Show:	*Cabaret*
Year:	1963
Key:	B♭

This song is more advanced beginner because: even though the melody is quite sustained, breaths are still every four measures. There are sustained F4s, but on a descending melody. The vowels are friendly for belting and the sustained quality can also assist in finding an open sound.

Title:	"I Chose Right"
Composer/Lyricist:	Maltby and Shire
Show:	*Baby*
Year:	1983
Key:	G

This song is more advanced beginner because: the melody is speechlike with sustained sounds on D4 and E4. The patter feel could be challenging to some, especially with breathing, but could help others lighten up. There are two moments of an F♯4 and G4, but they are short.

Additional songs in this category could include:

"Grow for Me" from *Little Shop of Horrors* by Menken and Ashman
"What Would I Do If I Could Feel" from *The Wiz* by Smalls
"Where Do I Go?" from *Hair* by Ragni and Rado
"Who I'd Be" from *Shrek* by Tesori and Lindsay-Abaire

More Intermediate Belt/Contemporary Sounds

Title: "Never Ever Getting Rid of Me"
Composer/Lyricist: Bareilles
Show: *Waitress*
Year: 2015
Key: F

This song is more intermediate because: there is a speechlike quality through most of the verses that move quickly. There are belted notes on F4 and G4 with good belt vowels, but then there are moving phrases through the E4–G4 range that can be challenging. There is one short B♭5 that moves into a descending phrase through the passaggio then middle range.

Title: "Boundaries"
Composer/Lyricist: Jackson
Show: *A Strange Loop*
Year: 2019
Key: A

This song is more intermediate because: much of the song is in the middle range with lots of descending melodies. There are two phrases that start on A4s but descend in a scale like motion through the upper range into the upper middle.

Title: "Keys (It's Alright)"
Composer/Lyricist: Stew and Rodewald
Show: *Passing Strange*
Year: 2008
Key: G

This song is more intermediate because: there is a speechlike quality in the upper-middle range with frequent pops to a G4. The tessitura remains in the E4–G4 area once the song gets into the chorus, which can be challenging. There is a section for ad lib toward the end, and the song asks for a rock style.

Additional songs in this category could include:

"Anthem" from *Chess* by Ulvaeus, Andersson, and Rice
"At the Fountain" from *Sweet Smell of Success* by Hamlisch and Carnelia
"Better Than I" from the animated film *Joseph* by Bucchino
"Close Every Door" from *Joseph and the Amazing Technicolor Dreamcoat* by Webber and Rice
"Forest for the Trees" from *The Spitfire Grill* by Valq and Alley
"Goodbye" from *I Love You Because* by Salzman and Cunningham
"It's Not Easy" from *Bradical* by Allen
"Lost in the Wilderness" from *Children of Eden* by Schwartz
"My Petersburg" from *Anastasia* by Flaherty and Ahrens
"Old Red Hills of Home" from *Parade* by Brown
"Role of a Lifetime" from *Bare* by Intrabartolo
"Run Away with Me" from *The Mad Ones* by Kerrigan and Lowdermilk
"This Is Not Over Yet" from *Parade* by Brown
"This Is the Moment" from *Jekyll and Hyde* by Wildhorn
"When She Smiles" from *Lysistrata Jones* by Flinn
"Why God, Why?" from *Miss Saigon* by Schönberg, Boublil, Maltby

More Advanced Belt/Contemporary Sounds
Title: "Michael in the Bathroom"
Composer/Lyricist: Iconis
Show: *Be More Chill*
Year: 2015
Key: E♭

This song is more advanced because: the range is B2–A4 and the song is almost six minutes in length. There are fourteen full-voice A4s and fifty-one full-voice A♭4/G♯4s, and almost all are approached from an ascending pattern. Some of the higher notes are sustained and some are not. The bridge of the song builds dramatically with a repeated pattern in the passaggio as it changes keys. There is a dramatic, ascending phrase from E4–A4 that repeats multiple times. There are multiple key and feel changes throughout. There is the option for falsetto at the end, and the song has a pop feel.

Title:	"Good Kid"
Composer/Lyricist:	Rokicki
Show:	*The Lightning Thief*
Year:	2018
Key:	G

This song is more advanced because: the song has a high tessitura, with forty-two G4s and six A♭4s with only two G4s having the option of falsetto. The range is F3–A♭4, with the option for riffing and falsetto. There are fast moving notes and many sustained notes throughout the upper range. The song has a rock drive and has a mix of ascending and descending phrases. There are meter shifts galore causing the feel of the song to shift frequently.

Title:	"Waving through a Window"
Composer/Lyricist:	Pasek and Paul
Show:	*Dear Evan Hanson*
Year:	2015
Key:	A

This song is more advanced because: the range is A2–B4, with four G♯4s, nine A4s, nine B4s, with only two G♯s and two As with a falsetto option. There's a mix of sustaining and moving quickly, including multiple sustained B4s at the end of the song. The song stays in a 4/4 pop groove but has some feel changes in the bridge. There is one dramatic key change.

Additional songs in this category could include:

"For Forever" from *Dear Evan Hanson* by Pasek and Paul
"Gethsemane" from *Jesus Christ Superstar* by Webber and Rice

- "Heaven on Their Minds" from *Jesus Christ Superstar* by Webber and Rice
- "I'm Not That Guy" from *Bloody Bloody Andrew Jackson* by Friedman
- "Man" from *The Full Monty* by Yazbek
- "Memphis Lives in Me" from *Memphis* by Bryan and DiPietro
- "Right This Way" from *Bandstand* by Oberacker and Taylor
- "Runnin'" from *Beau* by Lyons and Pakchar
- "Santa Fe" from *Newsies* by Menken and Feldman
- "Sarah" from *The Civil War* by Wildhorn
- "Soul of a Man" from *Kinky Boots* by Lauper
- "Take a Chance on Me" from *Little Women* by Dickstein and Howland
- "Thin Air" from *Amélie* by Messe and Tyson

WHERE TO FIND REPERTOIRE

Now that you have a system for organizing and looking at repertoire functionally, the challenge becomes finding new repertoire. Luckily, there are websites that serve as excellent resources to find new material, composers, and shows. Be sure and visit these sites frequently to learn about new composers and their repertoire. ♪

FINAL THOUGHTS

It is my hope that this chapter not only gives you ideas for repertoire selections, but also, and more importantly, that it gives you tools on how to select repertoire on your own. The more objectively you can look at repertoire, the better you will get at selecting material for yourself or your singers. There is no one way to select repertoire. I encourage everyone to use the framework in this chapter as a starting point for your own repertoire journey, freely adding categories that arise that are of value to you. The more time you spend finding and analyzing repertoire, the better equipped you become at picking the perfect song for every singer.

NOTES

1. Warren Freeman, Kathryn Green, and Philip Sargent, "Deciphering Vocal Demands for Today's Broadway Leading Ladies," *Journal of Singing*, 71, no. 4 (2015): 491–95.

2. We will talk more about repertoire in the chapter on auditioning, where we will discuss the types of songs in musicals and how to select songs for auditions.

3. John Nix, *From Studio to Stage* (Lanham, MD: Scarecrow Press, 2002), vii.

4. Nix, *From Studio to Stage*.

5. Laura Collins Hughes, "In This *Oklahoma!*, She Loves Her and He Loves Him," *New York Times*, August 15, 2018, https://www.nytimes.com/2018/08/15/theater/oklahoma-same-sex-oregon-shakespeare-festival.html.

6. There is more information on working with kids in a later chapter.

7. Lynn Helding, *The Musician's Mind: Teaching, Learning, and Performance in the Age of Brain Science* (Lanham, MD: Rowman & Littlefield, 2020), 83–84.

9

THE MUSICAL THEATRE ACTOR

Songs in musical theatre usually propel plot or reveal character—neither of which is achievable without believable acting. Being a good singer is typically not enough to create a sustainable career as a musical theatre artist. You must be a convincing actor. The greatest musical theatre performers are those that can seamlessly integrate their singing and acting to create cohesive storytelling, breathing life and creating depth into their characters. In this chapter, we will examine some basics of acting that can be easily integrated into the voice studio.

ACTING GROUNDWORK

Many people are drawn to musical theatre because they love performing. Performing typically gives people a rush of adrenaline that feels satisfying. It should be noted that there is a difference between performing for one's own satisfaction and embodying a character for the purpose of the story.[1] This is our aim when we sing in musical theatre. We are singing to serve the story, not revel in the beauty of our own voice or depth of expressivity.

There is no shortage of acting methods and strategies, nor is there one way to approach acting. In this section we will explore a few basic acting foundations that can be helpful for the musical theatre singer. Many of these can be applied in the voice studio to help achieve vocal and dramatic goals.

Inside Out/Outside In

Most acting methods work in one of two ways—inside out or outside in. Inside-out approaches work from a place of emotional or psychological connection that leads to physical and/or vocal adjustments. Approaches that work from physical and/or vocal adjustments that lead to a changed emotional or psychological connection would be considered outside in.[2] Neither approach is superior. Every performer will connect to a different way of working. In fact, many will connect to both under different circumstances.

The Magic "If"

Acting teacher Konstantin Stanislavski coined the term *magic if*. The magic "if" asks the question, "How would I act *if* I were in this situation?"[3] This question is the basis for most contemporary acting methods. The goal is to put yourself in the situation found in the text and attempt to find some truth in your response. The best actors respond in ways that feel believable, or truthful, to the audience. The magic "if" gives you permission to spark your creativity and imagination. You, as the actor, take on the journey of the character.[4]

For instance, if you are singing "Burn" from *Hamilton*, ask yourself how you would react in the character's situation. Eliza has just found out that her husband has been cheating on her. He made his affair public, breaking her heart. The magic "if" would ask you how you would react if you were in Eliza's position. By thinking through the specifics of the character's situation, you can come up with a more truthful response.

Given Circumstances

The given circumstances are facts about the character and the story. This information is gathered from the script and might include age, gender, likes, dislikes, physical attributes, race, ethnicity, disability, personality traits, relationships, social standing, physical environment, and other relevant information. These given circumstances might appear from things the character says about themself but could also come from what other characters say or do. When reading a script or lyrics of a song, be sure and look for any information that helps you understand the given circumstances of the character. The given circumstances help bring the world of the character to life.[5]

Characters fall in love in musicals all the time, but their given circumstances will impact their love story. Tony and Maria in *West Side Story* fall in love at first sight. Their eyes meet across the dance floor, and they are instantly in love. Their given circumstances will ultimately impact their trajectory. They are teenagers who come from different ethnicities and cultures. During the time, this meant their love was forbidden. They know that it is dangerous to be together, so they keep their love a mystery until others eventually find out. Ultimately, their love ends in tragedy with Tony's death. In *Hamilton*, Eliza and Alexander also fall in love at first sight. Their eyes meet across the floor at a party in a similar fashion to Tony and Maria. However, their given circumstances mean that their fate is different. Eliza is wealthy and able to marry whomever she pleases, so she and Hamilton are married and live happily ever after (well, almost). The given circumstances of these two musicals are different, which leads to different situations, responses, and outcomes. Given circumstances make characters who they are and help us, the actor, understand how they will react in certain situations.

Substitution

Substitution is the act of replacing one thing with another to serve the same purpose.[6] The great acting teacher Uta Hagen taught substitution as a way to find more truth in your acting. When there is a given circumstance that does not feel truthful to you, you can find a similar circumstance that does feel truthful and use it in its place. For instance, in *9 to 5*, Judy's husband cheats on her and leaves her for another woman. In act 2, he comes crawling back, hoping she'll forgive him. She puts her foot down, stands up for herself, and tells him no with the song "Get Out and Stay Out." An actor working on the role of Judy might not have ever been married or even been in a relationship. This circumstance might not ring true to them. An easy substitution might be to find either a real situation they have experienced, or a more realistic situation they could relate to more easily. Maybe a friend or parent had told them they weren't talented enough to pursue performing, making them feel small and devalued, similar to how Judy's husband made her feel. The actor might imagine singing "Get Out and Stay Out" to this friend or parent when they come groveling back after a huge performing success. This substitution still honors the script but creates a more vivid connection for the performer, making it personal, which leads to a more specific and dynamic performance.

Your Scene Partner, or "Other"

Most of the time when you are working on a solo musical theatre song for performance or auditions, you are alone on stage. There is rarely another human on stage with you acting as your scene partner. This also happens in the context of shows. Many songs are sung alone on stage. Even when there is no visible scene partner, there is always an "other" present in the actor's mind.

Your relationship to whom you are singing sets the tone for your performance. When working out of context or looking for a substitution, it is important that you select a scene partner that sparks an active response in your brain and body. To use the earlier example of "Get Out and Stay Out" from *9 to 5*, choosing that friend or parent who demeaned you in the past might be a more visceral relationship than singing to a former lover or partner. An active, strong relationship choice will conjure up an emotional quality that makes a great starting point in your acting journey.

Once you've identified to whom you are singing, you should examine the type of relationship you have with this other person. Relationships can be complicated, so it is important that you understand how you relate to the other characters to which you are talking or singing. It is especially important to understand the power dynamic in the relationship. This understanding can bring about more details regarding the nature of your relationship.[7] For instance, choosing to sing to your father could mean a lot of things. For one actor, their father could be their mentor, but for another, their father could be their adversary. Choosing the same "other" could yield drastically different responses from two different actors, so it is imperative to understand your relationship with your scene partner fully.

Objective

Your objective is what you want from the scene or song. A super objective is what the character is in pursuit of the entire show, whereas an objective might be a smaller objective that is present in a song or scene. This is the driving force behind acting. We are always in pursuit of something. In the song "Telephone Wire" from *Fun Home*, Alison is trying to work up the nerve to have a difficult conversation with her father. Her objective is to get him to open up about his sexuality. While she doesn't fully succeed, this objective fuels the entire song. It can be helpful to physicalize an objective. For instance, Alison may know that her father is listening to her if he takes her hand or looks her in the eye. Having a physical realization of an objective can make a performance come to life even more vividly for the actor.

Obstacle

An obstacle is anything that gets in the way of what you want. In "Telephone Wire," the main obstacle is that her father won't talk to her. He is resistant to admit what she wants him to admit. She keeps trying, but this obstacle is ever present. The obstacle creates frustration for her, which impacts how she sings the lyrics. Obstacles can feel even more urgent if you give yourself higher stakes, such as a time limit. If your other is about to board a plane and leave forever, you only have a short amount of time to convince them to stay. Choosing obstacles that have the greatest stakes create more tension in the scene, giving you more to work with.

Actions

Actions, or tactics, are the things that we do to get what we want. In "Telephone Wire," Alison might begin by trying to relate to her father. Once she realizes that isn't working, she might shift her action to challenging her father. Her final tactic might be to plead with him. These shifts represent changes in actions to achieve an objective. Verbs work well for tactics because they tend to elicit an active response from the actor. Specific actions help your work come alive. They provide a spontaneity to an actor's work, which can lead to a more interesting and watchable performance.[8]

What is exciting about actions is that no two actors will choose the same ones. Two different actors playing Alison in *Fun Home* might choose completely different verbs. This is what can yield different, unique performances of the same material.

Beats

Beats refer to sections of text that can be organized into a unit based on objectives, obstacles, or actions. A beat shift is when you move from one unit to the next either because you achieved, abandoned, or replaced your former objective or tactic.[9] In our "Telephone Wire" example, Alison realizes that her approach of relating to her father is not working. She abandons that tactic and shifts to challenging him. Those shifts represent beat changes. In songs, beat changes often occur alongside musical changes. Moving from the verse to the chorus could be a beat change, as could the second verse key change.

Subtext

Many times, humans don't say what they mean. While one might compliment you on your hair, if the compliment is said with a tone of disgust, the subtext is obvious—they don't actually like your hair. Subtext is crucial in musical theatre. Characters don't say everything they mean or mean everything they say. For example, in "Calm" from *A Funny Thing Happened on the Way to the Forum*, Hysterium sings about how calm he is. However, the subtext under the song is that he is anything but calm.

When acting a song, musical subtext comes into play as well. The underscore or accompaniment usually informs the audience of the character's subtext. In "If I Loved You," the characters are talking about how they would act *if* they loved each, but they are adamant that they do not. However, the accompaniment would tell us otherwise. The swelling, lush, romantic music clues the audience into how Julie and Billy really feel about each other—they are obviously in love. As a singing actor, it is important to understand the musical subtext of every song you sing, but it is vital that you actively play the actions, objectives, and subtext of the lyric. "If I Loved You" works when the actors actively play the action of the lyrics and don't allow themselves to be swayed by the romantic orchestrations.

Inner Monologue

Our inner monologue is the constant stream of thoughts, feelings, and impulses that happen while we are acting.[10] This inner monologue drives our tactics and our beat changes, and helps our acting come alive. As we sing a song, we are constantly evaluating how successful we are in the journey of achieving our objective. This evaluation allows us to shift beats and tactics as needed.

Moment Before

In a musical, songs have context, something that prompts a character to sing. We call this the "moment before." To use the example of "So Much Better" from *Legally Blonde*, in the moment before the song begins, Elle sees her name on the internship list. Seeing her name propels her into singing "So Much Better." The song would not happen without the specific moment before. Anytime there is musical accompaniment before you begin singing, you want to fill that time with your "moment before." This can help ground your performance. They say "acting is reacting" and a "moment before" is what we're reacting to that makes us burst into song.

IN (OR OUT) OF CONTEXT

When working on musical theatre songs outside of a show, actors have a choice of context. They can work on the song in the context of the show, meaning they use the given circumstances of the character and show to guide their work. Their objective, obstacle, and actions would line up with the characters'. They could also choose to create their own circumstance for the song, ignoring the given circumstances of the show, similar to substitution. This allows an actor to create their own circumstances, objectives, obstacles, and actions. It can be a great exercise to take songs out of context of the show. This allows an actor to flex their creative muscles. When first learning how to act a song, using show circumstances can be helpful. The structure of the script is a helpful tool in learning how to identify objective, obstacle, actions, and beats.

When working with songs that are not from musicals, you will have to work out of context. This happens with many songs from the Great American Songbook, jazz standards, and pop/rock material. These songs do not come with given circumstances, so we must invent them. Whether working with the given circumstances of a show or creating your own, it is important to flesh out as many details as you can. The more specific you are in terms of relationship dynamics, environmental considerations, time of day, weather, location, moment before, and so on, the more specific your work will feel.

BASIC QUESTIONS

There are a multitude of questions that an actor could be asking themselves when working on breaking down a song. There are, however, four basic questions actors should always ask themselves when working on a song—who am I, what do I want, what is standing in my way, and what am I going to do to get what I want? These questions will allow you to begin the work on crafting an acting journey for your song.

Who Am I?

Asking yourself who you are allows for a full examination of the given circumstances. You can look through the script for details about your age, physicality, education, social standing, relationship to those around you, hopes, dreams, desires, and so on. If you are working out of context, you have the opportunity to create the world on your own. Allow your creativity to take over as you build given circumstances for your made-up world.

What Do I Want?

The next question to ask is about objective. You want to know what it is that you want in the song. The script will help guide you to understand what is on the line during the song, or you could create or substitute your own objective. You could also examine *why* you want what you want. This helps you understand the motivation of the character more clearly.

What Stands in My Way?

This question is focused on obstacle. You must know what stands in your way of getting what you want. If there was no obstacle, we would have no theatre. With no obstacle, we would achieve our objective in the first verse of the song, making all songs very short. Obstacles keep us working toward our goals and keeps the audience engaged.

What Am I Going to Do to Get What I Want?

This last basic question is about actions, or tactics. What am I specifically going to do to overcome my obstacle and achieve my objective? This is where picking specific, actionable verbs is valuable. Actions always work better when they are between the words "I" and "you."[11] Examples would include I *beg* you, I *support* you, I *conquer* you, or I *trick* you. All these actions are active and easy to play throughout your song.

ACTING WHILE SINGING

Working through these acting strategies is necessary for musical theatre singers. The emphasis on acting and storytelling of each song is something that makes musical theatre unique. It can take time to fully integrate the art of acting and singing into one cohesive action. It is recommended that singing actors spend just as much time working on their acting skills as they do their singing.

Ideally, there should be a symbiotic relationship between acting and singing. One should be making vocal choices based on the acting needs of the song, while also making acting choices that support the vocal needs of the song. For instance, if a singer needs to back off vocally in a section of the song to in order to pace themselves appropriately, they need to make acting choices that support the backed-off sound quality.

On the other hand, if a song builds musically and dramatically to a big, sustained note at the end of a song that is the peak of the objective, the singer needs to meet that demand vocally. Choosing to sing the big note quietly in head voice is probably not going to meet the acting demands of the moment. It takes time to integrate these skills, but the payoff of a fully realized performance is well worth the effort.

FINAL THOUGHTS

All of these acting strategies can be implemented in the voice studio to create more vivid performances, but they can also help elicit vocal changes. When singers begin to connect to their acting, their voice tends to come alive. They begin to sing with intention and purpose, which can help activate the breath, body, and voice. Sometimes it takes time to work through multiple circumstances to find the one that works fully for each singer. Fine-tuning your acting takes time and technique, just as it does for singing.

NOTES

1. Joe Deer and Rocco Dal Vera, *Acting in Musical Theatre: A Comprehensive Course* (New York: Routledge, 2008), 9.

2. Deer and Dal Vera, *Acting in Musical Theatre*, 11.

3. Deer and Dal Vera, *Acting in Musical Theatre*, 8.

4. William Wesbrooks, *Dramatic Circumstances* (Milwaukee: Applause, 2014), 9–10.

5. Jennifer Thomas and Robert J. Vrtis, *Inclusive Character Analysis: Putting Theory into Practice for the 21st Century Theatre Classroom* (New York: Routledge, 2021), 61.

6. Uta Hagen, *Respect for Acting* (Hoboken, NJ: John Wiley and Sons, 1973), 35.

7. Deer and Dal Vera, *Acting in Musical Theatre*, 22.

8. Marina Caldarone and Maggie Lloyd-Williams, *Actions: The Actor's Thesaurus* (London: Drama Publishers, 2004), xiii.

9. Deer and Dal Vera, *Acting in Musical Theatre*, 15.

10. Deer and Dal Vera, *Acting in Musical Theatre*, 18.

11. Caldarone and Lloyd-Williams, *Actions*, xix.

10

THE MUSICAL THEATRE ATHLETE

Musical theatre performers are rarely stationary while singing on stage. They are often dancing, sword fighting, running, changing costumes, or even flying while singing. This movement impacts breathing, posture, tension, and body connection. While a singer might have excellent alignment and breathing in the studio, once blocking is incorporated onstage those skills might not translate. It's important that musical theatre singers learn how to use their bodies and voices together.

BREATH MANAGEMENT STRATEGIES

There is no shortage of information out in the world about breathing and singing. Pedagogues have been writing about the importance of breath for hundreds of years. Voice teachers are often impassioned about the breath and spend a great deal of time making sure a singer's breathing technique is proper and aligned. While this is well intentioned, once the physical demands of performing come into play, many breathing techniques suffer. As Scott McCoy stated earlier in this book, all singers will breathe in slightly different ways. Both the physical demands of the role and the performer's own facility and body type will play a role in selecting a breathing strategy.[1]

There are a few breathing strategies that singers may employ. While some teachers may feel certain that one strategy is superior to the rest, it is helpful to understand all breathing options.[2] Singers often use a combination of strategies when performing. A singer's breath management and their individual approach is dependent on a wide variety of factors, including choreography/movement, restrictive costumes, or if a singer has an injury, physical limitation, or disability. Additionally, many times singers don't accurately understand their breathing. They may feel certain that they are using a particular breathing strategy, when they may actually be using a combination of multiple strategies.[3] It is important to understand the various ways one could breathe in order to find the strategy that works best for each singer. Additionally, sometimes singers need to isolate one aspect of their breathing to find a balanced breathing strategy.

Clavicular Breathing

This type of breathing is named for the movement of the clavicle upon inhale. The clavicular breath is higher in the body than other strategies and tends to be considered an inefficient style of breathing. One of the reasons this strategy is considered less effective is because it does not allow for a full expansion of the rib cage or a release of the abdominal muscles, both of which are important for control of the exhale. Raising the clavicle can also cause the shoulders to lift and the neck to tighten, which could bring about excess tension. Despite these less-than-ideal consequences of clavicular breathing, sometimes musical theatre singers use elements of clavicular breathing successfully. Clavicular breathing could be the strategy of choice if the singer is playing a character experiencing anxiety. The higher breath may be just what they want to convey anxiety or panic to the audience. Clavicular breathing could also work if the singer is in a compromised position while singing. They may only be able to fill their ribcage higher by raising the clavicle.[4] It was even noted by belting pedagogue Jan Sullivan that breathing while belting is often higher than traditional classical breathing strategies.[5] Additionally, many contemporary styles of singing use more conversational approaches, which sometimes call for more conversational breathing strategies.[6] While this may not always be the most effective or efficient way to breathe while singing, it is important to know that sometimes this strategy can work well for some singers.

Thoracic Breathing

This breathing strategy focuses on the thorax, or ribcage. The goal here is to feel the ribcage expand upon inhalation. This type of breathing is great for training the intercostal muscles. Thoracic breathing is particularly important when engaged in a physical activity while singing, especially dancing. Feeling the ribcage open can help dancers get enough air in to sing a long phrase after engaging in movement. They may feel winded or short of breath but focusing on the ribcage expanding often helps them ground themselves and get enough air in their body to sing.

Abdominal Breathing

Abdominal breathing focuses solely on a release of the abdominal muscles during inhalation and the engagement of the abdominals during exhalation. This strategy can be valuable for singers who struggle with abdominal release. Many musical theatre singers are dancers or engage in physical fitness, which means they are likely conditioned to enlist their core muscles when dancing or working out. The act of releasing the abdominals might prove to be challenging. Focusing on abdominal breathing could be an effective way to introduce abdominal release. This type of breathing might also be the only strategy available to a singer who could be wearing a restrictive costume, such as a tight corset, or for a singer who wears a binder in daily life.[7] These singers may only be able to access abdominal release when singing.

Balanced Breathing

Balanced breathing is my term for a breathing system that incorporates elements of multiple breathing strategies to create a well-balanced breathing approach. Balanced breathing will look and feel different on every singer. It is also important to note that a singer's strategy might shift from role to role based on the movement, costumes, or other physical demands. For instance, when playing Cassie in *A Chorus Line*, a singer might be leaning on thoracic strategies, with the occasional need for a clavicular breath to make it through the lengthy song and dance number "The Music and the Mirror." The same singer might utilize more of a balance between thoracic and abdominal strategies when playing a non-dance role, such as Celie in *The Color Purple*. Breathing strategies should remain flexible as to adapt to the physical demands of the role and the needs of each singer.

Checking Action and *Appoggio*

Checking action is the process by which you check, or hold back, your airflow while speaking by continuing to engage the muscles of inspiration.[8] This is something that many people do instinctively.[9] If you have a lot to say, your body will often intuitively take in the right amount of air for the thought, and then pace how fast the air will escape while you speak. If your body did not do this, you would find yourself frequently running out of air mid-sentence. When checking action is applied to singing, it is often called *appoggio*.

The word *appoggio* can be confusing for many people. It is a word that has been interpreted in a multitude of ways, which has led to lack of clarity of the term.[10] Simply put, *appoggio* is another name for checking action. This means it is the act of engaging your inhalation muscles while exhaling to better control your exhale. Remember, people often instinctually do this. The trick with singing is learning how to control this maneuver for both long and short phrases. As we have already noted, everyone will breathe differently.[11] This means that *appoggio* breathing will look and feel different on all humans.

INHALATION EXERCISES

Before you can begin to work on *appoggio*, or controlled exhalation, you should make sure your inhalation is balanced and effective. Many folks like to lump inhalation and exhalation together, but I find it more effective to always be specific about whether an exercise is meant to target inhale, exhale, or both. This isolation helps you focus on one specific aspect of breath management.

Before beginning any of these physical exercises, please make sure you are cleared for movement from your doctor. Most of these exercises can be done sitting or standing, so if you have an injury, disability, illness, or personal preference, please feel free to choose the option that works best for you. You are also welcomed to modify all exercises to fit your exact needs. Additionally, make sure the exercise is appropriate for the singer before beginning. For instance, a singer wearing a binder might not benefit from the inhalation exercises that focus on ribcage expansion. In fact, too aggressive of ribcage expansion while wearing a binder can be harmful because of the constrictive nature of binding.[12] In addition, a singer with asthma or a similar pulmonary disease might need more care when participating in any of the inhale or exhale exercises. Please use your best discretion when selecting physical exercises for yourself or your singers.

The "Singing Girdle"

Start by taking an exercise band and tying it around your ribcage so that you feel a small amount of pressure on your ribs as in figure 10.1. As you inhale, attempt to expand your ribs into the band. You might feel a small amount of resistance from the band, which is great. Because the band covers the entirety of your ribcage, it can help you feel a full expansion front to back and side to side. This full ribcage expansion often leads to a feeling of the abdominal wall releasing, which is another important aspect of inhalation. When musical theatre performers are in a show, they often wear a microphone pack attached to an elastic band around their ribcage. This can be helpful for recreating this exercise on stage.

A modification to the singing girdle entails placing the exercise band across the back while pulling the band forward. This allows the singer to focus on expanding the ribcage in the back. This is an important sensation for musical theatre singers who have to move on stage. Opening the ribs up in the back often provides a feeling of stability when out of breath from movement.

"Hug a Tree"

Another way to explore back of the ribcage expansion when inhaling is through a position I like to call "hugging a tree" as in figure 10.2. In

Figure 10.1. The band is tied gently over their ribcage to feel a full expansion on inhale. *Courtesy of the author*

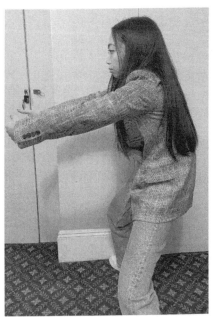

Figure 10.2. The singer is leaning forward with a hunched back and arms rounded in front to feel a full expansion of the ribcage. *Courtesy of the author*

this position, the arms are forward and rounded as if you were hugging a tree. The back can curve a bit to help feel more ribcage expansion.

Resistance Breath

Another way to explore a fuller inhale is to create some sort of resistance in the front of your mouth while inhaling. The easiest way to do this is with your finger, although pursed lips would also work. Inhale slowly while allowing the resistance to slow the inhale down even more. This slow, resisted inhale helps singers feel how much expansion they can get from their ribcage, as well as how much release they can get from their abdominal muscles.

Exhale before Singing

Taking in too much air is a common problem when working on a balanced breathing system and *appoggio*. When you begin to think about inhalation in the studio, inevitably singers will begin to inhale too much. One way to work on this is to have a singer take in what they think is an appropriate amount of air for a short exercise, but before they can sing the exercise, they must exhale half of the air they took in. Immediately after exhaling, they can sing the exercise. This shows singers who take in too much air that they need less air to execute short phrases.

EXHALATION EXERCISES

Training *appoggio*, or controlled exhale, in musical theatre singers requires flexibility. A balanced breathing approach will help singers begin to learn control over both their abdominals and intercostals, which is key in learning how to control the exhalation. Below are some exercises you can try to help gain control over your exhale.

The "Singing Girdle"

These exercises not only work for inhale, but also for exhale. After you inhale and feel the exercise band expand, try to keep it expanded as you exhale. Use the resistance from the band to help you keep the ribs up and out. See figure 10.1 for an example of what this exercise looks like.

Suspension Exercise

Another approach to learning control of exhale is through an exercise focused on suspending the ribcage.[13] This exercise will have a set number of counts for inhale, suspension, and exhale. For instance, inhale for a count of four, suspend for a count of four, and then exhale on a /ʃ/ or /s/ for eight counts. When suspending, you will keep your ribcage up and open without letting air in or out of your lungs. Be sure and keep your vocal folds open when suspending. It's easy to close the vocal folds and hold your breath, but you should be letting your ribcage do the work.

The aim of this exercise is to keep the feeling of inhalation in the ribs while suspending. This allows you to target external intercostal and diaphragmatic engagement.[14] Once you can recognize that sensation, you can try to keep that engagement going through the exhale portion of the exercise. As you get stronger with the exercise, you can start adjusting the numbers to include a longer exhale, or even a shorter inhale.

Exercise Band Pull

Take the exercise band and place it out in front you with your hands about six inches apart as in figure 10.3. Gently pull your hands away from each other as you exhale. This movement keeps your back muscles and external intercostals engaged while exhaling, which is a helpful way to feel the engagement needed for controlled exhalation. This exercise can help singers feel an anchoring in their ribcage and back when singing. This anchoring is particularly important when belting or sustaining long notes.

Sit and Twist

One of the tricky parts of exhalation is navigating abdominal movement. If you recall, the rectus abdominus is the outermost layer of the abdominals and is the easiest to engage.[15] This means that it is easy to overuse when singing. For instance, take the Valsalva maneuver. This

Figure 10.3. The singer is pulling the exercise band to feel more stabilization in the ribs and back. This is particularly effective when coupled with a plie. *Courtesy of the author*

happens when you attempt to lift something heavy, like a piano. If you try to lift the instrument, your upper rectus abdominus will engage, your ribcage will pull inward, and your vocal folds will close, creating a buildup of pressure under the glottis. This pressure buildup gives you something to push against as you attempt to lift the piano. In the past, some voice teachers used this as a fine example of "support." However, this type of engagement can be counterproductive to efficient voice use. Over engaging the abdominal muscles typically leads to over compression of the vocal folds. The abdominals should not be overly contracted with every exhale.[16] It is vital that singers learn to gently engage their abdominal muscles in an efficient way that helps their singing.

One way to work on the upper rectus abdominus is to twist your torso as in figure 10.4. This twisting motion helps disengage the upper portion of the rectus abdominus. You can twist while seated in a chair, or you can sit on the ground, cross one leg over the over, and twist over your knee. Try singing in this position and see if you notice abdominal engagement lower in your body. Ideally, the lower rectus abdominus, obliques, and transverse take over the work.

Figure 10.4. The singer is actively twisting as they sing in order to feel the work move to their lower abdominals. *Courtesy of the author*

Hands on Knees/Wall

The downside of the sit and twist is that your ribcage is somewhat compromised while twisting. The variation in 10.5 allows for more ribcage expansion when inhaling. Try putting your hands either on your knees while bending over or on a wall while leaning forward. In this position, you want the weight of your upper body in your hands. You want your abdominal muscles to be able to fully let go when you inhale, in addition to feeling your ribcage expand. Then when you exhale, try keeping your ribcage up and open while initiating the exhale from the lower abdominals.

BODY CONNECTION

Singing is a full-body sport. This is especially true in musical theatre where movement is an equal part of the storytelling. Musical theatre singers must have control over their entire bodies beyond just breath-

Figure 10.5. The singer has their body weight in their hands so that their abdominals can release and their ribcage can expand. *Courtesy of the author*

ing. The stamina to sing eight shows a week requires a strong, connected body. This connection is important to work in the studio, especially with adolescent singers whose bodies are growing and changing daily.

Yoga Positions

There are many yoga exercises that work well in the voice studio. Warrior position is a personal favorite because it helps singers feel an openness in their chest, hips, and pelvic floor, as well as a sense of being grounded. Many other yoga positions, like chair or tree pose, could also prove to be beneficial as well. Experiment with whichever position feels most appropriate for your body.

Balance Board

A balance board is a great way to feel abdominal engagement when singing, especially in the obliques and transverse abdominus. The balance board could also be a great tool for breath work. When balancing on a balance board, be sure and integrate your balanced breathing and controlled exhale. You want to avoid over squeezing your upper rectus abdominus. It is also helpful to balance near a wall or ledge of some sort to not fall.

Exercise Ball

A large exercise ball is a great way to explore connection to the hips and pelvic floor. Just the act of sitting on the soft ball can help some singers feel more grounded and connected to their hips. You can also try moving your hips in a circle, figure eight, side to side, or front to back while seated to explore more connection in this area.

TONGUE, NECK, AND JAW

It is not uncommon for singers to experience excess tension in their tongue, neck, and jaw. There can be numerous reasons for excess tension in these structures. The tension sometimes arises because of the movement the singer is required to do while singing. Certain choreography might leave the singer with a sore neck or tight jaw. However, sometimes singers carry tension in these structures independent of their movement requirements.

There are two aspects to tension that need addressing. The first is getting the muscles as relaxed and loose as possible. This can be accomplished with massages and stretches. The second aspect is retraining the body to make sound without recruiting the muscle. This is often an overlooked step. Our body learns muscle patterns, so to reduce tension, singers need to work on vocalizing without over engaging.

Please note that if any of these stretches or massages leave you sore, you have done too much. You want to use these exercises gently, but please listen to your body. A little goes a long way. Just as with the breathing exercises, please use your best discretion to determine which exercise is appropriate for you or your singer.

Tongue Out

If the tongue is chronically pulling back, try vocalizing with the tongue out. This position can help stretch the tongue and teach the singer to vocalize without excessively pulling the tongue back. Be sure and stick the tongue out without tightening the jaw or over opening the mouth as in figure 10.6.

Tongue Roll

A slightly more intense variation on this is the tongue roll. In this position the teeth are down on the tongue and sound will escape through the nose only as in figure 10.7. This makes this position act as an SOVT exercise as well. This position is useful for singers who pull their tongue back, or who suffer from tension in the middle of the tongue.

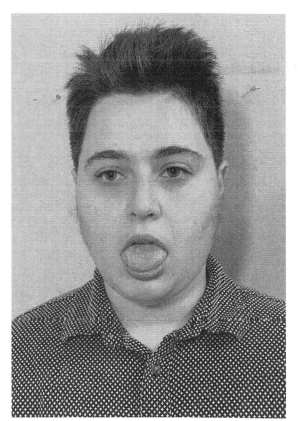

Figure 10.6. Singing with the tongue out can raise awareness of unintentional movement. It is especially helpful to use this tool with a mirror. *Courtesy of the author*

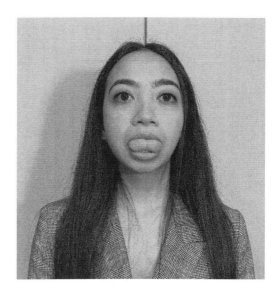

Figure 10.7. The tongue is in a rolled position, creating a deeper stretch in the middle. This stretch is more intense and should be used sparingly until the singer is comfortable with the position. *Courtesy of the author*

Gauze Stretch

Holding the tongue out with gauze is another way to stretch the tongue. Stretch the tongue out as in figure 10.6, but gently grasp the edge of the tongue with a piece of gauze. You can do this with or without making sound. If you add sound in, you are working on both stretching and retraining to not recruit the muscle when singing. Just as with the tongue out, be sure your jaw isn't over opening or tightening.

TMJ Massage

The temporomandibular joint (TMJ) is the root of discomfort for many singers. A gentle massage can help relieve mild pain or tension. Place a finger just in front of the tragus, or the small flap in the front of the ear, and gently open your jaw. You will feel a small opening in the jaw joint. Place your fingers in this joint opening and press forward toward the front of your face as in figure 10.8. Lightly massage the area.

Masseter Massage

Place your hands on your cheeks and gently bite down on your back teeth. You'll feel a chunk of muscle tighten on each side. These are

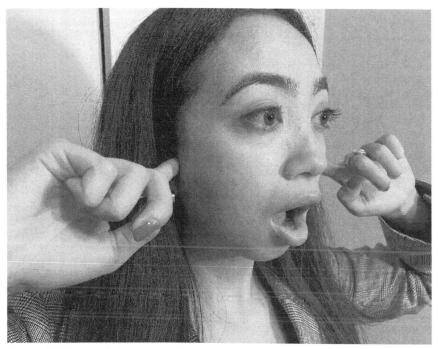

Figure 10.8. The singer is applying gentle pressure in a forward motion in order feel gentle pressure in the tempromandibular joint. *Courtesy of the author*

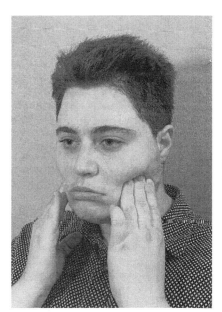

Figure 10.9. The singer is applying pressure in a circular motion. *Courtesy of the author*

your masseter muscles. Using either your palm or your fingers, gently massage the muscles in circles or downward strokes as demonstrated in figure 10.9.

Pterygoid Massage

This is a surprising massage that can provide relief for jaw discomfort, especially if you grind your jaw. Take your thumbs and hook them under your cheekbones, pressing upward. Begin to work your way back towards your ears. You will eventually meet your masseter muscle. Work your thumbs upward into the corner where the masseter and the cheekbone meet as in figure 10.10.

Figure 10.10. The singer is applying pressure upwards to find the pterygoid muscle.
Courtesy of the author

Dycem Stretch

Dycem is a non-slip mat that can be used to hold skin in place, which deepens a stretch.[17] The material often comes in a tube where it can be cut into small pieces. Take a small piece of Dycem and place it on your collarbone and pull your skin downward. Then stretch your head in the opposite direction. This helps intensify the stretch. Dycem can be used anywhere on the neck or jaw to help increase the stretch.

Handheld Massager

A small, handheld massager is a great way to loosen the muscles of the tongue, jaw, and neck. The vibrations help relieve tension, and regularly help singers feel more freedom and relaxation. Be sure and select a massager that is gentle and not too intense. The structures of the jaw, tongue, and larynx can be more fragile than more intense muscle groups like your quadriceps or hamstrings, so select a massager wisely.

DANCERS

Musical theatre performers come from various backgrounds. Sometimes those that come from strong dance backgrounds might have a limited understanding of the mechanics of singing. Some may have taken voice lessons alongside their dance training, but occasionally dancers seek out voice training later in their lives once they realize the importance of singing in musical theatre. There are some fundamental differences in how dancers and singers use their bodies, which can sometimes make training frustrating for the teacher and student. The more you understand how a dancer uses their body, the better you will be at translating the mechanics of singing to dancers.

The Core

Many of the dance styles used in musical theatre rely heavily on the core muscles, as many turns, jumps, and other movements initiate from the core. This core is often activated by pulling the ribcage in and engaging the abdominals, especially the upper rectus abdominus. A strong core is a strength for singing, but the movement of pulling the ribcage in and engaging the upper rectus abdominus is often counterproductive. The expansion of the ribs with the release of the abdominals is sometimes challenging for dancers because of the opposite nature in which they have been trained.

It is important to note that dancers need a pulled-in, tight core to dance safely. Attempting to have them drop their breathing down too low with fully relaxed abdominals might not always be a strategy they can use safely when singing and dancing. Oftentimes a compromise must be found to ensure that singing dancers are able to do both tasks simultaneously. This is when a higher, thoracic-focused breathing strategy could prove more effective. The earlier exercises focusing on ribcage movement can be particularly helpful for dancers.

Physical Exertion

When dancers dance, they exert a lot of energy. Their form of expression is physical. While singing is also physical, it is a different use of the body than dance. It is common for dancers to work too hard physically when they sing. They often want to overuse their abdominal muscles, their articulators, and their throat. This is not an issue that is unique to dancers, but it is something that is common in this demographic. One approach to working on this is to approach body and breath work in the voice studio as if it were choreography. Use the earlier exercises to explore body and breath as if the movement was delicate choreography they needed to master. This mindset can be helpful when working with dancers.

PHYSICAL FITNESS AND BODYWORK

Musical theatre requires a level of physical fitness that can be enhanced with training. Just as with any sport, sport-specific training will improve overall strength, stamina, and accuracy.[18] Musical theatre singers will benefit from partaking in some elements of physical activity outside of their performing. Before beginning any fitness routine, you should make sure you have been cleared to train by your medical professional.

Good cardiovascular fitness will help increase your stamina as a singer.[19] Partaking in a cardio regimen will be beneficial for breathing and the ability to fight fatigue. We also have habits when it comes to how we choose to hold our bodies. Working in a modality that seeks to identify and adjust alignment can be beneficial. The more balanced our alignment is, the easier it is to sing in an efficient manner. Methods like the Feldenkrais Method and the Alexander Technique can provide less physically strenuous work on balance, alignment, and stability. These methods are focused on replacing less efficient ways of moving the body with new, more harmonious movements and alignment.[20] Body Mapping can also be helpful in teaching a singer how to understand their somatic map more accurately. Once their internal map is clarified, their movement becomes more efficient.[21]

Many musical theatre singers rely on strength in their muscles to stabilize their bodies when singing. This allows for efficient engagement of muscles when breathing, singing, and moving onstage.[22] When engaging in a weightlifting routine, it is imperative that you pay attention to your breath. Many fitness programs encourage a held breath to increase the subglottic pressure under a closed glottis. This pressure helps stabilize the torso, which can make lifting weights or tightening muscles easier. Singers need to be aware of this over compression of the glottis and seek out ways to continue breathing through movement. When partaking in exercise, especially weightlifting and Pilates, you should be aware of this tendency toward breath holding. Even in a breath-focused practice, like yoga, you can find yourself holding your breath. Reconnecting to your breathing pattern in yoga is an asset.

Exercise routines should also emphasize balance and stability and come with clear functional goals, not simply aesthetic ones. It can be tempting to work out with the desire to change how the body looks, but all body types and shapes are welcome in musical theatre. Focusing your exercise routine on improving muscle function for performance will yield clearer, more tangible results. Yoga, Pilates, weight training, and cardiovascular work can be excellent ways to improve balance, stability, and function.

One of the most important aspects of physical fitness is modifying as needed.[23] If you experience discomfort when engaging in exercise or massage, listen to your body. All exercises and movements can be modified to be more comfortable for your body's needs. Bodywork such as massage, physical therapy, and myofascial release can also prove to be helpful for the musical theatre singer. These practices help reduce tension in the body and even help restore function after an injury or physical setback.

FINAL THOUGHTS

Singing in musical theatre is rarely stagnant, with singers often engaging in physical activity while singing. The more physically engaged a musical theatre singer is in the studio, the more likely they will be successful when moving from studio to stage. By using the strategies in this chapter, singers can begin exploring their connection to their body in the studio. This body connection can lead to more sustainable singing eight times a week in addition to providing a satisfying, full-body experience for the singer.

NOTES

1. Jennifer Cowgill, "Breathing for Singers: A Comparative Analysis of Body Types and Breathing Tendencies," *Journal of Singing* 66, no. 2: 141–47.

2. If you have not yet read the voice science chapter, please take a moment to do so. Dr. McCoy gives a full explanation of the anatomy and physiology of breathing.

3. Kari Ragan, *A Systematic Approach to Voice: The Art of Studio Application* (San Diego, CA: Plural, 2020), 25.

4. I once had to lie across a table on my back with my head and neck dangling off while belting into a handheld microphone. I can assure you that my breathing technique included some clavicular breathing to manage this body position.

5. Wendy D. LeBorgne and Marci Rosenberg, *The Vocal Athlete, Second Edition* (San Diego, CA: Plural, 2021), 123.

6. Jeremy Fisher, "Breathing—Let's Get Real! Jeremy's Second Rant," Vocal Process, https://vocalprocess.co.uk/breathing-lets-get-real-jeremys-second-rant/.

7. A binder is an undergarment worn to flatten breasts that is typically made of constrictive materials like cloth strips or spandex. Rib expansion is hindered while wearing a binder, so it is important that teachers have breathing strategies available to these singers that do not require extensive rib expansion.

8. "Anatomy and Physiology Series: Physiology of Exhalation (and breath support)," *New Voice, New Career Blog*, June 16, 2011, http://newvoicenewcareer.blogspot.com/2011/06/anatomy-and-physiology-series.html.

9. This is assuming there are no vocal fold injuries or respiratory issues. Both could cause an issue with the natural process of checking action.

10. "Appoggio Breathing," VoiceScienceWorks, accessed August 23, 2021, https://www.voicescienceworks.org/appoggio.html.

11. Cowgill, *Breathing for Singers*, 141–47.

12. "What Is Chest Binding?," WebMD, April 9, 2021. https://www.webmd.com/a-to-z-guides/what-is-chest-binding.

13. A version of this exercise was introduced to me by the fabulous Dr. Pam Phillips, former conservatory director of CAP21.

14. Just remember to not confuse your diaphragm with your rectus abdominus!

15. Please review the voice science and anatomy chapter for an explanation of these muscles.

16. Deirdre Michael, "Dispelling Vocal Myths Part 1: 'Sing from Your Diaphragm!,'" *Journal of Singing* 66, no. 5: 547–51.

17. Visit https://dycem-ns.com/ for more information.

18. Claudia Friedlander, *Complete Vocal Fitness: A Singer's Guide to Physical Training, Anatomy, and Biomechanics* (Lanham, MD: Rowman & Littlefield, 2018), xiv.

19. Friedlander, *Vocal Fitness*, xv.

20. LeBorgne and Rosenberg, *The Vocal Athlete*, 82–87.

21. LeBorgne and Rosenberg. *The Vocal Athlete*, 88.

22. Friedlander, *Vocal Fitness,* xv.

23. Friedlander, *Vocal Fitness*, 86.

YOUNG MUSICAL THEATRE PERFORMERS

In 2018, theatre critic Peter Filichia wrote, "Nationwide, there have been more performances of *Disney's Aladdin JR.* than the combined Broadway runs of *Cats*, *The Phantom of the Opera*, *The Lion King*, and *Chicago*. . . . That means over 37,200 performances."[1] Young performers are participating in musical theatre in their elementary schools, middle schools, junior highs, and high schools, as well as in their community centers. If you teach young singers, chances are you have worked on musical theatre songs in the voice studio.

Children are going to sing, whether we help them or not; this is especially true if they love musicals. If they are belting out showtunes in the car, we owe it to them to help them learn how to use their voices more efficiently. Plus, we don't want to miss the opportunity to use singing to inspire a lifelong love of music. Sports science tells us that when young athletes learn proper technique for their sport, they get injured less frequently.[2] It would stand to reason that when kids learn about singing technique, they stand a better chance of singing successfully. Additionally, there is no evidence that teaching young singers is harmful for their voice or vocal development.[3] This chapter will explore some unique considerations for working with young performers in musical theatre.

DEVELOPMENTAL OVERVIEW: PREPUBERTY

The most important thing to understand when working with young folks is that they are not simply miniature adults.[4] We cannot teach children in the same way we teach adults, and even more important, we cannot expect the same results. These changing expectations present unique challenges when working with young voices on musical theatre repertoire. While there are roles written specifically for children, much of the music that young people are drawn to is written for adults. It's helpful if we understand where children and teens are in development so that we can create realistic expectations for their singing.

The Larynx

At birth, our larynx behaves differently than in other stages of development. An infant's larynx sits high in the vocal tract near the jaw. This height allows babies to breathe while feeding.[5] The small vocal tract in infants also limits the available tone colors and ability to make vowels.[6] This does, however, allow for high pitched, loud sounds to be easily produced. The vocal folds themselves do not contain the layered lamina propria or a vocal ligament.[7] The lack of layers contributes to the lack of ability to create a variety of tones.

In the first seven years of life, the larynx begins to descend, although it is not anywhere near adult placement yet. The cartilages of the larynx begin to grow and become more mobile.[8] The larynx is relatively clumsy at this stage, which means young singers have a reduced range and that rapid pitch changes are challenging.[9] The vocal ligament begins to take shape, but the layered lamina propria is still less defined than in adulthood.[10] This lack of definition reduces the vibrational amplitude of the vocal folds, which means that dynamic ranges are still limited.[11] Therefore, when working with young children in this age range, it is helpful to keep their pitch range and dynamics limited.

As children move past seven years old up until puberty begins (around twelve), their larynx continues to grow. The layers of the vocal folds become more defined, as does the vocal ligament.[12] This layering allows young singers to have more control on higher pitches, although they do not have an adult range yet. They are also able to increase the complexity of movement within the larynx, such as quicker passages and more dynamic variability. As they move into this age group, they can begin exploring their higher range and can start to play with a slightly more expressive dynamic range.

The Respiratory System

An infant's lungs are substantially smaller than that of a child. Their ribs also sit in a more horizontal position, which means that they are much less flexible. Infants breathe primarily through diaphragmatic and abdominal movement because they lack the ability to move their ribcage.[13] Once they reach about eight years old, the lungs have dropped lower and grown. This growth allows children to begin exploring more rib cage expansion in their singing. They are also able to begin playing with slightly longer phrases. Despite these somewhat larger, lower lungs, we cannot expect children in this age range to have adult expansion, nor can we expect them to sustain phrases as long as adults. The younger the child, the more frequently they need to breathe in a song.

Musicianship

As young as infancy, we can identify melodies, no matter the key.[14] As our brains mature, we begin to learn language through observation and mimicry. Toddlers and young children learn simple songs quickly, which is why songs make an excellent learning tool. As young singers get a bit older, they can begin learning more about music, but they learn best when music is experienced as play.[15] Vocalizes are best approached as games with young children.[16] It is valuable to develop young singers' ears as well as their ability to read music, as long as there is balance between the two skills.

DEVELOPMENTAL OVERVIEW: ADOLESCENCE

There are three stages of adolescence—early, middle, and late. Early adolescence happens between about ages ten and fourteen, middle happens between fifteen and seventeen, and late occurs between eighteen and twenty-four.[17] The average age of the onset of puberty varies between cultures and regions. Puberty can be as short as a few months or could last up to four years.[18] It is during this time that we experience the biggest changes to the vocal system.

The Larynx

Before puberty there is little to no difference between children's larynges. Physical activity may play a role in children's respiratory function, which is why active children might produce louder, stronger singing.[19] Once puberty begins, laryngeal changes do occur. The exact type of changes is dictated by the hormones present in the body. Adolescents with ovaries will produce estrogen, and adolescents with testicles will produce testosterone.[20] It is these hormones that determine what effects puberty will have on the larynx.

Estrogen-producing adolescents will experience approximately a 34 percent growth of their vocal folds, in addition to growth of the laryngeal cartilages.[21] While this is not nearly as much as their testosterone counterparts, there are still impacts to their voice. The growth of the vocal folds causes a destabilization in vibrational patterns, which can lead to many changes in voice quality. One may experience the speaking voice dropping in pitch, a breathiness or roughness to the voice, more frequent voice "cracks" or "breaks", laryngeal register transitions becoming more noticeable, instability in the extremes of range, and an increased effort level.[22] These adolescents often have a gap in the back of their vocal folds due to weaker adduction muscles. This gap keeps the vocal folds from closing fully when voicing and is a physiological explanation as to why a breathy sound and a higher effort level are so common in this demographic. When menses starts, it can exacerbate these already present problems, especially in the days leading up to the start of the cycle. It may take time before a young singer's menstrual cycle stabilizes, which takes patience in the voice studio.

Testosterone-producing adolescents will experience a 65 percent growth of the vocal folds, in addition to major growth of the laryngeal cartilages. The thyroid cartilage grows predominately front to back with a sharper angle at the front giving the appearance of an "Adam's apple." This "Adam's apple" is a small notch at the front of the thyroid cartilage that is present in all humans. It is seen more prominently in testosterone-producing folks because of the sharper angle that appears during puberty. The vocal folds grow in length and thickness, which causes the speaking pitch to drop substantially. These adolescents often experience a reediness or roughness to the voice, a frequent change in timbre, intermittent "cracks" or "breaks" in the voice, increased effort level, inconsistency from day to day, and decreased control, especially in the higher range. Consistent range is limited, so it can be challenging to find musical theatre repertoire to work on during the voice change. Additionally, these instabilities could last anywhere from a few months to a few years, which is why it is imperative to practice patience and encouragement in the voice studio.

All adolescents experience growth spurts, which indicate that voice changes and destabilization will follow. Muscles increase in length before they increase in strength, so muscles will be least coordinated directly after a growth spurt. Additionally, despite all the growth that happens in the larynx during puberty, the larynx will not drop down to the adult position until late adolescence once the body is done with growth spurts.

The Respiratory System

Adolescents' lung size grows nearly to adult size during puberty. However, they do not achieve adult function of vital capacity and total lung volume until late adolescence. This limitation means that the young adolescent with a changed, adult sounding voice does not yet have the respiratory capabilities of adults until they reach about eighteen to twenty years of age.[23] Dynamics and range may still be somewhat limited because adolescents cannot create the same subglottic pressure of adults. During puberty, not only do the lungs grow, but the ribcage also gets larger. This larger, more expansive ribcage is often a new discovery for singers during puberty. They can begin to explore ribcage expansion and control in ways they could not before puberty.

Musicianship

Musical identity is crucial during adolescence. Many times, the music that we loved during adolescence remains our favorite type of music as we get older. Adolescence is a time where musical tastes are developed, and friendships are made over these shared musical tastes. Adolescence is a great time to expose teens to a multitude of music from a variety of genres. The musical theatre canon is excellent for this because of the wide variety of music present. While adolescents are becoming adults during this time, one should be reminded that they are not adults yet. Their cognitive abilities are growing, and they can learn more complicated musical concepts, but their instruments might not be ready to execute too complex of a passage.

INACCURATE SINGERS

It is not uncommon to run into a child who has trouble with pitch accuracy. The vocal mechanism is complicated, and many young singers do not have adequate control over the system, which can lead to inaccurate singing.[24] These children are often written off as "tone deaf" or "out of tune," both of which come with negative and ableist connotations. Referring to these singers as inaccurate is a more precise descriptor since pitch accuracy is something all singers need to work on.[25]

Inaccurate singing can be particularly challenging when working with a group of singers, like in an ensemble of a musical. When possible, try working with the inaccurate singer one on one to help them find more accuracy in their singing with the following suggestions.

Speaking on Pitch

Try speaking a short phrase like, "Hey, how are you?" in a rhythmic, intoned fashion and have the singer speak it back in the same rhythm and intonation. Try a variety of phrases at various pitches to get the singer used to the energy and resonance of different ranges.

Use Your Voice

Children can have a hard time deciphering timbre, or tone quality, from pitch, so using an instrument, like a piano, might only increase their inaccuracy. Their brain can be overwhelmed with the overtones of the instrument, making pitch hard to decipher.[26] Singers will have an easier time matching to another human voice, rather than an instrument. Because of this, it often is most effective to teach music to young performers using call and response, where the instructor sings a short phrase and the singers respond back, to ensure more pitch accuracy.

Match Their Pitch

Instead of always asking them to match the pitch you're playing or singing, try reversing it. Have them select a pitch and then match that pitch with your voice or on the piano. This can help them begin to understand what pitch-matching sounds and feels like.

Short Phrases

Inaccurate singers will work best with shorter, easier phrases of music or exercises. Try working in small sections so as not to overwhelm the singer. As they become more comfortable, you can begin putting smaller sections together to build toward singing a full song.

Give Time for Audiation

A key element of singing in tune is audiation, or hearing the music inside your head before singing.[27] It is important that all young singers, not just inaccurate ones, are given time to hear an exercise or melody in their head before attempting to sing. This helps increase their musical abilities and ultimately their pitch accuracy.

Singing Technique

As mentioned, the process of singing is complex. We must have control of the laryngeal and respiratory system. The more we help young singers understand how to use their voice in a balanced, efficient way, the better their ability to control their pitch accuracy will become.[28]

Appropriate Range

These singers will have more success in a range that is appropriate for their voice. Lower is not always better. For instance, I once had a teenager who had trouble matching pitch and he had been encouraged in the past to sing low and in his middle range. We began working on his upper range and he found it much easier to match pitch higher. Once he could match pitch in that range, we were able to bring that into the middle range for better accuracy all around.

REPERTOIRE CONSIDERATIONS FOR YOUNG PERFORMERS

Selecting musical theatre repertoire for young voices can be challenging. Kids are often drawn to songs that are written for adults that come with adult-sized vocal requirements. We've already seen that children and adolescents cannot be expected to sing in the same range as adults, nor can they be expected to sustain notes as long or sing with as many dynamics. Luckily, there are roles written for young people, which can help with selecting musical theatre repertoire. If you haven't read the chapter on repertoire yet, be sure and do so. All the information in that chapter applies to working with young singers. In addition, here are a few additional considerations for selecting material for young voices.

Keys

Changing keys for young singers is an acceptable, and encouraged, practice. Many sheet music websites now allow you to change keys of purchased music, which makes the process simple. When a song sits outside of a young singer's range, consider lowering or raising the key to make it comfortable. Changing keys might even apply to songs that were written for young voices as no two voices are alike. Changing keys can be especially important during puberty when the voice is changing.

Breaths

We've learned in this chapter that children and early adolescents cannot sustain notes as long as adults can. This constraint means that they need to breathe more frequently. Adding in breaths for young singers is a helpful way to accommodate their growing lungs. When there are longer phrases in a song, make sure the tempo of the song is appropriate to help the young singer meet the demands of the phrasing. Sometimes a tempo needs to be pushed slightly to make the longer phrases manageable.

Dynamics

Young singers also have limited dynamic ranges. It is helpful when their material avoids extremes, like pianississimo (*ppp*) or fortississimo (*fff*). When needed, feel free to adjust the dynamics of the song to be more comfortable.

Cuts

Consider working on a 16- or 32-bar cut of a song if the song is long, as are many songs written for adults. You can build up to the entire song over time by working short, targeted sections one at a time. This could also be a good opportunity to teach a young singer about how to cut music for auditions by helping them select a short cut of the song that includes their favorite parts.[29]

Lyrics

If there are lyrics in the song that do not feel age appropriate for the singer, consider picking a different song. If the questionable lyric is minor and the song won't be used for performance, you could consider altering or omitting the lyric. Be mindful that this is only acceptable in the studio where the focus is on the learning, not on performing. It is important to always honor the author's intent and understand that this practice is not recommended for auditions or performance, especially in a professional setting.

REPERTOIRE LIST

Below is a list of songs that are written for children and young teen characters in musical theatre. Some are duets, some are solos, and some come from animated musicals. This list is not complete but is a starting point for you to begin your repertoire selection journey. When looking through these songs, remember to think about the information in the repertoire chapter to determine if the song works for the young singer you have in mind. Just because a song is written for a child or young teen does not mean it will work for all young singers.[30]

"Awoo" from *Because of Winn Dixie* by Sheik and Benjamin
"The Bare Necessities" from *The Jungle Book* by Gilkyson
"Be Kind to Your Parents" from *Fanny* by Rome
"Born to Entertain" from *Ruthless* by Laird and Paley
"Candle on the Water" from *Pete's Dragon* by Kasha and Hirschhorn
"Castle on a Cloud" from *Les Misérables* by Boublil and Schönberg
"Different" from *Honk!* by Stiles and Drewe
"Dites-Moi" from *South Pacific* by Rodgers and Hammerstein
"Do-Re-Mi" from *The Sound of Music* by Rodgers and Hammerstein
"Do You Want to Build a Snowman?" from *Frozen* by Lopez and Lopez-Anderson
"Dolls R Stupid" by Rokicki
"Electricity" from *Billy Elliot* by John and Hall
"Everlasting" from *Tuck Everlasting* by Miller and Tyson
"Ev'rybody Wants to Be a Cat" from *The Aristocats* by Huddlestong and Rinker
"Expressing Yourself" from *Billy Elliot* by John and Hall
"For the First Time in My Life" from *Little Miss Sunshine* by Finn
"Gary, Indiana" from *The Music Man* by Willson
"Getting Tall" from *Nine* by Yeston
"Giants in the Sky" from *Into the Woods* by Sondheim
"Good Girl Winnie Foster" from *Tuck Everlasting* by Miller and Tyson
"Goodnight, My Someone" from *The Music Man*
"Happiness" from *You're a Good Man, Charlie Brown* by Gesner
"Hey It's Me" from *Freckleface Strawberry* by Kupper

"Home" from *Wonderland* by Wildhorn and Murphy
"How Far I'll Go" from *Moana* by Miranda
"I Always Knew" from *Annie Warbucks* by Strouse and Charnin
"I Don't Need Anything but You" from *Annie* by Strouse and Charnin
"I Just Can't Wait to Be King" from *The Lion King* by John and Rice
"I Know Things Now" from *Into the Woods* by Sondheim
"I Need to Know" from *Tarzan* by Collins
"I Want More" from *Lestat* by John and Taupin
"I Whistle a Happy Tune" from *The King and I* by Rodgers and Hammerstein
"I Won't Grow Up" from *Peter Pan* by Styne, Charlap, Comden, Green, and Leigh
"I'd Do Anything" from *Oliver!* by Bart
"If I Only Had a Brain" from *The Wizard of Oz* by Arlen and Harburg
"If Only You Would Listen" from *School of Rock* by Webber and Slater
"If Momma Was Married" from *Gypsy* by Styne and Sondheim
"I'll Believe in You" from *Elf* by Sklar and Beguelin
"I'll Never Have That Chance" from *Lestat* by John and Taupin
"It's The Hard-Knock Life" from *Annie* by Strouse and Charnin
"It's Possible" from *Seussical* by Flaherty and Ahrens
"Let Me Entertain You" from *Gypsy* by Styne and Sondheim
"A Letter from Charlie Bucket" from *Charlie and the Chocolate Factory* by Shaiman and Wittman
"Little Lamb" from *Gypsy* by Styne and Sondheim
"Little People" from *Les Misérables* by Boublil and Schönberg
"Maybe" from *Annie* by Strouse and Charnin
"Middle of a Moment" from *James and the Giant Peach* by Pasek and Paul
"Much More" from *The Fantasticks* by Jones and Schmidt
"My Best Girl (My Best Beau)" from *Mame* by Herman
"My Father's a Homo" from *Falsettos* by Finn
"Naughty" from *Matilda* by Minchin
"Never Never Land" from *Peter Pan* by Styne, Charlap, Comden, Green, and Leigh
"Noah down the Stairs" from *Caroline, or Change* by Tesori and Kushner

"On Your Way Home" from *James and the Giant Peach* by Pasek and Paul

"One Pal" from *Polkadots: The Cool Kids Musical* by Lyons and Borowsky

"The Perfect Nanny" from *Mary Poppins* by Sherman, Styles, and Drewe

"Quiet" from *Matilda* by Minchin

"Red Ryder Carbine Action BB Gun" from *A Christmas Story* by Pasek and Paul

"Reflection" from *Mulan* by Wilder and Zippel

"Reluctantly" from *Monstersongs* by Rokicki

"Ring of Keys" from *Fun Home* by Tesori and Kron

"A Round-Shouldered Man" from *The Secret Garden* by Simon and Norman

"Shake Your Badonkadonk" from *Little Miss Sunshine* by Finn

"Silver Bullet" from *Monstersongs* by Rokicki

"Sing Your Own Song" from *Dear Edwina* by Goldrich and Heisler

"So Long, Farewell" from *The Sound of Music* by Rodgers and Hammerstein

"Stepsisters Lament" from *Cinderella* by Rodgers and Hammerstein.

"Talk to Her" from *Big* by Maltby and Shire

"The Girl I Mean to Be" from *The Secret Garden* by Simon and Norman

"There Is a Santa Claus" from *Elf* by Sklar and Beguelin

"Time to Play" from *School of Rock* by Webber and Slater

"Tomorrow" from *Annie* by Strouse and Charnin

"Top Secret Personal Beeswax" from *Junie B. Jones* by Goldrich and Heisler

"Tree" from *The Me Nobody Knows* by Friedman and Holt

"Us Two/Chitty Prayer" from *Chitty Chitty Bang Bang* by Sherman

"Wendy" from *Peter Pan* by Styne, Charlap, Comden, Green, and Leigh

"What a Strange Life We Live (reprise)" from *In My Life* by Brooks

"What If" from *The Addams Family* by Lippa

"When I Grow Up" from *Matilda* by Minchin

"When We Grow Up" from *Free to Be You and Me* by Lawrence and Miller

"Where Is Love?" from *Oliver!* by Bart
"Who Will Buy?" from *Oliver!* by Bart
"Why Am I Me?" from *Shenandoah* by Geld and Udell
"World's Best Dad" from *Amélie* by Messé and Tyson
"You're Never Fully Dressed without a Smile" from *Annie* by Strouse and Charnin

In addition to these songs, there are many songs in the musical theatre canon written for adults that work well for developing voices. The information contained here and in the repertoire chapter should help you discern when a song works for a young, developing voice.

MUSICALS FOR KIDS

When it comes to selecting shows for kids to participate in, there are more options than you might think. It is suggested that you look at educational versions of shows for a few reasons. The first reason is that the length of the show is reduced to make it more manageable for young kids. These shows are often thirty or sixty minutes in length. The shows are also adjusted to include as many cast members as possible, which is great for getting more young people involved in theatre. One of the biggest reasons to select an educational version, though, is because the keys of the songs are changed to be appropriate for unchanged voices. These kid-friendly keys make navigating the vocal demands of the show much easier. Most educational versions also come with a variety of resources for the director to help make the production run smoothly. When it comes to selecting shows, be sure to consider the cultural and historical context of the show in question to make sure it reflects your student population, your school's culture, and the social location of your community.[31]

Music Theatre International (MTI)

MTI is a licensing company that is home to the Broadway Junior, Broadway Kids, and School Edition collections. Broadway Junior is a collection of sixty-minute musicals that have been adapted for middle school–age students. Broadway Kids is a collection of thirty-minute musicals that have been adapted for elementary-age students. The School Editions are shows that have been adapted for high schools. These high school shows often contain fewer changes, but will sometimes come with key options, are often edited for content, or have changes that make producing the show at the high school level more manageable.[32] Some of their shows include *Aladdin*, *Annie*, *Beauty and the Beast*, *Elf*, *Fiddler on the Roof*, *Frozen*, *Hairspray*, *Guys and Dolls*, *High School Musical*, *Legally Blonde*, *The Little Mermaid*, *Matilda*, *Mary Poppins*, *Seussical*, *Rent*, and *Shrek*.

Concord Theatricals

Like MTI, Concord has musicals that are adapted for elementary, middle school, and high school students. Their Youth Editions are sixty-minutes and geared toward elementary and middle schoolers, while their Teen Editions are longer and focused on high schoolers.[33] Some of their shows include *Be More Chill*, *Cats*, *A Chorus Line*, *Chicago*, *Crazy for You*, *Heathers*, *The Lightning Thief*, *Rock of Ages*, and *The Sound of Music*.

Broadway Licensing

Broadway Licensing has two educational categories. Their Junior Varsity (JV) editions are sixty minutes and aimed at middle schoolers, while their High School Editions are for high school aged students.[34] Some of their shows include *A Bronx Tale*, *Emma*, *Head over Heels*, *High Fidelity*, and *Polkadots*.

Theatrical Rights Worldwide (TRW)

TRW has a line of School Editions geared for high school students. Additionally, their Young@Part series comes in sixty-minute adaptations for middle schools, and thirty-minute adaptations for elementary schools.[35] Some of their shows include *The Addams Family*, *Curtains*, *Memphis*, *Miss Nelson Is Missing*, *Miss You Like Hell*, and *Spamalot*.

VOCAL HEALTH FOR YOUNG PERFORMERS

When young performers are participating in a musical, their vocal health is of the utmost concern. There are some concepts we can teach young singers so that they will begin to take charge of their vocal health.

Moderation

Teaching young performers to pace themselves can be a huge challenge. They tend to go nonstop until they run out of energy. The same goes for their voice use—both singing *and* speaking. It is not uncommon for young singers to use their voice until a noticeable voice change. Once their voice quality diminishes, they have gone too far. It's important that we teach them to use their voice in moderation in both their singing and speaking so that they don't push themselves to hoarseness.

One way to monitor vocal fatigue is through vocal dollars.[36] Everyone has a certain amount of "vocal dollars" that they can use throughout the day. An easy starting point is 100 dollars. Play rehearsal might cost 30 dollars, singing in choir might be 25 dollars, and then their voice lesson might take away another 25 dollars. That only leaves them 20 dollars for socializing with friends. If they wake up under the weather or vocally fatigued, they may be starting their day with only 75 dollars instead of 100 dollars. Once they hit their allotted dollar amount, they need to shut their voice down and rest. This can be a fun, easy way for young singers to start evaluating their vocal load throughout the day.

Red Flags

After moderation, the next most helpful thing we can teach young singers is to recognize red flags in their voice. It is important that they know that things like extra effort, loss of range, or raspiness are all signs that they may have overexerted their voice. Any red flag that shows up might indicate that they have exceeded their vocal dollars and need to rest.

Hydration

Teaching young singers to hydrate is essential. Encourage them to always have a water bottle in a voice lesson or musical rehearsal.

Consider having a hydration challenge in your voice studio or cast where students try to reach a certain number of healthy ounces in a day. If you have preteens or teens involved, you might even create a hashtag for the challenge so they can post their water pics to social media. This allows them to follow their friends and see how they are doing with the hydration challenge as well.[37]

Warming Up

Teaching young singers the value of warming up is paramount. Just as they learn to warm-up physically before playing sports, they should learn to warm-up vocally before singing. A warmup doesn't need to be too long or involved, but this habit sets them up for less fatigue and strain. It also helps set precedence for good habits as they get older.

Straw Phonation

One of the most fun things for young singers to do is blow bubbles in their water bottle. This activity is not only fun but also serves as an excellent semi-occluded-vocal-tract (SOVT) exercise.[38] It can help them warm-up before rehearsal, stay warm during rehearsal, and help them navigate fatigue. The straw can also be used without the water for a great vocal boost. Teaching young singers to use their straw when they feel fatigue kicking in is a great way for them to take control of their vocal health.

Vocal Naps

Vocal naps are moment throughout the day where singers take a few minutes of vocal rest.[39] Teaching young singers to do this when they are facing a big vocal load is advantageous. They could decide to eat lunch alone listening to music or doing homework instead of socializing with friends. This allows their voice to "nap." Help your students look for moments in their day where they can take a vocal nap. Learning the value of rest will help them keep their voice up and running.

FINAL THOUGHTS

Working with young singers can be incredibly rewarding. As we have seen in this chapter, kids are not miniature adults, and therefore cannot be treated that way in the voice studio. Having an understanding and appreciation for where young performers are in development will not only help strengthen their vocal technique but can help instill a lifelong love of music and singing.

NOTES

1. Peter Filichia, "Filichia Features: *Aladdin JR.* Takes a Giant Leap," Musical Theatre International, February 8, 2018, https://www.mtishows.com/news/filichia-features-aladdin-jr-takes-a-giant-leap.

2. Jenevora Williams, *Teaching Singing to Children and Young Adults*, second edition (Oxford, UK: Compton Publishing, 2019), 12.

3. Robert Edwin, "Vocal Parenting Revisited," *Journal of Singing* 70, no. 3 (2014): 341–44.

4. Edwin, *Vocal Parenting*, 343.

5. Williams, *Teaching Singing*, 25.

6. Williams, *Teaching Singing*, 26.

7. Kevin D. Skelton, "The Child's Voice: A Closer Look at Pedagogy and Science," *Journal of Singing* 63, no. 5 (2007): 537–44.

8. Williams, *Teaching Singing*, 28.

9. Maria Runfola and Joanne Rutkowski, *TIPS: The Child Voice* (Lanham, MD: Rowman & Littlefield Education, 2010), 50.

10. Skelton, *The Child's Voice*, 539.

11. Williams, *Teaching Singing*, 28.

12. Williams, *Teaching Singing*, 49.

13. Williams, *Teaching Singing*, 26.

14. Williams, *Teaching Singing*, 22.

15. Williams, *Teaching Singing*, 50.

16. Edwin, *Vocal Parenting*, 343.

17. "Adolescent Development," *Association of Maternal and Child Health Programs*, http://www.amchp.org/programsandtopics/AdolescentHealth/projects/Pages/AdolescentDevelopment.aspx.

18. Williams, *Teaching Singing*, 62.

19. Skelton, *The Child's Voice*, 538.

20. Steven Downshen, "Everything You Wanted to Know about Puberty," Teenshealth, https://kidshealth.org/en/teens/puberty.html.

21. John M. Cookscy, *Working with Adolescent Voices* (St Louis, MO: Concordia Publishing House, 1992), 7.

22. Cooksey, *Adolescent Voices*, 7–8.

23. Williams, *Teaching Singing*, 57–63.

24. Kenneth H. Phillips, *Teaching Kids to Sing* (New York: Schirmer Books, 1996), 30.

25. Phillips, *Teaching Kids*, 31.

26. Williams, *Teaching Singing*, 19.

27. Phillips, *Teaching Kids*, 34.

28. Be sure to read the chapter on voice pedagogy in order to understand how to work on the various sounds needed in musical theatre.

29. The next chapter has more information about how to cut music for auditions.

30. Additionally, many of the songs in the repertoire chapter would work really well for young voices, despite being written for adults.

31. For a more detailed discussion of this, please see the chapter on repertoire.

32. Please visit https://www.mtishows.com/ for more information.

33. Please visit https://www.concordtheatricals.com/ for more information.

34. Please visit https://broadwaylicensing.com/ for more information.

35. Please visit https://www.theatricalrights.com/ for more information.

36. Thank you to Christine Estes, MM, MA-CCC/SLP for this amazing idea.

37. Thank you to voice teacher Chris York for this idea.

38. Please see the chapter on pedagogy for more information on semi-occluded vocal tract positions.

39. Wendy D. LeBorgne and Marci Rosenberg, *The Vocal Athlete*, second edition (San Diego, CA: Plural Publishing, 2021), 844.

12

MUSICAL THEATRE AUDITIONS

There is an aspect of musical theatre that is unavoidable at all levels—the audition. From elementary school productions to Broadway, most performers go through an audition process to be cast in a show. This chapter will explore some aspects of auditioning that are important for musical theatre singers.

THE AUDITION BOOK

Your audition book is a collection of music with a selection of songs that you are prepared to sing at an audition. This book is typically an actor's lifeline. It includes songs that have been preselected and carefully prepared to show a wide range of vocal function, vocal style, acting ability, and musicianship. These songs should also be reflective of the characters that a singer would be appropriate and enthusiastic to play. Actors should be prepared to sing anything in their book at any audition.

Some auditions will provide material that they would like prepared, but those that do not will ask you to bring in your own song. This is where the audition book comes in handy. When you are auditioning frequently, as most professional musical theatre performers are, your book keeps you from having to learn a new song for every audition. While you will still occasionally need to learn a new song, your book serves as an arsenal of tunes you can pull from.

The Working Book

Having a second book can be valuable for musical theatre performers. I call this this your "working book." This book is where you keep material that is not for auditions. It's great place to keep songs that you are using for skill development in your voice lessons, songs you are prepping for your audition book, new songs you are learning, and songs you love to sing in lessons or repertoire coachings.

CONTENTS OF THE AUDITION BOOK

Your audition book should consist of a wide range of material that reflects the type of shows for which you are auditioning. You want a variety of time periods, tempi, vocal function, musical genres, and dramatic contexts or characters represented. One of the most important aspects of your audition book is that the songs reflect your skills as a singing actor. You want to tailor your book to the type of auditions that you attend. Your book should look different than your friends' books. We are all unique and bring different qualities and skills to each audition.

There is no one way to put your audition book together, but the following are suggestions for song categories to explore. You'll notice that much of this is reflective of what was discussed in the earlier chapter on genre.

Jazz Standards

Standards are songs that typically were written before the golden age, particularly in the jazz era. Composers of this time period might be Duke Ellington, Fats Waller, Richard Rodgers, and George Gershwin, to name a few. You might need a standard to audition for shows like *An American in Paris*, *Sophisticated Ladies*, *Crazy for You*, *Ain't Misbehavin'*, and *Bullets over Broadway*.

Traditional Musical Theatre

Traditional musical theatre could include songs that were written through the golden age and transitional time periods that have a more traditional musical theatre feel. Shows like *Guys and Dolls, The Unsinkable Molly Brown, West Side Story, Annie Get Your Gun*, and *Gypsy* all use traditional musical theatre sounds. You might also find pastiche songs from more contemporary musicals that beckon to traditional musical theatre. For instance, much of Millie's music in *Thoroughly Modern Millie* is a throwback to traditional musical theatre.

Legit Musical Theatre

The legit category could include a lot of music from the golden age and transitional eras where writers were writing songs that had inklings of a classical sound. You can find older legit musicals, like *Carousel, The King and I*, and *She Loves Me*, as well as more contemporary legit musicals such as *The Light in the Piazza, Gentleman's Guide to Love and Murder*, or *Death Takes a Holiday*.

60s/70s/80s Musical Theatre (Transitional)

The transitional time period is the post-golden age, pre-contemporary era of musical theatre. This era typically encompasses the 1960s–1980s where musical theatre was growing and changing due to the integration of pop/rock music. Much of the music of the 1960s, 1970s, and 1980s musical theatre does not sound contemporary to our modern-day ear, but it does not sound quite like the traditional musical theatre of the earlier decades either. Shows like *Cabaret, Company,* and *Baby* all evoke a musical theatre sound from this era. Singing a contemporary musical theatre song might not be right if you were auditioning for any of these shows. A more traditional, golden age song might not feel right either. If you find yourself auditioning for shows from this era, you'll want to make sure you have material from this time period in your book.

80s/90s Musical Theatre (The Pop Opera)

The 1980s and 1990s were the mega-musical decades, which gave way to what is sometimes referred to as the "pop opera." Shows like *Les Misérables*, *Miss Saigon*, *Evita*, *Cats*, *Jekyll and Hyde*, *Chess*, and *The Scarlet Pimpernel* were all musicals that had pop-inspired scores, with elements of legit musical theatre thrown in. This type of music is specific and feels linked to the popular sounds of 1980s and 1990s musical theatre. Having something from this genre in your book, is helpful when auditioning for these shows.

90s/2000s Musical Theatre (Early Contemporary)

By the 1990s, pop/rock was becoming a mainstay in musical theatre. In this period many new musical theatre writers burst onto the scene with their pop-influenced music. This is also when many audition notices started asking for pop/rock songs and not musical theatre songs for their auditions. Some of the songs from this time will feel contemporary, but some might feel as though they are specific to the 90s/2000s musical theatre era. Some examples include *John and Jen*, *Rent*, *Bare*, Lippa's *The Wild Party*, *The Last Five Years*, and *Tick, Tick . . . Boom!*

Contemporary

If contemporary means "existing or happening now," then this category will be ever evolving. You should always examine what type of shows are being written in the present and make sure you have material that sounds contemporary, knowing that contemporary will shift as the industry advances.

Contemporary musical theatre songs can sound more like pop/rock songs, or they can have more of a musical theatre feel. For instance, *Dear Evan Hanson* has a pop feel to the music while *Ordinary Days* has a musical theatre feel without as many pop/rock elements. One way to decipher between contemporary musical theatre and contemporary pop/rock musical theatre is to ask yourself if you would sing a pop/rock song to audition for the show or not. A pop song would be appropriate for *Dear Evan Hanson* but might not be quite right for *Ordinary Days*.

Pop/Rock

You should have a wide variety of pop/rock songs in your book. These are songs that are not from musicals, but rather were made popular by a band or recording artist. The best way to decide what pop/rock songs you might need in your book is to examine what type of pop/rock shows you are right for. I suggest revisiting the chapter on genre and looking at the shows listed. It's helpful to think in terms of decade *and* genre. You want pop/rock songs from various decades, but you also want to make sure you have a variety of genres represented as well. Having a pop song from every decade since 1950 won't serve you as well as having a pop song, a rock song, a country song, and an R&B song, all spanning various decades.

If you are right for shows in a certain decade or genre of music, you should have a song in your book that is reflective of that sound. If there is a category of show you are not going to audition for, then you probably don't need to spend time finding a song in that genre. For instance, not everyone is right for a show like *Rock of Ages* or *Bat Out of Hell*, so some folks might not need a 1980s rock song in their book. It is still a good exercise to explore singing these genres in the voice studio because you never know when you might find that you fit into a pop/rock genre vocally.

Comedy Songs

Having a song that makes people laugh is incredibly valuable. Sometimes audition notices will specifically ask for a comedy song. You tend to find this in comedies like *Spamalot*, *The Producers*, and *Urinetown*.

One of the challenges with comedy songs in an audition setting is executing the humor. There are two ways to look for comedy songs. The first is finding a song that was written to be funny. These are songs that have clever lyrics designed to make people laugh. This is the most common type of comedy song. Songs like "Whatever Happened to My Part?" from *Spamalot*, "In Short" from *Edges*, and "My Big French Boyfriend" from *The Toxic Avenger* all fall into this category.

The second way to look at comedy in an audition setting is find a song that was not intended to be funny and make it funny through your performance. This can be challenging, but it often has a fantastic payoff.

When people are casting a musical that is rooted in comedy, they are often looking for actors who are well versed in finding the comedy in everyday situations. There is a huge difference in delivering clever lyrics and being able to create situational comedy. Neither choice is right or wrong when auditioning, but it is helpful to understand the tone of the show you are auditioning for to understand what comedic approach might be more appropriate.

Simple Songs

Everyone benefits from having a simple song in their book. This is a song that doesn't do anything flashy vocally or dramatically, but allows you to show simplicity, and often tenderness. These are songs that feel naturalistic in their acting and show a grounded, understated quality. Simple songs can work well as second songs in auditions, especially after you've sung something that is bigger or showier. My suggestion is to make sure that one of the songs from the previous categories is simple.

Specialty Songs

This category might consist of unique, rarely used songs that fill niche categories. This could include a song you sing while playing an instrument, a song in a foreign language that you speak fluently, a song you wrote, an English art song, an operetta song, or a musically complex song like those by Stephen Sondheim, Michael John LaChiusa, or Adam Guettel. Songs that are complex can be challenging for pianists to sightread if they are not familiar with the music, so they are often not a great go-to. However, it is helpful to have something that shows off your musical abilities when it's appropriate.

Avant-Garde

There is a unique category of musical that has popped up in recent years that one might categorize as "avant-garde." These are musicals that are experimental in nature and typically include an eclectic mix of musical genres. They often defy genre classification and structure.

These are shows that are often created and nurtured off- and off-off-Broadway. Composers like Dave Malloy, Cesar Alvarez, Grace McLean, Michael Friedman, The Bengsons, and David Byrne all write shows that can be avant-garde in nature. If you find that you audition for these types of shows, you will want to include something like this in your book.

CONTRASTING SONGS

You want to have songs in your book that contrast with each other, meaning they each show something different vocally, stylistically, and/or dramatically. Sometimes you are only asked to sing one song in an audition, but sometimes people want to hear two contrasting songs so they get an understanding of your range and flexibility as an actor and singer. There are many ways for songs to contrast with each other, and oftentimes songs will contrast on multiple levels.

Contrasting Tempo

You want to make sure you have a nice balance of up-tempos and ballads in your book. Often, performers are drawn to one more than the other and can end up with a book that has too many songs of one tempo. Ideally you will have songs that contrast in tempo in each category, meaning up-tempos, ballads, and mid-tempo songs.

Contrasting Vocally

Songs can require different things from you vocally. It's helpful to make sure you have a variety of songs that require you to belt, sing legit, and show your abilities to mix. A book consisting of only legit ballads won't serve anyone well in the current musical theatre landscape. It's also helpful to think about dynamic variety as well. Though it is important to show range and dexterity, you also don't want all your cuts to be the loudest, highest parts of the song. Showing vocal nuance is important.

Contrasting Stylistically

Songs can vary stylistically as well. You might have two contemporary musical theatre songs with one requiring slightly more rounded, legit tones, and the other requiring elements of rock style like growls, screams, and gravel. For instance, "Wondering" from *Bridges of Madison County* has a folksy, almost legit quality, while "Top of Mount Rock" from *School of Rock* asks for a high, rock belt. Both are contemporary musical theatre songs but come with drastically different stylistic demands. It can also be helpful to have a few songs in your book that are flexible in nature. These are songs that can be sung in various styles. This helps expand the depth of contrasting material you might have. A pop song sung with a slight twang might work for a country audition. A rock song slowed down might work as a pop tune. Sometimes we don't have time to rehearse and prepare the "perfect" audition song, so having flexible material allows your book to be shaped for your needs in the moment.

Contrasting Dramatically

It's important that your book not only showcase your voice and musical abilities, but also your abilities as an actor. Everyone needs both lighthearted and dramatic material. You also want songs that allow you to portray different types of characters such as funny songs, youthful songs, mature songs, silly songs, earnest songs, etc. You want a wide variety of songs to help you feel prepared. Additionally, just as you might have songs that are flexible stylistically, it is helpful to have a few songs that can be acted in a multitude of ways. This allows a song to become more useful in your audition book.[1]

CUTTING SONGS

Often, performers are asked to prepare a cut of a song instead of the entire song. This helps save time in auditions, which is particularly important in the professional world where there are hundreds of people auditioning for a show. The length of cuts was standardized when songs were written in a more predictable pattern, namely the eight-bar phrase. Older songs were easily divided into eight, sixteen, and thirty-two bars, which became typical in the musical theatre industry. Music has changed a lot since this was standardized, so it's helpful to think about these cuts beyond just measure numbers.

The 32-Bar Cut

The 32-bar cut is typically your longer audition cut. You can think of this as being about 32 bars, about a verse and chorus, or being between a minute and a minute and thirty seconds. When people ask for a "short selection" in an audition, this is typically what they are referring to.

The 16-Bar Cut

The 16-bar cut, as you can probably guess, is about half of the 32-bar cut. It's about 16 bars, about the length of a chorus, or about thirty to forty-five seconds long. You could also sing a 16-bar cut when asked for a "short selection."

The 8-Bar Cut

This is typically the most dreaded of the cuts. Eight-bar cuts tend to only happen at nonunion auditions where there are so many people in attendance, they need to substantially reduce the amount of time in the room. This cut is about eight bars, or under about twenty seconds long. You often want your 8-bar cut to include a "money note" or show an interesting passage musically, vocally, or dramatically to reveal a snippet of your skills in such a short time. While the 8-bar cut can feel like a let down to the auditionee, people do book callbacks from them. Most casting directors and creative teams have a sense if someone's a good fit for their show within the first few seconds of an audition, so being prepared with a few knockout 8-bar cuts will help you feel more prepared.

Sometimes your cuts might be all inclusive, meaning you have a 32-bar cut in your book and you use half of it for your 16-bar cut, and then half of that for your 8-bar cut. Sometimes they aren't. Sometimes you might use one part of the song for your 32-bar cut and a different part of the song for your 16-bar cut. It's also worth noting that not all songs will allow themselves to have 32-, 16-, and 8-bar cuts. Some songs need more time to work in the room, so you only have a 32-bar cut. This happens often in story songs and comedy songs that need more time for the dramatic payoff. Some songs cut beautifully into 16-bar cuts, but they become challenging to expand to 32-bar cuts. You don't have to have all lengths of cuts from every song, you just need to make sure you have all cuts represented in your book.

The Full-Length Song

In the professional world, it is rare to be asked to do an entire song, but it is helpful to have one full song in your book. When it does happen, it's often in callback situations or when the music is particularly challenging. They may want to hear you on an entire piece to see your full acting journey or see how your handle a demanding full-length song. You might also be asked for a full song in community theatre or other nonprofessional venues, in which case, having a book with a variety of cuts *and* one or two complete songs would serve you well.

PICKING AUDITION SONGS

When it comes to selecting the songs to put in your audition book, there are unique considerations. Singers can find material on their own or work with a repertoire coach that specializes in finding audition material. Whether you select the material on your own or with a coach, it's imperative that you spend time working on the material before you bring it into an audition. Working on the song with your voice teacher is valuable to make sure the song is strong vocally, as is working on the song with your repertoire coach to make sure the cuts work and that your acting choices are clear and specific. We've already discussed the elements of selecting repertoire for developmental concerns, many of which still apply here.[2] However, there are additional elements that should be considered when looking for audition material.

Identity

Just as with songs meant for development, singers should bring great thought and care into deciding whether it is appropriate for them to sing the musical theatre song they are considering. If a song was written for a specific racial or ethnic identity, a trans or nonbinary character, or a character with a disability, it is important that singers who identify that way sing the song. These considerations are always important, but especially important when auditioning.

Age Considerations

When picking songs for your audition book, you want songs that are either ageless and work at all stages in life, or songs that feel age appropriate. This means avoiding material that is written for characters that are vastly older or younger than you are, especially if the material discusses content that would not make sense for your age range. This means that you might outgrow songs in your book over time and should replace them as you move into a new age bracket.

Functional Execution

This may seem like common sense, but you need to be able to sing every song in your book well. A song that's just out of reach vocally is meant for your "working book," not your audition book. You should be able to meet all vocal demands of a song like range, tessitura, breathing, dynamics, registration requirements, and not struggle with any vowels of the song. If you're still working these things out, the song does not belong in your audition book. Remember that you should be ready to sing *every* song in your audition book at *every* audition, so if you are under the weather and have something you can't sing that day, you might consider removing it from your book. It is not uncommon for a casting director or creative team member to flip through your book, look at your table of contents, or simply ask you for a second song of a specific genre. You want to make sure you're up to date with and ready to always sing what's in your book.

Musical Execution

Singing in tune at auditions is of the utmost importance. If you are unable to stay in tune with your pianist, it will be challenging to have a successful audition. You want all songs in your book to be on par with your musical abilities. If you need an accompaniment that plays the melody along with you, make sure that is represented in your sheet music. If your song has an acapella section or a section where the piano is sparce, you need to be able to successfully navigate the section.

Stylistic Execution

If you're putting a 1990s punk song in your book, you need to be able to sing in that style well. If you struggle to make sounds that align with punk sounds, it might not serve you well to include that in your book. Choose another pop/rock genre to include instead.

Dramatic Execution

Are you able to act the song well? If it's a comedy song, you need to be able to find the humor. If it's a more dramatic song, you should connect to the lyrics in a way that allows you to tell a compelling story. All songs in your book need to be not only sung well, but also acted well.

Character Baggage

Character baggage refers to the silent expectations that come with musical theatre songs. In particular, it is the unspoken information about the character that is inherently part of the song. When you sing "I Cain't Say No" from *Oklahoma!* in an audition, people will immediately think of Ado Annie. It is hard to separate the song from the character. This can be either a tremendous help or hinderance when auditioning. If you are auditioning for a character that exhibits similar traits or has a similar story to Ado Annie, for instance Meg in *Brigadoon*, bringing that character baggage into the audition could be helpful. It gives the auditors a lens with which to see you. However, if you are auditioning for a character that is different from Ado Annie, such as Nellie Forbush in *South Pacific*, the Ado Annie lens might hinder your audition. It might make it hard for people to see you as Nellie when the character baggage is weighing you down.

Your book should have songs that have character baggage and songs that don't. If you are trying to make the team behind the table see you as the leading character, then singing a song sung by a leading character in a musical could be helpful. It frames your audition and helps the team know how you want to be seen. Equally important are songs with no character baggage. This allows you to walk in the room and do whatever you'd like with the material. You can put it in a key that works for you and act the song however you'd like. Standards, pop/rock songs, and songs from lesser-known or unproduced musicals tend to come with less or no character baggage.

Song Expectations

While some songs might not come with character baggage, it's important to note that many songs *do* come with some sort of expectation. These expectations are not "good" or "bad," but rather come from an iconic performance or from being well known. For instance, "I Wanna Dance with Somebody" by Whitney Houston is iconic. While there's no character baggage, if you choose to sing it in an audition, there might be expectations. Understanding song expectations can help you select material that works for your voice and acting abilities.

Audition Worthy

For songs to be the most effective in an audition setting, they need to be "audition worthy." This means that they show enough vocally and dramatically to showcase your skills. Not all songs need high notes or the most dramatic story, but your songs should show your voice and acting off in the best light. Songs that are active dramatically, clearly show your vocal skills, and have clear storytelling tend to work the best in auditions.[3]

TYPES OF MUSICAL THEATRE SONGS

In musicals, the songs typically serve one of two purposes—they either move the plot forward or reveal character. Occasionally they serve to expand or reflect on an emotional moment, but most songs in musicals function as a major part of the storytelling. Some types of songs work better for auditions than others, so understanding the type of songs in musicals can help you find audition-worthy material.

Opening Numbers

The opening number is at the top of the show. It typically establishes the world of the show and introduces the main players. It also sets the tone for the show and tells the audience how to watch. Some iconic opening numbers include the opening to *Ragtime*, *In the Heights*, *Lion King*, *Legally Blonde*, *Urinetown*, and *Into the Woods*.

"I Want" Songs

The "I want" song is a song that typically comes early in the show and is sometimes even the opening number. It is sung by the main character or characters and essentially reveals to the audience what the character desires. Some examples are "The Wizard and I" from *Wicked*, "Wouldn't It Be Loverly" from *My Fair Lady*, "My Shot" from *Hamilton*, and "You and Me (but Mostly Me)" from *Book of Mormon*. Some examples of opening number "I want" songs include "More Than Survive" from *Be More Chill*, "The Day I Got Expelled" from *The Lightning Thief*, and "Belle" from *Beauty and the Beast*. "I want" songs often make great songs for auditions because they express a clear objective and typically show the voice off well.

"I Am" Songs

Like the "I want" song, the "I am" song exists to reveal who a character is. Some examples include "I Cain't Say No" from *Oklahoma*, "I'm Alive" from *Next to Normal*, "Cockeyed Optimist" from *South Pacific*, "Backwoods Barbie" from *9 to 5*, "Dentist" from *Little Shop of Horrors*, and "Morning Person" from *Shrek*. "I am" songs also tend to work well in auditions because they express a need or reveal character in an exciting way.

Story Songs

Story songs are just what the name implies—songs that tell stories. Story songs can serve a lot of different functions in musicals. They sometimes give exposition or reveal character, and sometimes they do not move the plot forward at all but serve as a moment of levity for the audience. Some examples of story songs include "Meadowlark" from *The Baker's Wife*, "I'll Be Here" from *Ordinary Days*, "Nothing" from *A Chorus Line*, "Another Hundred People" from *Company*, "Three Failed Escape Attempts of Sheila Nail" from *Love in Hate Nation*, and "The Saga of Jenny" from *Lady in the Dark*. Story songs can be challenging in auditions because they often require more time for a dramatic payoff. When you must perform a cut in an audition, you often do not have time for this payoff.

Comedy Songs

While they may also serve other purposes, like revealing character, or moving plot forward, comedy songs do so in a way that makes the audience laugh. Some comedy songs get to the joke quickly, while others take time for a humorous payout.[4] Selecting a comedic song for your book can be challenging because not all comedy songs remain funny when they are cut. Some examples of comedy songs are "My Big French Boyfriend" from *The Toxic Avenger*, "I Am Playing Me" from *[title of show]*, "Great Big Stuff" from *Dirty Rotten Scoundrels*, "My Unfortunate Erection" from *The 25th Annual Putnam County Spelling Bee*, and "Whatever Happened to My Part" from *Spamalot*.

Charm Songs

Charm songs are typically written for secondary characters. They are often designed to be a break in the action or tension to give the audience a necessary moment of levity. They are frequently humorous, optimistic, and rhythmic in nature.[5] Older shows would often stage a charm song in front of a closed front curtain to allow for set changes. Now, with automated sets, we don't typically have that need. However, charm songs can still help with the storytelling and pacing of a show. Some examples include "Fugue for Tin Horns" from *Guys and Dolls*, "Shipoopi" from

The Music Man, "Officer Krupke" from *West Side Story*, and "Honey Bun" from *South Pacific*.

Pastiche Songs

Pastiche songs are written in one era, but are meant to evoke an era, style, or genre of the past. Pastiche songs are valuable for storytelling, especially in developing character or world building. For example, the score to *Follies* is written in a pastiche style that is evocative of the music of the vaudeville era, particularly the music of the 1920s and 1930s. Even though the musical was written in the 1970s, Sondheim was able to convey the feeling of the *Follies* with pastiche songs. Other shows that use pastiche songs include *Ragtime*, *Chicago*, *Bandstand*, and *High Fidelity*. Recognizing pastiche songs is important for auditions. For instance, if you are auditioning for *Follies*, you wouldn't sing a typical Sondheim song, despite Sondheim being the composer. You would want to find a song from the vaudeville era of the 1920s and 1930s, particularly a song from the *Follies*, because that is the intended style of the music.

Eleven O'clock Numbers (and "End of Act 1" Numbers)

The two biggest moments in a show are typically the end of act 1 and the end of act 2. These are often the most vocally demanding songs of the show, save for the "I want" song. Songs at the end of act 1 are often cliffhangers, making the audience excited to come back for act 2. They can sometimes be a moment of crisis or triumph. Examples include "Everything's Coming Up Roses" from *Gypsy*, "Right This Way" from *Bandstand*, "So Much Better" from *Legally Blonde*, "A New Argentina" from *Evita*, "And I Am Telling You" from *Dreamgirls*, and "Defying Gravity" from *Wicked*.

The eleven o'clock number is typically the climax of the show and usually puts the protagonist in the moment of decision or revelation. The name comes from the era when showtimes were later, so this climactic moment in the show typically happened around eleven o'clock in the evening.[6] Examples include "Gimme Gimme" from *Thoroughly Modern Millie*, "Rose's Turn" from *Gypsy*, "Make Them Hear You" from *Ragtime*, "Gethsemane" from *Jesus Christ Superstar*, and "Memory Song" from *A Strange Loop*. Both "end of act 1" songs and eleven o'clock numbers can make for great audition songs.

Song and Dance Numbers

Song and dance numbers are just what the name implies—songs with a substantial dance component. They are often designed to showcase a performer and use dance as part of the storytelling. They can have a dance break in the middle of the song or use dance throughout. Examples include "I Can Do That" from *A Chorus Line*, "All I Need Is the Girl" from *Gypsy*, "Cold Feets" from *The Drowsy Chaperone*, "The Music and the Mirror" from *A Chorus Line*, "There's Gotta Be Something Better Than This" from *Sweet Charity*, "America" from *West Side Story*, and "Forget about the Boy" from *Thoroughly Modern Millie*. Song and dance songs sometimes don't work without the dance component, which can make them challenging in auditions. However, many work without the dance component, making them usable in auditions.

Patter Songs

Patter songs are typically rapid songs that are sometimes a tour de force for an actor. They often feel like stream of consciousness coming from the character and sometimes appear in a moment of crisis. They can show verbal dexterity from the actor and often come from characters with great intellect or wit. Songs like "Getting Married Today" from *Company*, "My Eyes Are Fully Opened" from *Thoroughly Modern Millie*, "I Am the Very Model of a Major Modern General" from *Pirates of Penzance*, and "Lost" from *The Lightning Thief* are all examples of patter songs.

Torch Songs

Torch songs are ballads that are typically sentimental, often reflecting on love. These songs are typically sung by female characters. Torch songs in the musical theatre cannon include "Send in the Clowns" from *A Little Night Music*, "But Not for Me" from *Girl Crazy*, "The

Man That Got Away" from *A Star Is Born*, "On My Own" from *Les Misérables*, "Maybe This Time" from *Cabaret*, and "As Long as He Needs Me" from *Oliver*. Torch songs can work well in auditions if they have clear acting objectives and aren't too emotion centered. The pitfall of torch songs is that they can become too self-reflective, which often makes them better in a cabaret setting.

Reprises

A reprise is a repeat of a familiar melody or tune in a show. Recurring musical themes and motifs play an important role in the function of a musical. Audiences will already be familiar with a song, so when that melody is repeated, dramatic moments can become heightened. Reprises often use the same melody or musical theme but change the lyrics to reflect the character's journey. A popular reprise is the "People Will Say We're in Love Reprise" from *Oklahoma!*, which changes the lyrics from "people will say we're in love" to "*let* people say we're in love." This reflects how Laurey and Curly have changed their feelings about being public with their love. Reprises are often gems when it comes to auditioning. Don't discount looking at a reprise as a potential audition song.

Duets, Trios, and Quartets

Duets, trios, and quartets are songs that involve a few characters singing together. Sometimes a verse and chorus of one of these songs cut beautifully into a solo for your audition book. Some examples include "If I Told You" from *The Wedding Singer*, "Tonight" from *West Side Story*, and "Some Other Time" from *On the Town*. This is another often untapped area for finding audition songs that aren't sung as often.

Contemporary Cabaret Songs

This last type of song refers to songs that are *not* written for shows, but rather written as stand-alone, cabaret songs. They often feel theatrical, but since they are not written in the context of a story, they don't have the job of revealing character or moving plot forward. Oftentimes these songs explore more general situations or simply expand on an emotional idea.

Some writers write stand-alone cabaret songs that come from a character's point of view with a clear acting journey, while others don't use this approach. Some popular stand-alone contemporary cabaret songs include "Quiet" by Jonathan Reid Gelt, "Not Yet" by Georgia Stitt, "Broadway, Here I Come" by Joe Iconis, and "I'm a Star" by Scott Alan.

Cabaret songs can sometimes work well in auditions, but I encourage singers to understand the difference between cabaret songs and theatre songs. When a song is character or plot focused, as most theatre songs are, the acting objectives are more easily realized. Songs that have general lyrics or explore emotional states require more work from the actor to create a dramatic narrative. Therefore, theatre songs typically work better in auditions.

PUTTING YOUR BOOK TOGETHER

The three-ring binder that holds your audition materials is sacred. Think of it as your portfolio; it showcases the skills that you take to every job interview. If you're a professional musical theatre performer, you are going to job interviews *all the time.* These job interviews won't stop unless you reach a place in your career where you no longer have to audition, which is unfortunately not the case for the majority of performers.[7] Here are some things to keep in mind about the actual book itself.

Overall Impression

If your book is organized and well put together, it not only puts you at ease, but shows a level of preparedness for the audition. If your binder is broken with stained or torn music, it could leave the impression that you are disorganized, regardless of how well you execute your performance. A disorganized book that is unclear is stressful for both you and the pianist and might not give the best impression.

The Binder Itself

The actual book you put music into should be sturdy. It should be able to open fully and be placed on a piano without falling or closing.

Binders tend to break after time, so replace it when needed. Some people are moving digital and using tablets instead of a binder. While this might seem like a good idea, one downfall of this is that all sheet music programs and tablets operate differently. There is no assurance that the accompanist will know how to operate your specific device or program, making a tablet a bit of a risky move. If you choose this route, be sure your device is always fully charged and turned onto airplane mode to ensure you do not receive any calls or texts during your audition.

Double-Side All Music

Your music should always be double-sided to create fewer page turns. The more the pianist must take their hands off the piano to turn the pages, the more at risk they are for making a mistake. You want to lay your music out with the fewest page turns possible.

Cuts

Make sure all your cuts are *clearly marked*. Use a highlighter or some other clear, discernable way of marking your music. You also want to make sure your cuts make sense musically. Pay attention to key changes, time signature changes, chord patterns, etcetera. You also need to make sure that you don't have conflicting cuts marked on the page. For instance, if you have a clear cut for your 16-bar cut that doesn't apply to your 32-bar cut, consider having the song in your book twice to reduce confusion. If you are not a pianist, it is helpful to show your cuts to a pianist to make sure everything is clear *before* you go into an audition. You don't want to find out that your cuts don't work while you're in the middle of an audition.

Cuts on Page Turns

If you have a tricky cut in your music, you want to make sure you don't place it on a page turn. You want page turns to be predictable so that the pianist knows where they are going musically. This helps reduce errors in the room.

Sheet Protectors

Every pianist has a different opinion on putting your music in sheet protectors. Some love them because they make turning pages easier, but others don't because of the potential for glare. As the owner of the book, the sheet protectors can be nice because they, well, protect your sheet music. They help your music last a bit longer in the book and keep it from being ripped or torn. My advice is that if you are going to use them, be sure and use the non-glare type so that your pianist can see your music clearly.

Dividers or Tabs

Organizing your music in a way that makes it easy to find is helpful. My recommendation is to organize by time period and song type so that all of your golden age songs are in one section, your pop/rock songs are in another section, and so on. This system allows you, or another person at the audition, to easily find the type of song needed. You can use dividers and create sections, or you can tab each individual song (but keep them grouped in sections).

Table of Contents

Keeping a table of contents in the beginning of your book can be helpful. This is a list of everything you have in your book, organized by time period and/or genre. This makes it easy for the pianist, director, music director, or casting director to look at the contents of your book during the audition. This sometimes happens when they'd like to hear a second song and want to see what you might have available. If you keep a table of contents, you *must* keep it updated. You cannot keep songs on the list that are no longer in your book, and any new additions must get added to the list.

Photocopies

If you photocopy a song from a book, or print a pdf from online, make sure the entire page of music gets copied. Do not put music in your book that is missing the bottom or top line of the accompaniment, including chord symbols. Make sure all copies that are in your book are legible and crystal clear.

Keys and Arrangements

You need to make sure that the music you hand the pianist is in the key you want to sing it in and that the arrangement is what you envision. Pianists will play what is in front of them. They cannot be expected to transpose on sight. Nor can they be expected to know the specific arrangement you want if it's not reflected on the music. If you put the music to the Judy Garland version of "Somewhere over the Rainbow" from *The Wizard of Oz* in front of them, but ask them for the Israel Kamakawiwo'ole arrangement, you will be sorely disappointed.

Lead Sheets

You cannot expect a pianist to play from a lead sheet in an audition. You *must* have sheet music in your book, not just lead sheets or chords. If you are having trouble finding sheet music for a song you'd like to include in your book, consider hiring someone to transcribe the music for you.

FINDING AUDITIONS

Once you have your audition book ready to go, you'll need to find an audition to attend. Luckily there are online resources to help you find auditions. There are various types of auditions in the professional world that you should familiarize yourself with. Each type of audition comes with different requirements of what to prepare.[8] ♪

The EPA

The Equity Principal Audition (EPA) is an audition that is held for principal characters in a show. These auditions are for members of the professional performing union, Actors' Equity Association. The rules and regulations of the audition are set by the union.[9] These auditions may happen in person or online via a self-tape. EPAs typically ask for a 32-bar cut or a short selection. When EPAs are in person, members of the union sign up for a timeslot online. There are only a certain number of timeslots available, so there is also an alternate list where union members can be seen when time permits throughout the day. Actors who are not members of the union are only seen when the team permits, which is typically based on the number of actors in attendance. When these auditions happen via self-tape, there is more flexibility in who may submit an audition.

The ECC

The Equity Chorus Call (ECC) is an audition that is held for ensemble or chorus members for a show. These auditions are for members of the professional performing union Actors' Equity Association. The rules and regulations of the audition are set by the union.[10] These auditions may happen in person or online via a self-tape. ECCs for singers typically ask for a 16-bar cut. When ECCs are in person, members of the union sign up online. The day of the audition, the sign-up list is called in the order that folks signed up. Those that are present receive a number and will be seen at the call. Dance ECCs will typically see about twenty people in the room at a time. They will teach a combination and then have you perform it in small groups of two to five people. Singer ECCs will go in the room one at a time but will typically be limited to a 16-bar cut. After dance ECCs, some people might be asked to stay and sing a short selection (typically 16 bars). The same can happen at singer ECCs. Some singers may be asked to stay and dance after everyone has sung. Actors who are not members of the union are only seen when the team permits, which is typically based on the number of actors attendance. When these auditions happen via self-tape, there is more flexibility in who may submit an audition.

The Open Call

Open calls are auditions that do not fall under a union jurisdiction. The rules and regulations can be set by the producer. They may ask for 32-bar, 16-bar, or 8-bar cuts as they see fit. If attending an open call, it's most often first come, first served, and they can turn folks away at any point in the day.

Type

Type refers to the kind of roles that you are suited for. Type can refer to your age, voice type, physical attributes, race, ethnicity, disability, or your personality. If a character is supposed to realistically play a sixteen-year-old, then actors who look like teenagers would likely be considered. If you look older than a teen, you will probably not fit the bill, no matter how right the role might be for your voice or personality.

In the world of musical theatre, the classical *Fach* system plays no real role in casting. Everyone will have genres of music or ranges they prefer to sing in, but musical theatre singers need to be able to belt, mix, and sing legit. The word "soprano" or "tenor" simply indicates the range or style of singing expected. Roles aren't organized or categorized by voice type in the same fashion as within the classical community. In fact, in many shows, one character might move through a variety of vocal styles and musical genres. Glinda in *Wicked* is a great example. She belts, sings legit, and mixes throughout the entire score. She even does all three in the song "Thank Goodness."

Typing

Typing is the act of preselecting actors to audition based on type. Typing typically occurs under two circumstances. The first is during an open call or ECC that has a large turnout of auditionees. The creative team may collect résumés and select the folks they want to see based on their résumé or headshot. If the creative team chooses to type during an ECC, according to union rules they will not be able to see any nonunion actors for the rest of the day. The second reason for typing is when the team is looking for a very specific type for a role. This can happen when they need someone of a specific body type to fit into costumes that are already created or when they need someone to play a sibling of an already-cast actor. They may collect résumés or even have auditionees come into the room in a group to see them in person before deciding who they would like to see audition.

MAKING THE MOST OF YOUR AUDITION

Now that you have an audition book ready and have found some auditions to attend, you want to have the best audition possible. Below are some considerations to help you bring your best work to your auditions.

Clothing and Shoes

You should wear something to your audition that makes you feel good. No one will do their best work if they feel uncomfortable in their clothing or shoes. For some this will mean a dress and heels, but for others this might be jeans and a nice T-shirt. I recommend practicing in your audition footwear so you get a sense of what it feels like to ground yourself and sing while wearing those specific shoes. You might be surprised how many times people are thrown off because they are wearing a new pair of shoes in an audition. There is no exact dress code for how to dress at musical theatre auditions. It can be helpful to take note of what you are auditioning for and pick an outfit that feels evocative of the show. For instance, your outfit for a *Rent* audition should look different than your outfit for a *Guys and Dolls* audition.

Warming Up

Warming up for auditions can sometimes be tricky. In the professional world you might sit for hours before being seen. This sitting doesn't always help your voice feel ready to go once you do get into the room. The best strategy is to try to warm-up early in the day and then keep your voice warm as the day goes. If you have time to sneak away into a practice room while waiting at the audition, this is a great way to check in on your voice, especially if you've been waiting a while.

There are a few tricks to keeping your voice warm as you wait for your turn to audition. Using straw phonation at auditions is the easiest way to keep your voice moving while waiting. Straws are easy to carry with you and allow you to sing without being loud. You can use a straw on its own or in a bottle of water where you blow bubbles while vocalizing. I recommend always keeping a straw in your water bottle to get in the habit of blowing bubbles throughout the day to keep your voice feeling warm.[11]

The downside of straw phonation is that you cannot use your articulators. The Beltbox and Voice Cups are devices that you put over your mouth that muffles your sound, all while allowing you to use language.[12] This is a great way to sing full out without disturbing your fellow auditionees. Additionally, you can use a paper, plastic, or Styrofoam cup with a small hole in the bottom to help create the same effect. It is helpful to practice with the Beltbox or cups at home before using it in an audition, so you know how it feels to sing full out while using either device. You want to make sure you aren't holding back or overcompensating.

Your Best Friend: The Accompanist

Your biggest ally in the room is the pianist. They can make or break your audition. It is important that you present them with an audition book that is clear and organized. When you present your song to the pianist, be sure that the name of the song, the name of the writers, the tempo, the key signature, and the time signature are all present on the page. This information is vital for the pianist to play your song effectively.

No matter how common your song is, you will want to clearly explain your cut and tempo. To best convey your tempo, you should sing a snippet of the song. Choosing to snap or clap the tempo can be irritating, not to mention that singers make more mistakes when simply clapping or snapping the tempo. Singing a section while gently tapping the tempo on your own body is the most accurate way to convey tempo. When your audition is finished, be sure and thank the accompanist for playing for you.

Who Is Behind the Table?

When auditioning professionally, there will be a list of folks behind the table outside the room. This helps you know who you will be auditioning for. Sometimes it will just be the casting director or their assistant, but many times there will be people from the creative team present. This could include the director, choreographer, music director, producer, or any other team members that are part of the casting process. It is a valuable practice to keep track of who you audition for, what material you present for them, and any notes on the reaction in the room or feedback gained. This allows you to keep track of how often you are presenting similar material to the same folks, especially casting directors. It can be helpful to vary the material you are presenting when audition for the same folks frequently.

Slating

Slating refers to a formal introduction of yourself and the material that you will be singing. The most important thing about slating is to remember that it should feel casual and relaxed. Also, use your best judgment when slating. If you walk into the room and the team behind the table greets you by your name, there's no need to slate your name before your audition. If they do not greet you by name, it is OK to mention your name before you begin. Typically, a slate includes your name (when it's appropriate), your pronouns, and the name of the material you are singing. There is no need to supply additional information such as composers, show titles, or years, unless the team has asked you for those details. It is important that you know that information, but it only needs to be divulged if asked.

Monologues

Some auditions ask for monologues, so it is important for musical theatre performers to have at least one monologue memorized, ready to go at all times. While monologues aren't needed often, it is better to be prepared than caught off guard when asked.

Readers

Musical theatre performers are often asked to prepare sides in auditions. These sides might include a short selection of a song and/or scene from the show you are auditioning for. If you are asked to prepare scene work, you will likely read the scene with a reader. The reader is a person who is in the audition to read the scenes with the auditioning actors. Most of the time the reader will be seated off to the side and should be included in your audition. Readers may or may not be actors, and you will obviously not be able to rehearse with them, so you should be clear on your objectives and acting beats no matter what the reader may throw at you.

Nerves

Auditions can be nerve-racking. It is normal to feel anxious. Finding a breathing routine that works for you can be a great way to calm your nerves. Practice breathing slowly with the goal of lowering your heart rate while you're waiting on line, before your give your tempo to the pianist, before your slate, and before you sing. It's easy to hold your breath and let your heart rate get the best of you, but slow, measured breathing will help you remain in control.

Another way to prepare for auditions is to practice singing in various environments. If you're able to sing your material in a voice lesson, in a class, in a vocal coaching, and other locations under various circumstances, you will feel more confident singing in an audition. When you are used to only singing in one location, under the same circumstances, it is more challenging to move into an audition with ease.

Goal setting is valuable in auditions. Pick one tangible singing goal for your audition. Anytime you begin to feel anxious or start worrying about whether it's going well or not, focus back in on your goal. For instance, you could set the goal of feeling ribcage expansion when inhaling. If you start to get distracted mid-audition, focus your energy and mind on your ribcage expansion. Picking a tangible goal that you have control of can help keep you present in the room.

When you are waiting on line to go into the audition room, people may ask you questions or want to chat. That time is for you to prepare, so it is acceptable to let people know that you are focusing on your audition and are happy to chat afterward. You can also wear headphones to signal that you are not interested in talking before your audition.

A source of stress for actors is when someone right before you sings the song you were planning to sing. If this happens, I recommended sticking with your plan and singing what you prepared, even if someone else has already sung the song. The reality is that the team behind the table will hear songs multiple times in a day. Changing a song at the last minute can be risky. Unless you have something else appropriate that you feel just as prepared to sing, stick with your plan.

It should be noted that performance anxiety is a real, diagnosable condition. Singers who struggle with anxiety when auditioning or performing should seek help from a licensed therapist who has experience with performance anxiety. There are coping strategies that can be learned in therapy. Medication is also sometimes warranted.

SELF-TAPES

Self-tapes are prerecorded auditions that you submit to casting directors and creatives online. They have existed for years, but during the COVID-19 pandemic, self-tapes became the only way folks could audition for projects. As the musical theatre community began to move out of the pandemic, self-tapes remained a popular way to audition folks and will likely be popular for a long time. Here are some considerations for self-tapes.

Be Well Rehearsed

One of the issues folks run into with self-tapes is that they tend to record their material multiples times in a row attempting to get it "right." If you have to record your audition a dozen times to get a good pass, you are more than likely under-rehearsed. You should be able to get your material recorded in one to three takes (barring a technical difficulty like the camera turning off or your doorbell ringing). Make sure you dedicate time to practicing your material, not just filming it. In fact, you should be spending more time working on the material without the camera rolling than with. Remember, you would only get one shot in person, so you want to be just as prepared.

Filming Location

Choose a neutral background for your self-tape filming. A solid-colored background limits distractions when the team is watching your tape. There is no need to purchase a fancy background, although you are welcome to if you do not have a neutral background in your home. While professional sound equipment isn't necessary to film a self-tape, you should be mindful of the sound in whatever space you choose to film in. For example, rooms that are empty or lack soft materials (fabric, etc.) are often echoey.

Framing

Make sure that you are centered and framed nicely in your video. You want to avoid setting your camera at an odd angle, too far away, or too close. Framing yourself from the waist up is typically effective but be sure and read the breakdown in case there are specific requests, such as slating with a full body shot.

Equipment

You don't need expensive equipment to create a good self-tape. It is helpful to have a light, such as a portable ring light, so that you are well-lit when filming. A tripod is also helpful so you can set your camera at the appropriate height. Most cell phones are effective for self-tapes because of the high-quality camera and microphone. There is no need to purchase an expensive camera or microphone unless your phone is older or of lower quality. The last piece of equipment you will need is some sort of editing software so that you can edit your takes into one self-tape video. There are plenty of free video editing software programs available online.

Practice

You should find a good location in your home and set up your self-tape equipment for a dry run. This will allow you to test the volumes, sound balance, location, framing, lighting, editing, and so on so that when you have an actual audition with a deadline you can move more quickly.

COLLEGE AUDITIONS

Over the last few decades, musical theatre college programs have begun popping up everywhere. The process for admittance to these programs is becoming increasingly competitive. While there are a handful of texts dedicated to this subject that explore every aspect in extreme detail, here we will discuss a few basic concepts for college auditions.[13]

Selecting Material

It is critical that you pay close attention to the requirements stated by each school you are auditioning for. Some will ask for 16-bar cuts, while others will ask for a minute-and-a-half cut. Some schools might want one song pre-1965 with the second being post-1965. Other schools will ask for two contrasting songs of any time period or genre. You will more than likely need three to four songs to cover your bases, or at least two songs with a variety of cuts. You will probably sing two of them frequently, but there will always be an outlier that asks for something different. It is imperative that you sing material that is aligned with the audition requirements.

The college audition is different from professional auditions in that the goal is to introduce yourself to the faculty. You want to select material that you feel represents you well, not material that is focused on a specific character. We want to get to know you and decide if we want to spend four years working with you, so getting a sense of who you are is helpful. It is also essential that you sing your songs well, right now, with the voice you have. Stay away from material that does not showcase your vocal and acting strengths, even if you think it is a "flashier" or "better" song. You should also avoid material that is inconsistent in performance. You want to be able to execute the song well at every audition.

Prescreens

Many programs require prescreens, which are self-tapes. Prescreens are typically required when there are more people who apply than can be seen. The prescreen is your first round of the audition. If you pass your prescreen, you will be invited for a live audition. When filming your prescreen make sure you follow the earlier advice for self-tapes. Also, make sure you submit all the required materials, including dance and a wildcard, if asked. The wildcard is typically a video where you can do whatever you would like. It's a great opportunity to showcase any other skills you might have or do something fun and memorable that helps the faculty get to know you better. When given the opportunity to submit a wildcard video, you should *always* do so.

Extra Songs

It can be helpful to have two to three additional songs in your audition book when you go to your college auditions. Occasionally, the faculty might want to hear you sing something else besides the material they asked you to prepare. You should make sure that one of the extra songs you include is a pop/rock song. If you are not preparing anything legit or belted for the audition, it wouldn't hurt to include a legit or belt song as one of your extras in case they ask to hear that quality. Anything else you include should be songs that you love to sing that show different vocal and dramatic qualities than your prepared material.

Selecting Schools

When embarking on the college audition process, be sure and look at a wide variety of schools. You will want to explore BMs, BAs, and BFAs to understand the different course offerings in the various degrees. You'll also want to look at the campus and school life to get a sense of what you are looking for in the college experience. University musical theatre programs are highly competitive, so it is helpful if you have a large list of schools for which to audition. Ultimately, the most important thing is that you find a school that you feel excited to attend. It is easy to become focused on the more popular, competitive musical theatre schools. However, you can receive an excellent education attending a small, lesser-known school. You do not need to attend one of the bigger, more well-known universities to receive a good arts education. Find the school that is the right fit for *you*.

FINAL THOUGHTS

Auditioning can feel daunting when you first embark on the process. However, the more you audition, the more confident you become. Auditioning can even start to feel fun! No matter where you are auditioning, it is important to show up feeling prepared and ready. Using the tools in this chapter can help you arrive feeling equipped for success.

NOTES

1. For instance, I used to sing "And Then He Kissed Me" as my 1950s/1960s pop song. I could perform it like the earnest girl next door if I was auditioning for Sandy in *Grease*, the vamp if I was auditioning for Marty in *Grease*, or the awkward, nerdy friend if I was auditioning for Penny in *Hairspray*. The song was valuable in my book because of this dramatic flexibility.
2. If you have not read the chapter on developmental repertoire, I highly recommend you do so to understand those elements of song selection.
3. Revisit the chapter on acting for a review on how to shape a song dramatically.
4. Paul R. Laird, "Musical Styles and Song Conventions," in *The Oxford Handbook of the American Musical*, ed. Raymond Knapp, Mitchell Morris, and Stacy Wolf (New York: Oxford, 2018), 43.
5. Knapp, *Musical Styles*, 34.
6. Knapp, *Musical Styles*, 34.
7. This is referred to as "offer only" and is a typical status of successful performers.
8. These audition rules and regulations are based on Actors' Equity Association, which it the professional stage union found in the United States. It is the union that governs Broadway. There is a Canadian Actors' Equity Association, as well as Equity, the British creative professional's union. In addition to these unions, there are numerous other unions that serve performing artists in both the United States and other countries. It is important to check with your local union's regulations when preparing to attend an audition.
9. The rules of the EPA change from time to time, so it is best to check with Actor's Equity Association for the most up-to-date guidelines.
10. The same applies to the ECC. Please check with Actor's Equity Association for the most up-to-date guidelines.

11. See the pedagogy chapter for a full explanation of semi-occluded vocal tract exercises, including straw work.

12. Please visit https://www.beltyafaceoff.com/ to learn more about the Belt Box. Check out https://voicestraw.com/ for more information on their cups and straws.

13. For a more thorough exploration of college auditions, see Mary Anna Dennard, *I Got In! The Ultimate College Audition Guide for Acting and Musical Theatre* (self-published, 2021): Tim Evanicki, *The College Audition: A Guide for High School Students Preparing for a Degree in Theatre* (self-published, 2018): Amy Rogers Schwartzreich, *The Ultimate Musical Theater College Audition Guide: Advice from the People Who Make the Decisions* (New York: Oxford, 2019).

⑬
MUSICAL THEATRE PROFILES

MEGAN HILTY

Megan Hilty is probably most recognizable for her portrayal of Ivy Lynn in the NBC Musical Drama *Smash*. Before that, Hilty started her career on Broadway, playing Glinda in *Wicked*, Doralee Rhodes in *9 to 5. The Musical*, and Brooke Ashton in *Noises Off*. Other stage credits include Audrey in *Little Shop of Horrors* (Kennedy Center), Annie Oakley in *Annie Get Your Gun* (Encores/NY City Center) and Lorelei Lee in *Gentlemen Prefer Blondes* (Encores/NY City Center). Her numerous television credits include *Sean Saves the World* with Sean Hayes, *Difficult People*, *Braindead*, *The Good Fight*, playing the iconic Patsy Cline in *Patsy and Loretta* and Lily in NBC's *Annie Live!* Megan's voiceover work spans from audiobooks to kids animated favorites like *TrollsTopia* on Hulu, *TOTS* on Disney, *Madagascar* and *It's Pony!* on Nickelodeon, and even some shows for adults like *Family Guy*, *American Dad*, *Robot Chicken*, and *Tuca & Bertie*. Hilty continues to tour her cabaret show with her band, which has been taped for *Live from Lincoln Center* on PBS, and regularly appears with world-renowned orchestras including the New York Pops, Boston Pops, and the National Symphony Orchestra.

How did you first get interested in musical theatre?
My parents exposed me to a lot of different types of music and took me to a lot of live music events. My mother read an article during my early childhood about tone deaf mothers and how they should never sing to their children because then their children would be tone deaf too. I don't know if this is true at all, but my mother took it to heart. She still swears that she can't carry a tune (I've never heard her sing!). So, naturally, I became obsessed with singing. My parents would play me all kinds of different music like Dolly Parton, Whitney Houston, *The Music Man*, Manhattan Transfer, the Beach Boys, and I became obsessed with listening to music. I would sing along and try to sound like the singers. I don't think I knew what I was doing, but I would try! My mom said I was just "always singing" and I didn't know what that really meant until I had my daughter, and she is *always singing*. She plays with tones and sound without even thinking about it!

My mom made sure I saw lots of community theatre, and since I grew up in Seattle, I would see national tours that would come through. When I saw *Jekyll and Hyde* on tour, I remember that at intermission, I had this feeling inside me, like, "I don't know what this is, but I want to be part of it!" I knew I wanted to make people feel the way I was feeling in that moment.

What is your experience with formalized voice lessons?
I started taking voice lessons when I was about ten from Merry Kimball and we focused on classical singing. She said that I had a voice for classical music, so we trained solely in that direction. Merry was also blind. She couldn't see what I was doing when I was singing, so she didn't know that I was mimicking all these bigger voices that I had heard. I was developing jaw tension that she couldn't see, so I was this ten-year-old with a wobbly jaw trying to make big sounds. When I was twelve, I started competing in classical voice competitions and the adjudicators kept pointing out my jaw, so Merry was able to help me by making me practice with a mirror every lesson to make sure that it was still, and I had to tell her if it started to wobble so she could help me work around it. Merry was my teacher until I went away to college. She exposed me to all kinds of singing. I was singing arias, Italian art songs, and I devel-

oped a great appreciation for that type of music. I even started seeing shows at the Seattle Opera because of her.

I have always been extremely grateful that I trained classically first because I feel like it gave me the building blocks to help me transition into different styles. I kind of liken it to a dancer learning ballet first and really understanding how to command those different muscle groups so that later you know how to adjust them. I'm grateful that I had those strong building blocks, especially at such an early age. I get nervous when parents ask me about teaching their babies how to belt. I am not a vocal coach or voice teacher, but there's something about that that makes my brain go "Oh, be careful with those young voices."

I know that you took a gap year between high school and college. Can you expand on why you made that decision?
I took two years off actually. I went to a performing arts high school that turned out to not be fully accredited by the time I would graduate, so we had to pivot quickly. My mom signed me up for an independent study program where I finished the few classes I had left. I ended up graduating early. It was very anticlimactic because there was no graduation—I was just done. One of my teachers had a friend in Southern Oregon who ran a community theatre and I ended up spending two years there. My mom's very progressive, and she was always very supportive of a gap year or—in my case—two. Thinking back now, you're making all these huge life decisions as a baby, so before I committed myself to four years of intense training (and potentially going into hundreds of thousands of dollars of student loan debt) we all wanted to be very certain that this is what I wanted to do. I took those two years, and I did dinner theatre, community theatre, and every terrible job you could imagine to support my theatre habit. I wanted to make sure that my heart was in the right place for this. And it was. I auditioned for Carnegie Mellon after the first year and I got in, but I decided I wasn't really done living life in Southern Oregon, so I took another year off. They were nice enough to let me defer for a year.

Something I constantly find myself telling people is, if you line up one hundred people who have made it to Broadway and you ask them how they got there, everybody will have had a wildly different path. Broadway isn't a destination. There's no right way to get there, and once you've gotten there, it's a constant struggle to maintain. There's no right way to have a career and there's no time line. I'm extremely grateful that my mom gave me the grace of those two years, because by the time I got to Carnegie Mellon, I was extremely self-sufficient. I knew how to take care of myself. I knew how to do my laundry and feed myself. I knew all those life skills before I got there, whereas a lot of my peers were struggling with life issues on top of the immense amount of work that we had to do at school. I was ready to work.

What were the most influential training experiences you had outside of formalized lessons?
When I went into *Wicked*, I learned quickly about the importance of placement for the character so that I could sustain the whole show. I wasn't trying to emulate Kristin Chenoweth's voice, but I knew that placement was so key to the character. Nobody can sound like Kristin, but I knew that very high, forward placement was going to be helpful in getting me through, especially with the speaking voice. A lot of times actor's voices go out in plays from not supporting their speaking voices correctly. When you're singing, you know how to support because you have to sustain the notes. But, in speaking, you can get in a lot of trouble. You can get lazy and sit back vocally. It can start to really wear and tear your voice, so with *Wicked*, that's where I made the conscious effort to emulate that placement. I knew it would help with the character and it would help with seamlessly going from speaking into singing too.

How do you maintain your voice while doing eight shows a week?
Well, I'm going to back up a bit, and this might seem like I'm taking a turn, but it actually has something to do with what this question. I did the Summer Conservatory at the San Francisco Opera, and I spent several weeks there training classically. It was there that I realized that musical theatre was probably going to be more for me because I never wanted to be as precious about my voice as the people around me had to be. It was such a necessity in the classical world. So many people didn't speak until they stepped on stage, which I couldn't wrap my mind around. That, and the fact that you probably won't work until your mid-thirties because that's when a woman's voice matures. I thought, "Whoa,

what?" That sounded like an eternity to my sixteen- or seventeen-year-old self. I've always wanted to take care of my voice, but I didn't want it to rule my life, which is why musical theatre sounded like much more of a correct path for me. And I've always felt that way. I'm not the type of person who doesn't speak until the show. I just can't do that. I have total respect for people who do—I just can't.

My regime has changed since I've gotten older. When I was younger, I could go out until one or two in the morning, drink, and get up and do a matinee *and* an evening show of *Wicked,* and pop up to the high E6 like it was no problem. Today, that would be a very different. But even back then I realized the importance of drinking enough water and getting enough rest. Those have always been the two big things for me: hydration and rest. I've learned how to power nap and not just for energy, but for my voice. I realized that a good twenty-minute rest, even if you're not sleeping, is excellent. I'm also one of those people that drinks a cup of coffee before every show. I know you're not supposed to have caffeine, but I have done it ever since my twenties. I did four and a half years in *Wicked* and I had a giant coffee and a cookie before every single show. We needed a lot of energy! I do that to this day before my concerts too.

Everybody has their own routine, and I have different warmups that I do. I try to take care of myself, but not be too precious. For each thing I do, I have a short vocal regimen, even for my animation work. The regimen is tailored to the type of day that I've had—how tired I am, etc. I also have these little checkpoints. For instance, if I have this note this easily in this way, I'm good.

I don't really cool down vocally, but I do have a sort of cooldown routine. I had a neck injury while doing a play on Broadway and it was impacting my voice. I thought I was going to have to miss a show, which I never did during the run. My ENT sat me down and asked me what I do after my shows, and I said, "Nothing. I get out of there as soon as I can." He suggested that I stop by my costume and say goodbye to my character before leaving. Something about that made complete sense, and I've done it ever since, even with my concerts; I say good night. There's something about it that tells my brain that I'm turning off and I'm walking away from the show. That's my cooldown.

You are known for having a versatile voice. Was your training focused on multiple styles, or did you feel as though you honed in on one more than the other?

I panicked when I went to Carnegie Mellon. I was thinking that I would be this sweet ingenue, since I'm a trained soprano, and then I quickly realized that the stuff that was happening on Broadway didn't have sopranos anymore. Everybody was belting and I didn't know how to belt, so I decided that if I wanted to work after school, I had to learn how to belt. I shifted my mentality from soprano to belt. I pretended like I didn't know the soprano stuff, and I focused solely on belting. It got to a point where when I was a senior, *Wicked* had just opened on Broadway and my classmates were going to New York to see it. They would come back and say, "Oh my gosh, Megan! You have to audition for this musical. It is so great and there is a part that is so perfect for you. The only problem is that you'd have to paint yourself green every day!" They thought that I would audition for Elphaba! That's how much I was working on belting at school. Nobody had any idea about the other stuff my voice could do. When I got the audition for Glinda, even I thought, "Why am I auditioning for this? That's not the role I'm supposed to play!"

I learned how to sing pop music on the fly as well. That was a huge learning curve. Once I started *Smash*, they told me I'd be singing pop songs. Thankfully, the producer, Andy Zulla, was encouraging. At first, he told me to take the Broadway out of it and I kept asking, "What do you mean take the Broadway out of it? We're doing a show about Broadway!" Then we started really understanding each other, and I started listening to recordings more closely. I had never really recorded stuff before. Everything I had done required projection and filling up a large space, and now I was learning how to sing in a confined space in an intimate fashion. I had never done that before, so I was learning on the job. I was lucky to have a producer like Andy who was patient with me and helped me stop and listen to what I was doing. I've grown to really love listening for those technical things. I love those small adjustments that make a huge difference. I think that's why I enjoy voiceover and animation so much. I appreciate the minutia and the kind of nerdy way to speak about the voice and how to manipulate it in certain way. That's so necessary for each individual character and scenario.

Marrying acting and singing is one of the challenging aspects of musical theatre. What are your thoughts on the relationship between acting and singing?

I always think it's so funny when people ask me if I like singing or acting better. To me, they are the same thing—at the end of the day, we're telling a story. Period. There is no separation between acting and singing. It's why I fell in love with the curriculum at Carnegie Mellon. In their program, musical theatre students were actors first who sang and danced on the side. It was really a double major as far as they were concerned because we did everything that the actors did, plus the singing and the dancing. And that was really appealing to me because I knew we were telling a story first and foremost. Some of the greatest performers in musical theatre are not the greatest singers, but they're so powerful because they know how to connect to the text. That's what's always been important to me.

Anytime I work with young people, I tell them that I don't care about the singing part because that's going to come if you are training with a good voice teacher. The important part is to focus on how you're telling the story. It's always about the text first, supported by the vocal technique. When you get a piece of music, the first thing you do is take out the lyric and you study the words like a monologue. Then, you start looking at your map, which is the music. The notes, the rests, the crescendos, and the decrescendos are the map that tells you how to interpret the song. You take what you've learned from the storytelling of the text and you infuse it with your own personal angle.

I often see young singers in master classes do great work and connect to their song . . . until the high note. Then I see them detach from what they're singing about and focus instead on trying to get the note out. Without fail, if I ask them to stop thinking about singing and think about their intentions and what they're saying, the note is there. Nine times out of ten, it's seamless and even more powerful. Even if the singer must cut the note short or make it a little different—i.e., not as loud or soft as it's supposed to be—it's powerful because the intention is clear. When you start panicking about the notes, you completely remove yourself from what you're talking about. This makes the audience remove themselves from the moment too. You have to trust that it's all there. If you've done the work with your voice teacher and coach, you can shift focus to your intentions. If the intention is right, the support is going to be there too. It's not there when you're panicking about how to sing the note. Everything tenses up and the support is gone, but if you really believe in what you're saying, and you have a clear intention in your mind—who you're talking to, why you're saying it, and why it's important that you're not just saying it but you're *singing* it—the notes will be there.

We rarely stand still while singing in musical theatre. How do you navigate singing and athleticism at the same time?
Even though I am a *terrible* dancer, I've still done very athletic things while singing in shows. Musicals have demanding physical elements—even just running around backstage is a marathon. It's a physically taxing job. Even though I'm not a dancer, I think I probably pay more attention to loosening up my body than I do my voice because they're so connected. With my vocal warm-up, I don't want to tire myself out. I simply want to check to make sure everything's where it needs to be. But I need to be fully in my body. I need to make sure that my neck is relaxed, my shoulders are relaxed, my hips are stretched out, my jaw is sufficiently loose, my tongue is massaged, and when I'm taking a breath, I want to make sure my breaths are deep enough and not sitting high. If anything is tense in my neck or my shoulders, it's going to really wreak havoc with my vocal folds, and my voice is going to have to take on more responsibility.

Who had the most influence on you, your career, and/or your training?
Well, as far as idols go, Bernadette Peters has always been mine. When I when I was younger, we didn't have YouTube, but I had cast albums. I'll never forget getting that CD of *Into the Woods*. I would pull the libretto out and listen while following along. The second I heard Bernadette Peters' voice, something inside of me lit up. There's something about her spirit that comes through her voice and her storytelling that made my body come alive on a molecular level. This is why she is who she is, and why live performances are so powerful. It literally resonates in spots inside our bodies. If it's recorded correctly, then that comes through without Auto-Tune, which is why I feel that it was such a powerful

recording. I was literally feeling the resonance from her voice in in my body. Not to totally nerd out on it, but I remember how powerful it was to hear her performance vocally. Her storytelling was perfection, and that got me excited. It made me want to do a deep dive into researching her career. I saw that she did everything—voiceovers, concerts, film, TV, theatre, recording artist work, etc. I knew that I couldn't be like her since she has a singular talent, but I knew I wanted my *career* to be like hers. I wanted to span over all these different genres too. Then during *Smash* they told me that not only was she going to be on the show, but she was going to be my mom and we were going to sing and have all these scenes together! I realized then after getting to know her that on top of this monumental talent, she is just one of the greatest people. She is a vulnerable, giving, nurturing person and that really reads in her performances. She'll always be at the tip-top of my list of idols. She has been, and always will be, the best.

What advice would you give an aspiring musical theatre performer?

Something I wish that I would have known as a young performer is that who I am and what I bring to the table is enough. It's more than enough. It's a gift. Not just me, but what everybody brings to the table. What you have is a gift. I panicked when I was younger, and I still do—I'm not saying that I ever got over it—but it's gotten easier as I've gotten older. I've always panicked that that I wasn't "insert whatever adjective" enough: I wasn't skinny enough. . . . I wasn't a good enough singer, etc. I was always panicked (even after I got jobs) that somebody would turn around and say, "Hey, you don't belong here because you're not this and you're not enough of that." It wasn't until I was a standby in *Wicked* that a stage manager turned around and said "Hey, you have to stop watching the show. Go back and make the role your own." Going into *Wicked* was one of the scariest things I've ever done because the bar was set so high after Kristin Chenoweth, who was amazing. I had to come to terms with the fact that I wasn't Kristin, and I wasn't the equally genius Jennifer Laura Thompson who had taken over for Kristin. I wasn't either of those people. I had to figure out what I could contribute to this role. Figuring out what that was and coming to terms with the fact that some people might not like it, was life changing. But it would be OK, because what I brought to the table was enough. I wish that I was confident in that at an earlier age, because I could have saved myself a lot of agony. When you are auditioning for a certain role, they might have something in mind for what they want, but what they really want to see is how *you* tell that story—*not* how you think they want to see the story told. There are many reasons why you might not get a job but being true to yourself will never be a detriment. If anything, it's what makes you more solid and comfortable in your skin. That's what people want to see. They want to see *you*.

What advice would you give a musical theatre voice teacher?
I would encourage any voice teacher to celebrate the uniqueness of your students and not try to make them into something that they're not. I think it's along the same lines with my advice for aspiring performers. The most successful people that I have witnessed or worked with are people that are very solid in their own skin and their uniqueness. They find the things that really make them different. There are so many programs that turn out a lot of people who work, but the people who have longevity are the ones that are unique and are very solid in that uniqueness. For any teacher, I would really encourage them to seek out that uniqueness and foster it. Help your students shine through because that will only make them more confident.

JUSTIN GUARINI

Justin's Broadway credits include *In Transit* (Trent; dir. Kathleen Marshall), *Wicked* (Fiyero; dir. Joe Mantello), *Romeo + Juliet* (Paris; dir. David Leveaux), *American Idiot* (Will; dir. Michael Mayer), *Women on the Verge* . . . (Carlos; dir. Bart Sher), and the Encores! production of *Paint Your Wagon* (dir. Marc Bruni). Regionally, he has been seen in *Once Upon a One More Time* at Shakespeare Theatre Co. (Prince Charming), *Rent* (Roger), *Chicago* (Billy Flynn), *Joseph . . . Dreamcoat* (Joseph), *Company* (Bobby), *Moonshine* (Gordy), *Ghost Brothers of Darkland County* (Drake), *Mamma Mia!* (Sam), *Cake Off* (Jack), *The Unsinkable Molly Brown*(Vincenzo) and more. His albums include *Revolve* (EP), *Stranger Things Have Happened, Justin Guarini*. Television credits include *American Idol* Season One Finalist, and Lil' Sweet for Diet Dr. Pepper national commercials.

How did you first get interested in musical theatre?
I first got interested in musical theatre when I was in elementary school. I used to be a latchkey kid and instead of going home to sit on the couch and watch cartoons, my school had an after-school program. They would roll in the AV cart with the TV strapped on it and the VHS machine and one day they put in this tape and up on the screen the words *West Side Story* appeared. From that moment on, I was hooked. I remember leaving the after-school session so clearly. I was poorly doing the Jerome Robbins choreography down the hall. I felt like I could fly. That, for me, was my moment that I knew, "Oh my God . . . I absolutely love this." It was this beautiful intersection of all the things that I loved to do. I loved to dance and sing, and then I could sing *and* dance *and* do all this emoting up on the stage. It was the perfect blend.

What is your experience with formalized voice lessons?
I started out in the Atlanta Boys Choir. That was my first big vocal experience. Choral singing would be a large part of my upbringing in the Atlanta Boys Choir, then the Philadelphia Archdiocese Choir. I started as a boy soprano. Then sometime during junior high my voice changed, and I went from being an alto to a tenor. Choral singing was the basis of my vocal education. I went to a Westminster Choir College camp, and that was when I took my first formal solo vocal lesson. I was classically trained from the beginning and I'm grateful because it gave me such a wonderful technical foundation. Singing in Latin and learning to blend in choir, especially learning how to fit into the larger sonic picture was valuable. I'm grateful for these experiences, because they made the longevity of my voice much easier to maintain.

What were the most influential training experiences you had outside of formalized lessons?
Well, that's where musical theatre comes in, because it's the integration of movement and vocalization. Even before I started my Broadway career, I found myself touring with *American Idol*. I was running on the stage and doing choreography, but we were also singing live. That

on-the-job training was crucial for me because I realized I could move, but I also had to maintain the core strength and breath support while I'm doing all that movement. This is why I love musical theatre and especially the role I'm doing right now in *Once Upon a One More Time*. We are athletes and not only are we doing athletic things just like any professional athlete, but we're doing it while we're singing.

Can you talk about your decision to delay your Broadway debut to do *American Idol*?
In 2002 I was working for a bar and bat mitzvah DJ company. I was singing and dancing on the weekends entertaining thirteen-year-olds. Between 1998 to 2002 I also auditioned off and on for *The Lion King*. I had been doing master classes, and work sessions, and did everything but set foot on the stage. They said to just be patient and that they wanted me for the show, but just didn't have room yet. I didn't hear anything for six or eight months . . . maybe a year. And then a show nobody's ever heard of called *American Idol* comes along they gave me a yellow piece of paper, told me it's a golden ticket, and that I'm going to California. Then, maybe four or five days before I got to California I get a call, and of course it's the casting director's office telling me that I'm going to make my Broadway debut in *The Lion King* and when can I start? I was like, "Wow . . . there's a show out in California I have to do. Can I call you in a week?" Fast forward to a week later, and I am exhausted. "Hollywood week" is designed to wear you down to see if you can handle the big show. I was at the Pasadena Civic Center where Hollywood week was filmed, and I remember looking over and seeing all my friends/competitors sitting in the orchestra seating section. I remember looking up at the stage and seeing the lights and the smoke and the *American Idol* logo. I was in the theatre, and you could smell the wood, and the age of the place and in that moment, I realized that I had to make this decision between the show nobody had ever heard of and the show that I had been wanting to be in for the better part of four or five years. I started weeping. I was not a big crier at the time, and I got myself together, and when I stopped and I listened to my inner voice, I knew I had to do *American Idol*. I was not in the top thirty yet—I wasn't even sure that I was going to be in the top thirty (let alone the top ten). I could have been cut the very next day, but I yielded, and I said, "OK." I called up

Jay Binder, the casting director, and said, "Thank you so very much for this offer. It is a dream to be on Broadway for me, but I have this other project and there's just something about it. I have to go with it."

The beautiful bow on this story is that ten years later—after the lights of *American Idol* had gone down and I had been in Hollywood through the ups and the downs and everything that my career was over those ten years—I would find myself debuting on Broadway in *Women on the Verge of a Nervous Breakdown*. Our opening-night cast party was in Times Square in a hotel conference room that was the exact room I had sat and waited in to audition for *American Idol*. I came full circle and yet I think, had I gone into *The Lion King*, I might have been successful. I might have been groomed to be Simba which would have been lovely. But I also could have been horribly injured, because of the raked stage and all the other injuries that people get on that show. But I ultimately came back to musical theatre in a much, much stronger position. If *Once Upon a One More Time* goes to Broadway, it will be my seventh Broadway show. I think it all worked out the way it was supposed to.

How do you maintain your voice while doing eight shows a week?
My routine is to always have a rhythm. When I get out of the rhythm, it's a challenge for me. Most people don't have a rhythm and they wonder why they're inconsistent. Developing your rhythm and learning via other peoples' rhythms is paramount. What I mean by that is that the voice is a muscle, just like any other muscle in the body. You have to warm it up. There are so many people who don't have a warmup routine that is the same every single time, and one that is tailored to their voice. That's why it's so important to find a good teacher who can guide you. I had an amazing voice teacher named Ron Anderson who completely changed my voice. He taught me how to go from the basement effortlessly through my passaggio all the way into the stratosphere.

Making sure I have a routine is imperative. I go into the theatre an hour and a half before the show. If I don't do that, I feel rushed. I do a seven-minute workout that warms up my body. Then I warm-up my voice, then I do my hair, then I do my makeup. I make sure that I do everything that needs to be done in a specific order. It's different for everyone. Just today, I went to the chiropractor/physical therapist, and they suggested a couple of exercises that I can do after my workout to target some very specific muscle groups to make sure that they start firing when my body gets tired to keep me from pulling out of alignment. Having vocal exercises that work the same way is essential as well. My routine and rhythm help my body get used to having what it needs. If you listen to your body, it will tell you what it needs and how it needs it. Your routine becomes the rhythm that helps you stay consistent during the show

We rarely stand still while singing in musical theatre. How do you navigate singing and athleticism at the same time?
Trust. Trusting in my body. There's a moment in every single show where I toe the line. Most people are afraid of going to the limit and they stop and say, "No, I don't want to go there." There's a point in *Once Upon a One More Time* where I have to do a major piece of choreography while singing very high and when I'm done, I feel like my toe has come right up to the line. It's the feeling that maybe I'm going to start to pass out or black out, but instead of freaking out, I trust my body. I trust the process. I say, "This feeling is OK. I'm going to now turn and walk upstage, take the biggest breath I can, and gather myself." It really comes down to trust, and you cannot trust yourself unless you are willing to go to a place that feels a little scary. You don't know your boundaries until you test them. If you're not willing to test your boundaries, you don't know how far you can go. You can teach yourself to go a little bit further, and then eventually you get to a place where it's feels OK. You know the limit, but you also know that you can get right up to that line and still be safe and healthy.

Marrying acting and singing is one of the challenging aspects of musical theatre. What are your thoughts on the relationship between acting and singing?
Again, trust. Trust what's on the page. What's on the page is designed to guide you. In musicals, the characters don't sing because that's what the writer wrote—the characters sing because they *must* sing. The characters feel or think a certain way and through the song, we are given a window into the thought process or the evolution of feeling or action. This then guides us to a new revelation at the end that moves the plot

forward. When you have a well-written musical theatre piece, and you trust the words on the page and the notes associated with the words, then you can look for action words, you can look for color words, you can look for emotional words and then marry it all together to understand the phrasing of music. Everything starts to come together. But you have to start from the perspective of trusting what is on the page and then giving yourself over to understanding that there are clues sonically with the notes and there are contextual clues in the words. You have to be a detective and know where to look. They're there and when you learn to look for them, and when you learn to trust the text and how the writer has put the text and the words together, they stand out like beacons and all you have to do is lean into it.

Who had the most influence on you, your career, and/or your training?

There's a lot of people! Technique-wise, definitely Ron Anderson. He is, hands down, the greatest vocal teacher I've ever had. He's amazing and he's still actively teaching. He was an incredible operatic tenor in his own right and he influenced me from a vocal technique perspective for sure. In musical theatre, I can't particularly point to one person that was the most influential, but I would say when it comes to mixing dance with vocals, there's no one better from my generation than Michael Jackson. He was able to take theatricality mixed with dance and soaring, powerful vocals in a way that no one had at the time. The modern music video is thanks in large part to "Thriller." That was groundbreaking and had a huge influence on me.

One of the things that has created my career and is the reason why I adapt so quickly to situations is because I'm always listening, watching, and learning. I'm not watching and learning from an employee mindset—I'm watching and learning from a producer or director mindset. If I'm doing a film, I'm always watching the camera, or what the DP (director of photography) is doing and paying attention to everything. When we pay attention to the behind-the-scenes stuff, especially what the producers and directors do, it helps us to learn how to do our jobs better and in a way that is more in alignment with how they see the world. We end up meeting in the middle.

What advice would you give an aspiring musical theatre performer?
This is one of those things where I think people are going to read this and then hopefully come back to it in a few years and read the same exact thing and hear something completely different, because I know that's the way it was for me. My advice is to know your brand. The word *brand* and *branding* are words that are all too foreign to most musical theatre actors. We think branding is what you wear or the pictures you put up on your social media, but it goes much deeper than that: it's your story. It is the messaging that you put out into the world that lets people know your unique selling proposition. Because the reason why we buy the clothes we buy and the reason why we love the musicals we love or the reason why we watch the TV shows we watch—basically why we consume anything that we consume—is because we are being marketed to by corporations and organizations who understand their brand and their audience. They create messaging that hooks people in and makes them want more. If we can begin to apply that to our own careers as artists, and begin to move away from the employee, the scarcity, the starving artist mindset and move towards the producer, the creator, and the financially independent mindset, we find more success.

What advice would you give a musical theatre voice teacher?
One of the greatest gifts, you can give your students (besides vocal technique) is the ability to understand what the black dots on the page mean. Music theory is vital as a musical theatre performer because when you are asked to learn a song in one day, two days, or three (if you're *really* lucky), it's much different learning that music when you're solely reliant on someone else to put in the work to play it for you and teach it to you. But when you can say, "Oh, that's a fourth and that's a third," for example, you at least have some reference of how to sing your way through the material. Music theory, in a way, allows you to have that little bit of an advantage over 99.9 percent of people who don't know anything about it. Incorporating music theory into your training is valuable. You will do your students a world of good and ultimately you will raise the musical intelligence of our entire community over time.

MUSICAL THEATRE PROFILES   355

SHAKINA NAYFACK

Most recently Shakina made television history as the first transgender person to be cast as a series regular on a network sitcom, with her starring role in the NBC's *Connecting*. . She can also be seen in Amazon's GLAAD Award–winning *Transparent Musicale Finale*, which she helped write and produce, and Hulu's *Difficult People*, for which she was a writing consultant. Her play *Chonburi International Hotel and Butterfly Club* premiered on Audible in 2020 in collaboration with Williamstown Theatre Festival and was recognized with a 2021 Drama League Award for best audio theatre production. She is the founding artistic director of Musical Theatre Factory, where she helped to develop hundreds of new musicals including Michael R. Jackson's Pulitzer Prize–winning *A Strange Loop* and her own autobiographical glam rock odyssey *Manifest Pussy*. Shakina is currently developing several projects for television and writing lyrics for the musical adaptation of *Come Back to the Five and Dime Jimmy Dean, Jimmy Dean*, with composer Dan Gillespie Sells and book writer Ashley Robinson. Recognitions include the Lilly Award for Working Miracles, the Theatre Resources Unlimited Humanitarian Award, the Kilroys List, and two-time Drama League fellow and two-time OUT 100 honoree.

How did you first get interested in musical theatre growing up?
I grew up in a musical family. My great uncle was a renowned percussionist, and my aunt was a musical theatre director and choreographer. She was the director of a nightclub act called *The String of Pearls*. They were a jazz group, and I would watch them perform when I was a kid. My family would also take me to musicals. Music was in the fabric of my family growing up. We're the kind of family that would burst into song because we all would know the words.

I loved singing and I had cast albums, but in seventh grade, my best friend (who was also my first crush) was in this extracurricular choir. It wasn't part of school and it felt like "real" singing to me. So, I auditioned and joined, and was part of the choir during middle school and early high school. I also did musicals in high school. I remember that before I started high school, I went to see the school's production of *Carousel* and was totally blown away. I was an eighth grader being like, "Wow, that's amazing!" I did *Godspell* my sophomore year and it kind of saved my life. It gave me a place to go and a connection with my higher power.

What is your experience with formalized voice lessons?
In college, I started doing trans performance art when I came out. I was performing but I didn't want it to be drag; I wanted it to be different. I also knew that I wanted to sing in these performances. *Aida* had just come out, so I wanted to sing "My Strongest Suit." I worked with a graduate student in the voice department and that was my first time having a private voice teacher. She taught me songs like "Amarilli, mia bella" because they didn't do musical theatre at the school. The most valuable thing I learned in those lessons was how to warm-up. And I gained confidence. So much of my journey at that point was about being confident using my own voice in my transgender performance work.

What were the most influential training experiences you had outside of formalized lessons?
One of the things that I'm still learning is how to ask for what I need. I had stopped singing and performing for about a decade before I created my first solo show, which I was using as a vehicle to fundraise for my gender confirmation. So, when I started singing again and got back on stage with that piece, I was still kind of under the assumption that a higher voice equated a feminine voice, or equated womanhood, and so I was really blowing my voice out and not hitting these notes that I was aiming for. I was pushing myself to achieve a sound that was hard on my throat and body. One of the things I've learned is how to get into the deeper registers of my voice and own that full sound as something feminine and womanly because it was coming from me. And so, when it came time to move out of the world of solo performance and into workshops and being cast in musicals, I had to learn how to have a conversation with a music director or composer about changing a key to a song. I had to learn how to tell them that I might not be able to give them something they were wanting. You want this note that is just not realistic for me to hit after dancing a two-minute dance break. It has taken me a long time to learn how to speak up about that stuff because I felt disempowered as an actor in general, and then I think further disempowered as a trans person trying to achieve this female standard.

That's something I'm still working on. It definitely requires active work. I think the industry is opening up, at least in casting—for instance, making music available in multiple keys for auditions. But part of it is about owning the full range of sounds that my body has the capacity to make. They are congruent with my identity because they're coming from me.

I would love to talk about your process of creating new work and how you found your metaphorical voice as a writer and creator. Finding my voice as a writer and as a singer was parallel with finding my voice as a woman and stepping into my body as a trans person. All of this happened around the same time, and not really until my thirties. I was focused on being a director in my twenties and my early thirties. When I knew that I was going to transition, nothing like that had happened in the Broadway community before. I knew I was going to have to figure out how to tell everyone what was going on. Since we all speak this language of theatre, I figured that if I could put it into a show, then people would understand it. The narrative would be on my terms because I would be constructing the story. That was the emphasis to create my one-woman show which told the story of my life from a very early age until my decision to pursue gender confirmation. It was an autobiographical reflection piece. That was the first time that I had to sing in public in over ten years. It felt really good, and I was getting a lot of positive feedback about it. I could feel my confidence growing as I performed the show more and more. When I came back from gender confirmation, I booked my first major television role. I was now an actress. It became a real thing. I also had a yearlong recovery for my surgery, and the only way I knew how to put a benchmark twelve months ahead was to have a performance on the one-year anniversary. That's how I created my second show, which told the story of my pilgrimage to Thailand for gender confirmation. The show featured a bunch of original music written by composer colleagues and friends of mine, some of which I wrote lyrics for. Both of those shows were born out of storytelling. I would have these occasions where I would gather close friends and tell them some stories about my life or about this journey. I would record myself telling the stories and then I would transcribe them. I'd figure out how to make them funny and streamline them. Many of these stories were potential song moments for the show. After I'd performed post-op, I realized the real show was the two of those things together—my life leading up to gender confirmation and the pilgrimage to get it. *Manifest Pussy* was me merging the two shows into one with some new interstitial material written to weave them together.

At that point, I had written a lot about my process and a lot about myself. There were so many other people who touched my life and intersected with me in a deep way through that process. I wanted to write something to honor all of them and that's where I got the impetus to write *Chonburi International Hotel and Butterfly Club*.

Marrying acting and singing is one of the challenging aspects of musical theatre. What are your thoughts on the relationship between acting and singing?
My foundation as a performer is rooted in this discipline called Body Ritual Movement that was started by Diego Piñón in Mexico. It's inspired by Japanese butoh dance and indigenous Mexican dance and ritual. It's a cultural fusion dance I studied for many years in Mexico with Diego. It is a practice of performance as energy work, so when I am performing a song, I view that song as a container that I'm filling up with a very intentional energy to transmit and share with an audience. I'm operating on a lot of different cylinders. I've usually crafted a sort of mind map for myself that has a lot to do with physical acting and internalizing imagery that's embedded within the song. Then I step into that imagery and experience it while I'm singing. What I'm communicating is really vibrating with the cellular experience I have of being completely enmeshed in the environment and the images that I've conjured to tell the story. For example, I have a song called "Down the Shower Drain" and it's about the first time I took a shower after my gender confirmation surgery. The song is written by Julianne Wick Davis and it is a really gorgeous ballad that has all this beautiful imagery about a natural park with a river and shrine of glory with a baptismal font. The song has gorgeous images and so I crafted a score that I'm seeing with my eyes while I'm singing the words of the song. At one point when I was performing the song, I literally tore through the multiverse and the space-time continuum and when the song ended and I opened up my eyes for the last line of the song and I had somehow superimposed the hospital bathroom on top of the theatre that I was in, and while I could

see my music director to my left, and I could see audience in front of me I could also see the hospital bed to my left and the mirror to my right. Both worlds were existing in at the same time. That's my aspiration. That's where I try to go whenever I'm singing. I try to conjure a reality and let the song be the bridge but not just on an auditory level on a real multisensory level for the audience to join me.

We rarely stand still while singing in musical theatre. How do you navigate singing and athleticism at the same time?
I have a few thoughts. On one hand there are production numbers, where you are dancing, covering a lot of territory, and doing a lot of things with your limbs. That requires a certain kind of breathing. I did a musical once where I had to sing while boxing. For that activity, your breathing mechanism is working in a totally different way; you're trying to support a specific kind of movement. Even with some of the songs I sing in a cabaret setting (where I'm standing in front of a microphone) there is a specific choreography, even if it's imperceptible to the audience. Audience may not realize that I'm doing the same thing with my body—or at least following the same pathway with my body—every time. It helps me to create a container through which I can control the energy.

What is your routine like when you are performing?
I am at my best when I'm performing. I've never had a long-running show, but I dream about what that would do for the rest of my life because the amount of discipline I'm able to conjure when I'm performing is amazing. I performed in seven cities in eight days when I took my show on the road to North Carolina. I was driving long distances in a van with the band and putting on shows in rock clubs, hookah lounges, and a metal bars. I had such a sense of calm around me because I know that when I'm called to perform—which I view as my spiritual discipline and my ministry as well as my creative work—I'm able to put up parameters around healthy practice that I can't seem to conjure in a regular way in my normal life. I love warming up physically and vocally before performing so that I feel ready. There are times when I was on the road when I would get to the last song in the ninety-minute show and I would say, "Ah, now I'm warm!" As I've gotten a little older, I realized

how important it is to stretch my whole body. There are many different fascial systems pulling on my breathing mechanism and my posture. I began rolling out and doing myofascial release massages. I adjust my diet and eat differently when doing a show. I adjust my caffeine and alcohol intake as well.

Who had the most influence on you, your career, and/or your training?
Definitely my aunt, Marilyn Bradford. She worked in the business, and she was a jack of all trades. During most of my young life she was no longer working in the theatre and was in Hollywood working as a producer. When I was very young, I would go see her and the jazz group she directed and choreographed. She would take me to musicals and tell me stories about when she did Anita in summer stock. She directed a number of musical reviews in Los Angeles. Carol Burnett came to see one of her reviews and asked my aunt to create a show for her. She also had this Gershwin Broadway review called *Let's Call the Whole Thing Off*. The show nearly made it to Broadway. It was slated to go to the Helen Hayes and was then bumped for *My One and Only*. The Gershwin estate felt that they could only have one review on Broadway at the time. That story is legendary in our family. So, since I was about eight or so, I knew that I was going to complete that legacy. She was my earliest coach and fan. I remember, I was doing a summer program at UCLA when I was in high school, and I was staying with her. I was looking for songs to sing and she had just shown me the original cast recording documentary of *Company* and I knew I wanted to sing "Being Alive." She looked at me, a sixteen-year-old gay boy at the time, and told me I couldn't sing that song until I was thirty. I took her advice and didn't sing it until much later because I had so much respect for her.

What advice would you give an aspiring musical theatre performer?
I came to New York to insist that trans people didn't need to be relegated to downtown theatre. I wanted people to know that we had a place in the mainstream. That we had a place on Broadway. We have gotten a small place and we're getting a bigger place. I think it's important for people to know the space they want to fill. You know the exercise in your

acting 101 class or your modern dance class where you walk around the room looking for the empty space to fill? It's just like that—you need to look for your space in the industry. Don't worry about type, just know in your heart the space you're meant to fill and what that is for you. Not just the kind of character you want to play, or the part of town you want to live in, but what purpose your soul brings to this field. If you can be in touch with what you must share as a performer, then no matter what is thrown at you, you know you can integrate it and make something magical out of it. And don't be swayed by convention. It's important to know the classics, the standards, and the hits, but you should also know, you know, the misfires, cult classics, and the off-center. Especially because that's what people are craving now as audience members. I would encourage folks to continue the task of bringing work from the margins to the center.

What advice would you give a musical theatre voice teacher?
Help your students find work that exists on the margins. Help students on the margins find their pathway to the center, as well as acknowledging that there can be multiple centers. It's not just Broadway. The center is the place where you are meant to be and where you stand in your greatest power.

I would also say there's probably nothing more valuable than taking the time to get to know your students. You should see them as full human beings before the training begins. The voice is such a psychologically and spiritually intimate thing. To help someone unleash the full capacity of their voice, you really must see and understand the full capacity of their being. Even in a lesson, if you can make those first few minutes about grounding person to person and taking in the whole of that person, then when you get down to work, you're just coming at it from a place of wholeness rather than a narrow cross section of who they are.

This is especially important that when you're working with someone from a background other than your own, especially if that background might imply that that student has come from a particular experience of oppression. It's important to understand how oppression gets internalized and placed onto the voice through stereotype, silencing, and trauma. The hard part of vocal practice is working through the constraints that those types of traumas and alienation have placed on the voice and spirit. I think working from a place of awareness is so important. That stuff is laden with power, privilege, and discrimination, and being able to talk through that and break that down is essential to truly train the voice.

TELLY LEUNG

Telly Leung is a New York City native, Broadway performer, recording artist, and theatre arts teacher. His Broadway and national touring credits include Aladdin in Disney's *Aladdin*, *In Transit*, *Allegiance* (with George Takei and Lea Salonga), *Godspell*, *Rent*, *Wicked*, *Pacific Overtures*, and *Flower Drum Song*. In 2010, he starred as Angel in *Rent* at the Hollywood Bowl opposite Wayne Brady and directed by Neil Patrick Harris. Regionally, Leung has performed at Philadelphia Theater Company, Pittsburgh CLO, the St. Louis Muny, Dallas Theater Center, The Shakespeare Theater Company in Washington, D.C., North Carolina Theater, and North Shore Musical Theater. Television audiences will remember him as Wes the Warbler on *Glee*, as well as his guest star appearances on *Instinct*, *Odd Mom Out*, *Deadbeat*, and *Law and Order: Criminal Intent*. Telly is featured as a coach for the Jimmy Awards in the PBS documentary, *Broadway or Bust*. He can be heard on many original Broadway cast recordings and has released two solo albums—*I'll Cover You* and *Songs for You*. His EP, *You Matter*, is a collection of five songs made during the 2020 pandemic with composer and arranger Gary Adler and profits will benefit Broadway Cares / Equity Fights AIDS. He holds a BFA from Carnegie Mellon University's School of Drama. He has taught master classes and courses at many American universities, including NYU, Nazareth College, The University of Michigan, Carnegie Mellon, and Point Park and has been a guest teacher at drama programs internationally from Edinburgh to Tokyo.

How did you first get interested in musical theatre?
It was the original Broadway production of *Into the Woods*. I grew up in New York City with immigrant parents. My mom worked in garment factories in Chinatown and my dad worked in Chinese restaurants. They

were blue collar, ESL, working, lower-middle-class parents who had one son because that's all they could afford. They were adamant that I do well in school. They had the traditional Chinese immigrant dream of me going to Harvard, being a doctor, and having lots of Chinese grandchildren for them. (None of that happened.) They wouldn't let me watch cartoons unless it was Saturday morning so I could focus on my schoolwork. They would let me watch educational TV though, so they would allow PBS. *Into the Woods* came on *Great Performances* and that's how I stumbled upon musical theatre. I didn't even know what it was. I was eight or nine when they showed *Into the Woods*, as part of their fundraising drive. I remember watching it thinking, "I know these characters from fairy tales but they're singing these clever songs and there are people watching them. . . . Where *is* this place?" Growing up in New York, I didn't realize that there was a Manhattan north of Chinatown. It wasn't until I was in high school that I found Union Square and midtown. I realized there were theatres where this happens all the time.

I went to a math and science high school called Stuyvesant High School. I did theatre for fun because I needed an extracurricular activity. I found my tribe of people in theatre. Growing up as an only child, I also found instant brothers and sisters. I spent a lot of time by myself with two parents that worked. Theatre fulfilled a childhood dream of having playmates, and it was somewhere I could use my very active imagination. Carnegie Mellon University was on my radar because there were so many people at Stuyvesant that went there for architecture or computer science. My theatre teacher suggested I think about Carnegie Mellon because they had a great acting program. This was also 1997 or 1998. There was no internet. You couldn't Google "Carnegie Mellon." You had to write the colleges and they would send you a brochure in the mail. That's what sold me on Carnegie Mellon—the brochure. I applied to all of my schools sight unseen.

What is your experience with formalized voice lessons?
I started voice lessons in high school for fun. I was doing musicals and I found that I was losing my voice a lot—I didn't know what I was doing. I found this wonderful teacher named Thomas Shepherd. He was the one that taught me to control my energy. My energy is still all over the place, but at fifteen, I was bouncing off the walls! He was the one to teach me

to slow down my breathing. He taught me that singing requires a certain amount of concentration, discipline, and coordination that you will not have if your energy isn't under control. He would calm me down so I could understand the sensations that I needed to have as a singer. He also had this wonderful Jessye Norman quote that he cut out of a magazine and framed on top of his piano. I can't remember the exact quote now, but it was something about how singing is not the sound you hear, it's the sensations you feel. That was something he imparted to me. As a kid in the 1990s, I would try to sing things like the Phantom in *Phantom of the Opera*. He would remind me that your voice is not the voice you think you hear through the cartilage of your ears, but what you feel. That was a good lesson for me. He taught me the basics of breathing, vowels, and creating space for singing.

Broadway is not about standing and singing (like in a voice lesson). You're asked to do such demanding things physically. Each show is so different. I feel like I've never had an easy show. I jumped on trampolines in *Aladdin*. . . . I sang for ninety minutes straight in the a cappella musical *In Transit*. . . . I never have had it easy. I realized as an adult that I needed voice lessons, and that I needed these lessons from somebody who not only gets the voice but gets the physical difficulty and the stamina that's required. I've been working with Liz Caplan since I was in *Wicked*. I met Liz because she was working with the witches in *Wicked*. I would sometimes grab a lesson with her when she was in Chicago, and we've worked together ever since.

What were the most influential training experiences you had outside of formalized lessons?
I feel like there's a lesson in every gig! I will say that the *Sitzprobe* is one of the most exciting days for a singer because you get to hear the whole band or orchestra for the first time. The first time we heard the orchestrations for *Allegiance*, which was a show I had been working on for five years, we all oversang. Even Lea Salonga, with one of the best voices in the world, overdid it. I had to remind myself that it's not what you hear, but what you feel because we were competing with horns and strings. I had to remember to not oversing . . . that's what the sound mixer is for. It's the adrenaline that kicks in, and I had to learn how to manage.

What's tough about musical theatre is that the fatigue is cumulative. That's another thing that I learned by doing eight shows a week. If you fatigue yourself on Wednesday, it's almost certain you're going to call out by Sunday. The goal is to make sure that you maintain a level of fatigue control. Of course you're going to be tired. You're using your voice in an athletic way, but learning to strategize fatigue is critical. You also learn that every show is different. What fatigue meant for me on *Allegiance*, which was emotionally exhausting, is not the same fatigue as *In Transit*. That show wasn't emotionally exhausting, but you sang in every part of your range with such specificity of the vowel, the blend, and the size of singing. That's taxing in a different way. In *Allegiance*, I was dealing with sinuses closing because I'm crying, and I was yelling because I was at war. Then *Aladdin* was a totally different experience. Everything from the neck down was sore all the time because of how physical the show was. I had to make sure that I didn't hoist my body up in a way that negatively impacted my singing. There's not an all-encompassing sensation of fatigue. It's specific to every show. The other thing is that you're human and you're going to get tired. On a five-show weekend, you're supposed to be tired. You should take a nap if you need one. I'm not a napper, but I had to learn to nap when it was necessary.

How do you maintain your voice while doing eight shows a week?
I drink a ton of water in the morning. It sounds so cliché but hydrating early in the morning is part of my routine. I drink two big glasses of water before I drink my coffee. I'm a coffee addict. I know some people don't drink coffee, and there are certain things that I do give up in a long run. I'm not going to drink a glass of milk or eat ice cream—cold dairy does my body no good. I don't do a ton of acidic food during a show either. But I can't give up coffee because I love it. I need the caffeine. I need a cup of hot coffee every day because the warmth feels good for me vocally.

In *Aladdin*, you literally get shot out of a cannon. Your first number is "One Jump," so you had to be twenty minutes into a high-intensity interval training (HIIT) workout before you start the show or you're going to hurt something. I have found that when I'm in a full sweat, I sing great because everything in my body is loose, limber, and warm. I'm taking in air efficiently because of the aerobic activity. Suddenly, my breath drops deep. I have also found that, especially in cold, freezing theatres, my sinuses tend to close with the air conditioning. I do not sleep with air conditioning at all. I've not slept with air conditioning my entire career. This is how I know my husband loves me, because we only have ceiling fans in our home. When I go on tour, my hotel room is 75 to 80 degrees with no air conditioning. I find that when the air is cold, I start to get stuffy and my sinuses close up. If I'm breaking a sweat, my nasal inflammation reduces. I love breaking a sweat right before going on stage, so oftentimes you'll see me off stage doing jumping jacks.

I also do a sinus rinse every morning. I don't do it before a show, only in the morning. For me, it's about whatever has been collecting in my sinuses while I've been sleeping. I also try to have some easy conversation in the morning because I feel like, finally, after voice therapy, I speak efficiently.

You are very outspoken about your vocal injury. Can you talk about your journey to recovery and your plight to destigmatize vocal injuries in the musical theatre industry?
When I did *Allegiance* out of town, the show was so hard. I didn't really know what I was doing. It was my first time leading a show. My voice cashed out on me, and I would do the show in San Diego pumped full of drugs. There were so many things that contributed to making the show hard. There were tons of rewrites that were happening, and I never really had a chance to put in those changes into my voice in a safe way. I just jumped in and did it. It was like, here's a new song—good luck. We're putting in this new scene where you're fighting a war and yelling at the troops—good luck. I never had time in a rehearsal room to figure it out vocally. I would get new pages around 2:00 p.m. and put them into the show that night. I never took the time to vocally figure out what it was that I had just been given. And there's a ticking clock because opening night is coming. This was the same time Billy Porter was doing *Kinky Boots* out of town, and I remember Billy saying to me, "Listen Telly . . . you're thirty. You have your thirty-year-old voice now, not your twenty-year-old voice anymore. Have them change the keys."

In my twenties, I would do *Rent*, then go sing a set of five songs at a bar and think nothing of it. I'd wake up the next morning and do another show. Our bodies recover more quickly when we're young. What Billy was saying was that I was older, and I can't do that anymore. Have them change the keys because nobody's sitting there with a pitch pipe checking keys. The show was written a good third higher in San Diego. So, I knew that if the show came to New York, I'd have them change the keys. The writers generously not only changed the keys, but they made my character older to reflect the keys being lower. When the show was in New York, it was a hard show to do, but I could do it eight times a week. If I got sick, I would call out. But I think I started to misunderstand my fatigue. I was starting to develop habits of creating muscular tension to get through the demands of the show either emotionally or vocally. The stuff that was off-site, like waking up early to do the morning show, going to the press event, taking pictures, doing interviews—all the stuff that is part of the job that no college prepares you for—was taking its toll. When you're leading a show, your voice is tired, but what I should have done is called out of more shows. Instead, I started to normalize that level of fatigue. The tension that was driving the song emotionally was making me work harder, which I started to feel as normal.

When I got to *In Transit*, I was working *so hard*. I now had to sing in every part of my range, from falsetto to bass parts. I had to beatbox. It required a certain amount of looseness that I did not have. To go from the pressure of holding the show up in *Allegiance* to suddenly making totally different sounds in *In Transit* was hard, and I developed a lesion on my vocal folds. It was unclear how long it had been there, but it was now large enough that I wasn't able to bring my folds together and make clear sound easily. I started to have a break in my voice toward B♭4, which used to be easy for me. That part of my voice only happens with good technique, and I couldn't muscle it anymore. There was no way I could sing this ninety-minute acapella show. I ended up taking six weeks off the show to have surgery and recover. I had an incredible team of surgeons, Dr. Lucian Sulica, and voice therapist Ellen Lettrich. Ellen started to give me voice therapy before the surgery, so I had an idea of what I was going to need to do post-op. She helped prepare me emotionally for a week of not speaking after surgery. And all of this, of course, was happening before opening night. I pushed myself to get through opening night, and I ended up hemorrhaging where the lesion was. I opened the show, got the reviews, they put in a replacement for me, and then I had surgery.

I was very thankful for voice therapy. The second week post-op, I could talk for five minutes per hour. I kept doing all sorts of voice therapy exercises like blowing into the straw in the glass of water. I was building a strong foundation. I realized during the process of voice therapy, that I didn't learn this in school. I think programs are teaching this now because shows are getting harder. Voice teachers are getting smarter about this kind of training. They know more about the physiological aspect of the voice. Back in the day, it was things like "imagine you are feather." With voice therapy, I started to understand what my vocal folds were doing and what was happening with my air. I realized this was my first time learning and feeling the sensation of what it means to speak properly and smartly. Voice therapy allowed me to use my articulators in a way that was more efficient. It was a good education for me. I felt like I learned so much through voice therapy. I started voice lessons up again with Liz about three or four weeks after surgery and was back in the show six weeks post-op. That whole six weeks between Ellen and Liz was about undoing all the tension that I had created that got me injured in the first place. I learned to do less and walked away with the understanding that if I don't do less, I might hurt myself again.

I had a whole new way of singing after surgery and therapy. My voice felt great, and I made it through the show. I didn't feel tired. I felt like I could sing the show again after I was done, but I will admit that, emotionally, I wasn't used to working less hard. I sweat through my costume because of my nerves. My body didn't know what to do when it wasn't gripping. It took a good two weeks for me to be in that show eight times a week and tell my body, "No, this is how we're singing now. This is what it feels like, and I know you are nervous, but just know that when you go home at night you won't be cursing yourself that you have no voice left to talk to your husband." I was really relearning the sensations of singing and then I finally got that quote that was on Thomas's piano when I was fifteen years old. It's the sensations you feel when singing.

I'm now forty-one and I think I sing better than I've ever sung before. I think back to Billy's advice about having a thirty-year-old voice and not a twenty-year-old voice and I think about it differently now. My forty-one-year-old voice is way better than my thirty-year-old, tired voice that I was schlepping through the business. It's not so much an age thing—it's a getting smarter thing and about learning to advocate for yourself.

It was the hardest thing in the world for me to tell those four writers on *In Transit* and Kathleen Marshall that I had a huge vocal injury and I might not be able to open this show. I made the decision to take steroids and push through opening night to help the show, and I have no regrets about it. It helped the production and helped them have time to put a replacement in the show.

Then there's the stigma of being injured. I didn't even tell my cast what I was going through. I think there was a fear that if the surgery goes wrong, that I'll never sing again. Singing is such a big part of my life and it's not only how the business has defined me, but in many ways, it's the way I've defined myself. I wasn't ready to tell everybody. I also knew that I got hired to sing and I felt like if I told the business that's why I was leaving the show they would think I was "damaged goods." I didn't want people to think I was a liability. So, I didn't tell anybody. I think that the official reason I gave was leaving for "personal, family reasons." After the surgery, when I ended up being totally fine, I told my doctor that I wished more people talked about their injuries. He told me that I'd eventually get to that place where I'd be able to talk about it openly.

I joined *Aladdin* shortly after *In Transit* and I was doing the show eight times a week with no issues. Somehow, someone had heard that I had had vocal surgery and they came to me and asked if I could help someone else in the show who was the same age as me dealing with some of the same vocal issues. That person ended up having surgery and went back into the show singing better than ever before. Then two more people in *Aladdin* asked for help with their vocal injuries, and once again, had surgery and went back into the show better than ever. I decided I was ready to talk about my injury publicly, so I wrote a show called *Sing Happy* about my injury and recovery. I premiered it at Birdland and then took it to San Francisco, Provincetown, and LA. I was talking about my vocal surgery in a funny, one man show/cabaret. I wanted to share so that people were less scared of vocal injuries. If we don't talk about it, we're just going to keep living in fear that we're going through this by ourselves when so many people are going through the same thing. Then, there was something that happened on Twitter where Caissie Levy tweeted about her vocal injury and surgery. Suddenly everyone in the Broadway community was responding about their injuries. Alex Brightman talked about his injuries and the Broadway fans were able to see what we go through and that we can recover. Alex was doing *Beetlejuice*, I was doing *Aladdin*, and Caissie was singing Elsa in *Frozen* every night. We all recovered and were smarter singers after our injuries. I hope someone reads this book and realizes that they aren't alone with their injury and that they will be OK.

Marrying acting and singing is one of the challenging aspects of musical theatre. What are your thoughts on the relationship between acting and singing?
For me they go hand in hand, but there is a technical aspect of singing that must happen first. I have to know how to make sound in a healthy way. I am very aware of that now after my surgery. When I get a piece of music, I put it in my voice first before I can put it in my heart. If I'm working on an original musical, I might ask for keys to be changed, or for a rhythm to be changed so I can catch a breath. I always take the time to figure the song out technically. Then I bring myself to the song in a way that feels good. I think I used to do it the opposite way and that got me into trouble. Your heart wants to jump right in, and your body just wants to commit, but then you remember that you have to sing it eight times a week. You must make sure that that is sustainable and then take the necessary steps to make it yours emotionally and tell the story.

We rarely stand still while singing in musical theatre. How do you navigate singing and athleticism at the same time?
Sometimes you don't know until you have to do it, so thank God for rehearsals. Figuring it out in rehearsal is crucial. One rehearsal you're going to jump around too much and forget to catch your breath and then not be able to sing at the end of the song or crack (or whatever), and that's OK. Don't be afraid to swing the pendulum both ways in rehearsal. For instance, be too physical and have no breath for singing, and then do too little and realize you can do more.

I enjoy a physical show because it helps me vocally. Doing aerobic activity helps warm-up my voice. I will do jumping jacks, burpees, or run in place because I feel that gets my body to do what it's supposed to do to get air in and out. I also think about my first voice teacher (when I was fifteen years old) trying to calm me down with slow breaths. So, I do both. I do my jumping jacks where I break a sweat, and then I have a moment where I slow the breath down. I like to breathe through a straw or exhale on a hiss. It helps me feel the expanse of my breathing apparatus. I like to remind my body that we will be breathing like this no matter what we might be doing physically. It's the juxtaposition of running around on stage or dancing but having to have total control of your breathing.

Who had the most influence on you, your career, and/or your training?
I had wonderful teachers at Carnegie Mellon. The person who taught me the nuts and bolts of acting and storytelling was Barbara Mackenzie Wood. I also have to say that Liz has been fantastic ever since I started studying with her in 2004. She has been a rock for me and really incredible. Ellen, my voice therapist, has had a huge impact on me as well. The process of what Ellen and Liz did to get my voice back together is something I carry with me. They taught me the importance of listening to my own body. That tickle sensation you're feeling is not good—your body is giving you a sign. I used to ignore those feelings all the time, but they taught me not to. I had to learn that I shouldn't feel that way and they helped me manage that.

What advice would you give an aspiring musical theatre performer and an aspiring musical theatre voice teacher?
My advice to *both* is to get scoped and to know the science behind what you are doing. If I could get scoped every day and see my vocal cords, I would. When I go to the gym, I can see my muscles improve. I can see my arms working. We don't see these things with singing. All we have is the sensation. I think that quote from Jessye Norman is really it. I'm starting to understand that now. I think understanding the sensations while seeing your vocal folds is the key. I learned so much when I would visit the doctor. He would take the videos and then he would slow them down and I would watch the oscillations. I would watch the air go through and the surfaces vibrate. That's when I really started to get it. I finally understood what I was doing. I started to understand the juxtaposition of how strong my cords were, all while being delicate. My advice is to understand the science behind singing. Go get scoped. Find a great laryngologist that's going to scope you and explain exactly what's happening when you make sound.

GLOSSARY

8-bar cut: A cut of music that is about eight bars, or under about twenty seconds long. The 8-bar cut tends to only happen at nonunion auditions where there are so many people in attendance that they need to substantially reduce the amount of time in the room.

16-bar cut: A cut of music that is about 16 bars, the length of a chorus, or thirty to forty-five seconds long. This cut is typically your shorter audition cut that you use at an Equity Chorus Call (ECC) or open calls.

32-bar cut: A cut of music that is about 32 bars, a verse and chorus, or about a minute to a minute and thirty seconds. This cut is typically your longer audition cut that you use at an Equity Principal Audition (EPA) or open call.

AEA: Actors' Equity Association.

ASCAP: American Society of Composers, Authors, and Publishers.

abdominal breathing: Breathing that focuses solely on a release of the abdominal muscles during inhalation and the engagement of the abdominals during exhalation. This strategy can be valuable for singers who struggle with abdominal release.

a cappella: Singing with no instrumental accompaniment. A capella is often heard in groups but can refer to solo singing.

acoustic registration: Timbral shifts that happen because of the interaction of harmonics and resonances throughout the range. There are four main acoustic registrations—whoop (or hoot), open, close, and yell (or call).

actions: The tactics we choose to get what we want. Actions are the specific, actionable verbs that we choose in a song to help achieve our objective.

Actors' Equity Association (AEA): American labor union representing professional stage actors and stage managers. AEA was formed in 1913 to create better working conditions for actors, including guaranteed pay.

adolescence: The period following the onset of puberty. There are three stages of adolescence—early, middle, and late. Early adolescence happens between about ages ten and fourteen, middle happens between fifteen and seventeen, and late occurs between eighteen and twenty-four.

American Society of Composers, Authors, and Publishers (ASCAP): A society that collects royalty payments on behalf of the writers. The nonprofit organization began in 1914 and is still operating today.

***appoggio*:** The act of engaging your inhalation muscles while exhaling to better control your exhale. *Appoggio* is a controlled version of checking action.

arrangement: Adapting music to fit the medium. Arrangements are essential to crafting the sound of a musical.

audiation: Hearing the music inside your head before singing. Audiation is important when working with inaccurate singers who need help matching pitch.

audition book: A three-ring binder of music with a selection of songs that you are prepared to sing at an audition. It includes songs that have been preselected and carefully prepared to show a wide range of vocal function, vocal style, acting ability, and musicianship.

avant-garde: Musicals that are experimental in nature with an eclectic mix of musical genres. They might defy genre classification and structure and are often created and nurtured off- and off-off-Broadway.

back pressure: Pressure that is reflected back down the vocal tract. Back pressure is increased when using semi-occluded vocal tract positions.

GLOSSARY

balanced breathing: A breathing system that incorporates elements of abdominal and thoracic breathing to create a well-balanced breathing strategy. A singer's breathing strategy might shift from role to role based on the movement, costumes, or other physical demands.

ballad opera: Racy operas with satirical plots that came about in 1728. They used more familiar music styles than opera, including preexisting songs, were written in English, and even used dialogue between the songs. *The Beggar's Opera* was the first ballad opera.

beats: Sections of text that can be organized into a unit based on objectives, obstacles, or actions. A beat shift is when you move from one unit to the next either because you achieved, abandoned, or replaced your former objective or tactic.

belting: A sound quality that aligns more with a call, or shout. This sound can be produced by all humans in various degrees of chest voice and is often most easily recognized on open vowels, despite being able to be produced on closed vowels. While belting tends to be louder and more dramatic when looked at contextually, it does not require a loud volume to be produced functionally.

bluegrass: A type of music that began in the 1940s in the Appalachian region of the United States. Bluegrass has roots in traditional English, Irish, and Scottish music, as well as jazz and blues. You typically hear acoustic instruments such as the banjo and mandolin in the orchestrations.

blues: A predecessor to rock and roll. Blues music incorporates syncopated rhythms in addition to other African musical elements, such as call and response. Blues music typically uses basic chord structures with the addition of blue notes.

book: The spoken dialogue in a musical. The book can also refer to the story, dramatic structure, and character development of a musical, even if there is no dialogue.

book musical: Musicals with fully integrated dialogue, music, and lyrics. In book musicals, every aspect of the show serves the plot or storyline.

Bollywood: Name given to the Indian Hindi language film industry based in Mumbai. A featured characteristic of Bollywood films is the music, often complete with song and dance numbers.

burlesque: A type of variety show that typically involved elements of mockery of the upper class, women dressed provocatively, and striptease. Burlesque could take the form of short musical shows or could be stretched into longer productions, and most shows loved to mock the more serious subjects of the day.

CCM: Contemporary commercial music.

CT: Cricothyroid muscle.

casting director: The person responsible for organizing the casting of a show. The casting director selects which actors will be given audition appointments and helps the creative team select the actors for the show.

character baggage: The silent expectations that come with musical theatre songs. In particular, the unspoken information about the character that is inherently part of the song.

charm song: Songs that give a break in the action or tension to give the audience a necessary moment of levity. Charm songs are typically written for secondary characters.

checking action: The process by which you check, or hold back, your airflow while speaking by continuing to engage the muscles of inspiration. Checking action is the basis for *appoggio*.

choreographer: The person in charge of creating the dance sequences in a musical. They work closely with the director and music director.

cisgender: A person whose gender identity corresponds with their assigned sex at birth. Cisgender refers to gender identity, not sexuality.

clavicular breathing: Breathing that is named for the movement of the clavicle upon inhale. The clavicular breath is higher in the body than other strategies.

comedy song: Songs that make the audience laugh. They may also serve other purposes, like revealing character, or moving plot forward, but they do so with humor.

comic opera: Operas with a lighthearted or comedic storyline. Comic operas first began appearing in the late seventeenth century and are sometimes called operettas or opéras bouffes.

concept album: An album where the songs hold more meaning together as an album than they do individually. Many concept albums are story or character driven with the entire album following a plot or a development of character.

GLOSSARY

concept musical: A musical where the concept takes center stage, not the plot. Hal Prince was instrumental in developing the concept musical in the 1960s and 1970s.

contemporary commercial music: A newer term for nonclassical music. It is a generic term that covers pop, rock, R&B, soul, rap, country, folk, electronic, and any other nonclassical genres.

contemporary musical theatre: Musicals that exist in the current era. Contemporary musical theatre will be ever evolving as the industry continues to move forward and adapt.

contrasting songs: Songs that show different qualities. Songs can contrast in tempo, vocalism, style, or acting.

country: A genre of music that combines elements of blues, spirituals, American folk music, and cowboy western music.

cricothyroid (CT) muscle: A tensor muscle of the larynx. When engaged, the vocal folds become longer and thinner, making less contact on the vibrational edge. This leads to a laryngeal registration that is commonly referred to as head voice, falsetto, thin mechanism, cricothyroid (CT) dominant, or vibrational mode two (M2).

DJ: Disc jockey.

DP: Director of photography.

disc jockey (DJ): The person who plays recorded music for an audience and often introduces the songs as well. DJs played an instrumental role in the creation and evolution of rap music.

director: The person in charge of the overall vision of a musical. They create all the staging in the show and work closely with the choreographer, music director, and the rest of the design team.

director of photography (DP): Also known as the cinematographer. The DP is responsible for the look of a film.

disco: Dance music that emerged in the 1970s. Disco gained popularity on the airwaves as many radio stations were leaning toward playing more conservative music, rather than the politically charged rock music that was prevalent early in the decade.

doo-wop: A subgenre of pop/rock music that emphasizes harmonies and group singing. Doo-wop originated among Black youth in the 1940s.

early contemporary musical theatre: Musical theatre from the 1990s and early 2000s. These shows often have a contemporary feel but might not sound as contemporary as modern day. Some examples include *The Last Five Years*, *John and Jen*, and *Bat Boy*.

ECC: Equity Chorus Call.

EDM: Electronic dance music.

electronic dance music (EDM): Music that is based in electronic sounds. The music is typically percussive and used for dancing.

eleven o'clock number: Typically the climax of the show, it usually puts the protagonist in the moment of decision or revelation. The name comes from the era when showtimes were later, so this climactic moment in the show typically happened around eleven o'clock in the evening.

EPA: Equity Principal Audition.

Equity Chorus Call: Audition that is held for ensemble or chorus members for a show. These auditions are for members of the professional performing union Actors' Equity.

Equity Principal Audition (EPA): Audition that is held for principal characters in a show. These auditions are for members of the professional performing union, Actors' Equity.

extravaganza: Sometimes called burlesque extravaganza. Complete with lavish staging, special effects, and opulent costumes, the comedic focus was often multifaceted, lampooning everyone and everything from famous persons to popular books, popular culture, and more.

FTP: Federal Theatre Project.

Federal Theatre Project (FTP): A branch of the WPA that helped fund theatre projects across the country. One such production was *The Cradle Will Rock*, which persevered despite being shut down because of its political themes.

funk: A rhythmic, danceable form of music that combines elements of soul, jazz, and rhythm and blues. Originated in Black communities in the 1960s.

jazz: A form of music with its roots in ragtime and blues. Originated in the Black communities of New Orleans, Louisiana, in the late nineteenth century and early twentieth century.

gender binary: Classification of gender as two distinct, opposite forms of masculine and feminine. Gender identity and expression can go beyond the binary into forms that are not defined as masculine or feminine.

given circumstances: Facts about the character and the story. This information is gathered from the script and might include age, likes, dislikes, physical attributes, race, ethnicity, disability, personality traits, relationships, social standing, physical environment, and other relevant information.

golden age: Time frame spanning from 1943 to the early 1960s in Broadway history. The golden age began with *Oklahoma!* and the fully integrated musical and continued with a rush of musicals that continued to integrate acting, music, and dance. Many of the golden age musicals are still part of the musical theatre canon and performed frequently to this day.

gospel: Music that typically encompasses harmonies sung by a group or choir, with exciting lead vocals. The precursor to gospel was the African American spiritual.

groove: A combination of a rhythmic pattern with a "feel" that leads to an obvious style, pace, intensity, and mood. Some theatre songs could also be said to use a groove, but its importance in interpreting pop/rock music cannot be understated.

gunboat musicals: Several musicals played Broadway between 1902 and 1907 that all had essentially the same plot. The fear of the "other" that these musicals perpetuated was often reinforced by the harmful portrayal of non-White American characters, specifically those from Asian, Oceanic, and Latin American countries.

high intensity interval training (HIIT): A form of cardiovascular interval training. Interval training alternates short periods of anaerobic exercise with less intense recovery periods.

HIIT: High-intensity interval training.

Hindi film music: Songs featured in Bollywood films. More formally referred to as Hindi Geet or filmi songs.

hook: A catchy lyric or melodic pattern that pop/rock songs are built upon. It's essentially the part of the song that is meant to "hook" in the listener.

"I am" song: A song that exists to reveal who a character is. Can be sung by a main or supporting character.

"I want" song: A song that typically comes early in the show and is sometimes even the opening number. It is sung by the main character or characters and essentially reveals to the audience what the character desires.

inertance: The result of the balance between breath pressure from below the vocal folds and back pressure from above the vocal folds. Inertance is maximized when using semi-occluded vocal tract positions.

Indi-pop: A genre of pop music that came about as a competition to the popular Hindi film music. The term was first used in 1981.

indie/alt rock: A subgenre of rock that came about in the 1990s. Indie/alt rock was influenced by rock and traditional folk music.

inner monologue: The constant stream of thoughts, feelings, and impulses that happens while we are acting. This inner monologue drives our tactics and our beat changes, and helps our acting come alive.

jazz: A genre of music born in the Black community in New Orleans. Jazz music combines the syncopated rhythms of ragtime with an element of improvisation. The vocals have the emotional cry often found in the blues.

K-pop: Short for Korean popular music that originated in South Korea. This music draws its influence from many genres including pop, R&B, hip-hop, jazz, rock, and traditional Korean music

laryngeal registration: The mode of vibration of the vocal folds that is enacted by specific laryngeal muscles engaging. One registration uses short, thick vocal folds that come together robustly in an almost square-shaped fashion, and the other main registration uses longer, thinner vocal folds that make less contact on the vibrational edge. We commonly refer to these laryngeal registers as head and chest voice.

Latin pop: A pop subgenre that is a fusion of US–style music production with Latin music genres. This subgenre typically combines Latin beats with American pop music.

lead sheet: A form of musical notation that notes the chords, lyrics, and occasionally the rhythms. This type of notation is commonly found with pop/rock songs but is not appropriate for musical theatre auditions.

legit: Short for "legitimate" singing. Vocally it typically encompasses sounds that fall more in line with classical singing. This might mean more lush orchestrations and singers' use of rounded, pure vowels,

GLOSSARY 381

instead of the brighter, more speechlike sounds found in the non-legit traditional musical theatre shows. Shows like *Carousel*, *The Music Man*, *She Loves Me*, *Flower Drum Song*, and *West Side Story* all use legit music and legit vocalism.

M0: Mode 0

M1: Mode 1.

M2: Mode 2.

M3: Mode 3

magic "if": Asks the question, "how would I act *if* I were in this situation?" The goal is to put yourself in the situation found in the text and attempt to find some truth in your response. The best actors respond in ways that feel believable, or truthful, to the audience.

megamusical: Shows focused on extravaganza with lavish sets and special effects. These musicals began appearing in the 1980s and were often sung through.

minstrel shows: An entertainment form based on the denigration of Black culture. The minstrel show was the first form of musical theatre born on American soil. The racist underpinnings of the minstrel show are another example of how intertwined the development of musical theatre is with the American sociopolitical climate.

mixing: Most commonly refers to sounds that cannot be classified as legit or belt. These sounds almost sound as if your head voice and chest voice were "mixed" together, despite that not being physically accurate. Humans can make these sound qualities that sound "mixed" together in both head voice and chest voice and are often most successful when they are able to transition between chest voice and head voice seamlessly.

mode 0 (m0): A vibratory pattern of the vocal folds that occurs at the lowest notes. The vocal folds are loose with a lot of air passing through, which creates a creaky sound.

mode 1 (M1): A vibratory pattern of the vocal folds where the vocal folds come together robustly in an almost square-shaped fashion. This registration is commonly referred to as chest voice, modal voice, thick mechanism, thyroarytenoid (TA) dominant, or vibrational mode one (M1).

mode 2 (M2): A vibratory pattern of the vocal folds where the vocal folds make less contact on the vibrational edge. This registration is commonly referred to as head voice, falsetto, thin mechanism, cricothyroid (CT) dominant, or vibrational mode two (M2).

mode 3 (M3): A vibratory pattern of the vocal folds that occurs at the highest notes. The vocal folds are stretched out to create a sound that is commonly called whistle, or flageolet.

moment before: Something that prompts a character to sing. Acting is reacting and a "moment before" is what we're reacting to that makes us burst into song.

Motown: A musical genre that combines rhythm and blues, soul, and pop music. Motown got its name from the record label that was started in 1960 by Berry Gordy in Detroit, nicknamed the Motor City (hence Motown). Motown played an important role in the racial integration of popular music during the 1960s.

music director: Head of the music component in a musical. The music director is responsible for the overall music design of the show including the band, orchestra, and vocals. Sometimes called the musical director.

objective: What you want from the scene or song. A super objective is what the character is in pursuit of the entire show, whereas an objective might be a smaller goal that is present in a song or scene.

obstacle: Anything that gets in the way of what you want. Choosing obstacles that have the greatest stakes creates more tension in the scene, giving you more to work with.

off-Broadway: Theatres in New York City that are smaller than Broadway theatres. Off-Broadway was born in the 1950s as a response to the commercialism and expense of Broadway.

off-off-Broadway: Theatre created spaces in basements, cafes, and lofts, mostly in the downtown, bohemian neighborhoods of Greenwich Village and the East Village. Off-off-Broadway was focused on more experimental theatre that was created by younger artists in the 1960s.

one-nighter: Playing a theatre for one night only. This term originated on the vaudeville circuit but is still used today.

open call: Auditions that do not fall under a union jurisdiction. The rules and regulations can be set by the producer. It is most often first come, first served, and they can turn folks away at any point in the day.

GLOSSARY

opera: Fully sung-through entertainment with an emphasis on the character's emotion. Opera quickly became a popular source of entertainment for the wealthy all across Europe beginning in the 1600s.

operetta: Operas with a romantic plotline and an accessible, soaring score, always with a happy ending. They often took place in lavish settings, such as ballrooms and castles.

orchestration: fleshing out the melodic line with instrumentation. The orchestrator often decides what instruments will be included in the band or orchestra, which plays a huge role in genre.

patter songs: Rapid songs that are sometimes a tour de force for an actor. They often feel like stream-of-consciousness vocalizations coming from the character and may appear in a moment of crisis. They can show verbal dexterity from the actor and often come from characters with great intellect or wit.

passaggio: A word that refers to passages, or areas of transition, in the voice. Passaggio typically refers to registration changes in the voice, both laryngeal and acoustic registration.

pastiche songs: Songs that are meant to evoke an era, style, or genre of the past. Pastiche songs are valuable for storytelling, especially in developing character or world building.

phonation threshold pressure: The minimum amount of lung pressure required to initiate phonation. The phonation threshold pressure changes with SOVTs.

pop/rock: An umbrella term used to indicate songs that are not from a musical. This term typically encompasses *all* popular genres outside of musical theatre, not just pop or rock.

pop: Typically refers to music that is popular in mainstream culture. Pop music originated in the 1950s. Today it is typically music that is commercially successful, uses a standard verse-chorus-bridge format, is danceable, and has a memorable hook and groove.

pop opera: Musicals that had pop-inspired scores, with elements of legit musical theatre thrown in. These shows were popular in the 1980s and 1990s and would use full orchestras, with some also using electronic instruments. Examples include *Chess, Miss Saigon, Les Misérables, Jekyll and Hyde*, and *The Scarlet Pimpernel*.

Princess musicals: A series of popular musicals written for the Princess Theatre. Because of the small size of the theatre (299 seats), these shows had to focus on character and story instead of the lavish sets and spectacle that were common at the time.

producer: Overseer of all aspects of a theatrical production. They are particularly responsible for the financial and managerial operations of a production.

puberty: Period when a child's body begins to develop into an adult. The average age of the onset of puberty varies between cultures and regions. Puberty can be as short as a few months or could last up to four years.

Pulitzer Prize: An award recognizing achievement in writing. Prizes are given yearly in twenty-one categories, including drama. Ten musicals have won the Pulitzer Prize for drama including *A Strange Loop, Hamilton, Next to Normal, Rent, Sunday in the Park with George, A Chorus Line, How to Succeed in Business without Really Trying, Fiorello!, South Pacific,* and *Of Thee I Sing!*

punk: A subgenre of rock that appeared in the 1970s. It was born out of a push against the commercialism of rock, and it often has political, antiestablishment lyrics.

R&B: Rhythm and blues.

ragtime: A musical genre with rhythms based on the music of Black Americans. Ragtime is known for its syncopated rhythms.

range: How high and low a song goes. When singers are just starting out, or when they are working on a new skill, a smaller range will be beneficial.

rap: Music that began at block parties in New York City in the 1970s. DJs would extend the percussion breaks of funk, soul, and disco music, and eventually began talking in time over the musical breaks. By the 1990s, rap was part of the popular music lexicon, with rappers charting on the pop charts

reader: A person who is in the audition to read the scenes with the auditioning actors. Most of the time the reader will be seated off to the side and should be included in your audition.

relationships: How a character relates to their scene partner. Relationships can be complicated, so it is important that you understand how you relate to the other characters to which you are talking or singing.

reprise: A repeat of a familiar melody or tune in a show. Recurring musical themes and motifs play an important role in the function of a musical. Audiences will already be familiar with a song, so when that melody is repeated, dramatic moments can become heightened.

resonance: The amplification and enhancement of musical sound through supplementary vibration. For singers, resonance is typically experienced through sensory feedback. As sound passes through the vocal tract, sympathetic vibrations can be felt in the bones and tissues of the neck, mouth, sinuses, and head.

resonant voice: Easy voicing that produces oral and facial vibratory sensations. Resonant voice is one tool used in voice therapy to help people gain a clearer, more efficient speaking voice.

revue: Shows featuring a variety of skits, songs, and dance numbers. Revues could be political and satirical and feature scantily clad women, the acts playing in a set running order with the same performers for the length of the run.

rhythm and blues: A distinctly African American genre of music that combines elements of jump blues, big band, gospel, and jazz. Rock and roll was heavily influenced by R&B in the 1950s. As R&B evolved, it began to incorporate elements of pop, soul, funk, and electronic music.

riffing: A form of improvising on a melody. It can be as simple as changing one note in a melody line, or as complicated as improvising a new melody, including embellished runs.

scansion: How lyrics scan when put to the melody. Good scansion will preserve the natural rhythm, prosody, and emphasis of speech.

semi-occluded vocal tract (SOVT) position: Closing off, or semi-occluding, the vocal tract. This occlusion most commonly happens by partially closing off the mouth in some way. When you do this, you increase the back pressure in the vocal tract, which leads to a change in how the vocal folds vibrate.

simple song: A song that doesn't do anything flashy vocally or dramatically, but allows you to show simplicity and often tenderness. These are songs that feel naturalistic in their acting and have a grounded, understated quality.

slate: A formal introduction of yourself and the material that you will be singing. Typically, a slate includes your name (when it's appropriate), your pronouns, and the name of the material you are singing.

song and dance number: Songs with a substantial dance component. They are often designed to showcase a performer and use dance as part of the storytelling. They can have a dance break in the middle of the song or use dance throughout.

SOVT: Semi-occluded vocal tract.

specialty song: Unique, rarely used songs that fill niche categories. This could include a song you sing while playing an instrument, a song in a foreign language that you speak fluently, a song you wrote, an English art song, an operetta song, a song that's gender flexible, or a musically complex song like those by Stephen Sondheim, Michael John LaChiusa, or Adam Guettel.

split week: Playing a theatre for part of a week. This term originated on the vaudeville circuit but is still used today.

"story" song: Songs that tell stories. Story songs sometimes give exposition or reveal character, and sometimes they do not move the plot forward at all but serve as a moment of levity for the audience.

straight tone: Removing the periodic oscillations of the fundamental frequency when singing. This stylistic element is used in a lot of contemporary musical theatre and pop/rock music.

substitution: The act of replacing one thing with another to serve the same purpose. When there is a given circumstance that does not feel truthful to you, you can find a similar circumstance that does feel truthful and use it in its place.

subtext: The underlying meaning of what you are saying. Subtext can exist in lyrics and music. The underscore or accompaniment can inform the audience of the character's subtext.

TA: Thyroarytenoid.

tessitura: Where the majority of the notes of the melody sit on the staff. Songs that spend too much time in areas of the voice that are less stable will have an increased difficulty level.

thoracic breathing: Breathing strategy that focuses on the thorax, or ribcage. Thoracic breathing is particularly important when engaged in a physical activity while singing, especially dancing.

thyroarytenoid (TA) muscle: A muscle that relaxes and shortens the vocal folds. When engaged, the vocal folds are short and thick, coming together robustly in an almost square-shaped fashion. This laryngeal registration is commonly referred to as chest voice, modal voice, thick mechanism, thyroarytenoid (TA) dominant, or vibrational mode one (M1).

Tin Pan Alley: Nickname for 28th Street between Broadway and Sixth Avenue where music publishers were located during the early twentieth century. These songwriters and publishers dominated the music scene at the time.

Tony Awards: Awards that recognize excellence in Broadway theatre. Named after Antionette Perry, cofounder of the American Theatre Wing, the first ceremony was held in 1947 in a ballroom at the Waldorf Astoria Hotel, with seven awards being presented.

traditional musical theatre: A type of musical theatre that could include jazz standards and songs from the Great American Songbook, but could also extend into the golden age era and all the way today. Traditional musical theatre is typically what people think of when they think of "showtunes" or "Broadway songs." Shows that use traditional musical theatre include *Guys and Dolls*, *Annie Get Your Gun*, *The Pajama Game*, and *Hello, Dolly!*

transgender: People who have a gender identity or expression that differs from what they were assigned at birth. The word is sometimes shortened to *trans*.

transitional musical theatre: Refers to the time between the golden age and contemporary musical theatre, most commonly the 1960s to the 1990s. These are shows that have a musical theatre sound that does not quite fit into the sounds of the golden age but does not quite feel at home with modern-day musical theatre either. These songs might have some light pop influence, but still feel like theatre songs. Some examples might include *Cabaret*, *Pippin*, *Baby*, *Big*, *Company*, and *Falsettos*.

type: The kind of roles that you are suited for. Type can refer to your age, voice type, physical attributes, race, ethnicity, or your personality.

typing: The act of preselecting who will have the opportunity to audition based on type. Typing may happen by looking at a performer's résumé only or might happen after seeing the performer in the room to assess whether their physical attributes fit the needs of the show.

vaudeville: Entertainment that typically consisted of skits, singing, dancing, juggling, or any other type of simple, short entertainment.

Vaudeville became a popular form of entertainment, with many famous performers gaining valuable experience on the vaudeville circuit.

vibrational amplitude: The amount of lateral movement of the vocal folds during phonation. Vibrational amplitude is reduced with semi-occluded vocal tract exercises, which lower the collision force of the vocal folds.

vibrato: A periodic oscillation of the fundamental frequency and all its harmonics. An organic vibrato is controlled by the larynx. The modulation of fundamental frequency happens because of a contraction between two antagonistic laryngeal muscles. Vibrato appears when the structures of the larynx are in balance with the breath system.

WPA: Works Progress Administration.

working book: A book of material that is not for auditions. A working book is a great place to keep songs that you are using for skill development in your voice lesson, songs you are prepping for your audition book, new songs you are learning, and songs you love to sing in lessons or repertoire coachings.

Works Progress Administration (WPA): An initiative to create work opportunities for Americans during the Great Depression. The Federal Theatre Project was one branch of the WPA that helped fund theatre projects across the country.

INDEX

Abbott, George, 27
abdominal breathing, 267
Abyssinia, 12
acapella, 67, 316
ACCAI (American College of Allergy, Asthma, and Immunology), 94
accompaniments, 172, 216–17, 260, 261, 316
accompanists, 324, 330
acoustic registration, 169, 170, 228
Across the Universe, 57
acting: audition songs with, 312, 316; character analysis questions, 262–63; context choices, 261; methods and strategies for, 255–61; singing relationship with, 263–64, 345, 352–53, 370
actions (tactics), 259–60, 261, 263
Actors' Equity Association (AEA), 16, 21, 326–27, 337nn8–10
Adams, Lee, 26

Adam's apple, 290–91. *See also* larynx
Addams Family, The, 298, 300
Adler, Richard, 26
adolescents, 275, 290–92, 295. *See also* children
advice: for aspiring performers, 347–48, 354, 360–61, 371; for vocal coaches/teachers, 348, 354, 361–62
AEA (Actors' Equity Association), 16, 21, 326–27, 337n8
African Theater, 4–5
Afrobeat, 59
age-appropriate songs, 212, 295, 315
Aida, 60, 356
Ain't Misbehavin', 31, 51–52, 306
Ain't Too Proud, 38, 57, 65
AIR (Applying Intelligence to Reflexes), 161–62
air conditioning, 366
air humidification systems, 93
Aladdin, 35, 300, 364, 365, 369–70

389

Aladdin JR., 287
Alan, Scott, 323
alcohol, 7–8, 17, 97, 104, 343, 360
Aldridge, Ira, 4
Alexander Technique, 283
Alice by Heart, 63
Allegiance, 238, 364–65, 366, 367
Allegro, 24
"All I Need Is the Girl," 321
"All I've Ever Known," 47
All Shook Up, 57
"All the Things You Are," 226
"Alone in the Universe," 248
Altar Boyz, 62
Alvarez, Cesar, 311
Always . . . Patsy Cline, 57, 66
Amélie, 55, 253
"America," 321
American College of Allergy, Asthma, and Immunology (ACAAI), 94
American Idiot, 63
American in Paris, An, 52, 306
American Psycho, 61, 67
American Revolution, 3–4
American Society of Composers, Authors, and Publishers (ASCAP), 15
American Theater, The, 5
Amos, Tori, 54
amplification, electronic: basics of, 112–13; benefits of, 107, 109; compressors, 123–25; delay, 126–27; digital voice processors, 128; disadvantages of, 109; equalizers, 120–23; live sound system basics, 128–29; microphones, 113–20, 130; reverb units of, 125–26; voice alteration technology, 113, 127–28
amplitude: compression adjustments to, 123–25; with equalization applications, 120–21; of microphones, 116–18; as sound fundamental, 110–11; vibrato styles and, 197; vocal vibrational, 77–82, 168–69, 202, 288
Anastasia, 55
Anderson, Ron, 351, 353
"And I Am Telling You," 320
& Juliet, 62
"And Then He Kissed Me," 337n1
Annie, 1, 33, 300
Annie Get Your Gun, 24, 52, 307
anorexia, 90
"Another Hundred People," 319
"Answer Me," 167
antiheros, 23
anxiety: breathing styles conveying, 266; performance, 98–100, 106, 139–40, 153, 333; somatic marker hypothesis and, 163n6; teacher-to-student touching provoking, 157
Anything Goes, 20, 228
"Anywhere but Here," 213
Applause, 25
apple cider vinegar, 94–95
Applying Intelligence to Reflexes (AIR), 161–62
appoggio, 268, 271
Aristotle, 141, 145
arrangements, 50–51, 216, 326
Arthur (or the Decline and Fall of the British Empire) (album), 59
articulators, 71, 86–88, 102, 282, 368
arytenoids, 79
ASCAP (American Society of Composers, Authors, and Publishers), 15
"As Long As He Needs Me," 322
Aspects of Love, 34

INDEX

athleticism. *See* performance athleticism
attentional focus theory, 157–62
attention deficit disorders, 144–45
audiation, 293
audio enhancement technology. *See* amplification, electronic
audition books: accompanists and presentation of, 330; college auditions and extra songs in, 336; construction and organization of, 323–26; contents of, 306–11; contrasting songs in, 311–12; cutting songs in, 312–14; impressions made by, 323; purpose of, 305–6, 323; song selection for, 314–17; song types for, 317–23
auditions: accompanists for, 330; advanced preparation for, 332; casting personnel at, 330; clothing and shoes for, 329; college, 335–36; finding, 326; introductions at, 331; monologues for, 331; musicals about, 33; music selection for, 46; nervousness at, 332; readings and readers at, 331–32; self-tapes for, 333–34; types of, 326–28; union rules and regulations for, 337n8; warming up for, 329–30.
See also audition books
auditory target spectrum, 174–75
automaticity, 139, 157, 160–61
autonomic nervous system (ANS), 99, 139, 142, 160
Auto-Tune, 127–28
avant-garde, 310–11
Avenue Q, 38, 39
Avenue X, 67

Babes in Arms, 52, 231
Babes in Toyland, 13
Baby, 34, 53, 65, 249, 307
Baby It's You!, 57, 65
Bacharach, Burt, 31, 59
back pressure, 202, 206, 207
Back to the Future, 61
"Backwoods Barbie," 318
Bailey, Pearl, 30
Baker's Wife, The, 235, 236, 319
balance boards, 275–76
balanced breathing, 266, 267–68, 271, 276
Balanchine, George, 22
Ball, Loewenberg, 133
ballad operas, 2–3
ballet, 8–9, 22, 23
Bandstand, 253, 320
Band's Visit, The, 167, 247
Band Wagon, The, 25
Bare, 61, 308
Bareilles, Sara, 39
BASH'd, 65
Bat Boy, 54
Bat Out of Hell, 61, 309
Beach Boys, 58
Beatlemania, 57
Beatles, 57
beats, 260, 262, 332
Beautiful: The Carole King Musical, 58, 59
"Beautiful City," 248
Beauty and the Beast, 35, 36, 243, 300, 318
"Beauty Is, The," 227
Beehive, 57
Beggar's Opera, The, 2–3
Beilock, Sian, 158–59
"Belle," 318
Bells Are Ringing, 25, 26, 234

Beltbox, 330
belter bridges, 192
belting: breathing while, 266; components of, 169; definition, 165, 166–67; exercises for, advanced, 195–97; exercises for, beginning, 185–86; exercises for, higher range, 191–92, 193–94; history on, 184–85; musical genres using, 53, 54, 55; prerequisite training for, 185; repertoire selection for contemporary sounds in, 247–53; repertoire selection for high/contemporary, 236–40; repertoire selection for midrange/traditional, 232–36; variations of, 187–91
Be More Chill, xx–xxiii, 55, 246–47, 251–52, 300, 318
Bend It Like Beckham, 66
Bengsons, The, 311
Bennett, Michael, 33
Berlin, Irving, 14, 15, 16, 20, 24
Bernstein, Leonard, 25
Best Little Whorehouse in Texas, The, 31, 60, 66
Betsy, 17
Big, 53, 247–48
Big River, 34
Billboard (music chart), 39, 61
Billy Elliot the Musical, 38, 60
Biltmore Theater, 30
Birdie, Conrad, 26
Bjork, Robert A., 151
Black Americans: all-Black casts and productions, 13, 20, 30–31; belting vocal styles, 185; character stereotypes, 19; dance sensations based on traditional dances of, 13; early musical performances featuring, 4–5, 12, 13, 18, 20; entertainment forms as denigration of, 5–6; female musical composer/writers, first, 31; love songs performed by, first, 18; mixed-race productions featuring, 16, 30; music genres attributed to, 17, 57, 65; music styles based on music of, 14; opera singers, 13; ragtime composers, 14; segregated seating, 18; theatre companies of, first, 4–5
Blackbirds, 18
Black Crook, The, 8–9, 10
blackface, 5, 19
Black Patti's Troubadors, 13
Black Suits, The, 236–37
Blake, Eubie, 18
Blitzstein, Marc, 21
Bloody, Bloody, Andrew Jackson, 63
Bloomer Girl, 24
bluegrass, 47, 63, 66, 87
blues, 17, 31, 46, 47, 56, 63, 82, 199
Bock, Jerry, 26
body mapping, 283
Body Ritual Movement, 358
Bolton, Guy, 15
Bombay Dreams, 66
Bonnie and Clyde, 36, 66
Bono, 39, 62
book musicals: definition, 18; historical development of, 18, 19, 23, 24, 25, 26; most successful, 33
Book of Mormon, 318
Booth, John Wilkes, 7
Born for This, 65
"Boundaries," 250
Bowie, David, 39, 60
Boy from Oz, The, 38
Boyle's Law, 72

Boys from Syracuse, The, 241
Bozeman, Ken, 169
Brackett, Stephen, xxi
Bradford, Marilyn, 360
branding, 354
"Breathe," 213, 238
breathiness (singing style), 49, 55, 200
breathing: anatomy of, 72–77; for children, 295; children and, 289, 295; exhalation exercises, 271–74; during fitness training, 283; inhalation exercises, 268–271; management strategies, 265–68, for performance athleticism, 359; performance exertion and physical fitness for, 97–98; as repertoire selection consideration, 215; techniques for, 77, 100
Brice, Fanny, 16
Bridges of Madison County, 66, 312
Brigadoon, 24, 25, 245, 316
Brightman, Alex, 369–70
Bright Star, 66
"Bring Him Home," 246
Bring It On, 213
"Bring on the Monsters," 47
"Broadway, Here I Come," 323
Broadway Bounty Hunter, 59
Broadway Licensing, 300
Broadway productions: all-Black, 13; decline of, 22; early growth of, 10; financial challenges, 37; golden age of, 22–24; incorporation of, 35; jazz dance in, 15; longest running/most successful, 25; modern patron and revenue statistics, 1; music style history, 14, 17; 9/11 impact on, 37; pandemics and, 16; theatres in the round, 38; ticket prices, 33, 37
Broadway songs. *See* traditional musical theatre
Bronx Tale, A, 58, 300
Brooklyn, 65
Brown, Jason Robert, 36, 54
Brown, William Henry, 4
Bubbling Brown Sugar, 31
Buddy: The Buddy Holly Story, 57
Bullets over Broadway, 306
burlesque, 6–7
"Burn," 256
Burnt Part Boys, 66
"But Not for Me," 321
Bye Bye Birdie, 26, 212–13
Byrne, David, 67, 311

Cabaret, 28, 32, 53, 249, 307, 322
cabaret songs, 322–23
Cabin in the Sky, 22, 23
Cablevision, 35
Café La MaMa, 29
Caffe Cino, 29
caffeine, 94, 102, 343, 360, 365
Cage aux Folles, La, 34, 52
cakewalk, 13
callbacks, 313, 314
calling voice, 55, 169, 185, 186, 188, 193
Call Me Madame, 25
"Calm," 260
Camelot, 25
Candide, 25, 174
Cantor, Eddie, 16
"Captain of the Team," 237
"Caravan," 242
Carlos, Wendy, 66–67
Carousel, 24, 52, 166, 174–75, 244, 307

Carrie, 61
Carroll, Earl, 16
Carte, Richard D'Oyly, 10
cash prize traditions, 7
casting directors, 313, 315, 325, 330, 331, 333
cast recordings, xx, 53, 217
Cats, 34, 54, 300, 308
CCM (contemporary commercial music), 135, 165. *See also* pop/rock music; pop/rock subgenres
CEA (Chorus Equity Association), 16
censorship, 3, 21
character baggage, 316–17
"Charleston, The," 18
charm songs, 319–20
Charnin, Martin, 33
checking action, 268
Cheetah Club, The, 30
Chenoweth, Kristen, 174, 342
Cher Show, The, 59, 61
Chess, 34, 54, 61, 308
chest voice: belting exercises, 186, 189, 190–95; compression technology benefits, 125; E4–E5 range and transitions to, 170–71; laryngeal register transitions, 181, 183, 228; range and auditory targets utilizing, 177; resonant voice training, 19, 179; singing styles using, 166, 167; speech into singing training with, 180–81; straight tone exercises, 198; terminology and usage, 168–69
Chicago, 12, 32, 36, 300, 320
Chicago World's Fair, 14
children: developmental stages of, 288–91; musicals for, 299–300; musicianship of, 289, 291–92; opportunities for, 287; pitch inaccuracy issues, 292–93; repertoire selections for, 215, 294–99; singing lessons for, 287–88; vocal health for, 301–2
Chitty Chitty Bang Bang, 38
Choir Boy, 67
choking, 158
choreographers, 22, 24–25, 26, 32–33, 330
Chorus Equity Association (CEA), 16
Chorus Line, A, 33, 268, 300, 319, 321
chunking, 146, 161
Circle in the Square Theatre, 38
circuits, 8, 12
City of Angels, 34
civil rights, 4–5, 27, 30
Civil War, 7
Civil War, The, 36
clavicular breathing, 266–67, 268
Clear Channel Communications, 35
Cline, Patsy, 57, 66
close timbre, 169, 171
Clueless, 61
"Cockeyed Optimist," 318
Coffin, Berton, 205
cognitive science, 134. *See also* learning; motor (procedural) learning
Cohen, George M., 11
"Cold Feets," 321
college auditions, 335–36
college programs, 336
"Colored Women," 47
Color Purple, The, 65, 268
Comden, Betty, 25
comedies, 38–39
comedy songs, 309–10, 314, 319
"Come to Me, Bend to Me," 245
comic operas, 3–4, 9

INDEX

commentary songs, 28
Company, 32, 53, 307, 319, 321
compressors, 123–25
concept albums, 31, 58, 59, 60, 63
concept musicals, 28, 30, 32, 33
Concord Theatricals, 300
condenser microphones, 113–15
conductors, 26, 153
Connecticut Yankee, A, 17
constrained action hypothesis, 158
contemporary cabaret songs, 322–23
contemporary commercial music (CCM), 135, 165. *See also* pop/rock music; pop/rock subgenres
contemporary music theatre, 54–55, 236–40, 247–53, 308
contemporary pop/rock, 62–63
context, 261–62
contrasting songs, 311–12, 335
cooldowns, 102, 343
coproducers, 33
copyright laws, 9–10
costumes: breathing strategies for restrictive, 266, 267; cooldown rituals with, 343; of early musical entertainment, 6, 9, 16; glam rock, 60; typing for, 328
counterculture movement, 27, 29
country music, 31, 47, 50, 56, 60, 66
Cowgirls, 66
Cox, Ida, 185
Cradle Will Rock, The, 21
Crazy for You, 18, 52, 300, 306
Creole Show, The, 13
cricothyroid (CT) dominance, 81, 168, 169. *See also* falsetto
cricothyroid (CT) muscles, 80, 81, 168
cries, 55, 201–2

crossover, 129
Cry Baby, 57
Curtains, 300
cuts, 295, 312–14, 324

"Daddy's Son," 212
Damasio, Antonio, 142
Damn Yankees, 26
dance and dancing: breathing strategies for, 267, 282; choreographers in history, 22, 23, 24; early musical integration with, 8–9, 22, 23; jazz, on Broadway, 15; nightclub scenes with, 23; performance athleticism and, 281–82; for plot direction, 22, 23, 24; popular styles of, 13, 18; song and dance songs, 321. *See also* choreographers
Dancin', 32
"Day I Got Expelled, The," 318
"Dead Girl Walking," 212
Dear Evan Hanson, 55, 62, 167, 216, 252, 308
Death Takes a Holiday, 52, 307
Debbie Does Dallas, 66
declarative learning, 134, 135, 137–38
"Defying Gravity," 320
delay, 126–27
deliberate practice, 136, 152, 161
DeMille, Agnes, 23, 24
"Dentist," 318
Descartes, René, 141, 142
desire(s), 140, 141, 142, 161, 262
diaphragms: of human anatomy, 73–74, 137, 289; of microphones, 113, 116, 117, 119
diet, 90–91, 96–97, 365
digital voice processors, 128

directors: casting, 313, 315, 325, 330, 331, 333; music, 325, 330; musical, 12, 25, 27, 330
Dirty Rotten Scoundrels, 38, 319
Disappointment or The Force of Credulity: A New American Comic Opera of Two Acts by Andrew Barton, Esq., The, 3
Disaster!, 58
disco, 58–59
Dixie Duo, 18
"Do, Do, Do," 223
"D.O.A.," 47
Donkey Show, The, 58
Donna: The Donna Summer Musical, 58
Don't Bother Me, I Can't Cope, 31, 233
"Don't Get Around Much Anymore," 229
doo-wop, 56
Do Re Mi, 25, 26
"Down the Shower Drain," 358
Dracula, 36
Dreamgirls, 33, 65, 320
"Drive," 47
Drowsy Chaperone, The, 321
drugs: pharmaceutical, 95–96, 97, 98, 99, 333, 366; recreational, 104, 105
DuBarry Was a Lady, 20
Dude, 60
duets, 296, 322
Duke, Vernon, 22
Duncan, Todd, 22
Dunham, Katherine, 22
Dusty: The Dusty Springfield Musical, 58
Dycem stretches, 280–81
Dylan, Bob, 58, 63

dynamic microphones, 113
dynamics, song, 215, 288, 291, 295

Earl Carroll's Vanities, 16
early contemporary musical theatre, 54, 308
ears, nose, throat (ENT) specialists, xxii–xxiii, 343
Earth, Wind, and Fire, 59
eating disorders, 90
Ebb, Fred, 12, 28, 32
ECC (Equity Chorus Call), 327, 328
Edges, 309
Edwin, Robert, 175
8-bar songs, 313–14, 327
electronic dance music (EDM), 67
electronic music, 66–67
Elegies, 231
eleven o'clock numbers, 320–21
Elf, 300
Elves, The, 6
emotion, 141–42
empiricism, 134
Enchanted, 1, 230
Enchantress, The, 13
"end of act I" numbers, 320, 321
Entertainer's Secret, 92
ENT (ears, nose, throat) specialists, xxii–xxiii, 343
"Epic I," 47, 200
equalizers, 120–23, 129
Equity Chorus Call (ECC), 327, 328
Equity Principal Audition (EPA), 326–27
Ericsson, K. Anders, 136
esophagitis, 96
Ethel Merman Disco Album, The, 59
Eubie!, 31, 52
Everybody's Talking about Jamie, 62

INDEX

"Everything's Coming Up Roses," 320
Evita, 31, 54, 308, 320
exercise, physical, 97–98, 282–83
exercise balls, 276
exercise bands, 269, 271–72
exhalation exercises, 271–74
experimental theatre, 29–30
external intercostals, 74
external obliques, 74–77
extravaganzas, 6–7, 34

falsetto: compression technology benefits, 125; registration descriptions, 168; repertoire selections for, 245–47, 252; songs requiring, 216; terminology usage, 168–69; vocal exercises for, 203; voice anatomy and, 81
Falsettoland, 36
Falsettos, 36, 53
Fame, 47
fear, 33, 98–100, 106, 139–40, 142, 153
Federal Theatre Project (FTP), 21
feedback, 155–57, 170
Fela!, 59
Feldenkrais Method, 283
fellowships, 7
Fiddler on the Roof, 25, 26, 28, 300
Fifty Million Frenchmen, 20
Filichia, Peter, 287
Finian's Rainbow, 25, 222–23
Finn, William, 35–36, 38
Fiorello!, 26, 227, 235–36
fitness, physical, 97–98, 282–83
flageolet register, 168
Fleetwood Mac, 60
Flora, The Red Menace, 230
Floradora, 10

Florentine Camerata, 2
Flower Drum Song, 24, 52
Floyd Collins, 66
Fly with Me, 17
Fold, Ben, 54
folk, 47, 63
folk rock, 57, 58, 63
Follies, 32, 33, 320
Footloose, 61
Forever Dusty, 58
Forever Plaid, 56
"Forget about the Boy," 321
formants, 83–86, 116, 127, 133, 197
"For the First Time in Forever," 231
Fortress of Solitude, 59
Fortune Teller, The, 13
42nd Street, 34, 52
Fosse, 32
Fosse, Bob, 26, 32
Foster, Melissa, 46–47
Four Seasons, 58
Freak Out (album), 59
frequencies (pitches): children and inaccuracies in, 292; fundamental, 81; hormone development impacting voice, 173–74; multiples of, 81, 82, 111; resonant, 83–86; sound, 81–82, 110
Friedman, Michael, 311
Friml, Rudolph, 13
Frozen, 1, 231, 300, 370
FTP (Federal Theatre Project), 21
"Fugue for Tin Horns," 319
Full Monty, The, 38, 213
functional spectrum, 174
Fun Home, 259, 260
funk, 31, 47, 59
Funny Face, 18
Funny Girl, 26, 235

Funny Thing Happened on the Way to the Forum, A, 260

García, Manuel, II, 133, 162
gargling, 91, 94
gastroesophageal reflux (GERD), 96–97
Gay, John, 2
Gay Rap Opera, A, 65
Gelt, Jonathan Reid, 323
gender, 173–75, 212–13, 315
gender-swapping productions, 213
generalizability, 153
genres, musical, 45–51. See also *specific genres*
Gentleman's Guide to Love and Murder, 52, 227, 307
Gentlemen Prefer Blondes, 24, 26
George White's Scandals, 15–16
GERD (gastroesophageal reflux), 96–97
Gershwin, George, 15, 17–18, 20–21, 306
Gershwin, Ira, 15, 17–18, 20–21
"Gethsemane," 321
"Get Out and Stay Out," 239, 257–58
"Getting Married Today," 321
Ghost, 62
Giant, 66
"Gideon Briggs, I Love You," 225–26
Gilbert, William Schwenk, 9–10
"Gimme Gimme," 235, 320
Girl Crazy, 20, 185, 321
Girl Friend, The, 17
Girl from the North Country, The, 58, 63
"Give My Regards to Broadway," 11
given circumstances, 256–57
glam rock, 60, 355

Glee (television show), 1
"Glitter and Be Gay," 174, 228
Glorious Ones, The, 55
goal setting: for auditions, 332; for motor learning, 157, 160–61; for repertoire selection, 218; for vocal exercises, 171; to vocal instruction motivation, 140–41
Godspell, 31, 248, 356
Goehring, Jerry, xx–xxi
golden age, 22–27, 28, 52
Golden Boy, 28
"Goodbye, Little Dream, Goodbye," 228
"Good for You," 216
"Good Kid," 47, 252
"Good Morning Baltimore," 200
Good News, 223
Good Vibrations, 58
gospel, 31, 65
gottals, 55
Grand Hotel, 34, 52
Grant, Micki, 31
grants, 7, 37
graphic equalizers, 123
gravel (singing style), 49, 55, 312
Grease, 1, 31, 57
Great American Songbook, 51–52, 262
Great American Trailer Park Musical, The, 66
"Great Big Stuff," 319
Great Depression, 19, 20, 22
Green, Adolph, 25
Green Day, 63, 64
Green Grow the Lilacs, 23
Greenwillow, 26, 225–26
Grey Gardens, 52
groove, 48, 236, 252
growls, 49, 55, 217, 247, 312

INDEX

Guarini, Justin, 348–54
Guettel, Adam, 36
gunboat musicals, 11
Guys and Dolls, 26, 31, 52, 225, 300, 307, 319
Gypsy, 25, 26, 307, 320, 321

Hadestown, 46, 47, 63, 200, 247
Hagen, Uta, 257
Hair, 29–30, 32, 58, 65
Hairspray, 57, 200, 300
Hallam, Lewis, 3
Hallelujah Baby!, 26, 30, 236
Hallmark, 35
Hallowell, Edward, 144–45
Hamilton, 39, 65, 256, 257, 318
Hamlisch, Marvin, 31
Hammerstein, Oscar, II, 19, 20, 23–24, 32
Hands on a Hardbody, 66
hands on knees/wall exercises, 274
"Happy Working Song," 230
harmonic, 81–82
harmonics, 111
Harnick, Sheldon, 26
Harris, Wynonie, 56
Hart, Amos, 12
Hart, Lorenz, 17, 20, 23
Hazel Flagg, 26
Head over Heels, 61, 213, 300
head voice, 168–69, 170–71, 222–28. *See also* falsetto
Heathers, 212, 300
Hebb's rule, 147
Hedwig and the Angry Inch, 62
Hello, Dolly!, 27, 30–31, 52
Helpburn, Theresa, 23
Henry, Joshua, 208n17
Henson, Jim, 38
Herald Square Theatre, 12

Herbert, Victor, 9, 13, 15
Here Lies Love, 67
Here's Love, 26
Herman, Jerry, 27, 52
"He's Here," 232–33
Heyward, DuBose and Dorothy, 20
High Button Shoes, 26
"Higher," 238
higher-order skills, 135–36
High Fidelity, 38, 55, 300, 320
high-intensity interval training (HIIT), 365
High School Musical, 300
Hilty, Megan, 339–48
Hindi film music, 64
H.M.S. Pinafore, 9–10
"Holding Me Down," 237
"Hold On," 234
Holler If You Hear Me, 65
Holly, Buddy, 57
Home Street Home, 63
honey, as throat gargle, 94
"Honey Bun," 320
Honeymoon in Vegas, 213
hooks, 48
hormones, 174, 290–91
Hornback, Robert, 4
"How about Me?," 222
"How Lovely to Be a Woman," 212
How Now, Dow Jones, 232–33
How to Succeed in Business without Really Trying, 26
"hug a tree" exercises, 269, 271
Humidflyer, 93
hydration, 91–94, 102–3, 301–2, 343, 365
hyperhidrosis, 92

"I Am Playing Me," 319
"I am" songs, 318

"I Am the Very Model of a Major Modern General," 321
"I Cain't Say No," 316, 318
"I Can Do That," 321
"I Chose Right," 249
Iconis, Joe, xx, xxi, 323
"I Could Have Danced All Night," 174, 226
identity: gender, 173–75, 315; musical, 291–92; racial and ethnic, 213, 315; repertoire selections matching, 222, 315
"I Don't Care Much," 249
"I'd Rather Be Sailing," 246
"If I Loved You," 260–61
"If I Told You," 322
"I Got It Bad (And That Ain't Good)," 228–29
"I Got Rhythm," 185
"I Like Everybody," 243
"I'll Be Here," 319
"I'll Know," 225
"I'm Alive," 216, 318
"I'm a Star," 323
"I'm Not at All in Love," 232
improvisation, 49, 161, 199–200, 237
"I'm Sorry," 247
inaccurate singers, 292–94
"In a Sentimental Mood," 244
In Dahomey, 13
indie/alternative rock, 46, 47, 63
indie folk/alternative rock, 63
Indi-pop, 64
individuality, 49, 347–48
"Infinite Joys," 231
Ingram, Rex, 22
inhalation exercises, 268–71
inharmonic overtones, 82
injuries, xix, 343. *See also* vocal injuries

inner monologue, 261
"In Short," 309
inside out, 256
"Inside Out," 227
integrated musicals, 23–24
Interstate, 237
In the Heights, 1, 64, 65, 213, 238, 318
Into the Woods, 1, 34, 318, 346, 362–63
In Transit, 67, 362, 364, 365, 367, 369
In Trousers, 36
Irwin, May, 185
Isle of Spice, The, 11
It's a Wonderful Life (movie), 26
"It Took Me a While," 249
"I want" songs, 318, 320
"I Want to Go Home," 247–48

Jabara, Paul, 58
Jackson, Michael, 61, 353
Jagged Little Pill, 62, 217
Jagger, Mick, 59
jaw tension, 278–81
jazz, 17, 20, 51–52, 306–7
Jazz Singer, The, 19–20
Jekyll and Hyde, 36, 54, 308, 340
Jerome Robbins' Broadway, 34
Jersey Boys, 38, 39, 58, 216
Jesus Christ Superstar, 1, 31, 32, 60, 321
Joel, Billy, 54
Joe's Garage (album), 59
"Joey Is a Punkrocker," 236–37
John, Elton, 54, 60
John and Jen, 54, 249, 308
Jolson, Al, 19–20
Jonathan Larson Grant, 37
Jonathan Larson Project, The, 37
Jones, Sissieretta, 13

INDEX

Joplin, Janis, 60
Joplin, Scott, 14
Joseph and the Amazing Technicolor Dreamcoat, 54
Judson Poets Theater, 29
Jujamcyn Theatre, 33
jukebox musicals: descriptions and popularity, 37–38; genre selection and orchestration for, 51; Gershwin's music as, 18; pop/rock genre variations, 51, 56, 57, 58–59, 60, 61–62, 64, 65
Jumbo, 241
"Just Imagine," 223

Kandel, Eric, 148
Kander, John, 12, 28, 32
Keene, Laura, 6–7
Kennedy, John F., 25
Kern, Jerome, 15, 19, 20
keys, 294–95, 299, 326
"Keys (It's Alright)," 250–51
Kilgore, Mykal, 174
Kimball, Merry, 340
King, Carole, 58, 59
King and I, The, 24, 25, 307
Kinks, 59
Kinks Are the Village Green Preservation Society, The (album), 59
Kinky Boots, 61, 366
Kiss Me, Kate, 24
Kiss of the Spiderwoman, 36
K-pop, 64
Kuti, Fela, 59

labor strikes, 16
labor unions, 16, 21, 33, 337n8
LaChiusa, Michael John, 36, 310
Lady Be Good, 18

Lady in the Dark, 23, 319
La La Land, 1
Larson, Jonathan, 36–37, 54
laryngeal registration: acoustic registration impacted by, 169; descriptions, 167–69; exercises for, 181, 182–83, 194, 230, 231, 245; feedback resonance from, 170; range training and, 170, 177; sounds using, 167
laryngopharyngeal reflux (LPR), 96–97
larynx (voice box): adolescent development of, 290–91; anatomy of, 77–82; dryness of, 91–94, 95, 96; gender and, 173–74; prepuberty development of, 288–89; reflux conditions of, 96–97; smoking and cancer of, 105; vibrato styles, 198
laser beam visualizations, 198
Last Five Years, The, 54, 308
Last Ship, The, 63
Latin pop, 64
LaTouche, John, 22
Lauper, Cindy, 39, 61
Laura Keene's Theater, 6–7
Lawrence, Van, 91
Lazarus, 60
lead sheets, 326
League of Broadway Producers and Theatres, 27
Leap of Faith, 65
Learner, Alan Jay, 25
learning: definition of, 136–38; modes of, 134–38; multitasking effects on, 143–45; process of, 138–48; sleep deprivation impacting, 143. *See also* motor (procedural) learning

LeDoux, Joseph, 142
Lee, Tim, 148, 152
Legally Blonde, 261, 300, 318, 320
legit (genre), 52–53, 54, 55
legit (vocal style), 166, 222–28, 240–46, 307
Lehár, Franz, 13
Lennon, 57, 60
Lestat, 60
Let 'Em Eat Cake, 20
Let It Be, 57
"Let It Go," 1
Leung, Telly, 362–71
Levy, Caissie, 369
Lew Leslie's Blackbirds of 1930, 224
Light in the Piazza, The, 52, 166, 227, 244, 307
Lightning Thief, The: children's adaptations of, 300; "I want" songs from, 318; musical genres of, 47, 63; patter songs from, 321; racial/ethnic identity and songs from, 213; repertoire selection from, 240, 252
Lincoln, Abraham, 7
Lion King, The, 35, 60, 318, 350–51
Lippa, Andrew, 36, 54
lip trills, 176, 202, 206
Little Johnny Jones, 11
Little Me, 233–34
Little Mermaid, The, 300
Little Night Music, A, 32, 321
Little Shop of Horrors, 34, 57, 318
Little Women, 55, 167
Loesser, Frank, 26
Loewe, Frederick, 25
Lola Versus Powerman and the Moneygoround, 59
long songs, 215
"Look to the Rainbow," 222–23

"Lost," 321
Louisiana Purchase, 23
Love, Janis, 60
Love in Hate Nation, 319
"Love Me, Love Me Not," 238
"Lover, Come Back to Me," 224
"Love to Me," 244
LPR (laryngopharyngeal reflux), 96–97
lyrics: of book musicals, 18; character analysis and acting through, 257, 259, 261, 316; children and age-appropriate, 212, 295; comedy songs and delivery of, 309–10; musical theatre descriptions, 49–50; pop/rock *vs.* theatre music comparisons, 49; as repertoire selection concern, 212–13; reprises and changes in, 322

Mack and Mabel, 234
Mackenzie, Barbara, 371
Mackintosh, Cameron, 34
magic "if," 256
Magic Show, The, 31
"Make Them Hear You," 320–21
Malloy, Dave, 311
Mame, 28, 52
Mamma Mia!, 38, 59
"Man," 213
Manifest Pussy, 358
Man of La Mancha, 28
"Man That Got Away, The," 321–22
"Maple Leaf Rag," 14
March of the Falsettos, 36
Marvelous Wonderettes, 56
Mary Poppins, 38, 300
massages, 276–81, 283, 346, 360
master class syndrome, 150–52
Matilda, 300

Maxim, the, 159–60, 161
"Maybe This Time," 322
McDavid, Julian, 358
McDermot, Galt, 30
McLean, Grace, 311
"Meadowlark," 319
Me and Juliet, 24
Mean Girls, 46, 62
medications, 95–96, 97, 98, 99, 333, 366
Meehan, Thomas, 33
megamusicals, 34, 53, 308
Mell, Michael, xx
"Memories of You," 224
memory: consolidation of, 139, 142, 143, 145, 147; constructive, 138, 147; emotion impacting, 142; long-term, 145, 147–48; short-term, 145, 147, 148; working (active learning), 145–46, 147
"Memory Song," 321
Memphis, 47, 65, 300
mental health, 98–100, 106
Merman, Ethel, 20, 24, 58–59, 184, 185
Merrick, David, 27
Merrily We Roll Along, 32
Metaphysics (Aristotle), 145
"Michael in the Bathroom," xx, xxi, xxii, 214, 251–52
micro-choking, 158
microphones, 32, 113–20, 130
Miles, Aubrey, 18
Milk and Honey, 27
Miller, Flourney, 18
Miller, Richard, 134
Million Dollar Quartet, 57
minstrel shows, 5–6, 14
mis-accents, 50
Misérables, Les, 34, 54, 246, 308, 322

Miss Nelson Is Missing, 300
Miss Saigon, 34, 54, 308
Miss You Like Hell, 300
mixing, 167, 181–84, 228–32
MJ, 61
moderation, 301
moment before, 261
money notes, 313
monitors, 129
Monsoon Wedding, 66
Monstersongs, 247
Montero, Barbara Gail, 159
Monteverdi, 2
"More Than Survive," 318
"Morning Person," 318
Morrisette, Alanis, 62
Most Happy Fella, The, 26, 243
motor (procedural) learning: attentional focus for, 157–62; attributes of, 136; controlled *vs.* automatic processes, 154–57; definition, 135, 149; evidence of, 150; feedback for, 155–56; goals for, 157, 160–61; as learning mode, 135–36, 137–38, 148; performance shifts and unlearning, 150–52; practice strategies for, 152–54; requirements for, 148–50; teacher-to-student touching during, 156–57
Motown (genre), 31, 57
Motown (musical), 57, 65
movies, 1, 19–20, 38, 39, 57
MPA (music performance anxiety), 98–100, 106, 139–40, 153, 333
"Mr. Cellophane," 12
MTI (Music Theatre International), 299–300
Mueller, Jessie, 208n17

multitasking, 143–45, 151, 153
Murder Ballad, 63
musical theatre, overview: future of, 39–40; lyrics of, 49–50; as music genre, 51–55; performance satisfaction of, 225; popularity of, 1.
See also musical theatre history
musical theatre history: early development, 2; 1500s, 2; 1600s, 2; 1700s, 2–3; 1800s, 3–4; 1900s, 10–16; 1910s, 16–17; 1920s, 17–20; 1930s, 19–22; 1940s, 22–25; 1950s, 25–27; 1960s, 28–31; 1970s, 31–33; 1980s, 33–34; 1990s, 35–37; 2000s, 37–39
"Music and the Mirror, The," 268, 321
music directors, 325, 330
musicianship, 289, 291–92, 305
Music in the Air, 242–43
Music Man, The, 26, 52, 319–20
"Music of My Soul, The," 47
music performance anxiety (MPA), 98–100, 106, 139–40, 153, 333
music publishing centers, 14
"Music That Makes Me Dance, The," 235
Music Theatre International (MTI), 299–300
"My Big French Boyfriend," 309, 319
"My Eyes Are Fully Opened," 321
My Fair Lady, 25, 174, 318
"My Grand Plan," 47, 213
My One and Only, 18
"My Romance," 241
"My Shot," 318
Mystery of Edwin Drood, The, 34
"My Strongest Suit," 356
"My Unfortunate Erection," 319

nasal irrigation, 94
Natasha, Pierre, and the Great Comet of 1812, 67
National Association of Teachers of Singing (NATS), xxvii, 91, 95
National Center for Voice and Speech (NCVS), 88, 95
Naughty Marietta, 13
Nayfack, Shakina, 355–62
neck tension, 276, 280–81
Nederlander Organization, 33
nervousness, 332–33
Neti pots, 93–94
neuroplasticity, 148
"Never Ever Getting Rid of Me," 250
New Amsterdam Theatre, 35
"New Argentina, A," 320
New Brain, A, 36, 246
New Moon, The, 224
News Corp., 35
New York City, 4–5, 12, 14, 35, 37. *See also* Broadway productions; off-Broadway; off-off-Broadway
New Yorker Gay Divorce, The, 20
Next to Normal, 63, 167, 216, 318
Niblo's Garden, 9
Nice Work If You Can Get It, 18, 52
Night with Janis Joplin, A, 60
Nikola Tesla Drops the Beat, 67
Nine, 34
9/11, 37
9 to 5, 38, 239, 257, 258, 318
Nix, John, 211–12
"Nobody," 12
"No Good Deed," 216, 239–40
"No Moon," 245
nonbinary people, 173, 174, 175, 213, 315
Norman, Jessye, 364, 371
"Nothing," 319

INDEX 405

"Not Yet," 323
nutrition, 90–91, 96–97, 365

obesity, 90
objectives, 259, 260, 261, 262–63, 264, 322, 323
obstacles, 259, 260, 261
Octet, 67
Octoroons, The, 13
off-Broadway, 28–29, 30, 34, 36–37
Offenbach, Jacques, 9, 13
"Officer Krupke," 320
off-off-Broadway, 29–30, 34
Of Thee I Sing, 20
Oh, Kay!, 18, 223
O'Keefe, Laurence, 54
Oklahoma!, 23–24, 50, 213, 316, 318, 322
Oliver, 322
"Ol' Man River," 174
Once, 63
Once Upon a Mattress, 216
Once Upon a One More Time, 62, 348, 350, 351, 352
110 in the Shade, 24
"One Jump," 365
"One Knight," 62
one-nighters, 8
"One Perfect Moment," 213
One Touch of Venus, 230
"On My Own," 322
onsets, 200–201
"On the Other Side of the Tracks," 233–34
On the Town, 25, 322
On the Twentieth Century, 25
On Your Feet!, 61, 64
open calls, 327–28
opening numbers, 318
Open Theatre, 29

open timbre, 169, 171, 189
Opera of Flora, or Hob in the Well, The, 3
operas, 2–3, 9–10, 20
operettas, 9, 13
orchestration, 50–51
Ordinary Days, 308, 319
Orfeo, L', 2
Oriental America, 13
"other" (scene partner), 258–59
Our American Cousin, 7
outside in, 256
overhydration, 92
overtones, 81, 82, 111

Pacific Overtures, 32
Paint Your Wagon, 24, 25
Pajama Game, The, 25, 26, 27, 31, 232
Pal Joey, 23
pandemics, 16, 333
Panskepp, Jaak, 142
panto, 8
pantomime, 8
Papp, Joseph, 30
parametric equalizers, 121–23
parasympathetic nervous system (PNS), 139, 140
Paris, 20
Parton, Dolly, 39, 60, 66, 340
passaggio, 178, 214, 224, 225, 227, 249, 250, 252
Passing Show, The, 15
Passing Strange, 63, 250–51
Passion, 36
pastiche songs, 320
Pastor, Tony, 7–8
pathé, 141
patriotism, 11, 14, 21–22
patter songs, 321

Peggy Ann, 17
"People Will Say We're in Love," 322
performance: anxiety and fear due to, 33, 98–100, 106, 139–40, 153; choking and micro-choking during, 158; context choices, 261–62; definition, 149; learning goals compared to, 149–50. *See also* performance athleticism
performance athleticism: body connection exercises, 274–76;; bodywork for, 283; breath management strategies, 265–68; dancers and dancing, 281–82; exhalation exercises, 271–74; experiences with, 365; inhalation exercises, 268–71; physical fitness for, 282–83; preparation for, 346, 352, 359, 370–71; tension reduction exercises, 276–81
performance shifts, 150–52
Peter Pan, 25, 26
Peters, Bernadette, 346–47
Pet Sounds (album), 58
Phantom of the Opera, 34, 364
phonation: exercises for, 176, 202–4, 329–30, 368; onsets and, 200–201; vocal anatomy, 7–79
phonation threshold pressure (PTP), 92, 202
phonotrauma, 89, 100, 103, 106
phrasing, 49–50, 293
physical fitness, 97–98, 282–83
physical therapy, 283
Pinon, Diego, 358
Pippin, 31, 32, 53
Pirates of Penzance, 321
pitches. *See* frequencies
placement, 170, 342
playwrights, 3, 7

plot-driven musicals, 10, 15, 18, 19, 23–24
PNS (parasympathetic nervous system), 139, 140
Polkadots, 300
pop musicals, 31, 46, 59
pop operas, 53–54, 61, 308
pop/rock music: for auditions, 309; definition, 46; genre characteristics and comparisons, 47–50; musical theatre genres with influence of, 53–55; orchestration changes for, 40–41. *See also* pop/rock subgenres
pop/rock subgenres: acapella, 67; for auditions, 309; bluegrass, 66; contemporary, 62–63; country, 66; doo-wop, 56; electronic and electronic dance music, 66–67; gospel, 65; indie/alternative, 63; indie folk/alternative, 63; Indi-pop and Hindi film music, 64; K-pop, 64; Latin pop, 64; overview, 55–56; punk, 63–64; rap, 65–66; R&B, 65; 1950s, 47, 56–57; 1960s, 57–58; 1970s, 58–60; 1980s, 61; 1990s, 61–62; 2000s, early, 62
popular music, 14, 17, 26, 45, 47, 51. *See also* pop/rock music; pop/rock subgenres
Porgy and Bess, 20–21
Porter, Billy, 366–67
Porter, Cole, 20, 24
posttraumatic stress disorder (PTSD), 142
"Power Law of Practice" (concept), 148, 152
practice: for audition preparation, 332; deliberate, 136, 152, 161; effective strategies for, 152–54;

INDEX 407

as learning requirement, 148; overpracticing effects, 105; for self-tape auditions, 333, 334; for vocal training, 135–36, 148, 152
preattentive processing, 140
prepuberty, 288–89. *See also* children
prescreens, 335–36
Present Arms, 17
Prince, Harold (Hal), 26, 27, 28, 32, 33
Prince Ananias, 13
Princess musicals, 15
Priscilla, Queen of the Desert, 58
procedural learning. *See* motor (procedural) learning
producers, 15–16, 27, 33, 330
Producers, The, 27, 38, 309
Promises, Promises, 31, 32, 59
proprioception, 137
pterygoid massages, 280
PTP (phonation threshold pressure), 92, 202
PTSD (posttraumatic stress disorder), 142
Public, The, 30
Public Theatre, 30, 33
Pulitzer Prize, 20, 26, 37, 355
Pump Boys and Dinettes, 60, 66
punk, 63
Punk Rock Girl, 63
Purlie, 31
"Put You in Your Place," 240

Quadrophenia (album), 60
quartets, 322
Queen of the Mist, 55
"Quiet," 323
"Quiet Thing, A," 230

Rachael Lily Rosenbloom (And Don't You Ever Forget It!), 58

racial and ethnic identity, 213, 315
racism, 4–5, 11, 56
Racism and Early Blackface Comic Traditions (Hornback), 4–5
Rado, James, 29
Ragni, Gerome, 29
ragtime, 14
Ragtime, 36, 212, 318, 320–21
Rain, 57
Rainey, Ma, 185
Raisin, 31
range: child development and, 291; children and key changes due to, 294; child vocal health and loss of, 301; E4–E5, 170–71; inaccurate child singers and appropriate, 294; repertoire selection consideration, 214; training in higher, 178–79; training in middle, 176–77; vocal exercises and, 172, 173
rap, 46–47, 65–66
raspberries, 176, 202, 206
raspiness, 301
Ratey, John, 144–45
R&B (rhythm and blues), 56, 57, 59, 65
readings and readers, 331–32
recombination, 146–47
Red, Hot, and Blue, 20
Redfield, Liza, 26
registration: categories of, 167–69; definition, 167; in E4-E5 range, 170–71; repertoire selection and, 215–16, 228–32
Renaissance, 2
Rent, 36–37, 62, 300, 308, 366
repertoire selection: for belting/contemporary sounds, 247–53; considerations, 212–19; genre knowledge for, 45; for head voice

(falsetto), 245–47; for high and contemporary belting, 236–40; for higher voices, 222–28; for lower voices, 240–45; for midrange and traditional belting, 232–36; pedagogical concerns, 211–12; for registration work and mixing, 228–32; resources for, 253; for skill building, 221–22; student-selected, 219–21; style variety, 165; for vocal development, 217–19
reprises, 322
resistance breathing, 271
resonance: belting and, 190–91; definition, 82–83, 170; in E4-E5 range, 171; resonant voice development, 179–80; sensory feedback of, 170; tools for measuring, 86; vocal science and anatomy of, 71, 82–86
resonant voice, 179–80
respiratory infections, 94
respiratory system, 72–73, 289, 290, 291. *See also* breathing
retention, 140
reverberation, 125–26
revues, 15–16, 37. *See also* jukebox musicals
rhythm and blues (R&b), 56, 57, 59, 65
Rice, Tim, 31
riffing, 54, 199–200
"Right This Way," 320
Rink, The, 34
Rise and Fall of Ziggy Stardust and the Spiders from Mars, The (concept album), 60
"Road to Hell," 47
Roaring Twenties, The, 17

Robber Bridegroom, The, 31, 60, 66
Robbins, Jerome, 25, 26, 34
Robeson, Paul, 174
rock: musicals featuring, 31, 32, 36–37, 45, 47; rhythmic structure of, 47–48; subgenres of, 37, 59–60, 61, 62, 63
rock and roll, 26, 29–30, 31, 56–57
Rock of Ages, 61, 300, 309
rock operas, 59–60
Rocky Horror Picture Show, 60
Rodgers, Richard, 17, 20, 23–24, 306
Rogers, Ginger, 20
Rogers, Will, 16, 25
Rolling Stones, 57, 59, 60
Romberg, Sigmund, 13
Roosevelt, Franklin, 21
Root, Lynn, 22
"Rose's Turn," 320
Ross, Jerry, 26
routines, 351, 359–60
Royal Chef, The, 11
royalty payments, 15
Rumours (album), 60
Runaways, The, 11, 60
Runnin' Wild, 18
rush tickets, 37

"Saga of Jenny, The," 319
Sager, Carole Bayer, 31
saliva production, 96
saltwater, as throat gargle, 94
Saturday Night Fever, 38, 58
Scarlet Pimpernel, The, 36, 54, 308
schemas, 147
Schmidt, Richard, 148, 152
Schoolboys in Disgrace (album), 59
School of Rock, 60, 63, 312
Schwartz, Stephen, 31, 38
scoops, 50, 55

INDEX

Secret Garden, The, 234
segregation, 5, 18
self-tapes, 333–34
semantics, 191
semi-occluded vocal tract (SOVT) positions, 176, 202–7, 277
"Send in the Clowns," 321
sequels, 20
Seussical, 248, 300
Seven Sisters, The, 7
SFX-Entertainment, 35
Shakespearean theatre, 4–5
Shakur, Tupac, 65
sheet music, 10, 14, 45
shelf equalizers, 120–21
She Loves Me, 26, 27, 28, 52, 217, 227, 307
Shenandoah, 31, 60
Shepherd, Thomas, 363–64
"Shipoopi," 319–20
Show Boat, 19, 23, 174
Show Girl, 18
showtunes. See traditional musical theatre
Shrek, 300, 318
Shubert Organization, 12, 15, 33
Shuffle Along, 18, 52
Shuffle Along, or the Making of the Musical Sensation of 1921 and All That Followed, 18, 224
"Shy," 216
signal chains, 112–13, 129
silent obligations, 217
simple songs, 310
Sing Happy, 369
"singing girdle" exercises, 269, 271–72
Singing' in the Rain, 25
Sissle, Noble, 18
Sister Act, 58, 65

"sit and twist" exercises, 272–73
Sitzprobe, 364
Six, 62
16-bar songs, 295, 313, 314
1600 Pennsylvania Avenue, 25
slating, 331
sleep, 142, 143, 152, 343
Smash (television show), 1, 344
Smith, Bessie, 185
Smokey Joe's Café, 37
smoking, 7, 97, 104–5
Soap Opera (album), 59
Soft Power, 55
"Soliloquy," 174–75, 244
"Solitude," 241
somatic marker hypothesis, 142
"Someday," 47
"Some Other Time," 322
"Some Things Are Meant to Be," 167
"So Much Better," 261, 320
Sondheim, Stephen, 32, 320
song and dance numbers, 321
song expectations, 317
"Song Is You, The," 242–43
Sophisticated Ladies, 52, 306
soul music, 31, 47, 57
sound, 110–12
Sound of Music, The, 24, 300
Soundscan, 61
sound systems, 128–29
Sousa, John Philip, 15
South Pacific, 24, 316, 318, 320
SOVT (semi-occluded vocal tract) positions, 176, 202–7, 277
Spamalot, 38, 300, 309, 319
Spamilton, 65
spatial orientation, 137
speakers, 113, 129
speaking, 103–4, 165, 179, 292, 342–43

Spears, Britney, 62
specialty songs, 310
spectacles, 4, 33–34
spectrum analyzers, 86, 111–12
Spiderman Turn Off the Dark, 62
Spitfire Grill, The, 66
split-week engagements, 8
Spongebob Squarepants Musical, The, 47
Spring Awakening, 61–62, 63
Springfield, Dusty, 58
"Squip Song," 246–47
"Stand Up," 47
Stanislavski, Konstantin, 256
Star is Born, A, 322
Starlight Express, 34
steam inhalers, 92–93
Steel Pier, 227
Stewart, Michael, 26
Sting, 39
Stitt, Georgia, 323
story songs, 319
straight tones, 49, 50, 53, 54, 55, 166, 198–99
Strange Loop, A, 55, 250, 321
straw phonation, 176, 202–4, 302, 329–30, 368
stress management, 106, 332
Strike Up the Band, 20
Strouse, Charles, 26, 33
Styne, Jule, 25
subplots, 23
substitution, 257–58
subtext, 260
Subways Are for Sleeping, 26, 27
Sullivan, Arthur, 9–10
Sullivan, Jan, 266
Sultan of Sulu, The, 11
Sunday in the Park with George, 34
Sundberg, Johan, 133

Sunset Boulevard, 34
suspension, 272
"Swanee," 18
Sweeney Todd, 32
Sweet Charity, 28, 321
Sweet Smell of Success, 55
sympathetic nervous system (SNS), 139–40
Sympathy Jones, 58
synaptic pruning, 143

Taboo, 61
tactics (actions), 259–60, 261, 263
TA (thyroarytenoid) dominant, 81, 168, 196
Tambourines to Glory, 65
TA (thyroarytenoid) muscle, 80, 81, 168
task-switching, 144, 151
TC-Helicon, 128
tea, as throat gargle, 94
"Telephone Wire," 259, 260
television shows, 1
tempo, 215, 311
temporomandibular joint (TMJ) massages, 278
Tenderloin, 26
tension, 87, 276–81, 283
Tepper, Jennifer Ashley, 37
Tesori, Jeanine, 36
tessitura, 105, 214, 315
"Thank Goodness," 231
"Thank Heaven for You," 233
"That's Him," 230
Theatre (theatre company), 3
theatre companies, 3, 6, 12, 15, 33
theatre owners, 12, 15, 33
theatres in the round, 38
Theatrical Rights Worldwide (TRW), 300–301

INDEX

"There's a World," 167
"There's Gotta Be Something Better Than This," 321
They're Playing Our Song, 31, 58
32-bar songs, 295, 313, 314
thoracic breathing, 267
Thoroughly Modern Millie, 38, 52, 235, 307, 320, 321
"Three Failed Escape Attempts of Sheila Nail," 319
Threepenny Opera, The, 29
Throat Coat, 92
throat singers, 82
thyroarytenoid (TA) dominance, 81, 168, 196
thyroarytenoid (TA) muscle, 80, 81, 168
thyroid cartilage, 79, 290
Tick, Tick . . . Boom!, 1, 308
Times They Are a-Changin', The, 58, 63
Tina, 61
Tin Pan Alley, 14, 21
Titanic, 36, 245
TMJ (temporomandibular joint) massages, 278
tongue tension, 276–78, 281
"Tonight," 322
Tony Awards, 24, 27, 31, 32, 38
"Top of Mount Rock," 312
torch songs, 321–22
touring shows, 8
Townshend, Pete, 59–60
Toxic Avenger, The, 309, 319
Tracz, Joe, xxi
traditional musical theatre: for auditions, 307; genre descriptions, 52; pop/rock music compared to, 47–50; as popular music, 45; popular music influencing, 51; repertoire selection from, 232–36, 240–45; song purpose, 317–18
transfer, 150
transgender people, 173, 175, 213, 315, 355–62
transitional musical theatre, 53, 307
Trap music, 47
Treasure Girl, 18
trios, 322
Trouble in Tahiti, 25
TRW (Theatrical Rights Worldwide), 300–301
Turner, Kathleen, 174
Turner, Tina, 61
twangs, 50, 201–2
tweeters (speakers), 129
25th Annual Putnam County Spelling Bee, The, 38–39, 319
"Two Little Words," 227
type, 328, 361
typing, 328

Unsinkable Molly Brown, The, 26, 307
Urban Cowboy, 38, 66
Urinetown, 38, 309, 318

Valli, Frankie, 58, 216
Vandergelder, Horace, 30
vaudeville, 7–8, 12, 15, 18, 185
"Very Next Man, The," 235–36
Very Warm for May, 226
vibrational amplitude, 77–82, 168–69, 202, 288
vibrato, 197–99
Victor/Victoria, 36
Viet Rock, 29
Violet, 58, 63, 65
visualization, 98, 99, 198, 210n51
vocal coaching/teaching: advice for teachers, 348, 354, 361–62;

experiences with, 340–41, 344, 349, 353, 356, 363–64; feedback as strategy for, 155–56; teacher-to-student touching, 156–57; teaching methods of, 154–55; for vocal injury recovery, xxi–xxiii, 368. *See also* learning; motor (procedural) learning; vocal development and training

vocal development and training: belting exercises, 184–97; chest and head voice transitions exercises, 181; common styles for, 166–67; E4-E5 range, 170–71; exercises for, 101, 102, 105, 171–73; feedback as strategy for, 155–56; gender and, 173–75; higher range exercises, 178–79; as key to success, 165, 184; for longevity, 101–2; middle range exercises, 176–77; mixing exercises, 181–84; registration, 167–69, 170–71; resonance and sensory feedback, 170; resonant voice exercises, 179–80; semi-occluded vocal tract (SOVT) positions, 202–7; speech into singing exercises, 180–81; style variety and flexibility exercises, 171, 197–202; teacher-student touching during, 156–57; vocal exercise considerations, 171–73; working books for, 306, 315. *See also* practice; vocal coaching/teaching

vocal dollars, 301
vocal exercises, 101, 102, 105, 171–73
vocal fatigue, 106, 301, 367
vocal folds (vocal cords): abnormalities of, xxiv, 90; alcohol effects on, 104; anatomy of, 78–82; child development and, 288, 290, 291; health issues impacting, 96; hydration of, 92–93, 102; illnesses impacting, 100; injuries to, xxiii, 100, 367–68; injury prevention strategies, 102, 103–4; registration types at, 167–69; scientific understanding of, 133; semi-occluded vocal tract (SOVT) positions, 202–7; smoking effects on, 104–5; swallowing anatomy and, 91–92

vocal health: age and, 343, 366–67, 368; for children, 301–2; cooldowns, 102, 343; digestive issues impacting, 96–97; hydration for, 91–94, 102–3; illness prevention, 94; importance of, 89–90, 107–8; medications and, 95–96; mental wellness for, 98–100, 105; nutrition for, 90–91, 365; physical exercise for, 97–98; practice strategies for, 105; speaking well for, 103–4; substance abuse impact on, 104–5; throat gargles for, 94–95; training for, 101–2, 107. *See also* vocal injuries; warm-up exercises

vocal injuries: causes of, 89, 100, 106–7; experiences with, xx–xxiv, 366–70; prevention strategies, 98, 101–5, 107, 152, 153; stigma of, xxiii, 89, 369; symptoms of, 179–80, 301

vocal naps, 104, 302
vocal nuance, 311
vocal styles: audition song selection and execution of, 316; common, 197–200; contemporary music theatre, 55; early contemporary

INDEX

musical theatre, 54; genre-specific, 55; jazz, 51; legit music theatre, 52; pop opera, 54; repertoire selection and, 216; silent obligations to, 217; skills requirements, 171; songs with contrasting, 312; traditional music theatre, 52; transitional musical theatre, 53. *See also* belting
vocal therapy, xxi–xxiii, 179, 366, 367–68
vocal tract, 82–86, 111
Voice Cups, 330
Voice Foundation, The (TVF), 88
VoiceLive3, 128
voice pedagogy, 133–34, 162, 165–66. *See also* vocal coaching/teaching; vocal development and training
voice science: articulation, 86–88; components of, 71; pulmonary system, 71–77; resonance, 82–86; vibration, 77–82
vowels, 169, 173, 176–77, 216

Waitress, 62, 250
Walker, George, 12, 13
Walt Disney Company, 35
"Wandering," 312
warm-up exercises: child vocal training and, 302; personal practices, 343, 351–52, 365–66, 370–71; pre-audition, 329–30; purpose, 102; suggestions for, 105, 172
War Paint, 52
Washington, George, 3
Watch Your Step, 14
Waters, Ethel, 22, 185
"Waving through a Window," 214, 252

We Are the Tigers, 237
Webber, Andrew Lloyd, 31
Wedding Singer, The, 61, 322
Welles, Orson, 21
West Side Story: characters' given circumstances, 257; charm songs in, 320; composers of, 25; duets from, 322; influence of, 349; lyricists for, 32; music genre of, 52, 307; original direction/choreography for, 25; song and dance numbers from, 321; vocal styles in, 167
We Will Rock You, 61
"Whatever Happened to My Part," 309, 319
Wheatley, William, 8–9
"Where Did the Rock Go," 60
Where's Charley?, 26
"Wherever He Ain't," 234
whines, 201–2
Whisper House, 63
White, George, 15–16
Who, The, 59–60
whooping, 169, 177, 182
Who's Tommy, The, 37, 59–60
Wicked: auditioning for, 344; awards, 38; eleven o'clock numbers from, 320; "I want" songs from, 318; placement importance, 342; repertoire selections from, 231, 239–40; vocal styles in, 167, 216, 328; vowel challenges, 216
wildcard videos, 336
Wildhorn, Frank, 36
Wild Party, The, 36, 308
"Will He Like Me?," 217, 227
Williams, Bert, 12, 13, 16
Will Rogers Follies, The, 25
Willson, Meredith, 26

Wilson, Dooley, 22
Wiz, The, 31, 58, 65
"Wizard and I, The," 318
Wodehouse, P. G., 15
Wolf, George C., 18
Wonderful Town, 25, 26
Wonderland, 36, 62
woofers (speakers), 129
word-to-note ratios, 215
working books, 306, 315
Works Progress Administration (WPA), 21
World Trade Center attacks, 37
World War I, 14, 21–22
World War II, 21–22
"Wouldn't It Be Loverly," 318
Wulf, Gabriele, 158, 159

Xanadu, 38, 58
xenophobia, as theme, 11

"Yankee Doodle Boy," 11
yell (acoustic registration), 100, 103
yoga, 275, 283
"You and Me (but Mostly Me)," 318
"You Have Cast Your Shadow on the Sea," 241
"You Oughta Know," 217
Your Arm's Too Short to Box with God, 65
Your Own Thing, 58

Zappa, Frank, 59
Ziegfeld Follies, The, 16
Zulla, Andy, 344

ABOUT THE AUTHOR AND CONTRIBUTORS

Amanda Flynn is a New York City–based voice teacher, vocologist, and researcher. She is the owner of a private studio with clients who perform on Broadway, off-Broadway, on national and international tours, in regional theatre, and in their recording careers. In addition she teaches in the musical theatre program at Pace University. Her clients have been nominated for Grammy, Tony, Lucille Lortel, Outer Critic Circle, Drama Desk, and Helen Hayes awards. Amanda was the production vocal coach for the Broadway shows *The Lightning Thief* and *Be More Chill*, along with the regional premiere of *Love in Hate Nation*. Her film vocal coaching credits include Disney's *Encanto*, *BEAU*, and *One Year Off*. As a Singing Voice Specialist, she frequently works with injured singers, collaborating with laryngologists and voice therapists in New York City and across the country. As a performer, Amanda was an original cast member of the LA company of *Wicked*, part of the Las Vegas company of *Mamma Mia*, and toured the country on the first national tour of the Broadway revival of *Oklahoma!* After initially studying voice at Baylor University, Amanda began performing professionally. She completed her BS in Liberal Arts at The New School. Amanda holds a MM in vocal performance with a musical theatre concentration as well as an Advanced Certificate in vocal pedagogy, both from New York University. She completed the Vocology Mentorship at Mt. Sinai

Medical Center, the Distinguished Voice Professional certificate from the New York Singing Teachers' Association (NYSTA), and completed her Certificate in Vocology from the National Center for Voice and Speech (NCVS) and the University of Utah. A recipient of the Van Lawrence Fellowship, Amanda is an active voice researcher and has presented research at the Fall Voice Conference, The Voice Foundation, the PAVA Symposium, the VASTA Conference, and the NATS National Conference. She has served on the board of the New York Singing Teachers' Association as director of the Professional Development Program and on the board of the Pan American Vocology Association as the communications director. www.amandaflynnvoice.com

* * *

Matthew Edwards is associate professor of voice and voice pedagogy at Shenandoah Conservatory and artistic director of the CCM Vocal Pedagogy Institute. His current and former students have performed on and off-Broadway as well as on national and international tours, major motion picture soundtracks, and on Billboard music charts. Edwards is the author of *So You Want to Sing Rock 'n' Roll* and has contributed chapters to *Manual of Singing Voice Rehabilitation*, *The Vocal Athlete*, *Get the Callback*, and *A Dictionary for the Modern Singer*. He has authored articles for the *Journal of Singing*, *Journal of Voice*, *American Music Teacher*, *VOICEPrints*, and *Southern Theatre*. Edwards regularly presents workshops on functional training for the CCM singer at conferences and universities throughout the United States.

Lynn Helding is professor of practice in voice and voice pedagogy at the University of Southern California Thornton School of Music, and creator of its vocology curriculum. She is an associate editor of the *Journal of Singing* and founding author of its Mindful Voice column. Her forthcoming book, *The Musician's Mind: Teaching, Learning, and Performance in the Age of Brain Science*, illuminates current research in the cognitive, neurological, and social sciences. Helding's honors include the 2005 Van L. Lawrence Fellowship, awarded jointly by the Voice Foundation and the National Association of Teachers of Singing (NATS), and election by her peers to head the founding of the first nonprofit voice science association, the Pan-American Vocology Association (PAVA). She currently serves on the PAVA advisory board and the NATS voice science advisory committee. Her stage credits include leading roles with the Harrisburg Opera, Nashville Opera, Tennessee Opera Theatre, and Ohio Light Opera, as well as numerous solo recitals throughout the United States, Italy, France, England, Germany, Spain, Australia, and Iceland.

Wendy LeBorgne is a voice pathologist, speaker, author, and master class clinician. She actively presents nationally and internationally on the professional voice and is the clinical director of two successful private practice voice centers: the ProVoice Center in Cincinnati and BBIVAR in Dayton. LeBorgne holds an adjunct professorship at University of Cincinnati College–Conservatory of Music as a voice consultant, where she also teaches voice pedagogy and wellness courses. She completed a BFA in musical theatre from Shenandoah Conservatory and her graduate and doctoral degrees from the University of Cincinnati. Her original peer-reviewed research has been published in multiple journals and she is a contributing author to several voice textbooks. Most recently, she coauthored *The Vocal Athlete* textbook and workbook with Marci Rosenberg. Her patients and private students currently can be found on radio, television, film, cruise ships, Broadway, off-Broadway, national tours, commercial music tours, and opera stages around the world.

Scott McCoy is a noted author, singer, conductor, and pianist with extensive performance experience in concert and opera. He is professor of voice and pedagogy, director of the Swank Voice Laboratory, and director of the interdisciplinary program in singing health at Ohio State University. His voice science and pedagogy textbook, *Your Voice: An Inside View*, is used extensively by colleges and universities throughout the United States and abroad. McCoy is the associate editor of the *Journal of Singing* for voice pedagogy and is a past president of the National Association of Teachers of Singing (NATS). He also served NATS as vice president for workshops, program chair for the 2006 and 2008 national conferences, chair of the voice science advisory committee, and as a master teacher for the intern program. Deeply committed to teacher education, McCoy is a founding faculty member in the New York

Singing Teachers' Association (NYSTA) Professional Development Program (PDP), teaching classes in voice anatomy, physiology, acoustics, and voice analysis. He is a member of the distinguished American Academy of Teachers of Singing (AATS).